Advance Praise for
Tipping Point for Advanced Capitalism

"D.W. Livingstone's *Tipping Point* is the culmination of an illustrious career dedicated to scholarship aimed to make a difference. This is a far-reaching engagement and reflection upon class matters and structural transformation in the new economy at a critical juncture. The main empirical claim is the growth of professional employees as the skilled trades of the 21st century 'knowledge economy' and as pivotal agents of change. The book also contains a refreshingly new take on economic democracy. Livingstone's substantial evidence-driven work merits serious consideration and provides both a proud legacy and look ahead."

— Wallace Clement, chancellor's professor emeritus, Carleton University, co-author of *Relations of Ruling: Class and Gender in Postindustrial Societies* and author of *The Challenge of Class Analysis.*

"Nothing is more important than class for explaining how advanced capitalism works (and doesn't work). Yet simultaneously there is no single analytical concept more misunderstood, in both intellectual discourse and public consciousness. In this timely and powerful volume, D.W. Livingstone brilliantly wields quantitative and qualitative data to show that, yes, class still exists — and that understanding the dynamics of class conflict is vital for confronting the fearsome multiple crises facing humanity."

— Jim Stanford, director, Centre for Future Work and author of *Economics for Everyone: A Short Guide to the Economics of Capitalism*

"D.W. Livingstone's detailed and highly crafted study demonstrates the ongoing power of capitalist class divisions in Canada, and marks a welcome renewal of a focus on work and employment within class analysis. Anyone who doubts the importance of class divides in affluent nations should ponder this book with care."

— Mike Savage, Martin White Professor of Sociology, London School of Economics and author of *Class Analysis and Social Transformation* and *Social Class in the 21st Century*

"In this important book capping a distinguished career, D.W Livingstone argues that class analysis remains fundamental to understanding the multiple crises of advanced capitalism and the possibilities for social transformation. A key argument is that changes in the class structure and in class consciousness since the 1980s are heightening the contradiction between capitalism and growing public access to knowledge, setting the stage for new class alliances for democratic socialism."

— Andrew Jackson, former director of social and economic policy, Canadian Labour Congress and author of *The Fire and the Ashes: Rekindling Democratic Socialism*

"Are classes dead in modern capitalist societies as often claimed? *Tipping Point* clearly demonstrates that most citizens of the rich democracies don't think so. They have clear ideas about their own class locations and their social, economic, and political consequences. *Tipping Point* scans the changing class topography of the contemporary world and its likely implications for the future. Must reading for all those who have forgotten about the most fundamental cleavages of our daily lives."

— John Myles, professor emeritus, University of Toronto and co-author of *Relations of Ruling: Class and Gender in Postindustrial Societies* and *Old Age in the Welfare State*

"Most accounts of class now stray too far from relations at work. Livingstone redresses the balance, using a unique set of empirical data collected over decades to chart the comparative changes in class structures and class consciousness in developed capitalist societies. Central to these trends is the growth and proletarianization of non-managerial professional groups. This development provides cautious hope that forces are gathering that may make fundamental change possible. The challenges this book poses deserve serious engagement if the multiple crises facing the world are to be overcome."

— Bob Carter, professor emeritus, University of Leicester and author of *Capitalism, Class Conflict and the New Middle Class* and "A Growing Divide: Marxist Cass Analysis and the Labour Process."

TIPPING POINT for ADVANCED CAPITALISM

Class, Class Consciousness and Activism in the "Knowledge Economy"

D.W. LIVINGSTONE

Fernwood Publishing
Halifax & Winnipeg

Copyright © 2023 D.W. Livingstone

All rights reserved. No part of this book may be reproduced or transmitted in any form by any means without permission in writing from the publisher, except by a reviewer, who may quote brief passages in a review.

Copyediting and text design: Brenda Conroy
Cover design: John van der Woude
Printed and bound in the UK

Published by Fernwood Publishing
2970 Oxford Street, Halifax, Nova Scotia, B3L 2W4
and 748 Broadway Avenue, Winnipeg, Manitoba, R3G 0X3
www.fernwoodpublishing.ca

This book has been published with the help of a grant from the Federation for the Humanities and Social Sciences, through the Awards to Scholarly Publications Program, using funds provided by the Social Sciences and Humanities Research Council of Canada.

Fernwood Publishing Company Limited gratefully acknowledges the financial support of the Government of Canada through the Canada Book Fund and the Canada Council for the Arts. We acknowledge the Province of Manitoba for support through the Manitoba Publishers Marketing Assistance Program and the Book Publishing Tax Credit. We acknowledge the Nova Scotia Department of Communities, Culture and Heritage for support through the Publishers Assistance Fund.

Library and Archives Canada Cataloguing in Publication

Title: Tipping point for advanced capitalism : class, class consciousness and activism in the "knowledge economy" / D.W. Livingstone.
Names: Livingstone, D. W., author.
Description: Includes bibliographical references and index.
Identifiers: Canadiana (print) 20230460143 | Canadiana (ebook) 20230460208 | ISBN 9781773636405
 (softcover) | ISBN 9781773636450 (EPUB) | ISBN 9781773636467 (PDF)
Subjects: LCSH: Social classes. | LCSH: Class consciousness. | LCSH: Knowledge economy. | LCSH: Capitalism.
Classification: LCC HT609 .L58 2023 | DDC 305.5—dc23

Contents

Table and Figures viii
Acknowledgements xii
Foreword 1

Introduction 4
    Bringing Class Back In 5
    The Current Moment Is Different 9
    G7/Nordic Focus 13
    Basic Elements of My Approach 14
    Economic Democracy 17
    Starting Thoughts for Readers 19

1 Studying Classes in Advanced Capitalism:
    Standpoint, Framework and Method of Inquiry 23
    Intellectual Standpoints: Class Vantage Points and Alignments 24
    A Trans-Historical Conceptual Framework for Class Analysis 31
    Research Method: Identifying Determinate Abstractions 34

2 Popular Notions of Classes Today 46
    Perceptions of Class Structure 47
    Personal and Standard Class Identities 50
    Trends in Standard Class Identities 51
    Class Models and Class Identity by Social Background 55
    Ways of Seeing Classes: Steelworkers 57
    Leaders' Ways of Seeing Classes 61
        Corporate Leaders 61
        Labour Leaders 63
        Professional Association Leaders 65
        Poverty Group Leaders 65
        Class Conflict or Harmony? 66
    The Relative Invisibility of Class 68
    Next Steps 71

3 Advanced Capitalist Mode of Production: Drivers of
    Class Relations in "Knowledge Economies" 75
    Feudal Origins 75
    Capitalist Development 78
        Growth of Private Ownership 78
        Gaining Control of the Labour Process 80
    Advanced Capitalism 85

Emergent "Knowledge Economy" 88
Post-Capitalist Enclaves 93
More on the G7 and Nordic Focus 94
Concluding Remarks 96

4   The Changing Class Structure of Production
    Relations in the "Knowledge Economy" 99
    Disconnecting Class 100
    Renewed Marxist Approach to Class and Production Relations 103
    Employment Class Structure in Advanced Capitalist Workplaces 107
    Major Classes in Contemporary Production Relations 109
    Empirical Estimates of Changing Employment Class Structure 114
        Best Estimates of Employment Class Structure for the 1980s 115
        The G7 and Nordic Class Structure 116
        Trends in Employment Status 117
        Trends in Employment by Occupation 119
        The Challenge of Combining Employment Status and Occupation .. 123
    The Changing Employment Structure in Canada, 1982–2016 125
    Comparative Employment Class Structure, G7 and Nordic Countries 129
    Professional Employees as a "New Working Class" 130
    Employment Class Structure and Other Social Connections 132
        Employment Class Structure and Demographics 134
        Employment Class Structure and Working Conditions 137
        Employment Class Structure and Intergenerational Mobility 139
        Employment Class Structure and Wealth 143
        Employment Class Structure and Health 145
    Concluding Remarks 146

5   Advanced Capitalist Mode of Thought:
    Bourgeois Ideology 150
    Modes of Thought and Classes 150
    The Feudal Mode of Thought and Elite Omniscience 155
    Bourgeois Thought and Dominant Ideas 158
    Profit Squeeze and Neoliberal Offensive 164
    Emerging Post-Capitalist Rights and Visions 166
    Profit Maximization and the Right to Strike 172
        Profit Maximization 173
        Right to Strike 175
    Concluding Remarks 178

6   Class Consciousness in Advanced Capitalism:
    General Forms and Recent Trends 180
    Levels and Forms of Class Consciousness 181
    Overview of General Class Consciousness Studies 183
    Levels of Class Consciousness: Empirical Profiles 1980–2016 187

    Class Identity 188
    Oppositional Class Consciousness 198
        Oppositional Class Consciousness by Class Identity 207
    Hegemonic versus Revolutionary Class Consciousness 210
        Alternative Visions: Potential Defenders versus Transformers 213
    The Full Range of Class Consciousness 215
    Class Consciousness and Support for the Poor and Climate Change 218
        Class Consciousness and Support for the Poor 219
        Class Consciousness and Climate Change 220
    Concluding Remarks 222

**7 Connecting Class and Class Consciousness:
The Acid Test 227**
    A New Working Class? 232
    Overview of Recent Class and Class Consciousness Studies 233
        Corporate Capitalists' Privileged Views 240
    Class and Class Identity: Working Class versus
    Upper-Middle Class Links 241
    Class and Oppositional Class Consciousness 248
    Class and the Highest Levels of Class Consciousness 256
        Class and Potential Defenders versus Transformers 256
        Class and Hegemonic versus Revolutionary Consciousness 261
    Strategic Class Groups, Hegemonic or Revolutionary
    Consciousness and Public Policy 266
    Concluding Remarks: Tipping Points for Transformation 270

**8 Tipping Point for Advanced Capitalism:
This Time Is Different 276**
    A Different Time 278
    Critique and Protest 281
    Alternatives: Economic Democracy 289
        General Receptivity to Progressive Alternatives 292
        Organizational Forms of Economic Democracy 293
        Sustaining Energies 295
        Feasible Financing 297
    Strategic Agencies 303
    Concluding Thoughts 315

Appendices 321
    Appendix 1: The Challenge of Identifying Managers 321
    Appendix 2: Class Consciousness Composite Logic, 1982-2016 326

References 327

Index 350

Tables and Figures

Table 2.1 Recognition of Classes, Employed Labour Force, Canada, 2016 47
Figure 2.1 Responses to Question about Existence of Social Classes 47
Table 2.2 Class Models: Number of Classes Identified
 and Common Classes Named, 2016 48
Figure 2.2 Personal Class Identities of Those with Class Models, 2016 49
Figure 2.3 Distribution of Class Identities for Those with
 and without Class Models, 2016 50
Figure 2.4 Standard Class Identities, Canada 1965–2016 51
Figure 2.5 Standard Class Identity by Personal Income Level,
 Employed, Canada, 2016 (%) 55
Figure 4.1 Employment Class Structure, G7 and Nordic Countries, circa 1982
 (% of employed labour force) 114
Figure 4.2 Status in Employment, G7 and Nordic Countries, 2016
 (% of employed labour force) 116
Figure 4.3 Status in Employment, G7 and Nordic Countries, circa 1982 and 1992
 (% of employed labour force) 118
Table 4.1 Employment by Occupation, G7 and Nordic Countries
 (% of Employed Labour Force in 1992/2016) 120
Figure 4.4 Employment Class Structure, Canada, 1998, Two Sources
 (% of employed labour force) 123
Table 4.3 Employment Class Structure, G7 and Nordic Countries
 (% of Employed Labour Force in (1992/2016) 129
Figure 4.5 Intergenerational Class Mobility, Employed Labour Force,
 Canada, 2004 (%) 141
Table 6.1 Class Consciousness Items and Response Codes, 1980–2016 188
Table 6.2 Standard Class Identity, World Values Survey, 2017–2020 (%) 190
Figure 6.1 Standard Class Identities, Advanced Capitalist Countries, 1980s 193
Figure 6.2 Standard Class Identities, Canada 1982–2016 (%) 195
Table 6.3 Support for Right to Profit and Right to Strike,
 Advanced Capitalist Countries, 1980s (%) 201
Table 6.4 Support for Right to Profit and Right to Strike, Canada, 1982–2016 (%) 203
Figure 6.3 Oppositional Class Consciousness,
 Advanced Capitalist Countries, 1980s (%) 204
Figure 6.4 Estimates of Oppositional Class Consciousness, Canada, 1982–2016 205
Table 6.5 Proportion with Pro-Labour Oppositional Consciousness (%)
 by Standard Class Identity, Advanced Capitalist Countries, 1980s (%) 207
Table 6.6 Proportion with Pro-Labour Oppositional Consciousness
 by Standard Class Identity, Canada, 1982–2016 (%) 208

Table 6.7 Support for Non-Profit and Worker-Control Alternatives, Advanced Capitalist Countries, 1980s (%) 211

Table 6.8 Support for Non-Profit and Worker-Control Alternatives, Canada, 1982–2016 (%) 212

Table 6.9 General Defenders versus Transformers of Capitalism, Advanced Capitalist Countries, 1980s (%) 213

Table 6.10 Full Range of Consciousness, Advanced Capitalist Countries, 1980s (%) 214

Table 6.11 Full Range of Class Consciousness, Canada, 1982–2016 (%) 215

Table 6.12 Support for the Poor by Class Consciousness, Advanced Capitalist Countries, 1980s (% agree) 218

Table 6.13 Support for the Poor by Class Consciousness, Canada, 1982 and 2016 (% agree) 219

Table 6.14 Threat of Global Warming to Human Life by Class Consciousness, Canada, 2016 (% agree/disagree) 220

Table 7.1 Standard Class Identity by Class, Advanced Capitalist Countries, 1980s (% Upper-Middle-Class Identity / % Working-Class Identity) 241

Table 7.2 Class Identity by Class, Canada, 1982–2016 (% Upper Middle Class / % Working Class) 244

Table 7.3 Oppositional Class Consciousness by Class, Advanced Capitalist Countries, 1980s (% Pro-Capital / % Pro-Labour) 248

Table 7.4 Oppositional Class Consciousness, by Class, Canada, 1982–2016 (% Pro-Capital / % Pro-Labour) 251

Figure 7.1 Corporations Benefit Owners at the Expense of Workers and Consumers by Class Position, Canada, 1982–2016 (% agree) 252

Table 7.5 Defending versus Transforming Class Consciousness by Class, Advanced Capitalist Countries, 1980s (% Defender / % Transformer) 256

Table 7.6 Defending versus Transforming Class Consciousness by Class, Canada, 1982–2016 (% Defender / % Transformer) 259

Table 7.7 Highest Class Consciousness by Class, Advanced Capitalist Countries, 1980s (% Hegemonic / % Revolutionary) 262

Table 7.8 Higher Class Consciousness by Class, Canada, 1982–2016 (% Hegemonic / % Revolutionary) 263

Figure 7.2 Support for the Poor by Strategic Class Groups, Hegemonic or Revolutionary Class Consciousness, Canada, US, Sweden, Norway, 1980s (% Oppose / % Support) 266

Figure 7.3 Support for the Poor by Strategic Class Groups, Hegemonic or Revolutionary Class Consciousness, Canada, 1982, 2016 (%) 267

Figure 7.4 Threat of Global Warming by, Strategic Class Groups, Hegemonic or Revolutionary Class Consciousness, Canada, 2016 (%) 268

Figure 8.1 "Canada's capitalist economy is based on maximizing profits for the rich" by Class, Canada, 2020 (%) 286

Figure 8.2 Economic Democracy Index and Gini Index, G7 and Nordic Countries, circa 2020 290

Figure 8.3 "Canada's economy should be transformed into a more democratic system focusing on (a) the needs of all Canadians and (b) environmental stability" by Class, Canada, 2020 (%) 291

Figure 8.4 "I would vote for a political candidate who proposes to transform the Canadian economy to a more democratic system based on (a) the needs of all Canadians and (b) environmental stability" by Class, Canada, 2020 (%) 303

Table A1.1 Wright's Final Employment Class Structure circa 1982: Combined Status in Employment and Employment by Occupation, 6 Countries (% of Employed Labour Force) 321

Table A1.2 Employment Class Structure, Canada, circa 1982, Three Logics (% of Employed Labour Force) 323

Table A2.1 Class Consciousness Composite Forms Logic, 1982–2016 325

*To my granddaughters, Brooke and Leah,
and the others in their generation who see this tipping point coming
and act for ecological and economic justice*

Acknowledgements

Most of this book was written in the last few years but it has been a presence in my mind for most of my eight decades. From my early years growing up in a small town in close contact with the poorest to the richest, I have always had a sense that economic class mattered more than is commonly admitted by most people and by teachers and scholars in particular. Most of my research projects and publications can be seen as building blocks for this book. Many people have contributed to this work.

The Ontario Institute for Studies in Education (OISE) in the 1970s was an exceptional place to begin this inquiry, a hybrid research institute and graduate school. Clifford Pitt, director of OISE, invited me to lead the initial OISE Survey of Educational Issues, which for many years was the only regularly conducted, publicly accessible attitudes survey of education policy issues in Canada. This led to many opportunities to conduct other community-based surveys and case studies on work and learning issues, generally with a class perspective involved. I later led the founding of the Centre for the Study of Education and Work at OISE and two associated research networks, New Approaches to Lifelong Learning (NALL) and Work and Lifelong Learning (WALL). I am indebted to the Social Sciences and Humanities Research Council of Canada (SSHRC) for funding these networks and to the literally hundreds of faculty, students and community partners who contributed their efforts. Many of the results are available via the Centre for Learning, Social Economy and Work at OISE <https://www.oise.utoronto.ca/clsew>. The 1998 national survey used here was conducted as part of NALL and the 2004 survey as part of WALL. The 2010 survey was done with funds from my Canada Research Chair in Lifelong Learning and Work. The 2016 national survey was part of the Changing Work in the Knowledge Economy project funded by the SSHRC.

The empirical parts of this book would have taken quite a different shape if I had to rely more fully on my own sources. Erik Olin Wright led the Class Structure and Class Consciousness research network in the 1980s. Members were able to conduct comparable national surveys in several advanced capitalist countries and the data were subsequently made publicly accessible <https://www.icpsr.umich.edu/web/ICPSR/series/115>. One of the countries was Canada, and the survey was led by Wallace Clement and John Myles. Without easy access to the data from these surveys, the comparative analyses of class structure and class consciousness conducted here would have been much more limited. It is very disappointing that so little further comparable class research has been done in recent decades. It is now technically much easier for qualified researchers and progressive social organizations to conduct similar studies, and I hope they will use my more recent databases: see Canada Work Learning Surveys 1998–2016.[1]

I cannot list all the helpful colleagues and many members of the research teams here but some deserve special mention. Doug Hart, Milosh Raykov, Brendan Watts and Wally Seccombe have been essential in conducting astute statistical analyses of the various databases.

I have had the benefit of frank and helpful feedback on parts of this manuscript from people from quite different perspectives and walks of life, including Tracey Adams, Anne Bird, Bob Carter, David Camfield, Raewyn Connell, Ted Dakin, Elise Dintsman, Margrit Eichler, Barb Fenessey, George Martel, David Guile, Richard Hillman, Andrew Jackson, Jim McCarter, John Myles, Ken Pankhurst, Leo Panitch, Aminur Rahim, Herman Robers, Henning Salling Olesen, Peter Sawchuk, Antonie Scholtz, Errol Sharpe, Dorothy Smith, Warren Smith, Steve Somfalvi and Alison Taylor. I am sure most of them would still find something here to debate. I am also grateful to the publisher's anonymous peer reviewers for constructive suggestions on the penultimate version of the manuscript.

For many years my toughest and most constructive critic has been Wally Seccombe. Our debate continues as we work on the Comparative Political Economy Database, which we hope will be useful for many researchers in coming years.[2]

This book would never have seen the light of day without the support of my family in countless ways. In particular, my daughter Stephanie gave wise editorial assistance and produced the bibliography and index, and my granddaughter Brooke expertly created the Excel tables and figures in the text. To Angela, the love of my life, I owe much more than anyone else will ever know.

Notes

1. For a guide to the full set of research projects, publications and data bases, see https://discover.research.utoronto.ca/27054-dw-livingstone/.
2. As summarized more fully on its website, the Comparative Political Economy Database (CPEDB) is an SPSS file including twelve advanced capitalist countries and over 600 variables, most for over a forty-year time span.

Foreword

This book asks large questions — and answers them. It deals with social structure and social change in a time of massive inequalities, when we face great uncertainties about our collective future. It locates responsibility for the crises we face, and it gives us a new way of thinking about how to face those crises.

The landscape for D.W. Livingstone's discussion is the rich capitalist countries of the global North, since about 1980. They are seen against a long historical background and in the worldwide context of capitalism. The focus is class.

That is no easy matter to deal with. There is a huge, confused and inconclusive debate about class in modern societies. Class sometimes disappears from the public agenda, then is re-discovered. Some voices claim that class no longer exists, some say that it takes entirely new forms, and others declare that we already know all that needs to be known.

Livingstone takes a stance against this confusion and also against dogmatism. He draws from Marx's work some basic ideas about how capitalist economies work and how we might examine them — and then studies the evidence.

This book is full of the evidence. Since the 1980s, Livingstone and his colleagues have built up a remarkable information resource, in effect a rich library of data from carefully designed survey research (some already in the public domain and more to come). The information concerns occupations, education, labour forces, social consciousness, change over time and the character of social divisions. *Tipping Point for Advanced Capitalism* puts this resource to work, giving us many of the highlights — it is really worth reading the detailed tables in this book — and pinning the argument constantly to the relevant data.

Tipping Point works step by step through the big issues about class. It proposes a way of mapping class structure, particularly focused on employment class. It has much to say about the different forms of labour we now see in and around a complex capitalist economy. But it isn't simply economistic. The argument moves on to class consciousness in its different forms and the social contours of attitudes to class-linked issues such as poverty, profit and climate change.

Livingstone is well aware that class structures are not static — social change has long been a theme of his research, whether on the steel industry, on schools or on occupations. So *Tipping Point* tackles questions of class dynamics, the directions of change and the reasons for change. Here it confronts questions about the growth of middle-class identification, the growth of the knowledge economy, the decline of the industrial workforce and the paradoxical degradation of conditions among highly educated workers. On these issues Livingstone has distinctive and carefully argued views, which I find entirely convincing.

I won't try to summarize his arguments — readers can have the pleasure of following the track for themselves — but I do want to say something about his methods. For a book so packed with data, *Tipping Point* is unusually explicit about its logic. Livingstone carefully sets out the conditions for each step in his analysis and the background assumptions for the analysis as a whole. He makes a careful critique of the relevant concepts. His account of what is meant by the "knowledge economy" is particularly helpful and so is his demolition of the attractive but misleading idea of a "professional/managerial class."

But as well as patient argument and systematic presentation of data, the book is rich in insights, unexpected conclusions and striking phrases. I love the image of "trace elements" in the politics of class and the blunt recognition that a capitalist economy centres on "profits stolen from wages." I'm particularly impressed by the book's account of the underemployment of the capacities of an increasingly well-educated workforce. It makes one weep to see all the potential in knowledge and creativity that is simply wasted by an advanced capitalist economy!

Livingstone doesn't use the term "'ruling class" for corporate capitalists, but I do, and I've learnt a lot about them from this book. The corporate rich are statistically almost invisible but are enormously consequential in their power. The way their power is used, promoting the unfettered pursuit of profit at the expense of others — including the natural environment and the majority of humankind — is at the heart of the crises we now face. *Tipping Point* brings together some key pieces of information about the group that holds this power, especially its ideological coherence despite its economic divisions. The book raises exciting questions about the connections between the owners of corporate capital and key support groups, showing how those connections might be fraying.

It is easy to feel despondent when thinking about the ruthlessness of power, the deepening environmental crisis, rising inequalities of income and wealth, the persistence of violence and the degradation of living conditions for so many of our people. Yet *Tipping Point* is not a pessimistic book. The title itself calls up the idea that social change does happen and can be catalysed by activism. So the final part of the book addresses the possibilities that emerge from the situation that the analysis has revealed.

Some important news is in the data itself. *Tipping Point* shows that even in rich capitalist countries, capitalist hegemony is far from total. Oppositional ideas are quite widespread across major groups, including those who mostly identify as middle class. Overall, belief in the unrestrained pursuit of profit has been falling, while concern about climate change has been rising. What Livingstone calls revolutionary class consciousness is not widespread in the population as a whole but is present, at far from trivial levels, among the most exploited.

There are, then, social bases for system change, more extensive than usually thought. Livingstone adds to this information his reflections on the direction of change that is now possible. The ingredients for economic democracy are known; many examples of the cooperative production of goods and services are already present. System change is by no means a plunge into darkness.

Tipping Point for Advanced Capitalism is an important book, not just for empirical social science but also for social movements. It provides a mass of new information and ideas about key issues in class analysis. It offers new perspectives on large-scale social and economic change and the forces that might produce change. It recognizes that we are living in distinctive times, which demand new thinking. It sees the self-destructive dynamic in our present social and economic order. And it is, at base, optimistic, showing real potentials for fundamental change. We are not trapped in the current swamp — there are ways of digging ourselves out. If we have the courage to try.

— Raewyn Connell, professor emerita, University of Sydney, and author of *The Good University* and *Knowledge and Global Power*

Introduction

We are living in the most dangerous time for the human species since our early origins. We are near the tipping point for advanced capitalism. A tipping point is a critical juncture when an unstoppable change takes place. In social terms, this is a point when many people rapidly change their behaviour by widely adopting previously rare practices. Mounting evidence suggests we are close to a moment when a combination of ecological, economic and political thresholds will activate a basic change in the dominant way of life on this planet — either for good or for ill. This basic change may be led by democratic mass movements through which the necessity for sustainable alternative practices advocated by small numbers becomes obvious to many who had assumed existing conditions would continue, or provoked by pervasive crisis events that incite panic, chaos and autocratic rule. Defenders of capitalism continue to deny, divert or diminish a tipping point for this system, but it is hard for almost anyone to deny the imminent threat of global warming, evident signs of which are happening all around us, documented by science, covered by mass media and inspiring large social movements for change. Mounting economic inequalities and discriminatory barriers are also felt like a slap in the face every day by people of colour, women, the young and the old. These too are leading to more demands for major social change. To overcome such ecological and economic threats, social movements make broad appeals targeted at elected governments, large corporations and the general public, but there is still too little attention to developing these movements into strategic agencies to transform capitalism rather than merely modifying this system into forms that continue to reproduce degradation and exploitation.

How do the evident ecological threats connect with economic inequities and chronic underemployment, mounting skepticism and distrust with conventional politics, as well as the renewed spectre of nuclear war? What's largely missing from public debate and movements for fundamental change is a clear sense of how *class relations* are involved. This book focuses on class relations, which have been much ignored in recent studies of advanced capitalism, explores how they are driving toward these combined thresholds and identifies major class forces defending and fighting to transform this system.

Bringing Class Back In

In the wake of student and worker protests in the 1960s, some critical researchers devoted unprecedented attention to both class positions grounded in production relations and to higher levels of class consciousness beyond simple popular notions of class identity in advanced capitalist countries. Harry Braverman's (1974) pioneering inquiry into the capitalist labour process inspired numerous analyses of its connections with the structure and working conditions of objective classes. Michael Mann's (1973) original exploration of oppositional and revolutionary levels of class consciousness among the "western working class" was followed by various empirical searches. These studies led more rarely to others looking for connections between objective classes grounded in paid workplaces and expressions of higher levels of class consciousness. Erik Olin Wright (1989) led the most ambitious of these studies in the 1980s. Since that time there have been precious few sustained inquiries into either objective employment class structure or higher levels of class consciousness and almost none looking into their connections. The dearth of such studies and the need for them is underlined by periodic appeals to "bring class back in" to critical studies of advanced capitalism (e.g., McNall and Levine 1991; Gindin 2015). As Gindin argues, without strategic class analysis addressing the practical needs and democratic potential of non-managerial workers, little renewal of the labour movement is possible; deepening class analysis can enable working people in renewed unions and cooperative social movements to both defend their own class interests and respond to imminent tipping point issues more effectively.

Since the 1970s I have been involved in a series of research studies and publications focused on continuity and change in class relations in advanced capitalist societies. These studies have built upon the studies by Braverman, Mann, Wright and others to develop the conceptual models of class structure and class consciousness presented in this book. I have conducted a series of empirical studies from the 1970s onward that document (1) continuity and change in the employment class structure of advanced capitalism; (2) continuity and change in forms and levels of class consciousness; and (3) the connections between employment class positions and expressions of class consciousness. Throughout this time, I have revised and refined some of these class distinctions through reflection and debate. Parts of the evidence and arguments have appeared elsewhere over the years as attributed, but the version presented in this book is the fullest documentation of the changing class structure based in production relations, the higher forms of class consciousness and the connections between class position and class consciousness currently available in advanced capitalist countries. I profoundly hope that other studies will draw on the available research instruments and databases to conduct further inquiries, with confirmations, refinements and refutations as soon as possible (Canada Work Learning Surveys 1998–2016).[1]

At some level, everybody knows that economic class matters. In advanced capitalism, the inequities in material resources are so vast that they are evident to virtually anyone. The variation in distribution of material resources has become so extreme that a tiny number of billionaires lay claim to most of them while billions of people can claim virtually nothing. These inequities are far beyond the range of distribution of natural abilities or human needs. The extraordinary thing is that most people seem to have accepted tacitly the idea that these billionaires warrant such wealth because of exceptional ability or luck and that others could have more if they applied more effort or seized more opportunities. But this sentiment is changing. As recessions and pandemics graphically demonstrate, these inequitable conditions are leading to extraordinary suffering by multitudes in a world that has the technical capacity to provide for the basic needs of all. This book examines recent changes in economic class relations and class consciousness that could lead beyond this widespread suffering.

The capitalist mode of producing most goods and services now dominates the globe. Nearly all of us are involved somehow in the class relations between the direct ownership of the means of production in pursuit of profits and the pursuit of hired employment for livelihood. In this book, I generally distinguish employment classes in terms of production relations between (1) owners of businesses who hire numbers of employees and other owners who work by themselves in self-employment; (2) managerial employees with delegated authority over other employees; and (3) non-managerial employees. In all advanced capitalist economies, this tripartite employment class structure (i.e., owners/employers; managers; non-managerial hired employees) exists with varying potential alliances of class interest. Of course, there are substantial minorities outside the employed labour force who want paid employment and/or are dependent on others who have it. But, as we will see, researchers from varied perspectives are converging on recognition of such a tripartite employment class structure.

My assessment of class consciousness remains more distinctive in recent times. I document that class consciousness also has taken tripartite forms, including pro-capital, contradictory and pro-labour tendencies. The pro-capital and pro-labour forms have several variants, from highly pro-capital consciousness to revolutionary labour consciousness. There has been a lot of argument — based on limited empirical evidence — that contradictory class consciousness prevails among non-managerial employees. That is, it has been widely claimed that most non-managerial workers have mixed or inconsistent views about the rights of capital and labour and tend to pragmatically accept capitalism as inevitable. This turns out to be at least an exaggerated claim. It does appear to be true that — in a context of fairly widespread inconsistent or contradictory class consciousness — small class groups with strongly held views supporting their own interests can exercise powerful influence over others. This has clearly been the case for a highly coherent pro-capital mentality among the tiny corporate capitalist class, a view I document and call "hegemonic capitalist class consciousness." But there is also mounting evidence in the present analysis that when substantial proportions of those in disadvantaged classes hold pro-labour class consciousness and when smaller proportions mobilize around these views, major changes in social conditions can occur at both local and wider levels.

Through this class analysis, I have been increasingly convinced of two things. First, professional employees — the core "knowledge workers" — have become a substantial part of the non-managerial hired labour force in emergent "knowledge economies," and they increasingly share deteriorating working conditions and pro-labour attitudes with other workers. As Owen, an automation engineer puts it: "The freedom we have to plan our own work has decreased.... We are salaried employees, wage slaves really, and we're no different from any other worker."[2]

Second, the extent of higher levels of class consciousness among leading capitalists and their allies, as well as among non-managerial workers and their allies, are of central strategic importance for understanding alternative responses to tipping points. The most basic argument of this book is that workers directly involved in creating goods and services commodities are among the most productive and exploited workers in emergent "knowledge economies" and are therefore in a strategic position to influence progressive changes in paid work and in transformation from advanced capitalism. The continuing development of class consciousness among these leading class forces and their allies are vital indicators of trends toward tipping points.

Leading capitalists and allied intellectuals may instinctively deny the relevance of work-based class analysis as against their basic interests. More disappointing in recent decades are the otherwise progressive scholars who have dismissed or severely diminished the relevance of such class analysis on the grounds that it diminishes other forms of oppression and domination, effectively reducing them to lesser, secondary forms of social reality. I profoundly disagree. Age, sex, racial appearance and physical disabilities are all personal attributes that may often be seen at a glance and condition what one can do and think. There are many forms of oppression and domination in capitalism inside and outside paid workplaces on grounds of racialization, gender, age and disability. They have undeniable effects even among those who presently have the same class position. The forms of oppression cannot be reduced to class relations, nor do I suggest that class-based exploitation is more relevant to the lives of people who may in fact suffer more deeply from these forms of oppression than from their class existence, perhaps especially in their lives beyond paid workplaces. Class is less visible. As later chapters illustrate, class is constituted in other spheres of our lives besides our work, and our class position can change profoundly throughout our lives. Class is largely a relationship, a relationship based on exchange and accumulation of resources. The differential resources provided by others condition what I can do and think, and the differential resources that I and others provide to others condition what anyone can do and think. Our age, sex, racialization and physical ability are less contingent on our relations with others than our class is. All human life is based on cumulative experience, but class existence can change more quickly in response to different historical circumstances. Whatever contribution this book might make to class analysis, there is no intention to denigrate the irreducible importance of oppression and domination on the bases of racialization, gender, age or imputed disabilities. All of these forms of oppression and domination are lived simultaneously. It is just that the focus here is on class and class consciousness grounded in paid workplaces because, in spite of their pivotal relevance for comprehending capitalism, there has been very little focus on these class relations in recent times. There have been periodic hopeful appeals for treating all forms of oppression as a social totality (e.g., Albert and Hahnel 1978) as well as for advancing analyses of their intersectionality (e.g., McCall 2005). The class analysis in this book does consider some modifying effects of gender, racialization and age factors on class and class consciousness, as well as remaining open to more interactive analyses of multiple forms of oppression and liberation.

So, the big claims of the book are to provide an unprecedented tracking of the changing class structure of advanced capitalism based in production relations since the 1980s, to offer a rare assessment of higher levels of class consciousness based on the rights of capital and labour in general and among those in different major classes and, with a bit of luck, to bring class back in to critical analyses of current tipping points.

The Current Moment Is Different

Capitalism has been widely recognized as a mode of production inherently prone to both business cycles and long waves of expansion and recession. These cycles continue. Capitalists continue to blame workers' wage demands for price increases in spite of compelling evidence that excessive profits are typically the root cause. But this time, tipping points present a quite different context.

In terms of ecological conditions, pollutants from resource overuse with industrialization have unleashed irreversible self-amplifying global warming changes that have driven many species to extinction and are imminent threats to tolerable existence of human civilization. The Intergovernmental Panel on Climate Change (IPCC), the leading international scientific body for assessment of climate change, provides the most definitive report on these conditions (IPCC 2022).[3] In spite of very strong evidence for declaring a state of planetary emergency, corrective environmental measures to date have been marginal at best. Antonio Guterres (2022), United Nations Secretary-General, speaks for most of the world when he says:

> With fact upon fact, this report reveals how people and the planet are getting clobbered by climate change. Nearly half of humanity is living in the danger zone — now. Many ecosystems are at the point of no return — now. Unchecked carbon pollution is forcing the world's most vulnerable on a frog march to destruction — now. The facts are undeniable. This abdication of leadership is criminal. The world's biggest polluters are guilty of arson of our only home.... People everywhere are anxious and angry.... Now is the time to turn rage into action.

But the world's biggest polluters and resource overusers are far from evenly distributed around the globe. The high-income countries include mainly those that had become members of the Organization for Economic Cooperation and Development by 1972 (Wikipedia, "Organization for Economic Cooperation and Development"). These countries constitute the core of advanced capitalism. These countries bear massively greater responsibility for reaching the ecological tipping point than the rest of the world. They have contributed hugely more to overshooting resource use and pollution levels that would permit a sustainable human ecological footprint on this finite planet. The planet's ecosystems and resources are a commons to which all are entitled to an equal share. By conservative estimates, the advanced capitalist countries, containing less than 20 percent of the world's population, have been responsible for three-quarters of global excess material use since 1970. The US has generated about 28 percent of this global overshoot, the EU and UK 25 percent and the rest of Europe and high-income countries 24 percent. China is the main middle-income contributor and — with about 18 percent of world population — generates 15 percent overshoot (Hickel et al. 2022). All these figures do not take account of even more inequitable resource use prior to 1970. As Hickel et al. (2022, e348) conclude:

> A fair-shares assessment of resource use shows that high-income nations bear the overwhelming responsibility for global ecological breakdown, and therefore owe an ecological debt to the rest of the world. These nations need to take the lead in making radical reductions in their resource use to avoid further degradation, which will likely require transformative post-growth and degrowth approaches.

To blame all who live in advanced capitalist countries for this ecological debt would be quite mindless. The driving economic force has been pursuit of profits by the tiny capitalist class. Accumulation of capital has been their overriding preoccupation at the expense of any other ecological, social or political considerations. With the concentration of capital into larger and larger transnational corporate blocs, income and wealth inequalities in advance capitalist countries are greater than any time since the Great Depression of the 1930s (e.g., Piketty 2014), becoming even greater and "ripping us apart" (Buchheit 2017). Employment conditions among the most highly qualified youth generation in history become increasingly precarious (Livingstone 2019a). As we will see later, most people in more subordinate class positions in advanced capitalism are not only very concerned about global warming and the threat of poverty, but are also losing faith in capitalism to do anything meaningful to address such problems. In any case, most of us living in advanced capitalist countries will have to find ways to do more with less in the transformation from capitalism to whatever succeeds it. This is the hard reality that profit-driven private corporations continuously try to get us to ignore through evermore appeals to consume more.

In terms of political conditions, austerity measures by state regimes to restore financial profitability have only served to increase precariousness (e.g., Streeck 2016). Public and private debt levels have increased greatly, skepticism about government capacity to respond to popular demands for environmental, economic and social justice grows, and mounting mistrust increases the vulnerability of political regimes. Popular support for real political alternatives gains greater expression (e.g., Saad 2019; John 2020), especially among the most exploited and oppressed, both in advanced capitalist countries and elsewhere. In geopolitical terms, all these conditions heighten threats of nuclear holocaust and cyber-warfare (Cimbala 2016; Klare 2019). In the view of a very recent observer (Satgar 2022, 1): "The contemporary world stands on the brink, facing extinction either through nuclear holocaust emanating from battle fields in Ukraine or from the ever-worsening climate crisis…. Precariousness, uncertainty, and complex risk have become the lived reality of deep globalization."

In the wake of recent ecological, economic and political conditions, existing class relations are challenged more than ever before, raising the general question of whether we are approaching the end of capitalism.

There still are ardent defenders of capitalism. Some believe that there are untold spheres of commodification that — with the aid of new information technologies — will generate both immense profits and lives of comfort. Others hope that large-scale feats of geo-environmental engineering will master multiple pollutants and lead to a greener capitalist future. Still others argue that the growth of intellectual capital and the emergence of a "knowledge economy" will nurture sufficient human ingenuity to figure our way out of the current unprecedented combination of challenges through enhanced productivity. Whatever the wisdom of these various projections, two things should be clear. First, a capitalist mode of production based on maximizing profits in ever more commodities keeps most people in increasing relative poverty in subordinated economic classes, regardless of how much per capita income may increase. Second, there is little likelihood of sustainable transformation unless substantial proportions of people in relative poverty cease their tacit acceptance of this system as inevitable. Realizing a more equitable, sustainable way of life requires strategic numbers to deepen their genuine concerns about the limits of capitalism, as well as the emergence of class conscious agents responsive to these concerns and able to lead mass movements toward alternative ways of life.

Regarding the distinctiveness of the current economic moment in advanced capitalism, I make three more specific introductory points:

1. Transnational corporate assets are more concentrated than ever before, with a very small number of financial consortia controlling a huge number of enterprises in many sectors (Vitali, Glattfelder and Battiston 2011; Rugemer 2019). This quasi-monopoly situation is leading to super-profits for some capitalists while increasing material and financial difficulties for many people and serious deprivation for others. Such high financial concentration leaves this system vulnerable to quick destabilization from several possible economic tipping points. The situation is likely to continue unless and until counterforces provoke widespread progressive changes globally.

2. State systems in all advanced capitalist countries took up a much greater proportion of gross domestic product (GDP)[4] over the twentieth century up to the early 1990s, from under 10 percent to well over 40 percent of GDP in many. The state has served as the key safety valve in relation to labour demands and social welfare concerns of

entire populations in ways that were inconceivable in the prior era of more competitive capitalism. Even in the more recent period of neoliberal austerity, capitalist state provisions have saved capitalism from serious reform demands. But conventional government economic policies coupled with fiscal and monetary measures only bring state systems closer to collapse.

3. Given the high concentration and mobility of global capital as well as the increased centrality of capitalist states in maintaining social and economic order, conventional public debt levels are becoming unsustainable. With each potential tipping point, the largest financial consortia, the major international monetary regulators and the G20 governments have moved to an increasing series of pump-priming policies/practices to re-stimulate economic growth. These debt levels are likely to continue to grow, along with increasing impoverishment, especially for growing numbers outside decent paid employment.

If wages continue to stagnate, and deferred wages provided by pension plans dissipate and consumption capacities decline, will this capitalist system break down in current life-threatening ways? Or will emergent labour, environmental and other allied mass movements be able to transform this system beyond its continual history of cyclical crises? I have no crystal ball, but I am arguing that whatever happens to the capitalism system in its high-income advanced countries in the foreseeable future is likely to be affected profoundly by the uneven relations between economic classes. Progressive forces should make every conceivable effort to understand these class relations and take them into account in mobilizing for ecological, economic and social justice.

G7/Nordic Focus

Beyond global indicators of these multiple crises, the empirical evidence in this book is focused on class relations per se in advanced capitalist countries. In particular, these countries include the G7 largest economies (Canada, France, Germany, Japan, Italy, UK, US) and larger Nordic countries (Denmark, Finland, Norway, Sweden) with their somewhat varied class relations. The focus on advanced capitalist countries is not because these countries deserve greater concern. Indeed, advanced capitalist countries deserve less in the sense that their global imperial reach and resource overuse have created greater suffering in much of the Global South. As the dominant economic and military power of the post–World War II period, the US bears much greater responsibility for unspeakable suffering than the others.[5] Much greater proportions of disadvantaged economic classes live in the Global South, and there might even be greater potential there for transformation among the disadvantaged. But because of ecological debt and material advantages, all advanced capitalist countries do have greater responsibility to contribute to moving sustainably beyond the tipping point.

The standpoint I bring to this inquiry is grounded in and limited by living in an advanced capitalist country. Much of the most relevant evidence about changes in class positions based in production relations and expressions of higher forms of class consciousness is most readily available for such advanced capitalist countries. Wherever possible, comparative evidence is used for these countries. Some of the most relevant recent trend data on class structure and consciousness is only currently available for one country, Canada, where I and colleagues have gathered it over the past forty years. This availability is generally true for the period after the 1980s and especially for the class consciousness of leading capitalists and their closest class allies. I assume that, if trends to a tipping point in material conditions and attitudinal dispositions of class relations are detected within one country, they are likely to be found in most other advanced capitalist societies. I hope that more directly comparative evidence will be generated soon.

Basic Elements of My Approach

The basic elements of my approach in organizing this book are as follows:

- establish a standpoint, general framework and method of investigation for this inquiry (Chapter 1);
- review simple popular notions of classes in recent times with empirical evidence (Chapter 2);
- provide an account of the driving material forces underlying class existence in the advanced capitalist mode of production (Chapter 3);

- present findings from a series of empirical studies of changing class structure of production relations in advanced capitalist countries since the initiation of austerity measures in the 1980s to the present (Chapter 4);

- outline defining features of the dominant bourgeois mode of thought and ideology in advanced capitalism with an emphasis on human rights, and compare the dispositions of leaders of different classes to either defend or transform these views (Chapter 5);

- identify levels of class consciousness and estimate general trends in forms of class consciousness in advanced capitalism (Chapter 6);

- connect changes in class structure with changes in class consciousness and document significant relations between them — the "acid test" (Chapter 7);

- finally, draw conclusions about the implications of class relations in advanced capitalist societies regarding prospects for major social changes in the near future (Chapter 8).

In Chapter 2, I examine popular notions of classes today. Some claim that classes do not exist, others insist that classes are not important compared to social divisions based on racialization/ethnicity, sex or age, and many more say that we are mostly "middle class." But it is impossible to credibly deny the existence of serious class differences in the face of large inequities in wealth, income and other possessions. I start from the simplest common perception of classes as status differences and aim for a more critical understanding of class relations today. Consider, for example, the following account by a male steelworker in Hamilton, Canada, in the 1990s:

> We know where the rich people are. And we know where the very poor people are, too. So, you've got your three different classes there. You could drive down any place in this city and you can almost see all three different classes in a matter of a short drive. It's probably gotten worse over the past ten years — no jobs. There are folks out there that were once middle-class people that are sitting there with nothing. (Quote from interview conducted for Seccombe and Livingstone 1999)

According to studies I and others have done with steelworkers in many countries, popular notions of classes are usually based on wealth or income and usually involve variants of distinctions between three basic groups, the affluent, working people and the poor. But most male steelworker breadwinner "jobs for life" vanished during the last decades of the twentieth century. Easy assumptions about existing in the middle of a class structure are declining and awareness that there are many poor people down at the bottom increased markedly (Seccombe and Livingstone 1999). There have been studies in some countries suggesting that the household *income-based* "middle class" has become a minority, perhaps signalling a demographic tipping point (e.g., Pew Research Center 2015).

There is also mounting evidence that most people in advanced capitalist societies, whatever their own class location, perceive a growing gap between rich and poor and place increasing importance on conflict between them (e.g., Morin 2012). Notions of classes and their relations are continually changing. My objective in this book is not to provide yet another descriptive snapshot of such notions of classes but to build from the fuller description offered in Chapter 2 to probe the underlying dynamics of class relations, the forces driving their continuity and change.

To undertake a more profound analysis of class and class consciousness we need a well-grounded view of the capitalist mode of production and the dominant bourgeois mode of thought. In order to adequately understand the existence of classes in advanced capitalism, we need to see them as related to the continuing development of capitalism as a mode of production as well as to the historical modes of thought that condition perceptions about the existence of classes. In this book I examine the basic tendencies of capitalism as a mode of production that continue to animate the structuring and change of relations between capital and labour. Then I document specific changing class structures. In particular, I examine the recent growth of professional employees who have been widely heralded as the leading knowledge workers in an emergent "knowledge economy."[6] After this, I suggest some distinguishing features of the dominant individualist mode of thought in the capitalist epoch that tend to limit consciousness of class relations. I offer some assessment of recent forms of and changes in class consciousness, with a special focus on comparing professional employees with the industrial workers who have led opposition to capitalism in prior times. A basic grasp of the development of both the capitalist mode of production and the associated individualist mode of thought are essential for understanding the conflictual reproduction and changes in class structure and class consciousness in advanced capitalism.

Economic Democracy

The sort of alternative to advanced capitalism that I favour is a version of economic democracy. Many modern versions of democracy can be traced to the Declaration of Independence of the United States of America to form a sovereign government against the tyranny of the British crown. The principle that all men (sic) are created equal with the rights to life, liberty and the pursuit of happiness, as expressed by the founding fathers in 1776, has inspired a wide variety of later freedom fighters, including originally excluded women, enslaved Black people and Indigenous peoples. Variants of economic democracy have been proposed and partially implemented in various times and places, including the US, especially since the rise of corporate capitalism in the 1880s. The most essential feature is the equal right to participatory control in all matters of socio-economic consequence. Two primary conditions of many variants are:

- workers control their own labour power through self-management of work organizations; and

- there is democratic control of investment for socially useful sustainable production.

I deal with the emergence of post-capitalist production enclaves and ideologies in early chapters, followed by assessments in later chapters of the extent of popular support in advanced capitalism for such alternatives as economic democracy in general and among specific classes. Here I merely register that feasible, preferable alternatives already exist. They contest the massive centralization and globalization of advanced capitalism and have massive potential to provide more meaningful participation for most people in more decentralized forms and forums.

From grassroots voices like Owen, the automation engineer, to pleas from the pulpit from the likes of Pope Francis (see Braun 2020), growing appeals are being made for more dignified fulfilling work for a global labour force increasingly overqualified for the sorts of jobs that profit-driven capitalism is now capable of offering. As long-time activist scholar Bill Ayers (2013), put it a decade ago in a passionate reflection about a book summarizing movements for economic democracy around the globe:

> Economic democracy requires popular control, wide participation, and decentralized decision-making, and it insists that the minimum requirements of life must be guaranteed — food, housing, clothing, education, and health-care.... Our struggle is for more participation, more equality, more recognition of human agency, and more transparency as we lean toward revolution. We must rouse ourselves, shake ourselves awake and perhaps shock ourselves into new awarenesses.... Without that vital sense of possible worlds, doors close, curtains drop, and we become stranded.... The tools are everywhere — humor and art, protest and spectacle, the quiet, patient intervention and the angry and urgent thrust — and the rhythm of and recipe for activism is always the same: we open our eyes and look unblinkingly at the world as we find it; we are astonished by the beauty and horrified at the suffering all around us; we act on what the known demands and we also doubt that our efforts made enough difference, and so we rethink, recalibrate, look again, and dive in once more.

Consider the following two voices speaking candidly about their jobs about fifty years ago:

> I'm a lonely animal in the jungle without a friend. Others are waiting for me to make a mistake to get my job. You have tremendous infighting for survival and clawing to the top.
>
> You never see the end result. Everybody should have something to point to. I just want to have a little respect. Lord, I wish I could do something else for a living.[7]

The first voice is a president of a conglomerate who later retired a wealthy man and lived out his days very comfortably. The second is a steelworker who lost his job in the mass layoffs of the next decade and struggled to make ends meet until the day he died. Both professed to hate their jobs. Their fuller life stories suggest they were people of quite equal talents, but with profoundly different material conditions and prospects.

Working conditions may well be worse generally today, but we certainly have enough shared knowledge of the demands of our times to see and rouse ourselves to realize workplaces that enable many people to have more fulfilling lives than such alienated steelworkers and friendless corporate capitalists.

The following chapters demonstrate that there is now a sufficiently informed and qualified population committed to democratic rights in many advanced capitalist countries to realize effective transition at all levels to genuine participatory control of workplaces, finance and civil rights, while recognizing and respecting basic individual and environmental rights.

Starting Thoughts for Readers

It should be apparent that this study builds on numerous insightful contributions to class analysis, especially from historical materialist or Marxist perspectives. The book is organized in a progression from framing the general orientation, to outlining the historical context, to presenting findings on recent trends in class structure and class consciousness, to drawing out implications for activism. Those most interested in getting to the heart of the matter might consider reading Chapters 4, 6, 7 and 8 first, followed by the others in numeric order to more fully appreciate and engage with the basic perspective on class analysis.

If the study is to be of any lasting relevance for understanding and acting on class relations in contemporary societies, it should provide readers with some basic ideas for further research and practice that can be taken up in various capitalist settings. So, here are a few starting thoughts for your further reading:

- It is pretty well recognized that the capitalist mode of production took over from feudalism and other pre-existing modes of production as it found them, starting for example from long-distance trading enclaves on the periphery of feudal modes. Post-capitalist modes are likely to be doing the same.

- The bourgeois mode of thought also emerged through infiltration of and interactive contrast with previously dominant feudal modes of thought; we may be in the midst of transition to post-capitalist modes of thought.

- At the same time as we are witnessing unprecedented concentration of global capital, we also see massive increases in public access to knowledge. The basic contradiction that Karl Marx identified between privatized ownership of the means of production and socialized forces of production likely continues to drive class relations in advanced capitalism.

- A very small bourgeoisie of owners of large private property became dominant powers in capitalism through a series of alliances with other classes; a small emergent class group to lead progressive transformation from capitalism could be based in access to specialized knowledge but would likely need critical alliances with other classes.

- In the wake of the unprecedented scope, scale and simultaneity of current ecological threats, economic inequalities and political trust crises, the tipping point for advanced capitalism is very likely imminent.

Capitalism has offered freedom from bondage to the land, but its unceasing drive to turn everything into a source of profit has generated today's world of inhumane inequities in resources for living and environmental degradation that threaten life itself. Increasingly universal access to and collective application of useful knowledge by those who have been previously dispossessed is potentially empowering the widespread emergence of more equitable and sustainable alternative ways of life. The animating thought behind this book is the recognition that we now have the technical capacity to provide decent lives for all humans at the same time as we face the real and ever-present danger of destroying or at least irrevocably degrading all life on Earth. If the book offers any insight into this dilemma from the standpoint of current relations between classes in advanced capitalist societies, it will have been worth the effort.

Notes

1. For a guide to the full set of research projects, publications and data bases, see https://discover.research.utoronto.ca/27054-dw-livingstone/.
2. Engineer quoted in Livingstone (2019b, 141).
3. See also Bellamy-Foster et al. 2010; Lenton et al. 2019; and Camfield 2022 for more supportive documentation.
4. There are now a variety of national indexes of well-being, such as a gross national happiness index (International Institute of Management n.d.), that include several

dimensions of human living conditions beyond the fixation of GDP with levels of commodity consumption.
5. For a most insightful documentation of this imperial process, see Panitch and Gindin (2012).
6. Professional employees are defined in this book as non-managerial workers with specialized post-secondary education job requirements. Further features and distinctions from other class positions will be specified in later chapters.
7. These two quotes are adapted from Terkel (1974). See especially pp. xxxiv and 407–408.

1

Studying Classes in Advanced Capitalism

Standpoint, Framework and Method of Inquiry

I would describe my perspective when I began systematic study of contemporary societies — and right now — as an "inside-outsider." I grew up with exceptional access to the experiences and thoughts of people from very different ways of life, at least in economic and some cultural terms. But as long as I can remember, there was a wider comparative view that kept me questioning some of these practices and beliefs. There were always some aspects that kept me from full immersion in any group. This chapter starts with different standpoints for studying classes in advanced capitalism and establishes my current standpoint as an intellectual inside-outsider aligned with subordinate class groups. Then, I briefly outline the general conceptual framework I work from, the landscape in which the following empirical explorations of class relations are developed. Finally, the method of social inquiry of class relations I use is discussed. Marx developed a method of "determinate abstractions." His analysis of capitalism began with the simple notion of a single commodity and of the wealth of societies as merely an immense accumulation of commodities. Through an investigation of the exchange value of commodities, he found the basic determining source of profit and wealth from commodity sales to be in the unpaid labour of hired workers — the labour theory of value. In Chapter 2, I begin with the simple notion of class in current popular understanding.

Intellectual Standpoints: Class Vantage Points and Alignments

I start with the general assumption that there are different standpoints from which to study classes in advanced capitalism and that these different standpoints for studying classes may lead to different perceptions of the phenomena and conclusions about their nature. If we agree that classes exist, then at least three basic types of classes can be identified: (1) a dominant class or classes that have overarching power as a consequence of owning the major means of production sufficient to hire and use others' labour power; (2) a subordinated class or classes excluded from such ownership and dependent on whether or not they can sell their labour for a wage; and (3) intermediate or marginal classes existing contingently between or somewhat outside the dominant and subordinate class positions who may possess sufficient assets to avoid complete dependence on selling their wage labour to the dominant class(es). I develop these class distinctions later. For present purposes, we need to recognize that we all begin from one of these basic classes of origin and that such points of origin continue to influence our later views.

It is an indisputable social fact that work remains the central material activity in most adults' lives in contemporary capitalist societies. It is equally indisputable that substantial divisions of paid and unpaid labour persist in all modern societies. These divisions are likely linked with the ways people think of their work experiences and of themselves in relation to other groups of people. Such work-based relationships constitute primary criteria for interpreting the existence of classes in contemporary capitalist societies — as illustrated especially in Chapters 2 and 5.

The bulk of the recorded interpretations of class relations, as well as of social reality in general, have been provided by those whose primary work is with ideas and who are now commonly referred to as "intellectuals." In a basic sense we are all intellectuals, but in many societies some have been designated as proprietors of knowledge that offers models applicable beyond individual situations or with cross-contextual validity, knowledge that a society (or group) can use to orient its members. These proprietors of knowledge have been exempted thereby from the obligation of performing physical or routine labour (Konrad and Szelenyi 1979, 24–35). Ever since societies have been based on commodity exchange, intellectual labour has been distinguished from manual labour by "the use of non-empirical form abstractions which may be represented by nothing other than non-empirical 'pure' concepts" (Sohn-Rethel 1978, 66). My main interest here is in the standpoints of social scientific intellectuals, who attempt to accumulate and systematize knowledge.

The continuing production and co-existence of diverse perspectives and results within most fields of science underline the fact that scientists, as all intellectuals, have different subjective dispositions related to their *vantage points* in society, i.e., the primary social locations in which they live and from which they work. At the same time, the proliferating marketing and unintended uses of scientific work beyond the scientific community's control make it clear, mostly by negative example, that scientists have their own distinct if not autonomous interests. They are not merely the neutral instruments of society as a whole or, for that matter, the empty-headed conduits of the dominant, subordinate or marginal group vantage points from which they come. In short, genuine scientists are being drawn to an awareness that scientific work in socially divided societies is contingent on not only the scientist's vantage point in dominant, subordinate or intermediate social groups but also their extent of *alignment* with or commitment to such social interest groups.

So, in identifying different intellectual standpoints for class analysis, we need to distinguish between vantage points and alignments.[1] Vantage points denote actual locations within class relations and other spheres of social activity. Those in dominant, subordinate and intermediate positions have different arrays and ranges of experience. Those lodged within a dominant group or locked into a subordinate one usually have many restrictions on the range of experience upon which they can draw to interpret society as a whole. The relatively comfortable material existence of dominant groups rarely has provoked sustained efforts to interpret social life in their societies in penetrating terms. The most subordinated groups — however intensely troubling their life experiences and however strong the impulse to make deeper sense of them — have hardly ever possessed the time and means to record and effectively distribute their reflections for posterity. New social media now at least offer further means.

Being in an intermediate class vantage point opens one to the contradictory realities of both dominant and subordinate vantage points, and more often, the time and means for recording and distributing ones' reflections are relatively accessible. One's class vantage point of origin may be distinct from one's later vantage point of arrival. Through whatever combination of talent, effort and circumstances, one who begins in any of these three basic class positions may end up in one of the others, with different combinations of privileges and restrictions in their views.

The *class alignment* one takes is as important as one's vantage point, which does not necessarily determine intellectual alignment. Such choices may be made intentionally or tacitly. Intellectuals may align themselves with their own class of origin or with their class of arrival, or with another class. Conversely, they may assume non-alignment with any of these classes and regard themselves as classless or class-free, or they may even see intellectuals as an autonomous community, a class in themselves.[2]

A prevalent tendency over the past century was to presume intellectuals' non-alignment with the major classes and to believe that they must pursue independent, "value free" inquiries to ensure objectivity. One variant of non-alignment with major classes asserts that intellectuals are autonomous from other social groups and can generate knowledge that is free of the values of such groups, or universally valid, and are "class-less" themselves (Mannheim 1985 [1929]). A further variant similarly assumes intellectuals' autonomy but asserts that their grasp of knowledge leads to a tendency for them to become a "class in themselves" (Benda 1928) and even sees them as an increasingly influential force in a knowledge-based "post-industrial" society (Bell 1976).

But many argue that such independence and value-free inquiry is impossible, that intellectuals remain inescapably class-bound and that their alignments with major classes — consciously chosen or tacit — should be made apparent for assessing the standpoint of their analyses (Gramsci 1971; Mills 1963). Gramsci in particular distinguished between "organic intellectuals," who consciously articulated the views of the class with which they were aligned, and "traditional intellectuals," who ignored their class alignment or professed non-alignment. For Gramsci, organic intellectuals aligned with the dominant bourgeois class played a central role in shaping the ruling ideas and ideology of capitalist societies, while traditional intellectuals, however creative, remained encapsulated within these dominant forms.

More recently, perspectives on class vantage points and alignments have become more complex and nuanced. For example, in terms of class-less approaches, Randall Collins (1998) assumes autonomy within intellectual worlds, but an autonomy mediated by varying external conditions and clusters of networks and rivalries. Pierre Bourdieu (1989; 1991) presents intellectuals as a class in themselves characterized as bearers of universal reason with invariant interest in pursuing autonomous fields of inquiry, but also comprising a dominated fraction of the dominant class. Among those who see intellectuals as class-bound, there has been considerable interest in the process through which intellectuals can become organic to specific classes, even influence the liberation of oppressed classes. But those interested in this process typically also register a series of necessary historical conditions and complicating social network patterns (Brym 1980; Karabel 1996).

If we were to consider origin in dominant, subordinate or intermediate/marginal classes, as well as mature class vantage point and alignment, dozens of possible combinations would be generated. The purpose of this overview is not to offer an exhaustive inventory of intellectual standpoints. Rather, it is to provide a context for situating the standpoint I use to study classes in this book. I take the position that both class of origin and mature class vantage point are likely to influence the views of intellectuals and that alignment should be made apparent for assessing the standpoint of their analyses. I also assume that the relationship between intellectuals' knowledge and power in advanced capitalism is highly mediated. Those intellectuals who intentionally or tacitly align themselves with dominant classes have been more likely to have their views quickly and widely disseminated by mass media; the views of intellectuals aligned with subordinate classes have been more likely to be relegated to specialized forums and less easily find popular resonance.

Some intellectuals have celebrated the epistemological privilege of marginality (e.g., Lefebvre 1971, xx). Marginalized intellectuals may be in position to perceive established values and settled norms of both dominant and subordinate classes more comprehensively than those embedded in these classes. But being at the margin hardly guarantees privileged insight. Marginalized intellectuals have often been prone to align themselves with either dominant or subordinate classes and attribute views to them without careful investigation (see Pels 1998), a point developed in Chapter 6 on class consciousness.

Distinct from marginalized individual intellectuals, groups marginalized by racialization, sexual orientation or impairment status have also increasingly been subjects of inquiry both by researchers who share the status and are considered to be members or insiders, as well as by non-members who stand at a distance, outsiders. Both positions have merits. Insider researchers may get privileged access and aid co-construction of knowledge (Chaudhry 2018). Conversely, outsider researchers could ask more challenging questions to deepen understanding for the marginalized group and more generally (Bridges 2017). Even in terms of vantage point alone, such binaries as "insider-outsider" or "privileged-oppressed" may be seen as simplistic. Arguments are made for adoption of an "in-betweener" researcher status located on insider-outsider continua (Chhabra 2020), but this direction could devolve into a complicating and discouraging relativism.

In general, the researcher position that I find most appealing in combining vantage point and alignment is *inside-outsider*.[3] These researchers align themselves with and are welcomed by a given social group but recognize that they are not full-fledged members of the group while seeking to develop collaborative knowledge.

Rather than assuming the superiority of any standpoint, it may be advisable to grant that different combinations of vantage points and alignments may be capable of generating insights and explanations about reality of class relations. In any case, intellectual standpoints should not be adopted as deep, primitive or essential vantage points beyond reflection. They should be explicitly constructed and identified as credible bases for conducting social analysis and remain accessible for interrogation in relation to empirical evidence.

Without assuming epistemological privilege, I observe that some outsider intellectuals who have aligned themselves with subordinate class groups have produced some of the most insightful and enduring contributions to understanding class relations in advanced capitalist societies. The examples of Karl Marx and Antonio Gramsci have been most relevant for me. Both aligned themselves with and were engaged with the labour movements of their times. Both were much more interested in the development of a critical analysis of capitalism than in reflecting on their own relationship with subordinate classes.

From around the time of Gramsci's imprisonment in the 1920s to the present, outsider intellectuals who have professed alignment with subordinate classes have generally had limited engagement with them and spent more time largely cloistered within expanding university settings.[4] More limited contact has also made differences between their own vantage points and subordinate classes more evident. So, it has been more difficult for outsider intellectuals to simply assume a proletarian standpoint, as Marx and Gramsci were inclined to do in their continuing engagement.

The illusion of neutrality and absolute objectivity continues to be furthered by the rarity with which academic social scientists recognize in any explicit terms the class vantage points and social commitments from which they work. Some with sympathies for subordinate classes may see such admission as undermining the objectivity claims of their research compared to value-free claims. But, if we recognized the existence of different standpoints, it is preferable to identify them in the research rather than hiding and confounding them with it.

Organic intellectuals, whether materially located within a major social group or only choosing to align themselves with it, can be among the most influential of scientists. Such associations are more easily observed over long historical periods and for the social sciences in particular. A recent example is the array of research consultants of the Trilateral Commission of global corporate leaders. Such researchers, while clearly aligned with transnational corporate capitalist interests, have carried out detailed, empirically grounded investigations of the world capitalist economy and its governability since the 1970s.[5] Despite their narrow elitist alignment and whatever propagandistic use may be made of their findings, such researchers can remain primarily scientists rather than ideologues for capitalism.

Scientific contributions that contradict current received knowledge and vested interests have to resonate with the experience or interests of emergent social groups in order to be considered seriously both within the scientific community and society at large. Scientists who align themselves with broader subordinate social groups should not be disqualified as scientists by such commitments. While traditional intellectuals are probably still the preponderant majority of scientists in most fields, the development of science in achieving general social truths should properly be understood as the result of cumulative works of traditional and organic intellectuals using intersubjectively verifiable methods and critically assessing the concepts, hypotheses and findings of those scientists with other values. All contemporary science remains class based. But a growing self-consciousness about the effects of different vantage points and commitments, as well as diverse methods, on past and present scientific work can aid scientists in establishing real truths about the world.[6]

My own interpretations of social reality and class relations are those of a social scientist with an outsider vantage point between dominant capitalist and subordinate working classes. My father's parents had a small store in a northern county during the Irish War of Independence. They went bankrupt and the family emigrated to Canada to start again on a small farm in the Lower Fraser Valley of British Columbia. My mother's parents ran a small hotel in northern BC in a town that burnt down. They also moved to another town to start again. Like many others, both families scraped through the Great Depression. My father found a job as an assistant municipal clerk. When I was growing up, he became city manager in Surrey, BC. In that job, he had to respond to demands of elected councillors and major local business owners, negotiate with leaders of the main labour unions and advise on welfare provisions for the most destitute people. I spent much of my youth in the Scout movement and a wide variety of sports teams. In our town, my friends included kids from the very poorest backgrounds to the very richest. As a teenager, I spent three wet weeks on a muddy hillside in the Philippines at a world jamboree with Scouts from over fifty countries. I left the Anglican church as a young teenager after an earnest reverend could not answer my Confirmation queries. I left the Scout movement soon after the Philippines, distressed by the inequities I saw that Scout doctrine grossly ignored. As a sociology student, I took a year out of university to backpack through Southeast Asia, the Middle East and Western Europe. By this time, I had developed strong sympathies for the life conditions of subordinate groups in Canada and globally. I decided to devote my further studies to understanding their life conditions and prospects for improvement.

I completed my doctoral studies at Johns Hopkins University in Baltimore with a dissertation on comparative economic, political and education development in many countries — and increasing unease with the "unreflected universalism" of the sociology I had been taught.[7] I obtained a faculty job at the Ontario Institute for Studies in Education of the University of Toronto. In this position, I was able to engage in research with various subordinate groups, ranging from community school activists in impoverished neighbourhoods to the largest steelworkers' union in the country. I was also centrally involved in establishing a research centre, the Centre for the Study of Education and Work (CSEW), that brought together academics, labour educators and community partners to understand and enable the often-undervalued work and learning practices of working people. CSEW developed research and teaching programs to help strengthen working-class and labour movement profiles as well as feminist, anti-racist perspectives within the University of Toronto.

In this context, I was able to work with several colleagues with similar sympathies, most notably Mary O'Brien (1981), Dorothy Smith (1987) and Margrit Eichler (1980), who taught me much about critical feminist inquiries. The Sociology and Equity Studies Department, in which we worked, was an exceptional site to engage in social inquiries devoted to and aligned with disadvantaged social groups. Through these experiences, I became increasingly intellectually aware of other social privileges that I had largely taken for granted as a white heterosexual male with no recognized impairment. But it is only now as I become elderly and hard of hearing that I can say I begin to understand the oppressive depths of these multiple forms of domination.

I have worked from this inside-outsider intellectual standpoint with the benefits of a relatively independent public institutional setting. I have tried to produce and present research on class relations in open forums subject to criticism from different standpoints. The objective has been to contribute to cumulative advance of intersubjectively verifiable knowledge mostly with and for interested communities of subordinate-class backgrounds. This is the standpoint from which I operate in presenting the research in this book.

A Trans-Historical Conceptual Framework for Class Analysis

I briefly outline here the trans-historical conceptual framework that has served to orient my own studies of class relations. This framework is a set of guidelines to identify basic aspects of social reality to be taken into account in developing class analyses in general and advanced capitalism in particular.

I assume that individuals always exist in a given society and natural environment and are at least partly determined by this milieu. The basis of social reality is the ensemble of relationships that people have established and continually reproduce or modify with each other and with their non-human environment. At least six general categories are invariably involved in this ensemble: the non-human environment, human biology, enduring material institutions and modes of thought, and the practical activities and consciousness of individual social beings. In short, human society is the effect of the interaction between nature, human biology and social relations, and it is crucial to a materially grounded approach that society be regarded as the product of this interaction. Nature and human biology are implicated in any account of social relations, even if social determinations themselves take precedence in historical explanation.

Within societies per se, I begin with *material production* and with the premise that the social production, distribution, exchange and consumption *of the means of subsistence* is the central problematic of human existence and the most fundamental historical act. The daily and generational *reproduction of the species' capacity for material production through household labour* of some form is equally essential.[8] In addition, *a third material activity essential to all human societies is communal relations*. These interactions across co-residence domestic groups create and modify languages, customs and social order, and thereby permit and facilitate the continuing production and reproduction of human collectivities.[9] The particular forms of institutions in which *production, reproduction and communal relations* are materialized may differ immensely across time and space, but institutions involving all three of these generic social activities serve as the irreducible material basis for the continuation of all human societies.[10]

Mental activities are always interwoven with material activities. Established patterns of thought also provide the social context for particular individuals' and groups' existence. Such thought patterns include both cognitive processes of how people think (e.g., perception, reasoning, imagination, abstraction and generalization, deduction and inference) and substantive forms of consciousness (e.g., signification structures, prevailing themes). Materially grounded methods of social inquiry should begin with reference to material social existence and should analyze mental life on this basis rather than disconnected from material context. Historical modes of signification and modes of cognition always characterize mental life and should be regarded as essential as modes of material production categories to an adequate analysis of the existing social context for historical individuals' activities in all human societies.

In the most trans-historical terms, then, the above account represents the general set of circumstances given by and transmitted from the past that are encountered by individual social beings. But it is always individuals who make history. Material institutions and modes of thought are historical social structures — not disembodied things but emergent summaries of social relationships which are continuously either reaffirmed or modified through individuals' acts, even though the mediated effects of human agents' acts are often remote from their intentions.

Individual acts involve the use of innate or acquired capacities or potentialities, whether as direct capacities or as efforts to acquire new capacities. I begin analytical inquiry of individual subjects by situating their practical activities in the material world, most essentially their material practices in institutional settings centred on production, reproduction and communal relations. Individual consciousness is best understood in the context of societal and individual material conditions as well as extant modes of cognition, individual phases of cognitive development and modes of signification, including prevailing patterns of "philosophy" (or ideology) and "common sense."

At least five conceptually distinguishable material sites of class relations are involved, namely the workplace, the household and the community as the major sites of everyday social existence where most essential production, reproduction and communal relations occur, as well as the marketplace and the state as "second-order" (i.e., not of irreducible necessity to the continuation of social life) institutions which have developed mainly from primary production and communal relations respectively to achieve increasingly pervasive influence in class societies. Such material sites are intimately interconnected and, particularly in pre-capitalist societies, may often be fused. But from the locus of advanced capitalism, where they are most fully developed, these respective material institutions are all relevant distinguishable sites for the constituting of class relations.[11]

In addition to different sites of material practices and modes of thought, approaches to studying class relations have generally tended to focus on either the conflictual or consensual nature of these relations. In conflict approaches, the interests of different classes or groups are stressed and primary attention is given to distinguishing the conditions and concerns of particular groups and the ways in which they relate to more dominant or subordinate groups. The central assumption is that their opposed interests make the legitimacy of social order problematic and vulnerable to continual change. In consensual approaches, individuals are regarded as generally sharing common value orientations and attention is given to identifying processes or forms reproducing the equilibrium and legitimacy of social order. In trans-historical terms, it is plausible to argue that processes of equilibrium between classes have been prominent in maintaining civilizations over long time periods, whereas in periods of their origin and decline, group conflicts are more likely to have prevailed. I assume that in all historical class societies, there has been inherent conflict between those who control surpluses from material production and those who do not, and that this conflict has been a continual source of potential change. But I do not presume the prevalence of either equilibrium or conflict; rather I take this as a question for empirical investigation of class relations within advanced capitalism.

This general trans-historical framework offers merely a starting point for more interpretive analyses of class relations in particular times and places with more specific theories of society and methods of inquiry. The remainder of the book narrows the focus to the development of class relations in advanced capitalism.

Research Method: Identifying Determinate Abstractions

Given the different standpoints of social scientific intellectuals, intersubjectively verifiable methods of inquiry are imperative in order to accumulate and systematize knowledge in any field, and particularly in fields such as class analysis where there are such evidently different standpoints. Techniques of investigation should aim for inclusion and representation of all relevant social groups and allow them meaningful expression of their views. Emile Durkheim (1964 [1895]) observed that we cannot understand a social fact unless we study it through the full range of its variation (although with other fathers of sociology he largely ignored women). Social science evidence never appears as stark objective information; it is as a combination of observations and hypotheses from particular standpoints. Basically, *descriptions* tell us in more or less detail *what* a phenomenon is as perceived by one or more of our senses. *Explanation* tells us *why* the phenomenon is the way it is. It is only by systematic efforts to penetrate beneath surface descriptive forms to discover the historical forces operating in social contexts that we can understand and explain the fundamental bases of class existence in any epoch.

The method of inquiry I have used in this research has three basic steps:

1. document simple forms of the notions of "class" and "class differences" as they appear in everyday life;

2. identify relations between classes in terms of forces that are posited to drive continuity and change; and

3. investigate interaction between simple appearances of class and driving forces of class relations in historically specific contexts.

This is a version of the experimental method, always starting from a real, concrete problem, proceeding to a more abstract hypothesis, and finally coming back to concreteness for verification. The first step can produce a plethora of materials that require selection for further investigation, but contending hypotheses about relations between classes can then be tested with similar bodies of empirical evidence. Contending hypotheses can be further tested through gathering of additional empirical evidence and hypotheses rejected, confirmed or revised. Whatever variation in specific techniques, this is ideally the basic process of advancing knowledge. I say "ideally" because frequently bodies of empirical evidence and hypotheses are tightly bound up and contend with each other in "paradigm wars." For example, among those who focus on social stratification, Weberian and Marxist approaches to class analysis have rarely tested their hypotheses with similar bodies of empirical evidence but chosen to refine their own hypotheses with their own selected evidence.[12]

In any event, I take the method of inquiry I am using to be close to a version of Karl Marx's basic approach to scientific understanding of social reality in his studies of capitalism. This approach was to locate in concrete historical materials determining abstract relations posited to animate concrete social reality and permit this reality to be accurately appropriated and reproduced in thought. This method of investigation entailed a continuing movement from the concrete to the abstract and back again.

This persistent effort to identify contingent historically determinate abstractions underlying and animating simple abstractions distinguishes Marx's method of inquiry from that of many other social scientists, friend or foe of his revolutionary commitment to subordinate classes. On the one hand, there are all those preoccupied with simple abstractions per se, ranging from social relativists such as ethno-methodologists, concerned with reconstructing common-sense interpretations of social reality, to naturalistic materialists who regard intellectual concepts as naively realistic impressions of objects themselves. On the other hand, there are all those formalist approaches that have reified particular concepts into universal abstractions and timeless logics, which are then presumed to underlie surface appearances in varied historical phenomena; this was a dominant intellectual tendency of bourgeois science as well as both Western and Soviet Marxism throughout much of the twentieth century.[13] Max Weber, perhaps the most gifted of all bourgeois social scientists, conducted detailed comparative historical studies. But he still tended to explain capitalism and bureaucracy as major manifestations of an all-embracing process of "rationalization" — a trans-historical concept that is generally treated as a continuous, inexorable progression rather than an historically specific phenomenon.[14]

As Marx (2010 [1879], 54) stated: "What I start from is the simplest social form of the product of labour in present day society, and that is the 'commodity.' That is what I analyse and I analyse it initially in the form in which it appears." That is, Marx begins studying the commodity in the forms that it has appeared in the popular notions of everyday life and in the concepts of the bourgeois economists, finding in it the correspondence to their concepts and ending up discovering the historical origins of the apparently timeless concept of "value." In Chapter 2, I begin the current inquiry by looking at popular notions of class and class relations in capitalist society today.

Marx came to regard the task of scientific history to be the determination of the laws regulating the movement of different epochs of history. In contrast to Weber, he recognized that general abstract historically indeterminate laws do not exist in history. A scientific conception of history could only be developed through the process of establishing the historically determining laws specific to each epoch and their corresponding concretely developed categories.

Marx's most general statement of the expository character of this historical materialism was probably the following: "The specific economic form, in which unpaid surplus labour is pumped out of the direct producers, determines the relationship of rulers and ruled, as it grows directly out of production itself and, in turn, reacts upon it as a determining element" (1967 [1894], 791–792). This statement has been interpreted in a multitude of ways by both friends and foes of Marx's method of inquiry. What is clear is that Marx came to see this labour theory of value as central to explaining change and continuity in the capitalist mode of production and class relations within capitalism. His own major task was to identify and explicate the development of dominant economic forms of the capitalist epoch of production. For instance, the simple category of "wage labour" had been known under various forms of social production before the capitalist epoch. The mobility of labour power became essential to the operation of the laws of motion of capital. But the historical specificity of "wage labour" as a concretely developed category or historically determinate abstraction — comparable to the abstraction of "capital" — derived not from the mere generalization of labour as a commodity but from its incorporation into surplus value producing enterprises. Generally, Marx's scientific study of the capitalist epoch culminating in *Capital* was, as Jairus Banaji (1977, 9–10) has summarized:

> the rigorous, systematic investigation of the laws of motion of capitalist production, in the course of which a series of simple abstractions (wage-labour, money, etc.) were historically concretized as bourgeois relations of production, or abstractions determinate to capitalism as a mode of production; that is, reconstituted as "concrete categories," as historically determinate social forms.[15]

More specifically, the underlying driving forces of the capitalist mode of production that Marx discerned and that I take as hypotheses of departure for current analyses of class relations are:

- inter-firm competition in pursuit of profits;

- competitive negotiations between employers and workers over profits and wage benefits; and

- continual revolutionizing of the forces of production.[16]

Marx thereby built his exposition of fundamental animating aspects of actual class relations in capitalist societies. These are the real determinate abstractions of surplus value (which is predominantly thought of in capitalism in the guise of "profits" and which wageworkers have sometimes identified in such terms as "getting a bit of our own back") and the historical laws of its extraction from labour power. Marx's labour theory of value and the centrality of extraction of surplus value from the labour power of workers have been subject to sustained attack by opponents and revision by supporters from the inception. For example, current debates rage about the relevance of the labour theory of value in relation to "intellectual" and "immaterial" forms of labour (e.g., O'Donnell et al 2006; Bohm and Land 2012). My studies of class relations start with an assumption of the continuing validity of this labour theory of value but also with the recognition of the continuing need to assess whether or not contemporary class relations are adequately explained by means of such previously established determinate abstractions.

The determinate abstractions that were Marx's points of arrival should not be turned into frameworks of timeless validity for widely varied historical studies and hence into formalistic abstractions. Marx's own basic contribution was to identify and specify a distinctive inner contradiction between the private character of capitalist relations of production and the social character of the productive forces of the advanced capitalist mode of production as it had developed up to his time. As we shall see, many of the concrete economic categories and laws of motion that Marx discerned in the 1860s largely on the basis of the English case may still be operative as capitalist relations of production have taken more fully developed forms in both the advanced and underdeveloped sectors of the contemporary world economy (e.g., Banaji 2010; Livingstone, Smith and Smith 2011). The point is to continue to regard laws of motion as historically contingent, not merely to seek the "facts" to further apply or verify them. Even with regard to the frequently presumed universality of the law of a fundamental contradiction between productive forces and relations of production, Marx (1967 [1894], 109) himself insisted — in contrast to many of those Marxist intellectuals who have followed him — that the "dialectic of the concepts of production forces (means of production) and relations of production [is a] dialectic whose boundaries are to be determined."

Historical materialist studies of contemporary capitalist societies generally and class relations specifically can draw on analytical distinctions and determinate abstractions established by Marx but should always verify and be prepared to modify them through reference to concrete social reality. Indeed, historical materialism is more accurately regarded as a methodological postulate than as a theoretical paradigm claiming to fully comprehend, or to provide timeless concepts capable of comprehending, concrete social reality. We should never turn prior simple abstractions and received laws developed through sensitive empirical historical inquiry into formalistic, reified versions of their generative forms.

Marx never claimed that he had identified all the tendential laws of motion of the capitalist epoch. Neither did Marx provide a full-scale theorization of class relations even in the sphere of production most narrowly conceived. In a last unpublished fragmentary chapter of volume three of *Capital*, Marx left his most explicit outline of the "big classes" in the capitalist production system. The chapter begins as follows:

> The owners merely of labour-power, owners of capital, and land-owners, whose respective sources of income are wages, profit and ground-rent, in other words, wage-labourers, capitalists and land-owners, constitute then three big classes of modern society based upon the capitalist mode of production. (1967 [1894]: 885)

Ever since his collaborator, Frederick Engels, edited and published this final volume, progressive scholars have bemoaned Marx's failure to develop this outline of classes further and speculated on the reasons — given that he lived and wrote for almost a generation after this fragment was drafted (Rikowski 2001). In my view, the basic reason is now obvious. When Marx wrote, the capitalist mode of production was still in transition to a fully developed form, as was its class structure. Ground rent to landlords had been an increasingly prevalent form of land tenure in rural regions (as distinct from more fixed common socage payments and other prior forms of feudal tenure, including serjeanty, frankalmoin and knight-service). But, particularly from the 1880s onward, private corporations based on large capital pools replaced family-owned firms and industrialization moved more people from land tenure to wage seeking. Rural landlords content with ground rent were increasingly replaced by capitalists hiring wage labourers to generate more profits from agribusinesses. In various places in his writings, Marx indicated some awareness of emergent classes in maturing capitalist production, including managerial overseers and service workers, but the specific class relations characteristic of capitalism were neither his priority nor as evident as they later became.

What Marx did do was to uncover a pivotal basis of the existence and contradictory development of classes in the distinction between necessary and surplus labour and in the extraction and appropriation of surplus value in capitalist production systems.[17] He identified the driving forces of the capitalist mode of production: inter-capitalist competition for profit maximization, struggle between capital and labour over relative profit and wage shares, and consequential continual modification of production techniques to enhance profits and limit wages. While the fully developed form of capitalist production was still in formation when he wrote, Marx discerned its basic tendencies rather well. These were concentration and centralization of larger and larger pools of corporate capital (manifest now in gigantic private equity firms like Blackrock) and generalization of the capitalist labour process (incorporating most forms of labour as wage labour) to extend around the globe and into most spheres of our existence. Chapter 3 provides an account of the development of the advanced capitalist mode of production. Chapter 4 builds on this basis to offer an outline of the main classes in advanced capitalist production relations. Just as the driving forces, class relations are continually changing rather than static categories. But in order to begin to comprehend prospects for progressive social change, we need to gain a sense of the magnitude and orientations of the "big classes" in advanced capitalism.

Marx's mature work has been of enduring relevance for class analysis in advanced capitalism because it does not depend on trans-historical abstract concepts but on historical abstractions regarding the material economic basis of society. While this method of inquiry initiated by Marx may still not be widespread nor even consistently applied by those who espouse it, it marks the beginnings of a fundamental departure from bourgeois science which takes as an underlying assumption the continuation of the capitalist mode of production. This historical materialist method cannot exist in a social vacuum. In some ways, historical materialism may still be encapsulated within the capitalist epoch of production and mode of thought. Certainly, historical materialism shares with bourgeois science a number of generic methodological properties of modern science. However, such properties are potentially just as usable against bourgeois rationalism as they were against feudal obscurantism, namely: a demand for evidence and appeal to common sense rather than social authority; a need for independent testing and judgement; a belief that knowledge is not self-evident and requires work; and an awareness that intellectual detours are sometimes necessary to solve problems (e.g., Levine 1981, 17). To characterize historical materialism as merely a "surface ripple" on the dominant mode of thought of the current epoch — as Foucault for example has done[18] — is both to presume formalistically a continuing absolute dominance of capitalist epochal structures and to ignore distinctive features of genuine historical materialist thought.

Marx's work was done when economics was the only developed social science, and the determinate abstractions he identified dealt primarily with relations of material production. As the trans-historical conceptual framework outlined above should suggest, in order to comprehend class relations more fully, inquiries into other material institutions, modes of thought and the practical activities and consciousness of individual social beings to identify simple abstractions and driving historical forces may also be identified and incorporated into class analyses. But it is probably fair to say that empirically grounded Marxist theorizing outside the sphere of material production relations is still largely at the level of comprehending history and identifying simple abstractions.

The above characterization of Marx's method, stressing its materialist epistemology, the centrality of history and the requirement of empirical verification, would be contested by several contemporary Marxist scholars (see Sayer 1979). Indeed, diverse theoretical currents of Marxist thought have been contending with each other in both methodological and substantive terms, often bitterly, for many years.[19] The purpose of the current research is not to enter into this largely philosophical debate but to apply Marx's method of determinate abstractions as I understand it to explore, explain and suggest further questions for comprehending class relations in advanced capitalism.

A few other features of the present method of inquiry should also be registered at the outset. First, as noted earlier, gender and race relations as well as age-group relations have all been increasingly recognized as essential features of social reality which are not simply reducible to or derivable from class relations per se. Women and those with marginalized gender and sexual orientations, minority ethnic groups, and young and old people all also experience particular forms of oppression and have had their vantage points submerged in advanced capitalist societies. More generally, biological differences in sex and age always provide potential material bases for gender and age-based subordination in all human societies. Geographically founded differences in physical distinguishability, language, religion and other ways of life always offer bases for ethnic subordination of distinct "peoples." While most of Marx's own work and the subsequent orthodoxy have been preoccupied with the production process and privileging the vantage point of subordinate producers in the direct relations of production, historical materialism remains essentially open to being combined with subordinate gender, ethnic and age-group vantage points for more comprehensive description, analysis and explanation of social totalities. There have been some promising initiatives toward drawing such links, both in contemporary social movements and intellectual work.[20] For those whose primary interest is in understanding class existence per se, the significance of these developments is twofold. They underline that classes themselves are constituted as lived associations in other material spheres of life as well, rather than simply derived from production relations and reproduced elsewhere; and in addition, they indicate that these other (i.e., gender, racialization and age-based) essential features of social relations, however entwined with class relations, are likely to have their own historically determinate effects on both class existence and the overall structure of societies. As Camfield (2016, 295) observes: "Anti-racist queer feminism offers two vital contributions to [historical materialist] social theory: a social ontology of oppression [as integral] and an understanding that forms of oppression operate simultaneously in social processes."

Second, I understand the Marxist phrase "being determines consciousness" as a methodological postulate for this inquiry. With growing documentation and analyses of the historical forms of the material sites of class relations and the interconnections between these sites, the material context of class existence in advanced capitalist societies is becoming clearer. However, classes themselves can never be reduced to material sites alone. As the trans-historical framework should suggest, classes are always constituted as lived associations at several material sites permeated by contending class-based modes of thought, through the consciousness and practical activities of particular individual subjects. Starting from material sites, the relations between material class location and class consciousness are approached as complex and interactive (see Seccombe and Livingstone 1999). Perhaps with the identification of historically specific material sites of class relations beyond the paid workplace whereby class consciousness is highly moderated, the analysis of class relations and the reproduction in thought of class existence as a concrete social reality can proceed on a more adequate basis.

The practical reality of liberatory action by subordinate classes has frequently occurred before intellectuals' theoretical awareness of it. If progressive intellectuals want to relate in genuinely liberatory terms to members of subordinate groups, they must not only listen and observe sensitively. They must also forego manipulative persuasion and continue to try to penetrate and share with these people the determinate abstractions that tend to animate all our lives and the contradictory social totality in which we live. This is the essence of Marx's methodological legacy that I pursue here.

Notes

1. For a brief earlier discussion of this distinction, see Livingstone (1983a, 12ff.).
2. For an extensive review of the alignments of intellectuals over the twentieth century as bound to major classes, class-free or a class in themselves, see Kurzman and Owens (2002).
3. For an accessible (but class-blind) account of inside outsider standpoints with reference to "some of the most innovative people in history," see Shahinian (2016).
4. Anderson (1976) provides an insightful outline of Western Marxist intellectual contributions in the post–World War I era, with defining features including remoteness from working-class movements. My only major dissent is with his decision to place Gramsci within the Western Marxist tradition; the inappropriateness becomes readily apparent as Gramsci is made the exception on nearly every point.
5. See, for example, Sklar (1980). Among the prominent social scientists associated with the Commission are economist Fred Bergsten, sociologist Michael Crozier and political scientist Samuel Huntington.
6. See, for example, Levine (1981) for a discussion of the relations between class science and scientific insight with particular reference to Euclidean geometry and Newtonian physics.
7. See Michael Burawoy (2016) for a critical reflection on the universalizing dominance of US sociology, the challenges of generating authentic perspectives in subordinated regions and the importance of researchers with "tentacles" in civil society to nurture critical standpoints globally.
8. See Seccombe (1992) for a well-documented account of how household and family forms and relations changed from the Middle Ages to the beginning of the Industrial Revolution and from peasant subsistence to the making of the modern working class.

9. "Community" is now widely regarded as one of the most elastic terms in social science. The term generally refers to the extent to which those in extra-familial settings share interests and identities. Debate continues about the extent to which geographical, occupational and cultural and other social groupings constitute effective communities. The basic point here is that such groupings reaching beyond household and workplace spheres continue to constitute political agency in most societies, the most coherent often being most powerful. For an overview of relevant literature, see Day (2006).
10. For earlier formulations of these three basic spheres of material human existence, see Livingstone (1976; 1983a).
11. For earlier applications of this trans-historical framework with reference to advanced capitalist societies, see Livingstone (1976; 1983a).
12. There have, of course, been some notable exceptions. See, for example Wright (1980) and Livingstone and Mangan (1996b).
13. For critical discussion of this point, see Sohn-Rethel (1978, 111-138), Anderson (1976) and Banaji (1977, 9-10).
14. See, for example, the sympathetic assessment of Weber's work in H.S. Hughes (1958, 278-335). Weber wrote with the benefit of a much more developed body of historical research than was available to Marx, and it is arguable that in his most mature work he identified a more complex array of institutional factors involved in the emergence of a world capitalist system than Marx had. Certainly, in his *General Economic History*, Weber (1961 [1923]) documents an intricate series of combinations of conditions occurring together in the origins of European capitalism, and he outlines continuing tension and balances among opposing elements in an open market or competitive capitalist economy. But Weber's bourgeois alignment and the idealistic logic of his method of inquiry still prevent him from perceiving relations of surplus value extraction in the production process as fundamental contradictions animating the capitalist epoch of production and dispose him to read history backwards from the presumption that "rational" capitalism as established in his time could indefinitely endure as an economic system. Randall Collins (1980, 927-928) so characterizes this approach in his valuable recuperation of Weber's mature analysis of capitalism.
15. Banaji (1977, 9-10) continues: "It follows that modes of production are impenetrable at the level of simple abstractions. The process of "true abstraction" is simultaneously a process of "concretization," of the definition of specific historical laws of motion.…Taken as a whole, across its various stages, the substance of Marx's analysis lies in its definition of the laws of motion of capitalist production: the production and accumulation of surplus value, the revolutionization of the labour process, the production of relative surplus value on the basis of a capitalistically-constituted labour process, the compulsion to increase the productivity of labour, etc. The "relations of capitalist production" are the relations which express and realize these laws of motion at different levels of the social process of production."
16. The classic exposition of these basic contradictory relationships in industrial capitalist production systems is in the writings of Karl Marx, particularly Volume 1 of *Capital* (Marx 1967 [1867]). For more recent treatments, see Castells (1980) and Livingstone (2009).
17. As Goran Therborn (1976, 394) has summarized Marx's view of economic classes: "The two polar classes of such an [exploitative] mode of production presuppose and precondition each other, and their relationship is not just logical, but material

— between exploiter and exploited, oppressor and oppressed. The classes are the two necessary poles of a common, specific mode of exploitation and oppression. Their interrelationship and their struggle are therefore determined by the development of this mode of production, a development which occurs in and through the struggle between the classes, as Marx demonstrates in the first volume of *Capital* (struggles over the working day, the introduction and use of machinery, wage levels, and the accumulation of capital). An exploitative mode of production, then, is contradictory in the sense that it is at the same time both a specific unity of opposing classes, of immediate producers and appropriators of surplus labour, and a conflict and struggle of these opposing classes."

18. See Foucault's (1970, 261-262) dismissive assessment of Marxism.
19. For overviews stressing such diversity see, for example, Kolokowski (1978) and Bottomore (1978).
20. Some of the most substantial work to date has been in the development of a feminist vantage point and has included both critiques of the silences and presumptions in classical Marxism regarding the specificity of women's situation and also attempts to apply a Marxist method of inquiry to document and analyze historical forms of patriarchy. As significant examples, see O'Brien (1981) and Smith (1987). With regard to ethnic relations, the British journal *Race and Class* has offered searching critiques of orthodox Marxism and applications of historical materialist methods from a vantage point of racial subordination. There is much attention to the general problems of youth and of aging, as well as to "passages" through the life cycle, in bourgeois social science. To my knowledge, no work comparable to the critical feminist and ethnic studies cited above but taking an age-based vantage point has yet appeared. Perhaps the fact that aging is the most universally shared feature of human lives is partly responsible for age categories of subordination being the hardest to perceive and analyze as historically constructed. For useful historical materials in this regard see, for example, Aries (1962).

2

Popular Notions of Classes Today

What does "class" signify to most people today? Differences in human abilities have always existed. In prehistoric hunter-gatherer communities there were divisions of labour based on the varied talents and experience of members. When rare surpluses occurred, they were either shared quickly or preserved for "rainy days" (Woodburn 1982). But with the development of agriculture and sustained surplus production, the notion emerged that some members, because of their distinctive merits, deserved more of whatever the community produced. Ever since, in nearly all societies with regular surplus production — whether extra grain or luxury products ranging from expensive automobiles to palaces — popular notions of class differences have been constructed to provide rationales for generally inequitable distribution.

If you asked most people in most historical societies what "classes" meant to them, you would probably have been given some version of divisions based on perceived social or economic status or privilege. Such divisions may have been seen primarily in terms of differences in wealth, income or other possessions. Some may have claimed that classes do not exist or are not relevant, but it is hard to deny the emergence of large inequities in material possessions in virtually all societies since the development of agriculture.

In this chapter, I look at popular notions of class differences among people in advanced capitalist societies today. In terms of inequity, there are blatantly massive material differences, for example, between the hedge fund managers who collect billions of dollars a year and the billions who barely survive, with precarious food and shelter provisions. But popular notions of class do not necessarily reflect such differences, and perceptions differ depending on the perceiver's social standpoint.

I begin with notions of the general sorts of classes and class structures that are recognized as important. I summarize where people identify themselves within class structures, and I also track changes in subjective class identity in recent decades. I briefly look at notions of conflict and harmony in class relations, and finally, I assess the perceived importance of class relations compared to other social divisions, such as racialization, gender, age and disability. Similarities and differences between those with different social standpoints are compared. I draw on survey evidence in Canada since the mid-1960s, especially a 2016 national survey.[1] Then, using quotes from interviews with Canadian steelworker families in the 1980s and 1990s as well as interviews with leaders of major social groups in the early 1990s and 2016, I provide further expressions of contemporary notions of classes. These profiles of change and continuity in simple popular ideas of class structure and class identity provide a basis for proceeding with more critical analyses in later chapters of class relations and class consciousness in advanced capitalism.

Perceptions of Class Structure

During the third quarter of the twentieth century, many researchers devoted attention to assessing images of class structure and political attitudes held by people working for wages (e.g., Bulmer 1975; Goldthorpe et al. 1969). Much of this interest concerned whether these workers were likely to revolt against their economic conditions. The conclusion was that, generally, workers were accommodating to current conditions. Interest then abated, with rare exceptions (e.g., Wallace and Junisbai 2003).

I start with questions about the existence of social classes and what sorts of images, if any, of different classes people hold today. The basic assumption is that responses to these questions provide initial approximations of people's awareness of classes and their own location within a class structure. When people in advanced capitalist societies have occasionally been asked directly in recent decades whether they think classes exist, the vast majority have typically responded that they do. Figure 2.1 summarizes the results of such Canadian surveys over the past several decades. About 90 percent in all surveys have recognized the existence of classes, whereas only about 10 percent either deny their existence or are unsure.

In recent decades, various political figures have proclaimed either that classes no longer exist, just individuals with different aspirations, or

Figure 2.1 Responses to Question about Existence of Social Classes

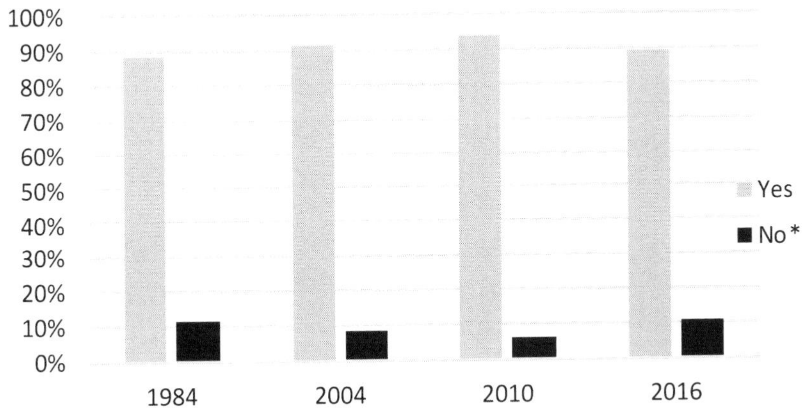

[Bar chart showing Yes/No responses for years 1984, 2004, 2010, 2016, with Yes responses around 90% for all years and No responses around 10%.]

*Includes those who responded "no" or "don't know" or refused to answer
Sources: 1984 Hamilton Families Survey (N=798) in Livingstone and Mangan (1996a); 2004 WALL National Survey (N=5590), 2010 WALL II National Survey (N=1193), 2016 CWKE National Survey (N=3007) all in Canada Work Learning Surveys. 1998–2016.

more commonly, that we are all now "middle class" (see Nunlee 2016). But, however pervasive ideological themes of classlessness or meritocracy have become, the vast majority from the poorest to most multi-millionaires still find it difficult to deny that classes exist.

In the 2016 national survey of the employed Canadian labour force, the many people who recognize the existence of classes were then asked how many classes they see and what their names are. The findings are summarized in Table 2.1. Around three-quarters of those in the employed labour force are willing and able to estimate the number of classes and around 60 percent can name them and provide more specific images of a class structure.

Table 2.1 Recognition of Classes, Employed Labour Force, Canada, 2016

Extent of Class Recognition	Percent
Recognize classes exist	89
Can estimate number of classes	75
Can name classes	62

Source: 2016 CWKE National Survey (N=2868) in Canada Work Learning Surveys. 1998–2016.

As Table 2.2 summarizes, among the three-quarters who estimate the number of classes, most indicate either three (47 percent) or four (27 percent) classes. The common classes named by those with three-class models are variants of rich, middle and poor classes. Those with four-class models tend to add either a very rich or a very poor class at one extreme. Those with simpler models identify only rich and poor. Some with more complex models add distinctions between those in the middle who are "comfortable" and those who are "getting by." Some offer more colourful language — such as "damn guys with way too much," "barely hanging on" and "truly destitute," or "thriving," "surviving" and "sinking," or "those with nothing," "living cheque to cheque" — but the basic pattern is clear. Most of those who perceive a class structure see it in terms of rich, middle and poor classes, with some refinements either at the top or the bottom.

Table 2.2 Class Models: Number of Classes Identified and Common Classes Named, 2016

Number of Classes Identified	Common Classes Named (and % with that Class Model)
2	Rich, Poor (7%)
3	Rich/Upper, Middle, Poor/Lower (47%)
4	Rich/Upper, Middle, Poor/Lower, plus either Very Rich or Below Poverty (27%)
5	Very Rich, Rich/Upper, Middle, Poor/Lower, Below Poverty (11%)
6	Very Rich, Rich/Upper, Upper (comfortable) Middle, Lower (getting by) Middle, Working/Lower, Poor/Lower, Homeless/Below Poverty (8%)

Source: 2016 CWKE National Survey (N=1864) in Canada Work Learning Surveys. 1998–2016.

A few respondents include either specific ethnic or racial groups (such as "Aboriginal"), recent non-white immigrants or people with physical or mental disabilities, probably because they perceive such groups as experiencing evident discrimination in terms of material possessions or opportunities.

It is evident both from the names they use and further comments that most of the respondents to the 2016 survey see classes in terms of wealth or income differences and consequential differences in consumption rather than political or cultural distinctions. Many prior studies also found that most people name either wealth or income as the main factor dividing classes, while small minorities mention occupation, education or family background (e.g., Lambert et al. 1986; Livingstone and Mangan 1996b).

Figure 2.2 Personal Class Identities of Those with Class Models, 2016

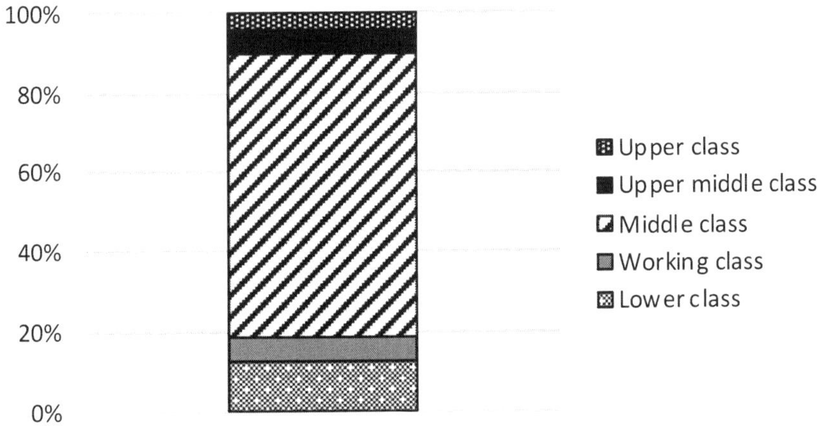

- Upper class
- Upper middle class
- Middle class
- Working class
- Lower class

Source: 2016 CWKE National Survey (N=1772) in Canada Work Learning Surveys. 1998–2016).

Personal and Standard Class Identities

Figure 2.2 shows the personal class identities of those who offer their own models of class structure; that is, they provide both the number and the names of the classes they see. While their personal terms for their own class may differ according to the classes named in Table 2.2, all can be translated easily into the standard class identities used in Figure 2.3 and later in this book. Nearly three-quarters of these people see themselves as right in the middle of their personal class model, i.e., as "middle class." About 10 percent see themselves above middle class, while 20 percent regard themselves below middle class — as either lower class or working class. So, among the majority of the employed labour force who have clear models of a class structure, the vast majority situate themselves in between the extremes of whatever classes their personal model holds.

Much more commonly, surveys have asked people to identify themselves in terms of standard pre-coded class identities. The typical terms are upper class; upper middle class; middle class (and/or lower middle class), working class and lower class. In the 2016 survey, all respondents were also asked to reply to this standard question. Figure 2.3 summarizes the standard class identity responses for those with clear models of class structure, for those without such models and for all respondents combined.

Once again, the common tendency, both for those with their own personal class models and for those without such models, is for people

Figure 2.3 Distribution of Class Identities for Those with and without Class Models, 2016

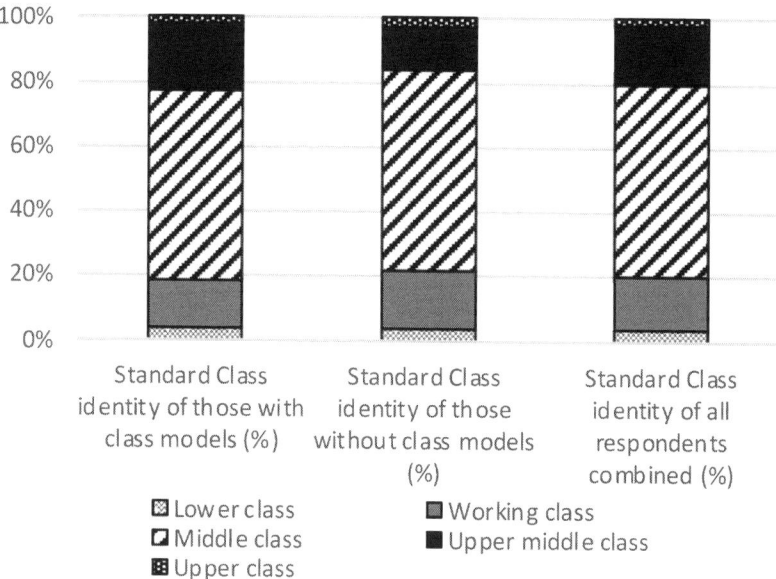

Source: 2016 CWKE National Survey in Canada Work Learning Surveys. 1998–2016. (N with class models=1772; N without class models=1096; total N=2868).

to identify themselves in the middle, with around 60 percent choosing "middle class." For those with their own class models, there are a few notable differences between class identities on their own personal class models and the standard pre-coded model. Some of those who think of themselves as "middle class" in their own terms opt for "upper middle class" when offered this standard label. Some of those who opt for "lower class" on their own class model choose "working class" on the standard model. This could mean that standard class identity options somewhat overestimate the proportions who generally think of themselves as either upper middle class or working class. In any case, a general bias to middle-class identity is evident.

Trends in Standard Class Identities

Comparable data on personal class models are not readily available for trend analysis. So, I use my data on standard class identities from 2004–2016 surveys in combination with earlier standard surveys of class identity to estimate trends in standard class identity. Figure 2.4 summarizes changes in such standard class identity terms in Canada over the

Figure 2.4 Standard Class Identities, Canada 1965–2016

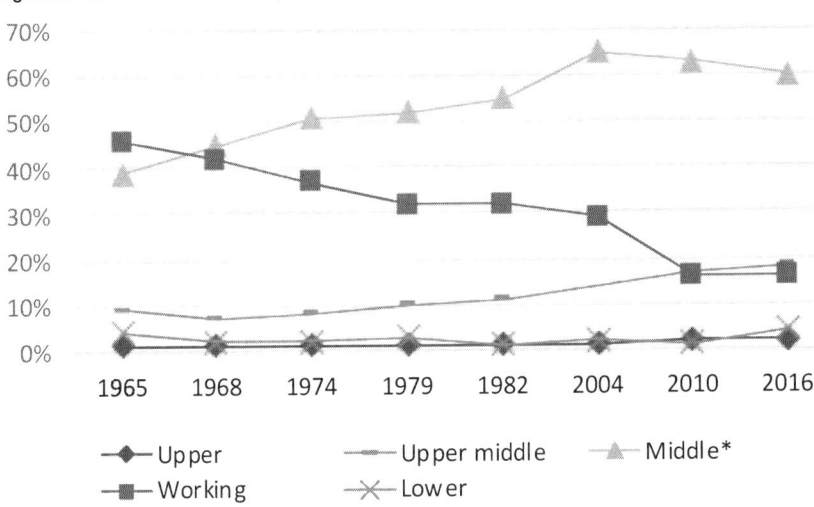

* Includes "lower middle"
Sources: 1965–1979 Clark, Kornblum and Mishler (1982) 1965 (N=2661); 1968 (N=2695); 1974 (N=2335); 1979 N=2517); 1982 Clement and Myles (1994) (N=808); 2004 WALL National Survey (N=5733), 2010 WALL II National Survey (N=1299), 2016 CWKE National Survey (N=2668) all in Canada Work Learning Surveys. 1998–2016.

1965 to 2016 period. Two trends are readily apparent. The frequency of reported working-class identity declined throughout the period. Nearly half of Canadian adults identified as working class in the mid-1960s. The proportion has declined to under 20 percent. Conversely, those who identify as middle class have grown from a minority to the majority. Similar trends have been found in the US (see Schreiber and Nygreen 1968; Jackman and Jackman 1983; Gilbert 2003) as well as in several other advanced capitalist countries where there are comparable time series data (e.g., Evans and Kelley 2004; Oddsson 2010).

In addition to the increasing trend to middle-class identity, there has been extreme reluctance to identify oneself at either the top or the bottom a social-class hierarchy. Only 1 or 2 percent of respondents ever declare themselves to be in the "upper class," and only the same tiny proportion or slightly more admit to being in the "lower class." Some upper-class identifiers may have delusions of grandeur, but most are probably too rich to deny it even to themselves. Some lower-class identifiers may harbour persecution complexes, but most are likely too destitute and desperate for delusions.

Perhaps more importantly, standard working-class identities — and likely personal working-class identities as well, to judge from the tiny proportion in Figure 2.2 — are claimed by dwindling numbers. Labour leaders and progressive researchers who try to appeal to the "working class" should probably recognize that many of those they are trying to address do not now see themselves in these terms. "Working people" and "working families" may be terms that more effectively resonate with those who see themselves as neither rich nor poor.

These tendencies to increasingly take on middle-class identity have been observed in advanced capitalist societies since the beginning of the post–WWII era of economic growth. These trends have commonly been attributed to increasing affluence or homogenization of reference groups (e.g., Evans and Kelley 2004; Curtis 2013). An obvious factor is the increasing mass production and consumption of standardized commodities. In all advanced capitalist societies, consumer products such as clothing, housing, food, entertainment, schooling, transport and information have become widely available in most basic spheres of life. Each of these tendencies is easily illustrated.

Clothing. Mass-produced clothing is widely available to most people in a diverse array of styles. Customized luxury wardrobes and accessories remain the preserve of the rich, while the very poor may depend on worn clothes from charities. But in a typical public space, the vast majority are indistinguishable except in the combinations of mass-produced clothing they choose.

Housing. Housing subdivisions, apartment blocks and condominiums have provided most people with a regular form of housing, whether fully owned, mortgaged or rented. There will likely be a "millionaires' row" of luxury homes and probably neighbourhoods of public housing for the poor, and there are some homeless people on inner city streets. But most areas of human settlement in advanced capitalism contain diverse mixtures of housing types.

Food. Mass-produced, processed foods sold through grocery chains and fast-food outlets constitute the bulk of most people's diets. There are exclusive clubs and fine restaurants for luxury dining, as well as food banks for the poor. But most of us have come to rely more and more on standardized packages of hothouse tomatoes and Big Macs.

Entertainment. If you attend a sporting event or musical performance at a public stadium, you will probably try to get reserved seating in one of many designated sections. There will likely be private boxes purchased by wealthy corporations. There may also be general admission to the "bleachers" that could become available at reduced rates if demand is low. But most people will try to buy either reserved seats or general admission at advertised rates.

Schooling. Majorities or near-majorities have attained some form of post-secondary schooling. Small numbers have completed post-graduate level training in arts and sciences, while smaller numbers have been unable to complete elementary and secondary schooling. But most people have an advanced level of schooling.

Transport. Most people have access to private or public transportation whenever they wish. For most this means owning or renting a private vehicle or having nearby public transit. Small numbers have private luxury autos with or without chauffeurs. Poor people are limited to public transit when affordable, the odd taxi or walking.

Information. With the profusion of information technology, most people have access to a wide array of sources of information most of the time. There is less to distinguish the rich in this regard, except that they can hire adepts to manipulate information for their own ends and may have more discretionary time to use it. The poor, on the other hand, may not be able to afford IT devices and be limited to using public sites.

In terms of employment patterns, continuing automation and computerization of manufacturing and extractive industries have served to greatly diminish the large concentrations of organized industrial workers that constituted the core of the traditional working class. Concentrations of immense wealth in large private corporations have greatly increased. Chronic, or structural, unemployment has also grown. The vast majority of the employed may have differing levels of qualifications and job security, but what they most have in common is that they work for a wage or salary.

If we consider all the dimensions of social differences in public spaces, signs of the existence of the rich, or upper class, and the poor, or lower class, are clearly evident. But the overwhelming appearance is of a large middle class taking up most of the space. So, it is not surprising that most of those who have their own class models perceive a large middle class and, when asked to locate themselves in their own or standard class groupings, they choose "middle class." Nor is it strange that most folks' class models include at least rich, middle and poor class groups, since versions of these differences are evident in most spheres of modern life.

So, what sorts of similarities and differences in class models and class identity are there between those with different social standpoints? I first look at general patterns and then consider a few representative voices.

Class Models and Class Identity by Social Background

There are few people from most social backgrounds who deny the existence of classes. Around 90 percent at all income and wealth levels, from the poorest to the richest, agree that social classes exist. There may be various reasons for some people to deny the existence of classes in modern society. Facing uncertain conditions themselves may lead some people not to recognize such differences. For example, in the 2016 survey, about 40 percent of the tiny minority with uncertain citizenship status deny classes exist. Similarly, most of the small minority who have uncertain occupational status do not have clear class models. Limited knowledge could also be a factor; about 40 percent of the tiny number in this survey who did not complete elementary schooling express ignorance of classes. Some of those in more dominant positions may wish to avoid humiliating subordinates or fomenting resentment by recognizing class differences (e.g., Thompson and Yar 2011, 100). In the 2016 survey, there is some suggestion that "rentier capitalists," whose main source of income is rent directly from others, are more likely (around 40 percent) to deny that classes exist. But majorities from all social backgrounds offer models with numbers and names of specific classes.

If material conditions have discernible effects on subjective perceptions, there should be some more general correspondence between different social locations and different personal class identities. Several decades ago — as working-class identities declined and middle-class identities rose — scholars were already documenting declining relations between standard measures of class identity and conventional measures of socioeconomic status (e.g., Goyder 1975). However, income and wealth levels continued to be recognized as central ingredients of socioeconomic status (e.g., Lambert et al. 1986). Figure 2.5 summarizes current relations between personal income level and standard personal class identity, according to the 2016 survey.

The first thing to register in looking at this figure is that those with personal incomes of over $100,000 in 2016 values were less than 10 percent of the labour force (Statistics Canada 2018) and those with over $150,000 were only a few percent. It is only among the small numbers in

Figure 2.5 Standard Class Identity by Personal Income Level, Employed, Canada, 2016 (%)

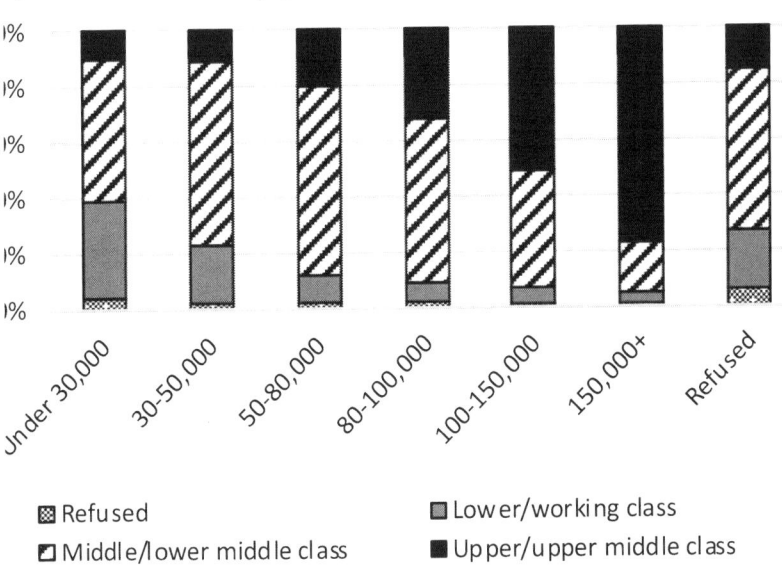

*Personal income distribution in the sample: <30,000=24%; 30–50,000=20%; 50–80,000=22%; 80–100,000=8%; 100–150,000=6%; 150,000+=2%; refused=18%
Source: 2016 CWKE National Survey in Canada Work Learning Surveys. 1998–2016. (N=2974).

these high-income groups that majorities identified themselves as upper middle class. Even in the highest income group with over $150,000, less than 10 percent identified as upper class (not shown in Figure 2.5). But there is a clear progression to greater upper-middle-class identity with higher personal income.

The dominant tendency for all those with incomes under $100,000 was to identify themselves as "middle class," even those in the lowest income groups. Similar patterns are found for both household income and levels of wealth. In the 2010 survey, which also included the unemployed, they too were just as likely as employed respondents to identify themselves as middle class. There now appears to be a very strong bias to see oneself in the middle of standard class schemes and even more so in the middle of personal class models, with limited regard for personal level of wealth or poverty. The conditions of mass consumption referred to above, as well as increasing visibility of minorities of both very rich and very poor people, surely encourage such mindsets. Of course, some people may have quite complex social relations, and material possessions may be less influential for some than racialization, gender and other cultural factors. But increasing middle-class bias does appear to be weakening relations between class identity and more objective measures of socioeconomic status even more than registered in the 1970s.

It is relevant to note here a classic study of British auto workers in the early 1960s. This study found that as these workers became more "affluent" they were more likely to identify themselves as middle class than working class and more concerned with consumption issues than labour relations (Goldthorpe et al. 1969). The publication of this research was followed shortly by militant strikes by the same workers (Mann 1973, 48). These researchers should have been more cautious in drawing conclusions from subjective class identity for class action. The same holds true today. I now look more closely at popular ways of seeing classes and class relations, first with attention to the views of rank-and-file steelworkers, then with the views of a range of acknowledged leaders of different class groups. The following quotes are drawn from interview transcripts.

Ways of Seeing Classes: Steelworkers

Through much of the twentieth century, steelworkers were widely considered to be at the core of the hired labouring class. They worked together in the largest industrial sites, produced a material essential to the expansion of capitalist economies and were centrally involved in the development of the organized labour movement. If anyone was likely to identify as "working class," it was a steelworker. For many years, I was involved in a research project that documented the lives of steelworkers (Corman et al. 1993; Seccombe and Livingstone 1999). This research began in the early 1980s in the wake of the largest mass layoffs in the history of the global steel industry. The study included a 1984 sample survey of steelworkers at Stelco's Hilton Works in Hamilton, Ontario, the largest industrial worksite in Canada at that time, in-depth follow-up interviews in both 1984 and 1994, and a comparable 1984 survey of the general Hamilton population (Livingstone and Mangan 1996a). The research continued until Hilton Works was reduced to a shell of its former might, with a few hundred workers, after being sold to US Steel in 2006 (Livingstone, Smith and Smith 2011). The class models and class identities offered by these steelworkers in interviews, conducted mainly in 1984 and 1994, may be fairly indicative of the organized working class in advanced capitalist settings.

In the mid-1980s, our surveys and in-depth interviews with Hamilton steelworkers found near unanimity on the existence of classes, with most naming either wealth or income as the main factor dividing classes. About three-quarters provided class models in their own terms. Most identified at least three distinct groups. The major distinctions that emerged were usually between the "rich" or "affluent," those who have to work for a living, or "working class," and the "poor."

> I think that there's the very, very rich, the very wealthy. Within the upper class, there's sort of a structure of people who have enough money to buy and sell you and me. Then you get your doctors and lawyers and others who make a fair bit of money. Then there's the working class.... There's nothing special about what we do for a living — anyone could do it with the right training.... And then unfortunately below that is anyone of a number of people that through bad luck or their own doing are not very well off one way or another.

> There are groups of people that have a higher standard of living than we do. They are able to do what they want when they want. They don't have to save for it or accumulate time off on holidays — they can go when they want. Working class have enough money to live on but have to work hard to get it.... Then there's the less fortunate. A lot of people in Canada will never have their own homes. They have to rob Peter to pay Paul every month.

> The right high class are snobs to begin with and, you know, they treat the working man like dirt, whether they knew you or not, the majority of them. The lower-class people, I get along great with them. Like I know a lot of people that are down in that bracket, eh.

As steelworker breadwinner "jobs for life" vanished during the last decade of the twentieth century, interviews in 1994 revealed increasing concern that positions in the middle of the class structure were declining, with more poor people at the bottom, and less explicit reference to the "working class" (see Seccombe and Livingstone 1999).

> There's fewer middle class, like the middle class that have lost their jobs and are now lower class. The upper middle class have become rich, but I think there have been more going down than going up.

> There have always been rich, middle and poor classes. But there are more poor in the last few years — food banks all over. You never had food banks when I was a kid. People who are higher class don't help the lower, the middle class do. You're in the middle, you could go down. You're closer to poverty.

In terms of personal class identity, steelworkers in the mid-1980s tended to locate themselves in the middle of the class structure, generally with a clear sense that there was a more affluent class above them. Both on their own class models and on the standard pre-coded class identity question, the vast majority of steelworkers saw themselves to be in the middle of the class structure and rarely at either its highest or lowest extremes. The terms "working class" and "middle class" were typically intermingled when steelworkers who chose "middle class" on the standard forced-choice question talked further about their own class identities.

> I would put myself in the middle working class. We're not rich, we're not poor. I work regularly, but we're not going to be millionaires. This is probably the only house we'll ever own. We probably could have moved up houses if we'd had less children. To me, that's materialistic and — you know, I enjoy my home, I don't mind the neighbours.

> We have got to get one thing straight. Is the working class the middle class or not? We will keep it to people who are working, who are making a wage, somebody who has to go to work for a wage. Blue collar, I guess that's what I am. I'm not a salary man, not working in the office, so I guess you can put me in the working class. In the upper part, because working at Stelco, let's face it, we make more money than a lot of people in this city. But I'm not saying that by making money you are a better person, because you can make $100,000 and be a bum.

A decade later, many of these steelworkers expressed much more insecurity and uncertainty about their own middle-class status, as well as less reference to a working-class identity.

> I guess if there was any kind of middle class left, I would say I was middle class. Depending on what type of year it was, I'd be upper middle or lower middle class. But I wouldn't consider myself poor by any means. There's always food on the table and we eat fairly good … and shoes and that kind of stuff…. We make payments on the car, it's gone through hell but now we can't afford to buy a new one, so we keep it. So, we're not rich but we're not poor.

> I don't really think the working middle class exists anymore. I see the poor and then we're pretty well next. I don't think there's that big of a line between the poor and the middle class, really, anymore. There used to be more of a distinction…. Like, to me, it wouldn't take much for us to go under, really…. I don't think our parents had that kind of fear. I mean, they went through their bad times, too, but they also went through the boom years when things were really great. My concern now is for the kids. Even education doesn't guarantee them something better. And I look at the rich as being really rich, untouchable.

This fear of falling out of middle-class living conditions grew as steelworkers, along with others in previously secure wage and salary jobs, faced the prospect of prolonged unemployment and stagnant earnings (cf. Ehrenreich 1989). However, regular reminders that the rich were getting richer and that there were increasing numbers of poor below them meant the truest response for employed steelworkers was to continue to identify themselves in the middle, even if just hanging on. This preoccupation with hanging on to what they've got in increasingly precarious job markets is probably also related to a decline of simple working-class identity, among both steelworkers in the 1990s and hired employees more generally today.

Leaders' Ways of Seeing Classes

In the early 1990s and with some further work in 2016, I and my research team conducted in-depth interviews with people who we identified through their own public prominence and the advice of key informants as influential leaders of major social groups in Canada. These groups could be characterized primarily as top executives of large private corporations, elected leaders of large labour unions and professional associations, and acknowledged leaders of poor peoples' groups. Over fifty interviews were completed. One of the first topics was class models and class identity. I present summary comments by corporate leaders, followed by labour union and professional association leaders and poverty group advocates.

Corporate Leaders

The leading executives of large private corporations who were interviewed in the 1990s generally spoke about several materially based class divisions. They tended to regard the rich as responsible for guiding society, to see those in the middle as just getting along and to express some form of concern about those in poverty. They generally saw themselves at the top of their class structure.

> Certainly there is a very large division between the rich, the middle class and the poor. For example, I think almost all single mothers in this country are poor. The rich tend to be intelligent, reasonable people contributing to society one way or another. The middle class just do their job. The poor tend to look upward. They're probably more aware of their class because in a very ugly stark way they live with poverty every day of their lives. The real heroes of this society are an awful lot of single mothers who are not on welfare but doing a hard job on minimum wage and bringing up children by themselves and suffer for it. Our society still tends to place you in a social class according to your paycheque. I'm rich. I think very rich people spend some time assessing what responsibilities they hold to society and to other classes. We generally tend to have a philanthropic strand in there somewhere. The middle class is too busy earning a living to contemplate what responsibilities they have to the poor.

> I think the class structure really only has three levels. The well-to-do, maybe 15 percent, have got a lot of things that twenty years ago people wouldn't have dreamed of. This includes a very small number, about 1 percent, who make huge amounts of money but there are a lot more people who live a very comfortable life. Then, the middle class are a huge group that don't have a lot of extra comforts but they have the basics. And then you have the people that are disadvantaged, having problems economically: single mothers, working poor, seniors with bare pensions. I place myself in the top group, the well-to-do. I'm not rich but I have a nice house, all kinds of food, vacations, new clothes. Anybody who has as much as I have must be in the top group in terms of good fortune.
>
> I see two types of social classes. One would be categorized by economic group. That is, well-off, middle income, lower income, poor and poverty-stricken. The other would simply divide people into empowered and powerless. A meaningful percentage would fall into the poor and poverty-stricken, The majority between lower income and middle income, a very small percentage in the well-off. Also, the majority do feel empowered but a significant minority, perhaps 20 percent, would feel relatively powerless in terms of the way they experience the world around them. There's a widening gap between the "haves" and "have nots" and the sense of powerlessness that comes with the latter. I'm in the upper end of the well-off and empowered.

By 2016 in Canada, corporate leaders tended to be somewhat franker about the existence of the very rich and the increasing poor.

> Well, there's the 1 percent of wealthy business folks, including successful entrepreneurs and the super wealthy, including some taking in much more than they're worth. There's the upper middle class, including senior managers and skilled professionals. Then there's the middle class in comfortable jobs, the working poor and increasingly the non-working poor, including poor suffering seniors. I'm in the 1 percent.

Labour Leaders

Leaders of labour unions in the early 1990s identified similar class divisions but tended to see larger changes, with many of the well-off with decent jobs falling into poverty as the rich get richer. Labour leaders saw themselves in the middle of the class structure, but they also tended to affirm affinity for working-class traditions and values, as well as expressing hopes for solidarity between middle- and lower-class groups.

> There's the homeless, the poor, the working poor, the lower middle class, then the upper middle class and the rich. I put the first three in the same block. I put the upper middle class and the rich in the same block. It's certainly a very biased class system. It's also racist, much harder for minorities, and much harder for women. The first block represents maybe 80 percent. One of the major challenges is to get them to recognize their common interest. A guy with a job in a manufacturing plant, his interest is the same as guy who doesn't have a house and nowhere to live. His interest is not with some guy who has made his million paying people minimum wage or ripping off the system for huge fees. It's a major challenge for the labour movement if it's going to survive. I would put myself in the lower middle class by way of my income. But I think it's what you represent and what your line of work allows you to do and how your line of work allows you to think. If I were to use traditional terms, I would certainly say I am working class. I have working class values and I am a socialist and damn proud of it!

> You've always had an elite group. But there are more high-income earners now than ever before, upper middle class. There are a lot of people in the financial community speculating on properties and housing, just playing a system that doesn't produce much for us. That's where the separation starts and then you have working people. You have a lot of people in manufacturing plants who, comparatively speaking, are fairly well off. Then you have a whole range of other working people who are light years behind that. But many who thought they were well-off are finding that a decent standard of living, a decent house is beyond their reach. There's many more who are going to consider themselves working class than ever before. Where I

am today, I guess you would say I'm in the centre of the middle class, if you're talking about financial. But I think I belong to the working class. If you ask me who my friends are, who I relate to — working class.

We are creating a society of very rich and very poor, and now we have a class of working poor that is on the increase working at substandard jobs, part-time and at minimum wages. There are working people who are making a reasonable standard of living, decreasing numbers of industrial workers, and skilled workers and professionals like nurses and teachers. There is also a class of professionals who control their fees or numbers of clients. Then there's the corporate structure becoming richer with more concentration of dollars. I probably have the skills to be in the skilled worker class. Right now, as an elected official, I'm probably at the upper end of it. Unelected, I'm not.

There's the poor, there's the middle income and there's the rich. But the poor are getting poorer. People are being thrown off unemployment insurance unjustly, and they're going to welfare and breadlines. As the rich get richer, they get greedier and they cut off even more of the poor.… So, there's definitely three classes and nobody can deny that. The evidence is there every day. I belong to the working class. There's working class that are working in the government, in industries making just above minimum wage and working class that have much better wages. I'm far from rich. I'm definitely in the working class.

By 2016, labour leaders tended to express greater awareness of the wealth of the rich and greater concern with the growing numbers on the edge of and falling into poverty, including themselves potentially.

There's the 1 percent, people that now own most of the country. Then the very well-off business owners and top managers are up there. There's doctors and lawyers and other well-off professionals. At the bottom end you have the more and more very poor who depend on welfare and other assistance. In between, you have a lot who are working in public and private union jobs and a lot who are working in non-union jobs, especially growing numbers working in retail who are mistreated more than anybody. I'm middle class now, a house, investments, but I don't feel middle class. The unjust cost of living increases in capitalist society make it inevitable that working people retire into poverty.

Professional Association Leaders

Professional associations usually represent people with specialized skills who may provide services across the social spectrum. As I documented elsewhere (Livingstone, Adams and Sawchuk 2021), these associations often represent professionals in quite different class positions. Their leaders typically regarded themselves as in an intermediate location and downplayed class differences generally.

> Yes, society is stratified on economic grounds but more so on cultural grounds. We're a multicultural society and we allow different cultures to flourish. I don't see any strong social classes. There are small numbers who are very well-off and more who are not very well off. But I think the middle class has expanded so far now that we have a pretty uniform society. We could do better at looking after the disadvantaged at the bottom edge of the economic scale. I don't like the word "class," different cultures if you like. Working class, it's very prosperous, even they don't think of themselves as working class; they think of themselves as middle class. I'm pretty firmly in the centre of the middle class.

> Certainly there's a wealthy elite. There's a large middle class with various striations and there's an underclass. Middle class now includes blue collar workers. The divisions are not as striking as they once were. Middle class now encompasses most people in society. I don't think problems are now much defined in class terms. I'm right in the centre of the middle class.

Poverty Group Leaders

People widely acknowledged as leaders of poor peoples' groups also tended to recognize rich, middle and lower classes but with more refined distinctions of sorts of poor people as well as different orientations among middle-class groups. The rich were either revered or feared.

There are the poor, the really poor, people who have been really marginalized, Native people, welfare mothers, street people. Then, there are those middle-class people who are more comfortably situated and employed within corporations, universities or what have you. Some of these have really bought into the belief — the house, the cottage, the boat and whatever –that they have really "made it" somehow. And there are those that are really dissatisfied and want to change the system while they hold on to the comforts within the system. Then there are those who are really affluent and powerful, the corporate elite group with an incredible amount of power. My gut responds as a welfare mother. That is exactly who I am and where I have been the greater part of my adult life. It forms everything I do and say. So, you would have to say "lower class" would be where I stood, where I am inside. Through opportunities and access to information I think I have a clearer social vision than either of the "other ends"; there must be thousands of us who haven`t yet cohered and are still looking to fit in somewhere.

Class Conflict or Harmony?

In addition to discussing their views of the class structure and where they were personally situated in it, leaders offered their views of the nature of relations between the classes. The class divisions were similar, but their views of relations between these groups differed markedly, in the most recent discussions as in the earlier ones. The corporate leaders clearly saw themselves as responsible for guiding from the top to keep others in the middle "busy," with some gestures to the poor. Labour leaders feared this class structure is changing to reduce more workers to poverty, and they showed ambivalence about their personal class identities in the context of what they see as a growing need to unite the middle and lower groups into a coherent "working class." Professional leaders tended to see themselves right in the middle of the class structure, trying to serve and to overcome barriers between others. Poverty group leaders clearly saw themselves at the bottom of a class hierarchy with hopes to develop more solidarity at the bottom as well as links with some disaffected in the middle. The following quotes are from four leaders — corporate, labour, professional association and poverty group, in that order.

I don't think there has been any noticeable increase in the conflict, say, between labour and management. You know, these things sort of bubble up to the surface occasionally. But in general terms, society's been relatively stable and harmonious. In my company, we all work together as a team and get along well. We are all friends. Conflict comes up from time to time on specific issues. But there's very little general conflict now in Canadian society. There is a danger in the fact that the rich are at least staying where they are if not getting richer, and the poor seem to be getting poorer with disincentive to work and real problems for the disadvantaged.

The big conflict is between corporate entities, big business, and basically everybody else. I think it's not just working people. It's not just a conflict between unions and employers but also a conflict between environmentalists and corporations, health advocates, poverty advocates, occupational health and safety advocates and corporations. The conflict is really between profit and social values.

Class differences are not as striking as they once were. I don't think social problems today are defined in class terms — even though there's not much movement between them. The fact that we find ways to resolve conflicts without violence is a very positive aspect.

It's complicated. The affluent group that has the controlling interest in this country has set up a scenario that places the other two groups in artificial conflict with one another. Probably the most threatening thing that could happen to the affluent group is if the rest of us started really talking to one another and looking at who is invested where and what. But there is serious conflict between groups working with issues of poverty, for example, between the labour movement of "gainfully employed" within the system and poverty movements and unemployed workers. Organized labour may be fighting for reform within the system but not really to shake up the status quo because they have an investment in maintaining it.

Critical review of all this interview material, the survey findings and a wide array of other observations have led me to the following preliminary conclusions:

- Only those at the very top and very bottom of perceived class hierarchies in advanced capitalism tend to own up to their actual class locations. Most others near either the top or bottom in terms of living conditions are inclined to see themselves in the middle because there are undeniably others above them and below them.

- There are many encouragements for most people to see most others in a common middle group of consumers, workers or voters. This tripartite class model of the rich and the poor with most in the middle is widespread in popular consciousness, in contrast to the status continua prevalent in much of academic research and mass media.

- Subjective middle-class identity, at least in the terms examined here, does not appear to be connected in a simple way with views about relations between classes or political attitudes. In particular, assuming a middle-class identity does not necessarily lead to acceptance of the political or economic status quo.

In light of these conclusions, in Chapters 3 and 4, I explore the driving forces underlying class existence in advanced capitalism and the changing class structure they animate, before returning to more critical ways of analyzing class consciousness in this context in later chapters.

The Relative Invisibility of Class

Perceptions of class structure and personal class identity are unlikely to be ever-present in most people's thoughts. In fact, many people may not think about class existence at all most of the time. For example, some sample surveys have found that fewer than half of respondents say they actually think of themselves in class terms (e.g., Schreiber 1980).

As noted in the Introduction, class identity is the least visible of major markers of social difference in our everyday lives. We are constantly reminded of our racial and gender identities by our bodily appearance and other peoples' reactions to our bodily appearance. Physical conditions of age and disability are often difficult to disguise or ignore. Alone or in combination, these aspects of the human condition can be more pertinent to our consciousness than class per se in influencing our thoughts and actions. In all advanced capitalist societies, racist, patriarchal, youth-centred and ablest biases remain embedded in dominant institutional practices to a significant extent. Racial discrimination continues to be widespread, and many visible minorities experience it as the greatest barrier to realizing their ambitions. Racial bias fused with religious persecution has often been a most potent form of discrimination; witness Islamophobia in the current moment. Gender bias against women and gender minorities persists in the home and in many other institutions. The very old and the very young are effectively excluded from exercising their human rights in a number of spheres, and the disabled still rarely receive the accommodations needed for them to do so.

In the wake of the biggest mass layoff in the history of the Canadian steel industry in 1982, steelworkers were asked about their general perceptions of relations among social groups in Canada (Seccombe and Livingstone 1999). In our 1984 survey, almost half of these Stelco workers thought conflict generally prevailed among social groups, nearly a third saw both conflict and harmony, and only 16 percent regarded group relations as generally harmonious. However, most steelworkers said they did not tend to think of group conflict primarily in terms of class relations. When asked in open-ended questions to identify which groups, if any, they thought were in conflict, more than a quarter of Stelco workers did not identify any specific major group conflicts. But the most commonly perceived types of conflict were ethno-linguistic ones — not surprising since Canada is one of the most ethno-linguistically diverse countries in the world and this was a period when francophone Quebec separation was a live issue. Around a third of all respondents mentioned either French–English or some other form of ethnic or racial conflict. Two versions of explicitly political conflict — between political parties or between the government and the "people" — were also mentioned by nearly half the Stelco workers. Explicit class conflicts were less commonly identified than either ethnic or general political ones. Fewer than a third of Stelco workers volunteered that class conflicts were among the most important group conflicts. So, within one of the largest groups of organized workers in the country, in the midst of an ongoing bitter struggle with their employer, it did not occur to most of these Stelco workers to identify class conflict as one of the most important forms of group conflict in Canadian society.

In in-depth interviews ten years later, most continued to speak of group conflicts primarily in terms of ethnic and racial conflicts, especially in terms of perceived threats to established traditions:

> It's mainly a racial thing. And I guess that's been a lot worse in the last ten years than better, unfortunately.... I think they should be a little more selective in who they're letting into the country. Like that plays a major part in a lot of social issues that the average person has to deal with — you know, crime and even preferential hiring. So, what's a white Canadian going to do? If they're segregating right now for government issue jobs, I don't know. It's pretty scary.

> There are conflicts with everybody else because the politicians say this is going to be a multicultural society and it won't work.... You know, there is too much of that garbage going on and all it's doing is pitting us against them. If we are all going to be Canadians, fine, let's all be Canadians and have like a big melting pot. You come into the country, you're a Canadian. You're not an Italian-Canadian, or a French-Canadian. You're a Canadian, that's it, the bottom line. You don't have any more rights than I do. We're not going to change any rules to satisfy you and that's it.

Some steelworkers who saw racial conflict as primary tried to put it in a broader historical perspective and challenge its more subtle forms:

> It's sad but I guess you'd have to say there's a lot of racial conflict.... The French in Canada, I mean, this has been going on for years.... So, I would still say the Jews have a hard haul of it, like the Pakistanis or the Indians — anybody that wears turbans seems to be — and the French. I can handle the downright racists because I can confront them.... It's the people that don't care that get me.... It's just sort of a non-caring and those people scare me because those are the ones that would, if something like [German fascism] ever happened again, they would fall right in and go along with it.

In our interviews, these steelworkers tended to express complex views of social group relations in general. They were unlikely to see social harmony prevailing, and they were probably somewhat more likely to see conflict in group relations than the general population. But, like the men and women of all social backgrounds in Canada's "steeltown" of Hamilton, they were most likely to identify easily and frequently visible ethnic or explicitly political conflicts as generally more pertinent than class conflict.

In terms of combined effects of social differences, there are still public spaces where able-bodied males are privileged with little regard for class differences, such as many sporting events and pubs. Older, disabled Black women remain excluded from many public spaces whatever their class position might be — but it will probably be lower class. And this is the larger point. It is usually difficult to disassociate class from other bases of social division. Through the historical development of advanced capitalist societies, those in dominant rich class positions have tended to be white, able-bodied males while those in the most subordinate class positions have tended to be disproportionately female, visible minorities, disabled and/or old. We should not expect that class identity will be seen by most people most of the time as the primary feature of their existence when there are many other visible features that they face more directly every day. But once more, none of this should lead us to conclude that differences in class positions have no connection with differences in political consciousness and action.

Next Steps

The starting point for my further analysis is the confirmation that most people in advanced capitalism can recognize the existence of a specific class structure and locate themselves within it. The pertinence of class relations within the complicated context of lived experience today is the subject of the remainder of this book.

As the findings reported here and in prior research (e.g., Vanneman and Pampel, 1977, 423) document, the widespread recognition of the existence of classes does not indicate agreement on the nature of relationships among those classes. As I have begun to illustrate, views of these relations may differ greatly from different social standpoints and at different times. Just one more example. In steeltown Hamilton, after experiencing a long and bitter strike in the early 1980s, about a third of steelworkers surveyed did consider classes to generally be in conflict. But the capitalist class of Hamilton was unanimous in denying that conflict prevails in class relations (Livingstone and Mangan 1996b). Most capitalist employers have probably had considerable experience of conflict with their workforces, although it is probably not in their best interests to admit that this condition prevails, even to themselves. However, even in conditions of sustained class struggles, both workers and employers may find their interdependent relationship to contain complex combinations of conflictual and harmonious aspects. One steelworker focusing inside the plant expressed relations a decade later as more harmonious:

> I don't see so much the management-worker thing anymore. We've got together. The idea of worker and manager is just not the same anymore. I think you are in it together to do something. You can't do something if you are fighting with someone all the time. You're losing track of what you are there to do…. I think that comes with maturity too, having your responsibilities and whatever, you tend to cool down and think "this isn't so bad." Now it's good to have a job.

Other steelworkers took a more general view and saw class conflict increasing overall in society:

> I think the classes thing sure is growing. There's a greater gap between the poor and the well-to-do. It's definitely starting to grow. Before, everybody was kind of moderate, like there wasn't a real high end and low end. But now I'm really seeing that it's really starting to develop…. I've seen guys lose their jobs, lose their homes and go down the tubes, have whole families splitting up, you know. And I've seen that happen a lot. And that's causing a lot of violence. If people haven't got anything, they go out and steal it, you know? … There is no safe place.

In more recent years, there is evidence that most people in advanced capitalist societies, whatever their own class location, perceive a growing gap between rich and poor and increasing conflict between them (e.g., Morin 2012). Notions of classes and their relations are continually changing. My purpose in this book is not to provide yet another descriptive snapshot of such notions of classes but to probe their underlying dynamics, the forces driving their continuity and change. The remainder of this investigation gives priority to the standpoints of working people, hired employees, those whom the poverty group leader above calls the "gainfully employed." With no disrespect intended for unemployed and other lower-class groups, it is non-managerial hired employees with whom I have engaged most closely and developed the deepest appreciation for their conditions.

General disrespect for working (class) people's intellectual capabilities has persisted in both research literature and dominant cultural forms. One of the most extreme and influential versions ever of such disrespect targeted steelworkers. Frederick Winslow "Speedy" Taylor, the father of scientific management in the 1890s, promulgated the image of "Schmidt," the strong-backed, weak-minded steelworker who was incapable of making intelligent judgements about the most efficient way to do a job without the aid of time-and-motion engineers. Similar forms of disrespect for working people's mental capacities have continued to be conveyed by the mass media through depictions of workers as dumb and narrow-minded, as well as by a scarcity of real blue-collar characters (e.g., Miller 1994). The review of working people's perceptions of class structures and class identities in this chapter suggests that they actually make more complex judgements about class issues than either mainstream researchers and propagandists, or revolutionary theorists, have usually recognized. Their understanding of contemporary class relations is often as subtle and nuanced as representatives of more dominant classes.

The interplay of short- and long-term personal and collective interests may often be complicated in the specific situations of working people and their households. Researchers have often been spectacularly inaccurate in their efforts to evaluate and predict the class sentiments of steelworkers and other blue-collar workers prior to militant strike actions (e.g., Spencer 1977, 12). My aims here are more modest. I trace changes over time in employment conditions and the general class structure and then assess the extent to which the expressed sentiments on basic issues of employers' prerogatives and workers' rights relate to these changes. This assessment relies primarily on further analyses of a time series of population surveys and on interviews with class leaders. Popular notions of classes and class relations may remain complicated and interactive, with various forms of overt racism, sexism, xenophobia, Islamophobia and other forms of prejudice and bigotry in the name of nationalism and patriotism. Class relations should not be reduced to *the* essential social relations, any more than they should be jettisoned for postmodern cultural analyses (Seccombe and Livingstone 1999). But the popular perceptions of class identity and class structure profiled here can serve as a valid starting point for critical analyses of class relations in advanced capitalist societies that at least pay fairly equitable attention to the standpoints of working people.

If extraction of surplus labour from direct producers of goods and services remains, as Marx discerned, the strategic "innermost secret" of class relations in advanced capitalism, then it is surely in the class interest of the owners of large private corporations and their allies to do whatever they can to disguise and deny the relevance of this relation. The purpose of the next two chapters is to expose this dynamic relation between owners and direct producers.

Note

1. Further information on the national surveys I conducted in Canada in 1998, 2004, 2010 and 2016 is presented in Chapters 6 and 7, and is fully available at Canada Work Learning Surveys 1998–2016.

3

Advanced Capitalist Mode of Production

Drivers of Class Relations in "Knowledge Economies"

Global capitalism is a relatively recent historical condition, and it is continually changing as a consequence of the underlying material relations and forces driving its reproduction. The main driver of change in capitalist economies has been competition for profits between private firms. The capitalist mode of production can be defined as production, distribution and sale of commodities for profits by competing privately owned enterprises using hired wage labour. This mode of production now pervades the globe, with a vast array of goods and services being produced and sold by increasingly international contending private corporations and with most paid employment offered by private companies. This chapter briefly sketches the context for the class analysis in the remainder of the book. It traces the transition from the feudal mode of production to capitalism, the development of the capitalist mode of production in terms of growth of private ownership and control of the labour process, the main features of advanced capitalism, the emergent "knowledge economy," the co-existence of post-capitalist enclaves and the later focus on G7 and Nordic countries.

Feudal Origins

Five hundred years ago, most people lived in feudal or other tribute-paying modes of production, in which they were tied to the land and compelled to provide labour beyond their subsistence to support the conspicuous consumption rituals and military forces of ruling classes. Pre-capitalist modes of production had their own dynamism, with gradual changes in production techniques, trade relations and political alliances. Before 1500, horses were already being used with iron-tipped ploughs, manure was being used to fertilize the soil, crop rotation had been introduced, wheelbarrows were in use, and water mills were grinding grain. Long-distance trade in luxury goods had gone on for centuries, but the fundamental motive force of the feudal mode of production was the social consumption needs of royal and religious ruling classes and manorial lords of feudal estates, who controlled virtually all the land. The production process changed much more slowly than it has in capitalism. The vast majority relied on the land they lived on for their subsistence and had little incentive to produce much surplus.

The version of capitalism that gradually emerged from feudalism — first in England, then in western Europe more generally — pivotally involved the development of private-property ownership and dispossession of serfs from feudal estates. Rebel lords sought relief from royal taxation and increasing property rights for themselves, as symbolized by the Magna Carta of 1215 and its many successors. Town merchants developed trading systems that offered peasant cottage holders more benefits from putting out goods than did their loyalty to local lords. Enclosure of feudal estates by lords for more profitable raising of sheep and cattle began to throw large numbers of rural workers off the land and made them available for employment in emerging city manufacturing sites. Growing numbers of private-property owners, large and small, began to assert their interests in producing surpluses for their own gain rather than giving them to crown and church.

Ever since that time, motivated by the drive of owners of goods and services to sell their commodities above cost for the greatest profit, labour has become freer from the land and more dependent on hired employment. Labour power has been continually combined with technical innovation, and long-distance trade has become more prevalent. In terms of labour time per commodity, capitalism has been by far the most productive form of economy, and it is still expanding both spatially and into new commodity spheres. But it did not spring to birth overnight. Nor was the transformation of capitalism into a new mode of production necessarily evident in the early stages.

Even when feudalism reached its most fully developed form as a producing organization in medieval western Europe, the feudal estate's consumption needs were sustained not only by its characteristic serf labour but by a variety of other forms of labour, including domestic servant-slaves, day labourers, part-time hired workers and free tenants. The appearance of hired labour — in the absence of a capitalist form of enterprise focused on profit making — remained an expression of feudal relations of production. Capitalist enterprises themselves initially were sustained not only by hired labour but by a variety of inherited forms of labour. Capitalist enterprises in which hired labour was prevalent only began to emerge seriously later, in the context of the expanding commerce of the sixteenth century (Banaji 1977; 2010).

At the outset, capitalist enterprises took over the labour process — the technical means and methods of production — as they found it. The highly significant departure was that labourers' production no longer responded to the consumption needs of their rulers at rates enforced by direct political and social means. For millennia, prior empires and civilizations had been driven by ruling classes demanding loyalty and labour through ritual and coercion. As Brenner (1976) observes, in pre-capitalist agrarian societies peasants generally effectively possessed the land, tools and labour power needed to carry out production on their own, and in virtually every case ruling classes depended on surplus extraction by extra-economic coercion to reproduce themselves. The growing need by merchants, moneylenders and landholders to make profit through trade led to expropriating more labourers from the land and their own tools of production, compelling them to sell their labour power in order to subsist. Such labour was conducted at increased levels of intensity, duration and continuity of production, with wage incentives and threats of job loss.

In pre-capitalist modes of production, ruling classes typically held both economic and political power. Capitalist owners of the means of production, commonly known as the bourgeoisie, have rarely taken absolute political power. They have concentrated on increasing control of the means of production and strongly influencing political state policy while remaining officially separate from state power. Modern state governments based on separation of executive, legislative and judicial powers originated in struggles between the crown, feudal lords and the "commons" (merchants, independent craftspeople and small landowners). Rebel lords and the "commons" increasingly asserted their property claims versus absolutist monarchs. The English Bill of Rights of 1689 is one of the clearest legal expressions of the challenge of these growing private-property rights to established feudal authority. As John Locke (1689,

368) summarized the political goals of these emerging classes: "The great and chief end … of men's uniting into commonwealths, and putting themselves under government, is the preservation of their property."

Capitalist Development

The continuing internal development of the capitalist mode of production is best understood in terms of the cumulative *expansion of the private ownership of property* and negotiations over *control of the labour process*.

Growth of Private Ownership

Over the past three hundred years, a most evident dimension of the development of the capitalist mode of production has been the expansion of the private ownership of property. Prior to that time, the few freed from feudal servitude to become small-scale property owners and independent craftspeople had occasionally asserted demands that property earned as the fruit of their labours deserved civil and political rights. However, in 1689, the required value of property in freehold land or chartered trading privilege only effectively gave a tiny fraction of English *men* the right to vote. By the late 1700s, still less than 3 percent of men were deemed to have sufficient land or chattel assets to be regarded as political citizens with the right to vote. The growth of modern industry in the nineteenth century was characterized by growing numbers of large and small independent business owners and much larger numbers of industrial wage earners, including craftspeople, who were also able to acquire significant property assets. In spite of this, further reforms of 1867 only extended the vote to about 8 percent of men.

The growing gap between private-property assets and economic independence on the one hand and narrow political rights on the other continually provoked protest movements for wider political rights. These social movements can be traced from the seventeenth-century Levellers (who wanted government elected by the male heads of all households) and the Diggers (who began to settle on and cultivate common land as a basic human right).[1] The Diggers' focus on the rights of the landless rural poor is reflected in a widening array of civil and political rights movements that have persisted to the present. Seen from the perspective of the historical development of the capitalist mode of production, such movements have been a correlate of both continuing expansion of private ownership of property and economic independence from pre-capitalist forms of subjugation.

The entrepreneurial capitalist of the manufacture phase succeeded in appropriating most of the actual means of production and consolidating full ownership in their own position. The enlarging scale of capitalist enterprises and the need to mobilize wider sources of capital later led to the emergence, especially from the 1880s, of private companies that invited numbers of small stockholders to invest in legal ownership for potential profits. Corporate capitalist firms became dominant. At least initially, such joint-stock companies reinforced the real economic ownership of big stockholders, who maintained actual control of the overall accumulation process in their positions as directors and executives of such enterprises.

Today, the early struggles over ownership of the immediate means of production are largely forgotten as capitalist enterprises' appropriation has become so extensive. Even most of the remaining self-employed farmers and artisans in North America, for example, are working with capitalist manufactured, heavily mortgaged means of production and are compelled by capitalist marketing processes. However, the conflict between capital and labour over ownership of production persists in many guises within contemporary enterprises. An indicative example is West Germany's Mitbestimmung law, which by 1978 purported to give workers' and trade unions' representatives co-determination with those of shareholders on the boards of management of the largest industrial enterprises (McGaughey 2015). This law conceded some legal claims and detailed ownership functions in the face of an increasingly socialized labour force and immediate capital shortages.

Most private land outside state ownership in advanced capitalist countries is now available for sale. Through much of the twentieth century many labouring families were able to purchase homes as well as growing amounts of other commodities. In addition, with the development of public stock exchanges, formal legal ownership of private capitalist enterprises did become more widespread, first through penny stocks, now through large investments of workers' pension funds. The real influence of such workers' funds has remained restricted, with corporate executives and directors typically maintaining control of the overall capital accumulation process.

However, modern capitalist enterprises have continued to develop by gathering more and more of the available means of production (land, tools, labour power and raw materials) under *concentrated ownership*, thereby appropriating the main profits of the existing labour processes. This production process has seen a drive to commodify everything, leading to the greater concentration of capital, the centralization of firms and the proliferation of reserve armies of labour. Along with the expanding scale and increasing concentration and centralization of capitalist ownership, effective economic ownership is much more concentrated in small numbers of corporate capitalists. This real concentration is distinct from the formal legal stock ownership claims that have proliferated since the 1880s (e.g., Crompton and Gubbay 1977). The realization of profits in the sphere of exchange is divided among industrial, service, financial, commercial and real property fractions of corporate capital. However, as Vitali et al. (2011) document, financial capital has become the most concentrated form of capital and dominates over other forms. In the early twenty-first century, a tiny number of private financial capital firms orchestrate global selling, buying and restructuring of banks and other major enterprises for growing profits with declining quality of work (Rugemer 2019). A few of these immense pools of private capital, such as BlackRock and Vanguard, have influential financial tentacles in virtually all major stock markets as well as the ear of many governments' finance personnel.

The struggle over ownership is not containable within the currently institutionalized forms of actual capitalist production. This is most evident where capital is striving to commodify new realms and appropriate the relevant potential means of production which all people had presumed as their birthright. One need only reflect on the development in recent generations of air cleaners, water purifiers and seabed mining and the proliferation of personal electronic devices to recognize the extent of capitalist appropriation of space and time. Such developments underline the continual relevance of the struggle over private or genuine public ownership of the means of production and of the means of life itself as the capitalist mode of production tries to reproduce itself.

Gaining Control of the Labour Process

The formal separation of labour from the means of production was critical in the transition to capitalism. The early resistance of labourers in different social formations to such formal separation has been widely documented. These forms of resistance included peasant revolts against crop seizures and land enclosures; struggles of guild members and independent artisans against mercantile capitalists' standards of subcontracting and "putting out" systems in appropriating their products; and general resistance to the abolition or undermining of independent private ownership and commercial use of small tools of production.

Capitalist enterprises have increasingly developed by gaining control over their internal labour processes. Marx analyzed the historical phases in this increasing control from simple cooperation through manufacture to "machinofacture." Machinofacture literally means making with the aid of machines. It was still in its infancy in the nineteenth century when Marx wrote. In its generic sense, machinofacture is the production process characterized by the use of machinery, conscious application of science and technology, standardization of work procedures and replaceability of labour, and conduct of production on an extensive scale. Given the inherent increasing productivity and labour-saving character of machinofacture, the possibility of reducing the absolute amount of labour we do and achieving a sustainable economy for all can be envisaged by both ecosocialists and advocates of people's capitalism (e.g., Rodrigues de Moraes-Neto 2013; Albus 1976). I revisit this possibility in the last chapter.

However, *capitalist* machinofacture has the following structural features:

- an elaborate hierarchy of social discipline;

- a division of labour into conceiving and fragmented executing elements; and

- a compulsive dependency on mechanization per se.

These features have tended to become generalized in the capitalist mode of production because they have been seen as required by most capitalist enterprises to maximize extraction of surplus labour from the direct producers of commodities as a prime source of profits. Capitalists' mere ownership of the various means and products of production proved an inadequate way to get more profit out of contracted labour. Owners brought hired labour together with tools and raw materials, but combining them efficiently was often impeded by workers' demands for more decent wages and working conditions.

Throughout the history of capitalist production, the labour process itself has become the major site of the struggle between capital and labour. But, after Marx, systematic analysis of the capitalist labour process was largely ignored until the working-class militancy of the late 1960s. Since that time, researchers, beginning with Harry Braverman (1974),[2] have more closely analyzed these three interrelated historical tendencies (i.e., hierarchical social discipline, fragmented division of labour and compulsive mechanization) in capitalist machinofacture's efforts to control the labour process for profit maximization.

First, capitalists have consistently tried to bring the social relations of production under their own systems of social discipline, from the initial gathering of workers under a single roof so they could be controlled effectively under supervision of the capitalist or their overseer, to more elaborate managerial structures. The expanding scale, concentration and centralization of capital within the production process necessitated that capitalists, while retaining overall control of the capital investment process, increasingly delegate direct managerial control (e.g., control of details of investment flow and resource allocation) to hired subordinates. The hierarchy of social discipline, including managers, supervisors and other middling administrative personnel, has generally grown proportionately as the production process itself has become more capital-intensive. The process has become increasingly mechanized, with more of the remaining productive workers responsible for tending machinery.

More recently, institutionalization of the hierarchical social power of capital in the form of company "work criteria" (i.e., detailed formal job descriptions and performance standards that appear to be more important than the will of managers and the whim of particular supervisors) may serve capital even more reliably and profoundly to allocate and differentiate jobs, enforce speeds and intensities, sanction poor quality and generally make capital's efforts at social control less visible. But, however subtly done, the more that discretion in organizing the way they work is taken away from those who actually do the work, the less conscientious they tend to become in performing that work. The objective alienation of workers from their products and the decline in the quality of their work may have been tolerable to capitalists generally when they have been able to use increased control of the social relations of production and the threat of the industrial reserve army to command greater gross productivity from workers and to realize greater profits. Increased measures of capitalist discipline have most typically been met by individualistic sabotage and other reactive efforts at "getting a bit of our own back."[3] However, the contradiction between worker discretion and profitability emerges in starker structural form in the most advanced industries. In order to try to release the potential productivity that remains locked inside the workers in such capital-intensive industries, capitalists continue to be driven to experiment with worker self-management schemes (e.g., Espinosa and Zimbalist 1978; Pink 2009). Such experiments have usually led to both higher productivity and substantial difficulties in containing worker initiatives within management systems of norms and rewards. As Richard Edwards (1978, 123) notes, "Capitalists themselves are led, even forced, to introduce the very schemes that threaten their grip."

Second, capitalists have tried to gain greater control over the technical relations of production, or workers' relations to the physical process of production per se. They have tried to monopolize knowledge and technical power over the design of production systems, imposing capital's objectives by appropriating the capacity to plan and coordinate the physical process of production and relegating many workers to fragmented, routine tasks.

But the generic technical requirements of labour in machinofacture come into contradiction with capital's imperative to gain and reproduce a monopoly over systemic knowledge of the production process in order to impose its valorization objective. While industrial capitalists "rent the veil" of the technical mystery and secrecy of earlier conservative labour processes with the development of machinofacture, they cannot reconceal such knowledge without threatening their own existence. Thus, while capital has continually tried to reduce the mass of labourers to standardized, fragmented tasks and to limit jobs requiring special conceptual or "intellectual" skills to as few workers as possible (e.g., design work, machine setting, maintenance and repair), the ongoing development of new products and new technologies demands versatile, technically knowledgeable labourers who retain the collective technical capacity to plan and coordinate the system of production themselves. Capital is compelled to revolutionize the instruments of production to achieve profitability, but to do so it must encourage the full development — in as docile a form as possible — of the technical aptitudes of the labourers for such varied work.

Third, during the machinofacture phase, capital has taken feasible opportunities to replace human labour with machinery in the material transformation process itself, thereby reducing the subjective, living labour element to a routine monitoring role in many instances. Noble (1986), for example, documents how twentieth-century manufacturing corporations frequently chose computerized control technologies that minimized worker mediation even at greater expense.

But, once again, capitalists' drive to replace workers by machines is also inherently contradictory and critically associated with profitability crises. In the long term, other things being equal, replacing living labour by the dead labour embodied in machinery diminishes the pivotal productive, or profit-creating, element in the production process and can lead to capital accumulation crises. From the standpoint of labour, while the time- and energy-saving potential of machinery remains ultimately in labour's fundamental interest, the introduction of machinery in its capitalist form threatens labour's immediate interests in job retention and has been resisted by many workers. From the standpoint of capital, the labour savings are immediately compelling to individual capitals, but ultimately disintegrative of substantial profit-making capacity and thus of capital itself. Capital can postpone this eventuality by increasing discipline and introducing new production techniques, and by concentrating, centralizing and generally speeding up economic relations in the sphere of exchange. But this requires the use of more labour beyond direct production of commodities, and such measures also serve to raise the level of the contradictions more closely associated with the other aspects of the labour process.

These three aspects of the labour process, namely social discipline, technical division of labour and mechanization, are often only analytically distinguishable, and the extent of capital's domination of actual labour processes varies immensely both among economic sectors and between social formations. Thus, the development of the advanced capitalist mode of production remains uneven. In all work settings, labourers still frequently resist capitalist control of the labour process. Such struggles are likely to continue as long as the capitalist version of the labour process prevails.

In sum, the capitalist mode of production in its contemporary, fully developed form can be understood as a continual conflict between two basic social forces. On the one hand, there are capitalist firms, conglomerates and consortia, whose controlling positions and agents must compete or collude to achieve the objective of profit maximization. On the other hand, there are the various forms of contributing labour, with their own broader social needs and aspirations, that the capitalist enterprise tries to subordinate to profit making. The two basic aspects of the antagonism between capital and labour, namely *ownership* of the means of production and *control over the labour process* of production, have been recognized at the level of simple dichotomous abstractions by many class analysts.

Since the 1970s, some Marxist scholars have focused their class analyses on dichotomous class characteristics associated with divisions within the capitalist labour process (e.g., owner/non-owner; supervisory/non-supervisory; intellectual/manual; productive/unproductive). But, as the foregoing account suggests, these basic aspects are dynamic historical relations, not simple categories. The development of capitalist machinofacture to expropriate real control over the production process itself has been associated with the most direct forms of resistance by contributing labour. The tendency of capital to appropriate to itself increasingly concentrated ownership of all the potential means of production has continually altered the forms of enterprises and terms of employment. These contradictory relations underlie more particular relations between capitalists and the variety of forms of labour in contemporary capitalist social formations. These relations per se remain important for understanding the formation of classes and the changing class structure in advanced capitalist societies, in which the production of knowledge is becoming a central commodity.

Advanced Capitalism

The primitive accumulation of assets in western Europe through plunder and unequal and often violent exchange with non-European societies also played a significant role in the origin and development of the capitalist mode of production in Europe and in the penetration of capitalist relations of production into many of these other societies. By the beginning of the twentieth century, capitalism had reached an imperialist stage in which large transnational industrial and financial corporations had become dominant on a world stage, the productivity of labour with technological innovation permitted extensive export of capital globally, and the division of virtually all large territories of the globe among the nation-states in which the largest capitalist corporations were centred was realized (Lenin 1973 [1917]). From early in the twentieth century until recent decades, the main capitalist imperialist states with large enough enterprises to be significant global net exporters of capital were the United Kingdom, France, Germany, Japan and the United States. Disputes between these states over resources and markets were centrally involved in the major wars of the twentieth century.

Some analysts distinguished social formations in this global system in terms of how extensive capitalist enterprises were within them and the proportion of the labour force engaged in wage labour. Four categories were identified: major imperialist, secondary imperialist, sub-imperialist and peripheral formations (Amin 1974). However, by the early twenty-first century, capitalist enterprises dominate production relations in most social formations around the globe. The late twentieth century saw massive increases in the proportion of the global labour force dispossessed of the means of production and seeking alternative work for wages. The world capitalist system is characterized by a hired labour force and a burgeoning relative surplus population located primarily in the previously "peripheral" world of Asia, Africa and Latin America (Neilson and Stubbs 2011). Advanced capitalist countries (i.e., major imperialists and secondary imperialists) are still characterized by larger shares of global capital, greater shares of relatively well-paid workers and lesser shares of surplus population in desperation.

Analyses of the global capitalist mode of production should still beware of confounding forms of labour with types of production. Neither industrial workers in particular nor hired wage labourers in general are any more identical with contemporary capitalist enterprises than serfs were with feudal enterprises. Global capitalism also requires a variety of forms of labour to sustain it in addition to industrial workers and other forms of privately hired labour. Self-employed producers, many hired state workers, several forms of peasant labour and numerous reserve forms of labour all function as other expressions of capitalist relations of production. The capitalist enterprise driven by its prime motive of profit maximization has become the dominant organizer of pre-capitalist, capitalist and post-capitalist surface forms of labour throughout the global capitalist economy. Even the most peripheral social formations within this system no longer combine capitalist and pre-capitalist modes of production. Some labourers on the plantations of some of the poorest countries might exist in a modern form of slavery, but such enterprises respond to similar profit-maximization motives as automobile plants and fast food franchises virtually everywhere. All these workers are exploited by capital. The continued existence of some pre-capitalist forms of labour and a few self-sufficient primitive economies in the most remote peripheries merely underline the overwhelming predominance of capitalist profit maximization in animating the most substantial forms of labour within the contemporary global capitalist economy.

Each of the major imperialist states of the early twentieth century (United Kingdom, France, Germany, Japan, United States) also invests substantially in and exchanges many commodities with the others. China has also emerged as a key global exporter and importer of capital. Capital flows at an unprecedented scale and accelerated rate through the global financial ownership system, which has both expanded enormously and become highly concentrated in the past three decades (see Vitali et al. 2011; Rugemer 2019). Information and transportation technologies facilitate widespread restructuring and relocation of production systems around the globe, and many transnational corporations originating in many countries have attained a global reach. In the post–WWII period, the US state coordinated and policed a generally hegemonic leadership worldwide (Panitch and Gindin 2012). But the territorial colonial expansion that was vital to the origin and development of capitalism is no longer a necessary aspect of the reproduction of capitalist accumulation in the twenty-first century (Sakellaropoulos and Sotiris 2015). With the global penetration of capitalist enterprises, major imperialists no longer require territorial control; rather, they need continuing access to profitable foreign resources and markets within territorially sovereign modern nation-states, as guaranteed to date by regional US military bases and institutional means such as international trade agreements.

The reach of large capitalist enterprises has continued to expand beyond nation-state boundaries both in terms of production sites and location of pools of capital to maximize profits. But such enterprises still require executive, legislative and judicial support of state agencies to ensure capital accumulation within most territories. By the same token, most of those who resist capitalist expansion still choose to rely on state agencies to mediate demands for decent living conditions and, more rarely, for limits on profit maximization. This global system is continuing to expand and is ever shifting, but most relations between capital

Emergent "Knowledge Economy"

Along with the growing global penetration of the capitalist mode of production, a recent shift from production based on transformation of objective materials to production based on mental knowledge and information has been widely heralded.[4] The emergence of the notion of a "knowledge economy" coincides with the decline of employment in the manufacturing sector and a corresponding shift into information-processing service sectors that began around the end of the 1960s. This change has been seen by some observers as the most significant economic shift in advanced capitalist economies since the widespread development of industrial machinery and the decline of agricultural employment in the nineteenth century. Many who had been forced off the land were drawn into the manufacturing plants that continued to expand into the mid-twentieth century. Steel, auto, petrochemical and electrical industries all created new mass-produced material commodities that became basic needs for urbanizing workforces throughout this period. But as automation increased and market capacity was exceeded, a spiral of mass layoffs of workers and the mergers or failures of remaining firms occurred in many manufacturing industries. Between 1970 and the early twenty-first century, advanced capitalist countries lost massive numbers of manufacturing jobs (ILO 2003). We have witnessed the general decline of employment in manufacturing in a more rapid way than the decline in agriculture in the previous two centuries. Service-sector industries focused more on information than objective material-based commodities grew proportionately.

But similar shifts in established patterns of production have occurred throughout the history of Western industrial capitalism in one key sector after another: in agriculture during the nineteenth century, in energy generation and transportation in the early twentieth century, in manufacturing most recently — and most likely in multiple service sectors presently. These periodic shifts share the following features:

- competitive capitals investing in a key employment sector to the point of massive overproduction capacity relative to consumer markets, followed by increased state intervention and increased concentration of ownership to maintain sector production;

- implementation of major existing technologies to multiply productivity and greatly reduce operating costs of surviving enterprises; and

- massive reduction in the key sector's labour force, coupled with negotiations to revise the social contract between capital and labour.

There has been a recurrent tendency toward capital-intensive, labour-displacing forms of technological change for increased productivity and assurance of profits in one sector after another. The upheaval in heavy manufacturing industries such as steel and the rapid expansion of less-secure service-sector employment are current manifestations of the fundamental underlying dynamics of the advanced capitalist mode of production which have prevailed in Western societies for roughly two centuries — namely, inter-firm competition in pursuit of profits and competitive negotiations between employers and workers over profits and benefits, along with continuing revolutionizing and mechanization of the forces of production.

All competitive capitalist enterprises are at least periodically impelled to invest in new technologies and new product lines and to undertake an intensive reorganization of their workforces in order to survive. The development of the capitalist labour process has entailed a wide variety of employer strategies and tactics in relation to their employees. These initiatives have usually revolved around profitability prospects of a particular production process and secondarily around concern about either controlling or deskilling workers.

Much of the literature heralding the "post-industrial society" or more recently the "knowledge-based economy" tends to exaggerate both the pervasiveness and distinctive character of recent economic changes. These changes are best understood as a widespread implementation by employers of a new set of technologies utilizing much smaller, re-combinable standardized components or modules (especially in microelectronics). These technologies are combined with strategies to motivate workers to use their discretion to operate these devices efficiently, in order to ensure the profitable production and marketing of diversified commodities. Neither the changing sectoral composition of employment from manufacturing to services nor accelerating rates of change in employment conditions and commodity markets should obscure the continuity of these underlying dynamics. The same capitalist logic of incessant commodification and periodic labour intensification is still at work. The contradictions in this logic are only more evident within key sectors that have reached a condition of overcapacity in relation to available markets and extreme underemployment of labour, as has been the case in many advanced capitalist societies' manufacturing industries in the past generation (e.g., Livingstone, Smith and Smith 2011).

However, it is true that increasing access to digital information sources via hardware, software and the internet is generating a growing array of intangible material labours (often misleadingly termed "immaterial labours") that are constituting a collective and collaborative productive force via online sharing platforms that have been relatively difficult for capital to control (see Carchedi 2022). The struggle over open access to and private appropriation of digital knowledge is at the heart of the current development of advanced capitalist economies.

Many observers would probably agree with the following social facts pertaining to most advanced capitalist economies today (see Livingstone and Guile 2012):

- declining minorities of jobs are in materials processing occupations, and growing majorities include computer-mediated information;
- growing proportions of jobs are designated as professional and technical occupations distinguished by specialized knowledge;
- growing proportions of labour forces are attaining post-secondary formal education and participating in adult education courses; and
- knowledge management has become a high declared priority of private corporations and governments.

But to argue, as many advocates of a post-industrial society or knowledge-based economy do (see David and Foray 2002), that an unprecedented acceleration of the speed of creation and accumulation of knowledge requires greater learning efforts from workers, more investment in "human capital" and the fuller development of a "learning society" in order to respond to a new economic imperative is to ignore other basic social facts.

First, all human economies are knowledge based. The most distinctive feature of our species has been the gathering of information from our environment and processing it into useful knowledge to cope effectively with changes in this environment. These forms of knowledge have ranged from basic language elements to highly sophisticated theories of life. All human civilizations have exhibited a wide range of forms of knowledge. The more we study both ancient and modern societies, the more we appreciate the depth of the knowledge, including informal and tacit knowledge as well as formally documented knowledge systems, they have relied upon to survive (e.g., Livingstone 2010). Second, knowledge is distinctive from most goods and services in that it cannot be reduced to a commodity. The more we use it, the more there is potentially for wider use. The typical commodity is used up soon after acquired and we are expected to purchase a replacement. Third, this irreducible character of knowledge coupled with its increasing centrality in information-based production systems makes it increasingly imperative for capitalist employers to try to control and manage workers' knowledge for profit maximization. This irreducibility of workers' knowledge leads knowledge-economy management experts to urge:

> This basic fact of skill development and knowledge formation makes systematic personnel development and lifelong learning a permanent management task in knowledge-intensive processes of value creation.... Most of the skills and competences needed are embodied and cannot be expropriated, but must be maintained and developed in and through the work processes in which they are used. All managerial activities ... therefore, are directed to achieve this. (Brödner 2000, 15, 22)

This permanent knowledge-management task continually contends with the expansive embodied irreducible nature of workers' knowledge and with workers' individual and collective motivation to share (or not share) it. This has been a familiar story in industrial and "post-industrial" societies. Approaches such as knowledge-economy theories that have not attended to the underlying contradictory dynamics of advanced capitalism — including conflicting aspects of the interest relationship between owners and paid workers — have misunderstood the nature and extent of changes occurring in both work and learning processes (see Livingstone 2009, 59–60).

This opposition between most peoples' widening access to valued knowledge and the efforts by business owners and managers to control knowledge as discrete intellectual property is a central feature of our times. Some express this opposition in terms of a contrast between aspirations for a "knowledge society," in which there is increasingly equal access to higher education, and constraints of a "knowledge economy," in which exclusive development and sale of intellectual products is an increasing preoccupation of private enterprise. Whatever the terms, the contest between democratic access to and use of knowledge versus its privatized control is a vexed issue with no easy path toward the dominance of one or the other. As long as capitalism survives, this opposition is most likely to persist.

Whether the focal commodities are produced primarily through objective or mental transformations of material, the quintessential motor of capitalism is competition between firms, which ensures that each of them must grow and reinvest its profits to survive. As Bellamy-Foster, Clark and York (2010, 109) remind us: "By its nature, capital is self-expanding, and accumulation is its sole aim.... The earth and human labour are systematically exploited/robbed to fuel this juggernaut." Regardless of how much knowledge-economy advocates and other mainstream economists focus on intangible aspects of the economy, it is clear that the scale of damage to the earth from continuing material production has reached unprecedented levels, along with the massive polarization of wealth and poverty around the globe, as discussed in later chapters. One of the deepest ironies of knowledge-economy discourse is that there has been precious little attention in it to the kinds of environmental knowledge that are needed to aid human survival in the wake of the negative environmental effects of the continual expansion of capitalist production. The knowledge that apparently counts in this context is that which can be applied to producing multitudes of commodities for continuing profit, and anything else, including human and ecosystem survival, remains secondary.

Aside from the indifference in knowledge-economy discourse to issues of survival, there is also a large contradiction in the presumption of skill deficits suffered by much of the current labour force, including a consequent call for more lifelong learning. These presumed deficits doggedly ignore the social facts of unprecedented levels of participation in higher education and adult education. Human capital theorists have long argued that investment in formal education leads to economic growth, but we have experienced a generation of unprecedented growth of advanced formal education along with economic stagnation and high unemployment. Many researchers have documented the existence of growing underemployment of formal knowledge attained in comparison to education requirements for available jobs (e.g., Livingstone 2009). In particular, while the ability to use computers and the internet are the most often demanded competencies for new labour market entrants, these are also the competencies where there is the greatest surplus of underutilized skills (Allen and van der Velden 2011; Livingstone 2019a). The dominant tendency is clearly for workers to have both unprecedented levels of formal knowledge/qualifications and increasingly recognized extensive embodied informal knowledge. There is compelling evidence of increasing underemployment and underutilization of workers' abilities. Surely then, the assumption of a major skill deficit as a significant barrier to further development of a "knowledge economy" is highly questionable. The deficit is much more likely to reside in the capitalist organization of paid work, which inhibits many workers from fully using their substantial abilities.

On the basic question of continuity and change in the prevailing economic system, the contradictory dynamics of advanced capitalism are still at play in driving both knowledge management of twenty-first-century firms and the lifelong learning of current and prospective workers. Numerous specific features of firms, workers and their strategic relations continue to change significantly, but overall, the "knowledge economy" remains a variant of the advanced capitalist mode of production which should provoke serious consideration of alternative ways of organizing economic life to utilize our knowledge for a sustainable future.

Post-Capitalist Enclaves

Alternative ways of organizing economic life have co-existed with capitalism from the outset. Small commodity farmers and skilled craftspeople tried to maintain independent ways of life as profit-driven production systems expanded. As corporate capitalism spread and took greater control of hired workers' lives, many who wanted to retain prior freedoms banded together in producer cooperatives. Since the 1880s in virtually all advanced capitalist countries, there have been substantial numbers of producer and consumer organizations based on principles of self-management and participatory decision-making for widely shared goals besides profits. In recent decades they have attracted relatively little attention as large private profit corporations penetrated more of our everyday existence. But, in fact, cooperatively owned organizations oriented to social needs have become widespread (see Alperovitz 2004; Quarter, Mook and Armstrong 2017).

In virtually every local community there are numerous publicly owned organizations that have provided needed services for a long time. Just think of public libraries, parks and blood banks, as well as many universities and hospitals. Community-owned social enterprises under many names are increasingly providing local and regional services — such as food hubs, housing, transit, internet access, financing and many other services — through mutual benefit corporations (e.g., Howard, Dubb and McKinley 2014). The qualifications of the members of the labour force in the advanced capitalist corporate world have mounted rapidly while their alienation and underemployment have also grown, along with poverty and pollution. In this context, the appeal of worker self-management in organizations based on socially useful, sustainable production (aka economic democracy) should also continue to grow among "knowledge workers," along with their prospects for decent jobs and human survival.[5] The extent to which coherent emergent visions of worker self-management and socially useful sustainable production are being advocated by class opinion leaders and how they resonate with broader publics are addressed in later chapters.

More on the G7 and Nordic Focus

The primary focus of this book is on advanced capitalist economies that are fully developed in terms of the dominance of private ownership of production and the prevalence of hired workers in the labour force, with particular attention to recent development of class positions in production and connection with expressions of class consciousness. The specific reasons for this focus are two operating assumptions. First, the most fully developed form of a mode of production will exhibit the greatest contradiction between the expansive capacity of its productive forces and the more restricted organization of the actual production process. Second, this contradiction is likely to be most clearly perceived by those who most directly experience it through the exploitation of their labour power in the production process. Whether or not these assumptions are ultimately proven valid for the global capitalist economy, I bring to bear the best available empirical evidence for a current assessment. The relative extent of oppression and exploitation of the employed population and surplus population may be even more severe in more peripheral capitalist formations facing continuing plunder and unequal exchange. It is certainly possible that transition from capitalism could occur in these countries first. Given the growing interdependence of this global system, significant change in any part should have major implications for other parts. I merely offer one test with the best available evidence for advanced capitalist economies.

More specifically, the empirical focus is on the G7 and Nordic countries. The G7 are the largest advanced private-market economies in the world in recent times (United States, Japan, Germany, France, United Kingdom, Italy and Canada). This Group of Seven constitutes an inter-governmental political forum. Along with the European Union, a non-enumerated member, they represent about 50 percent of net global wealth, while making up only 10 percent of world population (Wikipedia, "G7"). The most populous Nordic countries are Denmark, Finland, Norway and Sweden. These countries have historically had social democratic regimes and still have among the most highly unionized labour forces in the world. They are included because of the general assumption that they have made the furthest advances yet toward challenging capitalist ownership of the means of production and control of the labour process. This is admittedly a controversial assumption. The intent is to study advanced capitalism through the fullest range of its current development. Selected comparisons where relevant data are available permit assessment of the recent development of these countries' class structures as well as some expressions of class consciousness.

The data sources are specified further in the following chapters. They include estimates from 1992 to 2016 of class structure based on original syntheses of occupational and employment status trend data from the International Labour Office (2019) on *Key Indicators In the Labour Market* (KILM). Initial estimates of class structure and initial links with class consciousness rely mainly on secondary analyses of the 1980s national surveys in the Class Structure and Class Consciousness (CSCC) project led by Erik Olin Wright (1989). The most detailed and accurate trend estimates of both class structure and class consciousness are based on a series of national labour force surveys and related case studies I have led in Canada since the 1980s. These studies also include a twenty-year series of representative surveys of corporate executives, providing an exceptionally rare window into the class consciousness of the corporate elite. Where comparable evidence is available from other countries, it is incorporated in the text. The main surveys and data I used are readily publicly accessible (see Canada Work Learning Surveys 1998–2016). In any case, further studies should soon address more fully the patterns and relations in class structure and class consciousness identified here.

It is relevant to consider the nature of pre-capitalist production relations in these current nation-states and the forms and periods in which they were integrated into the capitalist world economy. A brief word specifically about the Canadian case, which is focal in some of the analyses by default because of the absence of relevant recent class-based data elsewhere. Among twentieth-century "secondary imperialists," Canada was previously seen as a "white settler formation" based on predominance of the simple commodity form of production and individual private-property ownership. As in the US, the construction of this settler state involved the near extermination of Indigenous Nations and the implementation of a system of white privilege. The country therefore had a capacity for relatively rapid achievement of a fully developed capitalist system of production, to be achieved with heavy dependence on foreign commercial capital and foreign sources of labour. In the comparative analyses throughout this book, Canada is considered as a fully developed advanced private-market economy but with somewhat less dependence on pre-capitalist modes of production than the other included countries.

Concluding Remarks

The profiles of contemporary class relations suggested in this text are primarily derived from production relations. While class relations should never be reduced to production relations, these relations should never be ignored, as they have been in many recent accounts of contemporary societies. The analysis in this chapter draws on insights into the contradictory determining forces of the capitalist mode of production discovered by Marx and confirmed by recent generations of critical scholars who have given primary attention to production relations per se. The private concentration and centralization of capital is becoming increasingly pronounced on a global scale and the capitalist labour process has become increasingly pervasive. At the same time, democratic demand for and public access to general and specific knowledge relevant to production — and to life generally — have widened through expansive means of communication such as public education and the internet. While capital concentration continues to grow, we see degradation of the physical environment and underutilization of capital for productive purposes. While the numbers of highly qualified workers and their engagement in lifelong learning activities may continue to increase, we see widely increasing underemployment. We are experiencing an increasingly global expression of the basic contradiction of the driving forces of the capitalist mode of production: the private concentration of capital and the socialization of knowledge are both becoming more pronounced as the capitalist world economy operates in its fully developed form. These contradictory tendencies are animating a wide variety of social forces everywhere. We ignore these driving forces at our peril.

But production relations do not represent the totality of class relations at any level of abstraction. The objective here is to emphasize briefly how the historical laws of motion of the capitalist enterprise unavoidably come into conflict with the broader social needs and aspirations of the mass of people. However, the relations between capital and labour cannot be generated and sustained at the level of the enterprise but only within social formations as a whole through complexes of social practices (see Brighton Labour Process Group 1977). Drawing on the transhistorical model outlined in Chapter 1, at least political and ideological aspects of class relations and social practices should also be considered.

Political relations involve organizing or integrating the operation of the social formation as a whole, in particular through the right to exercise constraint over others. These relations are currently most manifest within the structures of the capitalist state. Ideological relations involve the creation and transmission of worldviews from the standpoints of particular classes or groups. Such relations in capitalist societies are prominent in a range of sociocultural institutions, such as the family, church, school, mass media, social clubs, etc. The intangible nature of many aspects of ideological struggle continue to present inherent difficulties to any systematic analysis. Further consideration of modes of thought within capitalism in relation to dominant and subordinate ideologies is offered in Chapter 5.

The characteristic capitalist forms and dynamics of political and ideological class relations both within and beyond the production process remain far less developed than analyses of the production process per se. The current level of political and ideological class struggles should always be relevant considerations in conducting analyses of class relations in any mode of production. After the serious political protests by student and worker movements in 1968, critical investigations of both the historical and current impact of dominated groups on the shaping of political and ideological forms became more relevant to analysts. In the wake of 1968, Poulantzas (1975) offered a suggestive analysis of political and ideological aspects of class relations *within* the production process, in terms of supervisory hierarchies as the basis of political relations and the "mental/manual" division as the basis of ideological relations. Such dichotomous concepts remained formalistic abstractions and also tended to reduce political and ideological relations to parts of production relations. Since the 1970s, some Marxist scholars have continued to focus their class analyses on such dichotomous class characteristics associated with divisions within the capitalist labour process (i.e., owner/non-owner; supervisory/non-supervisory; intellectual/manual; productive/unproductive). Others have pursued studies of political and ideological class relations more removed from production relations. The analyses in later chapters address political and ideological class relations primarily through expression of class consciousness related to production relations. However, as discussed in the next chapter, many general class analyses have become disconnected from production relations entirely. The deepest class contradiction is found between the massive concentration of private capital and the universalizing access of workers to useful knowledge. I take this insight as a starting point for understanding the changing class structure of advanced capitalism.

Notes

1. As an introductory source on these property rights developments and social movements for broader human rights from the seventeenth century, see Wikipedia, "Right to Property."
2. The most substantial work to date is still Braverman (1974). See also Gorz (1976). Carter (2021) offers an insightful critical appreciation of the enduring significance of Braverman's work.
3. A most vivid, insightful account of this struggle in early twentieth-century English painting gangs is provided by Robert Tressell (1955 [1914]).
4. See Carchedi (2022) for an incisive analysis of the limits of this shift and the persistence of the divide between capital and labour, as well as the continued operation of the law of value.
5. For my own account of the development of some of the leading contemporary cases of economic democracy, see Livingstone (2004).

4

The Changing Class Structure of Production Relations in the "Knowledge Economy"

As noted in Chapter 1, Marx began his inquiry into capitalist production by studying simple commodities. I began this inquiry into class relations by reviewing popular notions of class in Chapter 2. These notions typically focus on evident differences in commodity consumption and accumulated monetary wealth. Many scholarly studies of classes focus on such differences in consumption levels or on occupational categories. Some studies ignore paid workplaces entirely to focus on cultural consumption issues. Either out of conceptual or empirical convenience, most contemporary studies that have analyzed class relations in paid workplaces have tended to focus on easily measured occupational categories, simple abstractions that ignore or obscure class relations per se. Such studies remain at the level of surface descriptions. As outlined in Chapter 3, when capitalism coalesced as a mode of industrial production, its major protagonists took shape and grew within its core production structure. The wellspring of capitalism's continuing expansion was seen by Marx to be the extraction of surplus value by capitalist owners of the means of production from the unpaid labour time of wage labourers who directly produced the commodities that capitalists sold to realize that value as profit. Both apologists for capitalism and many recent analysts of classes and the production process appear to be intent on ignoring this connection between class formation and production relations. I follow Marx's method to identify the class forces in advanced capitalism generated by the contradictory production relations involved in extraction of surplus value from direct producers by owners of the means of production.

To get to heart of class relations in advanced capitalism we need to identify these basic relations within the production process that underlie both popular notions and occupational categories. Class formation has continued to be linked to relations between capitalists and hired labour, albeit in somewhat more complex ways in advanced capitalism, and most recently — as we will see — with the growth of professional employees. We need to identify this changing class structure as a basic context for class practices in advanced capitalism. Among researchers who have continued to focus on class relations in paid workplaces, some operating from different vantage points and alignments have begun to converge on similar class models. From both Marxist and Weberian perspectives, tripartite class models identifying (1) capital in different levels of concentration, (2) non-managerial hired labour based on producing objective material goods, more intangible services or designing these good and services commodities, and (3) managers mediating between these forms of capital and labour are emerging in recent empirical studies.

I offer a brief critical assessment of recent approaches to class analysis and labour process analysis in advanced capitalism. Then I suggest a Marxist model of current employment class structure grounded in production relations between owners and hired labour. An empirical assessment of continuity and change in this class structure is provided, based on the best available comparative data since the 1980s on employment relations in advanced capitalist economies. Other connections of employment classes with demographic features, working conditions, intergenerational mobility wealth and health distribution are briefly noted. In later chapters, I draw on this underlying class structure to assess connections between class and class consciousness.

Disconnecting Class

The death of the economic and political significance of classes based in production relations in advanced industrial societies has been heralded since the end of World War II. Early farewells referred to increasing consumer affluence, political quiescence of industrial workers and the end of class-based ideologies (Bell 1962). Since the 1970s, the decline of manufacturing employment and industrial labour unions, coupled with an increasing capacity of large transnational companies to relocate production operations, have drawn death notices from intellectuals who see few signs that the industrial working class can act as a coherent political force (e.g., Gorz 1982). One of the most extended obituaries (Kingston 2000) claims that the production process itself is extremely unlikely to generate class formation because of diverse employment conditions, high occupational mobility and experience-diversifying technologies. The emergence of cross-class social movements based on civil rights and feminist and environmental concerns has been highlighted in critiques of the inadequacy of existing class analyses to deal with these issues (e.g., Pakulski and Waters 1996). Most recent analyses of classes in advanced capitalist societies have ignored relations in the sphere of production per se while focusing on exchange issues (marketable skills, income levels) or have taken a cultural turn that tends to disconnect class from paid workplaces entirely. Some of these approaches, such as those inspired by Pierre Bourdieu, purport to offer more holistic analyses of multidimensional class experience. Such approaches offer complex descriptions of current consumption patterns (e.g., Savage et al. 2013). Some who have taken this cultural turn do recognize the need to reconnect with employment characteristics (Atkinson 2009; Hebson 2013), but none of these approaches offer insight into changing class relations within the capitalist labour process.

After generations of neglect, Harry Braverman's (1974) book on the degradation of work in "monopoly" capitalism did effectively redirect some attention to the capitalist labour process and class relations within production. Braverman's research was followed by several class analyses with more specific attention to relations of production (e.g., Carchedi 1977; Wright 1978). The renewed interest in production relations generated more complex models of class structure, cores and peripheries, including "new" corporate elites, "new" working classes, "new" middle classes and "new" petty bourgeoisies. Braverman also inspired case studies of the detailed social and technical division of labour (see Thompson 1983) that challenged a long prevailing focus on labour *market* relations. A variety of efforts were made to revise Braverman's degradation perspective, including Friedman's (1977) identification of "responsible autonomy" strategies of labour control and Burawoy's (1979) attention to subjectivity and workers' consent. Thompson (1990) proposed a "core" labour process agenda that rejected Marx's labour theory of value while attending to structured antagonisms and a control imperative to ensure firms' profitability. While this "core" theory has animated a good deal of empirical research, it has done little to connect with broader analyses of class. Indeed, Smith and Thompson have called attempts to reconnect class analysis and labour process studies a "sterile functionalist project" (Smith and Thompson 1999: 219) that miss the ongoing centrality of ownership and profit maximization in shaping class relations. I agree with this centrality but suggest that rejecting the labour theory of value disarms class analysis by permitting the "dazzling appearance" of free market exchange to obscure the wellsprings of private capital accumulation in the exploitation of labour in production — the innermost secret referred to in Marx's method and traced in Chapter 3.

Since the 1980s, class analysis and labour process studies have become increasingly disconnected (see Carter 1995; Neilson 2007). Analytical Marxists have also dismissed Marx's labour theory of value as false and useless, defined class structure and exploitation in terms of possession of various assets and largely ignored production relations per se (Roemer 1982). Much employment class analysis has focused on complex arrays of occupational communities that are disconnected from actual relations of production (e.g., Grusky and Weedon 2001). Labour process research has devolved into either macro analyses of global corporate capitalist enterprise development or micro case studies of firms, both of which are disconnected from systematic employment class analysis (Jaros 2005; Tinker 2002). Once again, classes should not be reduced to production relations alone, but production relations cannot credibly be ignored.

My view is that classes are fundamentally grounded in production relations in all capitalist societies and simply cannot be comprehended accurately if these relations are evaded. This is the central assertion of this book. As noted earlier, classes cannot simply be reduced to production relations in the abstract. Class existence is lived both in production relations and beyond them in household and community relations (Livingstone 1983a; Seccombe and Livingstone 1999). Class existence is inextricably embedded in other irreducible features of our lives, especially gender, race and age relations. These features are often more enduring than the constant change of class positions in production relations, and they constantly inflect the lived experience of classes. Whites have been privileged over non-whites in virtually all class positions, as have men over women. The very young face large challenges to establish themselves in employment, while the very old face different challenges to remain in it. In contrast to those class analysts who effectively efface production relations, I seek to focus on them. But to grasp classes in production relations, class must be seen as irreducibly mediated through these other features of our lives. I look briefly at connections between employment class structure and some of these features at the end of this chapter.

Renewed Marxist Approach to Class and Production Relations

For Marx, the most basic driving force of class relations in capitalist economies was the exploitation of productive hired workers by the owners of private companies through the extraction of surplus value in order to maximize profits via the realization of that value in competitive commodity markets. The material interest of hired labourers to attain higher wages to improve their living conditions was a major counterforce. The dominant tendency was for techniques of production to be modified frequently to reduce the amount of living labour per unit of saleable commodities in order to continue to maximize profits. This production process was seen as a drive to commodify everything, including labour, and as leading to the concentration of capital, the centralization of firms and the proliferation of reserve armies of labour.

Ever since Marx worked out a labour theory of value that identified the extraction of unpaid labour from direct producers of commodities as a central feature of the reproduction of capitalist economies, this theory has been subjected to continuing dismissal and ridicule. Vitriolic criticisms have come from a wide array of defenders of the varieties of capitalism. Even among strong critics of capitalism committed to promoting economic alternatives, Marx's value theory has often been deemed useless (e.g., Wright 1997; 2010). But this theory of value continues to be resurrected in a search for explanations of capitalism's dynamism, conflict and crises.

As noted in Chapter 3, most of the hired labour force of the global capitalist economy is located in the Global South (Neilson and Stubbs 2011). Advanced capitalist countries are characterized by larger shares of global capital, greater shares of relatively well-paid "knowledge workers" and lesser shares of surplus population in desperation. My focus in the current analysis is limited mainly to the employed labour force in advanced capitalism — the primary basis of my experience and empirical evidence. The main operating assumption is that the exploitation of productive hired workers in advanced capitalism by private enterprise owners continues to be relevant to the constituting of the class structure and the development of class consciousness within advanced capitalism and beyond.

Within advanced capitalist centres, direct manual labour is widely assumed to decline with de-industrialization and increasingly mechanized commodity production, while more intellectualized and managerial work expands — the emergent "knowledge economy" discussed in Chapter 3. In such "knowledge economies," with growing amounts of work involving processing of information, mainstream analysts' fixation with labour productivity increasingly focuses on capturing knowledge. This is exemplified by a diffuse knowledge theory of value that is inattentive to knowledge workers' own interests or capacities (Jacques 2000). Workers with scientific knowledge are increasingly strategically located in many current sectors of advanced capitalist economies and play essential roles in the production process. I designate these non-managerial specialized knowledge workers as "professional employees." The value of their design, development and distribution labour in goods and service commodities tends to increase with every step toward capital intensification and displacement of more routine labour. From the standpoint of employers, more efficient utilization of their specialized knowledge is becoming a paramount issue for productivity and profitability. For management guru Peter Drucker (1998, ix), ensuring the productivity of such knowledge workers is the most urgent issue for twenty-first-century advanced capitalism: "The productivity of knowledge and knowledge workers will not be the only competitive factor in the world economy. It is, however, likely to become the decisive factor, at least for most industries in the developed countries." There has been a veritable explosion in recent decades of management tools to capture, codify and apply professional knowledge for organizational development and growth, with relatively rich benefits for a few professional enablers (e.g., Girard and Girard 2015; Wikipedia, "Knowledge Management").

Advanced capitalist production may increasingly centre on intangible services rather than objective material goods, but Marx's labour theory of value centring on the extraction of surplus value in the capitalist labour process is still being seen as essential to understanding capitalist development by lines of activists and scholars (e.g., Foley 2013; Hiroyoshi 2005). Although some seek to rebury the labour theory of value, it continues to be resurrected in a search for explanations of capitalism's economic changes. Few recent Marxist class theorists have attended closely to value relations. A notable exception is Resnick and Wolff's (1987) model, which focuses abstractly on the production/appropriation of surplus value as the fundamental class process. Prior empirical studies in both advanced capitalist and global settings found significant relations between rates of value exploitation of manufacturing workers and rates of protest actions (Cuneo 1984; Boswell and Dixon 1993). Various researchers are turning attention to specialized workers, who may be primary sources of surplus labour for profits and bases of resistance in the "knowledge economy" (e.g., Cockshott, Cottrell and Michaelson 1995; Huws 2014).

There are at least two reasons for the ongoing attraction of the labour theory of value. First, although value chains of production, distribution, exchange and consumption have become much more complicated, the extraction of unpaid labour from the direct producers of a vast array of goods and services commodities is still at the root of the profit making that defines and drives advanced capitalism. For example, there is suggestive evidence that the rate of exploitation of productive-sector workers increased greatly in the emergent neoliberal period of 1987–2008 in advanced capitalist economies (Carchedi 2011). Second, the extraordinary productivity — when compared with earlier periods of capitalism — of those whose labour is directly involved in the creation of objective and intangible commodities indicates the real potential alternative uses of labour time and free time both for such productive workers and for the growing numbers in the reserve armies of the unemployed, the underemployed and those relegated to jobs that do not produce use value for sustainability. A basic argument of this book is that workers directly involved in creating commodities are among the most productive and exploited workers in the emergent "knowledge economy" and are therefore in a pivotal position to influence the future development of paid work in and from advanced capitalism. I turn more fully to the question of alternatives to capitalism in the final chapter.

If the extraction of surplus value from productive hired workers by enterprise owners continues to be a basic driving force of advanced capitalism, then identification of such workers and assessment of their objective material and ideological conditions remain pertinent to prospects for change in and from advanced capitalism. Most value theorists would agree that manual production workers in private goods–producing industries (i.e., resource extracting and manufacturing) (hereafter usually called "industrial workers') are direct producers of surplus value. Most would also consider other hired employees involved in producing private goods to be productive workers. In an advanced capitalist economy, many other hired employees involved in creating diverse goods and services for private sale may also be considered as productive labourers and part of the "collective worker" (Carchedi 1977). But with transnational corporations, rapid currency exchange and long-distance supply chains, the value/price conversion process has become much more mediated, complex and obscure, and there is much dispute over which other workers do productive labour, especially in relation to saleable services (Bryer 2005; Moraitis and Copley 2017). For the purposes of the present analysis, I identify different class positions in terms of production relations, estimate recent structural changes in such class positions and later explore their association with expressions of class consciousness. It is of primary importance to distinguish owners of the major means of production who drive profit maximization from employees identifiable as producers of saleable goods and services as well as those who provide necessary labour to deliver these commodities.

In particular, the notion of "knowledge workers" needs to be specified in terms of class position and working conditions. Contrary to the optimistic claims of knowledge-economy advocates, many of those commonly regarded as advantaged knowledge workers, notably those I identify as "professional employees," appear to be experiencing degradation of their working conditions, increasing underemployment and relegation to the reserve army of labour, comparable to the historical experience of skilled labour (Livingstone 2009; Livingstone, Adams and Sawchuk 2021). But neither should it be assumed that such degradation is inevitable. As Tinel (2014, 8) observes: "Interactions between the tendencies to (class) polarization and the counter-tendencies identified by Braverman are much more uncertain than he suggested … the global outcome is likely to be more indeterminate and unstable."

More generally and in contrast to the complex surface descriptions of current class situations offered by those with a fixation on exchange and cultural consumption patterns, a focus on production relations can attend to connections between labour processes and differential class experiences.

Employment Class Structure in Advanced Capitalist Workplaces

The initial challenge to understanding classes in advanced capitalist workplaces is locating them in the division of labour. There are three basic dimensions to this division: ownership of the means of production; authority over others in the social division of labour; and discretion over skill use in the technical division of labour.

I agree with Marx that the most basic employment class division in capitalism is between the owners of means of production and those who must offer their labour to make a living. *Ownership* entails proprietorship of a private enterprise, either on one's own account or with hired employees. As outlined in Chapter 3, there has been a dominant tendency for ownership to become increasingly centralized and concentrated with the expansion of the capitalist mode of production and for capital assets to be held in proportionately fewer hands.

The *social division of labour* involves the exercise of managerial authority, a designated role to direct other hired employees. In Chapter 3, I outline how, with increasing commodification of production relations, there has been an increasing imperative for capitalist owners to ensure effective coordination and control of production for profit maximization by employing proportionately greater numbers of managerial personnel among hired employees.

The *technical division of labour* involves the extent to which the exercise of specialized knowledge and skills is required to perform one's job tasks. Chapter 3 outlines the inherent conflict between increasingly socialized access to advanced knowledge (through such means as the internet) and its privatized appropriation (through such means as intellectual property rights). I expect that, with increasing mechanization of the labour process, there will be increasing demand for remaining workers to use the labour power of their minds in interaction with both other workers' minds and machinery as parts of collective labour. There also will be increasing knowledge qualifications to obtain jobs in advanced capitalist production, but this process will be uneven and contested in terms of recognition of this knowledge.

So, I propose a reintegration of class analysis and labour process analysis using a model of class structure based on these three dimensions of production relations within paid workplaces. I use this model to investigate historically specific shifts in ownership and the organization of production. These class boundaries are more permeable than other social distinctions, such as age, sex and racialization. Many employers do *some* labour (e.g., manage labourers and accounts) and many labourers own *some* capital (e.g., pension plans), and there has been continuing movement between positions of capital and labour. Some class positions in the production process clearly perform the respective functions of capital and labour, while others have more mixed functions. But the model remains grounded in ownership relations, the extent of managerial authority and specialized knowledge exercised in production relations. Basic employment classes in advanced capitalism are identifiable in term of these three key dimensions.

Much research on employment classes in contemporary capitalist societies in terms of production relations suggests three basic types of class positions: (1) ownership classes of capitalist employers and a petty bourgeoise of self-employed; (2) intermediate class positions combining capitalist managerial functions and collective labour roles; and (3) class positions of non-managerial hired collective labour. Among Marxist scholars, these tripartite distinctions between class positions in the capitalist labour process have been most fully elaborated by Guglielmo Carchedi (1975; 1977), who proposed a conceptual model of the economic identification of classes in terms of ownership, functions of global capital and the collective worker, and the productiveness of labour. Erik Olin Wright's (1978; 1985; 1997) several employment class models were also initially based on capital, labour and contradictory class positions. Among Weberian researchers focused on the nature of the employment contract, self-employed owners and labourers as well intermediate service classes have commonly been distinguished (e.g., Erikson and Goldthorpe 1992; Goldthorpe 2016; Oesch 2006). My composite model is conceptually most similar to Carchedi's in recognizing the centrality of ownership, as well as capital and labour functions in production and the continuing pertinence of value extraction to class formation.

So, in simplest terms, we have enterprise owners, managerial employees and non-managerial labourers. Much of the recent dispute among class analysts involves who is included in the intermediate class positions. Two important points here. First, anyone with a formally delegated role as a manager or supervisor should be understood as part of the managerial hierarchy in capitalist economies. They are indeed intermediate as hired employees who both coordinate collective labour and control other employees on behalf of enterprise owners. They exercise some of the powers of capital, hiring and firing workers and making specific production process decisions.

But, second, hired employees with specialized skills are clearly part of collective labour and not typically delegated powers of capital beyond gestural voice. Wright (2005), for example, in his influential writings, persisted in seeing "semi-autonomous employees" or "experts" as in intermediate class positions — because their specialized skills and credentials were assumed to confer some discretionary control over some technical aspects of their own jobs. However, such employees are not intermediate in the sense of combined managerial and labour functions. They are clearly part of the collective labour process and mainly distinguishable from some other non-managerial hired labour by the specialized knowledge certified by post-secondary education required for their jobs.

Among the heralds of emergence of a knowledge-based economy, there has been a persistent promotion of the notion of a powerful "professional-managerial class."[1] In amalgamating managers with specialized non-managerial employees, this turns out to be one of the most confounding concepts in the history of class analysis. Even some earlier leading advocates have shifted dramatically to concede that "the professional middle class" is facing "the same kind of situation that confronted skilled craft workers in the early 20th century and all (American) industrial workers in the late 20th century" (Ehrenreich and Ehrenreich 2013, 3). Recent grounded research on non-managerial professional employees is certainly finding a loss of workplace power among them. As we will see, professional employees and managers are both substantial and probably growing portions of the employed labour force in advanced capitalist countries. Some professional employees may become managers, but managers themselves are becoming more polarized and there is little empirical support for growth of a coherent combination of professionals and managers (Livingstone, Adams and Sawchuk 2021).

Major Classes in Contemporary Production Relations

More specifically, among these three basic employment class groupings, I identify the following ten distinguishable major classes in contemporary production relations:

Owners
- corporate capitalists
- large employers
- small employers
- self-employed

Non-managerial workers
- professional employees
- service workers
- industrial workers

Managerial employees
- upper managers
- middle managers
- supervisors.

Among owners, corporate capitalists oversee investment in companies and corporations with multimillion-dollar assets and many employees; large employers include substantial owners of capital with more than ten employees;[2] small employers, typically in family firms or partnerships, tend to have exclusive ownership, smaller numbers of employees and continue to play active co-ordinating roles in the labour process of their firms. The self-employed remain in formal control of their small commodity enterprises but are reliant on their own labour.

On the other side of the capital-labour divide are those employees without substantial ownership claims and not delegated any official managerial authority. This includes industrial workers, who produce material goods in extractive, manufacturing and construction sectors; and service workers, who create or deliver wide array of sales, business, social and other services. Third, there are professional employees, who require specialized post-secondary education credentials for job entry; they are expected to design production processes for themselves and others and execute their own work with a relatively high level of autonomy, but they remain subordinated to employer and managerial prerogatives.[3]

Between owners and those who are clearly subordinated hired labour are other employees who tend to have mixed functions. Upper managers are delegated by owners to control the overall labour process at the point of production to ensure profitability but also contribute their labour to coordinate this process. Under the authority of upper managers, middle managers perform administrative and accounting staff services. Supervisors control adherence to production standards by non-managerial workers but may also collaborate directly with them in aspects of this work.

All these class positions are based on relations of production as distinct from occupational classifications that overlap them (see Wright 1980).[4] For example, a carpenter may own a business that employs one or more hired labourers; they may be self-employed working entirely for themselves; they may be a supervisor in someone else's business; or they may work as an employee for someone else. In each instance, the class interests and the power they can exercise differ according to position in these production relations. Professionals similarly may be located in such different classes (i.e., professional employers, self-employed professionals, professional managers and professional employees).[5] The large research literature on professional occupations has been reluctant to recognize different professional classes (see Livingstone, Adams and Sawchuk 2021). More generally, as we will see, a great deal of empirical research on employment differences has fixated on documenting occupational categories while ignoring or conflating their relations with ownership status.

Beyond the sphere of employment, the *relative surplus adult population* (i.e., surplus to capitalist production) includes many who play essential reproductive labour roles, including especially unpaid domestic labour and volunteer community labour (Livingstone 1983a). It also includes various pensioners who are excluded from paid labour by age and other benefit conditions and students excluded by preparatory training conditions. Most pertinently, the relative surplus population includes the reserve army of labour available for paid employment — from those actively looking for jobs to those who have become discouraged by repeated failure and have given up hope for jobs (Neilson and Stubbs 2011). In nearly all advanced capitalist economies, more than 80 percent of all adults between the ages of 25 and 64 are in some form of paid employment. Unemployment status is a continuum ranging from those with part-time jobs who need full-time jobs to those chronically without any paid work. Those outside paid employment at any point in time may have diverse orientations to class positions within the production process. Without denying the importance of those outside paid employment for class analysis, the current study is mainly limited to the majority of the adult population that is in some form of paid employment in advanced capitalist countries.[6]

These general employment class groupings reflect a convergence in contemporary empirical studies of class structure based on the foundational writings of Marx, as well as those of Max Weber (see Burris 1987; 1990) This convergence is grounded in models of class structure relying on ownership and control of employment criteria. In one sense, this convergence should not be surprising since, as Marx observed (1973/1939) 188–217), production, distribution, exchange, consumption and reproduction aspects of goods, services and material existence are intimately related. As noted in Chapter 1, Weber differed profoundly from Marx in his view of the primacy of market domination in constituting classes and societies, and the potential for transformation of capitalism. However, Weber followed Marx in distinguishing ownership and non-ownership ("negative privilege") of private property as the major class division. Like Marx, he recognized among non-owners a working class that sells its general labour to make a living, as well as the "declassed, debtors and paupers" comparable to Marx's lumpen proletariat and reserve army of labour. In addition, both Marx and Weber saw a petty bourgeoisie of independent owners who work for themselves (Weber 1978 [1922]: 302–305). Beyond these generally agreed class positions, Marx discussed the growing importance of hired managerial employees to coordinate and control subordinate labour in larger private enterprises, while Weber emphasized an inevitable development of centralized bureaucratic administrative management of an increasingly complex civilization. Marx had begun to problematize skill differentials among hired labourers while Weber identified other "middle classes" who make a living from their acquired skills.

Among related conceptual studies of employment class structure since the 1970s, the following sorts of nominal class positions have commonly been suggested: *owners*: employers (big/small); self-employed or petty bourgeoisie; *non-owners*: managerial/supervisory employees; elite/professional/specialized knowledge workers; proletarian/working class; marginal/reserve/redundant /lumpen/underclass (see Portes 2000). The most influential Marx-based (Wright 1978; 1985; 1997) and Weber-based (Goldthorpe and McKnight 2004) conceptual class models identify most of these employment class positions in some fashion and have continued to be widely relied upon by other empirical researchers of employment class structure. As noted previously, much of the dispute among later Marxian and Weberian class analysts has revolved around ignoring or conflating some of these class positions, as well as the significance of middle or intermediate class positions that remained more suggestive for Marx and Weber.[7] But a tripartite class structure including owners, hired labourers and intermediate classes with greater authority or control has become basic to much of this research.

There have been several systematic empirical comparisons of these different Marx- and Weber-based models of class structure. Leiulfsrud et al. have conducted conceptual and empirical comparisons: two versions of Wright's and another by Esping-Anderson with Goldthorpe's typology. Their most general conclusion, based on national surveys in over twenty western European countries, was that "there is a high degree of resemblance within the class schemes over time" (Leiulfsrud et al. 2005: 22). Bergman and Joye compared several of Wright's schemes, Goldthorpe's simpler and more complex ones and several other stratification scales. Their basic conclusion was: "The stratification schemes ... display a tremendous variety in terms of their theoretical underpinnings and methodological constructions. Despite this variation, it is surprising how strongly they correlate with each other and how similar they are with regard to predictive validity" (2005: 43). In fact, strong correlation is hardly surprising given the shared underlying tripartite structure.

In contrast to this convergence, there has been little continuing interest in value relations among class analysts. Weberian models deny the relevance entirely. Wright's (1997) class models devolved into treating exploitation diffusely in terms of the presence or absence of ownership, authority and skill assets, and followed Roemer in effectively dismissing the labour theory of value. Conversely, Resnick and Wolff's (1987) focus on surplus value as the fundamental class process effectively dismissed composite models that include property ownership and control of production as secondary, but they offer no compelling reason for doing so. Carchedi's (1977) general abstract model of capital and labour functions offers a clearer conceptual basis for identifying economic class positions in the capitalist labour process while not throwing out the value baby with the occupational status bathwater. I use essentially the same criteria to estimate continuity and change in more concrete class positions in this chapter.

Empirical Estimates of Changing Employment Class Structure

Before proceeding to empirical data analysis, a few significant limitations should be noted. The presumptively dominant corporate capitalist class is not adequately distinguished in any national surveys because of its very tiny numbers. There have been valuable studies tracking changing networks of the corporate capitalist class in specific countries and globally (e.g., Clement 1974; Carroll 2010). Close study of their actual roles in production relations has been largely prohibited. I later draw upon a unique series of representative surveys of the attitudes of corporate capitalists based in Canada.[8] But direct critical study of the production practices and attitudes of the most powerful remains largely off limits.

Equally importantly, the reserve army of unemployed labour is poorly represented in most sample surveys, including the ones I use. I recognize the importance of the currently unemployed within broader class struggles, but for immediate analytical purposes they are excluded from this analysis.

In addition, other studies I have been involved in have documented the relevance of household and community relations in constituting classes in advanced capitalism (Livingstone and Mangan 1996a; Seccombe and Livingstone 1999). But these relations remain largely beyond the empirical scope of the present analysis.

Most limiting in terms of employment class relations per se, there are yet very few available national-level surveys that provide sufficient data on ownership and social and technical divisions of labour to accurately estimate patterns and trends in employment class structure. As we will see in a moment, official national labour force surveys to date focus mainly on occupational categories. Some identify self-employed or employer statuses, but almost none permit simply combining employment status with occupational data to estimate ownership, managerial authority and specialized knowledge divisions simultaneously. Nearly all prior studies of classes based on employment relations have relied heavily on occupational labels "as the only viable option" (Svallfors 2006, 15). Fortunately, there have been a few national surveys conducted by critical social scientists that have gathered some relevant data. I use some of these to assist in estimating trends in employment class structure with official national census data, as well as drawing on these few national surveys to compare political attitudes.

Best Estimates of Employment Class Structure for the 1980s

The most extensive cross-national empirical effort to date to estimate employment class structure in relevant terms occurred in the 1980s. It was led by Erik Olin Wright in the US, and the Class Structure and Class Consciousness Series (CSCC) eventually included a dozen countries.[9] A standard basic questionnaire was designed, research teams obtained national funding in many of these countries, the survey was administered to representative random samples and the data were archived at accessible sites for further use. The questions enabled clearly distinguishing the self-employed and both large and small employers, as well as gathering information on specific occupational descriptions and managerial-supervisory authority. I discuss Wright's own use of these data a bit further on, but the archive permits the best available class estimates for the early 1980s according to the criteria discussed in the prior section. My estimates for the country surveys with fairly complete data are summarized in Figure 4.1. These estimates follow Wright's (1978) own original class logic, which distinguished "semi-autonomous employees" — who at that point approximated non-managerial specialized knowledge workers, the professional employees discussed throughout this book.

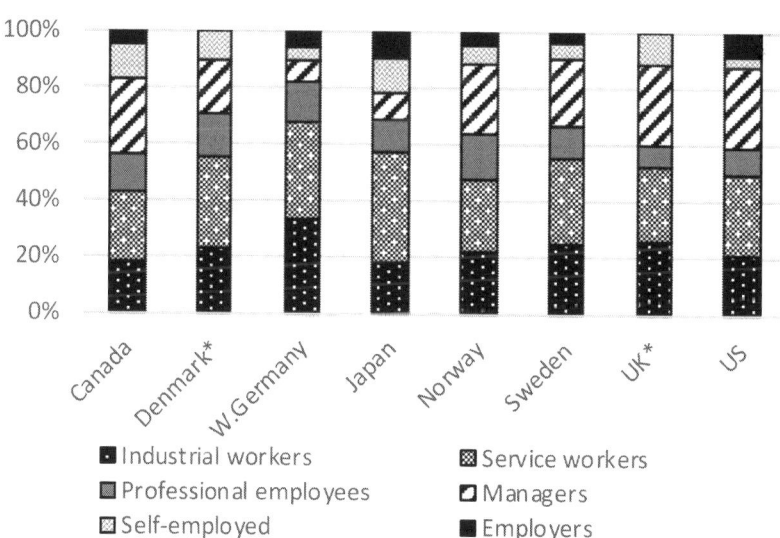

Figure 4.1 Employment Class Structure, G7 and Nordic Countries, circa 1982 (% of employed labour force)

*insufficient information to distinguish employers from self-employed
Source: CSCC Data archive. Canada (N=1888); Denmark (N=1128); W. Germany (N=1552); Japan (N=547); Norway (N=1676); Sweden (N=1137); UK (N=1306); US (N=1697).

Given the margins of error for sample surveys and a more limited comparability of 1980s occupational categories than more recently, I draw several preliminary conclusions here. First, owners of the means of production, including self-employed and employers, made up less than 20 percent of the employed labour force in most of these countries in the early 1980s. Second, the traditional working class of industrial workers and service workers made up around half of the employed labour force in most countries. Third, professional employees constituted a smaller portion of the non-managerial labour force than service workers or industrial workers in all countries. Finally, managers appeared to make up around a quarter of the labour force in most countries, with the exception of Japan and West Germany, where the numbers were much smaller. However, a major limitation of most of these surveys is the *inclusion* of virtually any respondent who indicated any informal supervisory role as part of the managerial hierarchy (see Appendix 1). It may be notable that in both West Germany, with its co-determination decision tradition, and Japan, with "kaizan" methods of labour process collaboration, there was less apparent individual concern among workers with being considered as part of management. In any case, these estimates offer rare and valuable benchmarks from the early 1980s for continuing studies of employment class structure in advanced capitalist countries.

The G7 and Nordic Class Structure

As noted in Chapter 3, the countries selected for comparative trend analysis of advanced capitalist class structures include the G7 and Nordic countries:

- the G7 consists of the largest advanced market economies in the world in recent times (United States, Japan, Germany, France, United Kingdom, Italy and Canada);

- the Nordic countries (Denmark, Finland, Norway and Sweden) are historically distinctive in having been led predominantly by social democratic political regimes with highly unionized labour forces.

The most readily available cross-national source of comparative data on recent employment class structures is the International Labour Office (2015) data set on *Key Indicators in the Labour Market* (KILM). The KILM report builds on the census data reported by countries to ILO and is supplemented by external statistical sources from other organizations including Eurostat, OECD, UNESCO and the World Bank. The KILM report relies on internationally comparable criteria derived from statistical standards agreed by the International Conference of Labour Statisticians. Comparable data for all 11 of these countries are available from 1992 to 2016.[10] Two variables are most relevant: *status in employment* and *employment by occupation*.

Trends in Employment Status

Status in employment is based on the 1993 International Classification by Status in Employment, which classifies the job held by a person at a point in time with respect to the type of explicit or implicit employment contract that person has with other persons or organizations. This is ILO variable KILM3. Three main categories are distinguished: (1) employees (also known as wage and salaried workers), (b) employers and (b) own-account self-employed workers. Contributing unpaid family workers are also counted. However, with the long movement of employment out of agriculture into the industrial and services sectors, those without any paid work have diminished to very small numbers in these countries, and hired wage and salary have replace much self-employed work. The 2016 distributions of status in employment for all eleven countries based on national censuses are summarized in Figure 4.2.

Based on these recent data, I draw the following conclusions about current employment status in these advanced capitalist national economies:

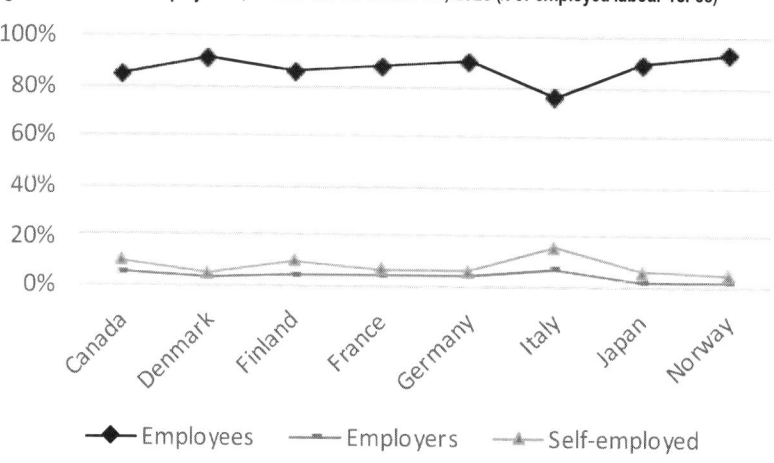

Figure 4.2 Status in Employment, G7 and Nordic Countries, 2016 (% of employed labour force)

Source: ILO KILM Report 2015.

- The vast majority of those in the employed labour force are hired employees. In most countries this amounts to over 85 percent of those employed;
- Employers and self-employed make up less than 15 percent of the labour force in most countries, and the self-employed are twice as numerous as employers.

There are few notable differences between these countries in these terms. Italy is somewhat distinctive in continuing to rely more on independent small commodity producers, particularly in agriculture, so it still has more self-employed and small employers than the others; it is also the only country that has somewhat greater than 1 percent of the labour force who are still unpaid family workers. But the dominance of hired employment is pervasive.

Estimates of trends in employment status from the early 1980s to the early 1990s are possible for some of these countries by comparing findings from Wright's CSCC project in Figure 4.1 with the ILO KILM3 data in Figure 4.2 for available countries. The results are summarized in Figure 4.3.

Very high incidence of hired employees prevailed throughout this period in nearly all these countries. Japan is the partial exception with self-employed small commodity producers in agriculture and other sectors declining significantly during the 1980s and hired employees only reaching 85 percent by 1992. Further trend comparisons of ILO KILM3 employment status data over the 1992–2016 period suggest that all advanced capitalist economies are converging on the employment statuses summarized in Figure 4.2 for 2016, in which the vast majorities are wage and salary earners, where self-employed own-account workers persist and continue to emerge in these economies to make up at least 5 percent of the labour force and where employers are slowly declining in numbers to generally less than 5 percent of the labour force. Most people's labour is for hire; small numbers still try to work on their own, but fewer and fewer are able to hire anybody else to work with them. The "entrepreneurial economy" lives on but in tiny "start-ups," most of which are either taken over by larger corporations or die.

Note that the ILO KILM3 census distribution of employers, self-employed and employees in Canada between 1998 and 2016 and the distributions found in my Canadian national sample surveys of 1998, 2004,

Figure 4.3 Status in Employment, G7 and Nordic Countries, circa 1982 and 1992 (% of employed labour force)

Sources: circa 1982 Wright 1997, Figure 2.1, 47; 1992 ILO KILM Report 2015.

2010 and 2016 used later in this book are consistently almost identical. This equivalence on status in employment with KILM3 indicates a solid representative sample basis to build fuller comparisons of employment class structure using my national surveys for Canada — particularly in the absence of adequate information on some class criteria for other countries to date.

Trends in Employment by Occupation

The International Labour Office (2015) KILM data set also provides *employment by occupation*, presented by major classification groups according to the International Standard Classification of Occupations (ISCO). ISCO has been developed since the 1950s through the work of the International Conference of Labour Statisticians.[11] ISCO is widely regarded as the "gold standard" for distinguishing types of occupations, particularly in advanced capitalist countries. The current (2008) version of ISCO, KILM5, includes the following main occupational categories:

- managers
- professionals
- technicians and associate professionals
- clerical support workers
- service and sales workers

- skilled agricultural, forestry and fishery workers
- craft and related trades workers
- plant and machine operators
- elementary occupations.

For purposes of comparative assessment of the occupational structure of the employed labour force, professionals and technicians and associate professionals are combined here as "professional occupations." It is important to register that non-managerial professionals, associate professionals and technologists/technicians all have specialized post-secondary education job requirements. Recent studies have also found that non-managerial workers in all three of these specialist occupational groups share similar levels of job autonomy and discretion (Adams and Livingstone 2020). Clerical support workers and service and sales workers are combined as "service workers." Skilled agricultural, forestry and fishery workers, craft and related trades workers, plant and machine operators and elementary occupations are combined as "industrial workers." Table 4.1 summarizes the 1992–2016 occupational distributions and trends in these KILM5 terms using census data for all eleven countries.

The data in this employment-by-occupation table allow the following conclusions:

- The numbers of those in professional occupations are increasing significantly and make up over 30 percent of the labour force in nearly all of these countries;
- The numbers of those in skilled trades, machine operators and other manual occupations are declining significantly and make up less than 35 percent of the labour force in all these countries;
- The numbers of those in clerical, sales and service occupations are also declining at least slightly in most of these countries and generally make up under 30 percent of the labour force;
- The numbers of those in managerial positions appear to have remained relatively small in these countries in recent years.

Given the demonstrated relative stability of "status in employment" in recent times in nearly all these countries, we can draw some tentative conclusions about differences between them in the prominence of pro-

Table 4.1 Employment by Occupation, G7 and Nordic Countries
(% of Employed Labour Force in 1992/2016)

Country	Managers	Professional Occupations	Service Workers	Industrial Workers
Canada	11 / 8	27 / 36	29 / 28	33 / 28
Denmark	4 / 3	32 / 43	30 / 28	34 / 26
Finland	5 / 3	26 / 43	35 / 25	33 / 28
France	7 / 7	31 / 39	29 / 24	33 / 30
Germany	5 / 5	30 / 40	28 / 28	38 / 28
Italy	3 / 4	25 / 33	28 / 30	44 / 34
Japan	4 / 2	21 / 26	44 / 42	31 / 30
Norway	14 / 8	23 / 45	30 / 27	33 / 21
Sweden	5 / 6	34 / 46	29 / 26	33 / 22
UK	10 / 11	34 / 38	28 / 28	28 / 23
US	9 / 11	31 / 36	31 / 29	29 / 24

Source: ILO KILM Report 2015.

fessional occupations. First, the Nordic countries have higher proportions of professional occupations than the G7 countries. There has been greater growth of professional occupations in Nordic countries, particularly Norway, since the 1990s. Well over 40 percent of the entire labour force in these countries is in professional occupations. This increasing relative prominence of professional occupations is in part attributable to larger public sectors with mandated specialized services requiring professionals, as well as state policies facilitating greater private sector development of specialized occupations in such areas as advanced information technologies and renewable energy; both developments continue to be aided by effective negotiation of highly unionized employees for professional jobs. At the other extreme, Japan continues to have the lowest proportion of professionals as well as managers. This is probably a reflection of historically entrenched hierarchical organizational structures whereby many people with specialized training have started out as low-level service workers. Virtually all Japanese workers are widely expected to share their working knowledge in "kaizen" modes and there may be less call for designated knowledge specialists. In addition, there is a relatively small Japanese public sector, with many support services still addressed within families and less demand for public sector professionals to provide them. Italy still has fairly low levels of professionals, which is related to higher continuing levels of agricultural and industrial employment. In all other G7 countries, professionals make up the largest of these occupational groups, at over 35 percent of the labour force.

There are, of course, important differences in economic structures related to geospatial origins and established institutional regimes. There are also a few other definitional limits on comparability of KILM statistics on employment by occupation between countries or over time: age coverage, inclusion of armed forces, minimum hours employed. But overall, the KILM5 data suggest that the general occupational structures of all these countries are moving in the same direction of growing reliance on professional occupations. As Table 4.1. indicates, the increasing proportions of professional occupations have been substantial in all these countries, reflective of a general shift toward specialized knowledge work and away from predominantly manual labour jobs in advanced capitalism.

More generally, efforts to document the changing occupational structure of the labour force have a long and torturous history in most countries (Boyd 2008). Canada has been a world leader in developing occupational classifications that have permitted comparing trends over time. The Canada Census Classification of Occupations (CCDO) of 1971 served as a vehicle for various earlier analyses of occupational distribution and change. One of the most commonly used schemes has been the sixteen-category occupational system for the Canadian labour force developed by Pineo, Porter and McRoberts (1977) based on the 1971 CCDO. This system offers a quite accurate way of aggregating many specific occupational titles into relatively coherent groups and provides a practical basis for comparing trends in such groups up to the present. I relied initially on this Pineo-Porter scheme in my national surveys to estimate changes in occupational groups in Canada over the 1982–2016 period. In particular, in re-analyzing the 1982 Canadian survey data from Clement and Myles, I relied on the Pineo-Porter classification of CCDO occupational codes. Later concordances were produced between Canadian occupational classifications and the ISCO occupational codes developed through ILO for more recent occupational data.[12] I applied these ISCO codes to my survey data for all years. It should be noted here that various new specific occupations (most notably in information technology) have, of course, emerged over this period, but most of these can be classified within the same general categories for general occupational trend analyses.

The Challenge of Combining Employment Status and Occupation

There are serious limitations to drawing further general conclusions about employment *class* structure from the above ILO-based tables. As Erik Olin Wright (1980) most cogently argued around the outset of his multi-country comparative class structure (CSCC) project in the 1980s, occupation should not be conflated with employment class. As noted previously, members of virtually any occupation could be employers, self-employed, managerial-supervisory positions or non-managerial workers. The main limitation of the ILO KILM occupational data sets, along with most other official national surveys, is the apparent impossibility of distinguishing owners from employees. Employers and the self-employed are mixed together with hired employees in Table 4.1, the KILM5 employment by occupation table. Many ISCO occupational titles include at least small numbers of both self-employed and employers. More seriously, numerous ISCO titles combine supervisory employees with non-managerial employees in the same occupations, thereby significantly underestimating numbers of managerial employees. This limitation is discussed in more detail in Appendix 1, with particular reference to the important contributions of Erik Olin Wright (1985; 1997). This limitation makes detailed employment class analysis difficult with KILM data per se — beyond trends for employers and self-employed vs employees using the KILM3 status in employment variable (as in Figures 4.2 and 4.3), and some rough estimates of changes in professional versus non-professional occupations using the KILM5 employment by occupation variable (as in Table 4.1). Nevertheless, the ILO KILM data offer the best available current comparative empirical starting point.

Fortunately, my later Canadian national surveys beginning in 1998 contain sufficient information to distinguish both employers and self-employed as well as ISCO employee occupations and specific managerial titles. I use these national surveys from 1998 onward and ILO census-based data for the same years on employment status and occupation to make comparative estimates for employment class structure with ILO KILM survey data. My Canada surveys for 1998 onward were weighted by Canada Census age, sex and education attainment figures, used standard questions to distinguish employers and self-employed, identified managers by job titles and otherwise used standard ISCO occupations to distinguish professional employees, service workers and industrial workers. As noted above, employers and self-employed cannot be distinguished in the accessible ILO KILM5 occupational data. But the proportions of employers and self-employed in my 1998 survey and all later surveys were almost identical to those found in the ILO KILM3 employment status reports. Therefore, the proportions who were employers and self-employed in the KILM 1998 Canada survey were first counted in and then the distributions of managers, professional employees, service workers and industrial workers in the ILO KILM5 data set were expressed as proportions of the residual. The resulting comparison of employment class distributions for 1998 based on my composite model applied to my national survey data and the ILO 1998 census data for Canada based on KILM 3 and KILM 5 codes appears in Figure 4.4.

The Canadian estimates for traditional (industrial and service) working-class positions, in my national surveys between 1998 and 2016 and the corresponding ILO census-based data sets to which ISCO KILM5 residual proportions criteria have been applied, are all very similar. As shown in Figure 4.4, in 1998, the results for the traditional working class of service and industrial workers in both data sets were at slightly over 50 percent. The estimates for employers and self-employed, as noted earlier, were virtually identical in all corresponding years. My surveys from 1998 onward still find somewhat more managers and fewer professional employees than the ILO data set. As mentioned previously, this is probably attributable to the fact that substantial numbers of managerial

Figure 4.4 Employment Class Structure, Canada, 1998, Two Sources (% of employed labour force)

Sources: ILO KILM Report 2015; Livingstone and Watts 2018.

employees are identified among the respondents to my surveys but in the census data they remain embedded in some non-managerial ISCO professional occupation codes. In any event, the general estimates of 1998–2016 employment class structure using my national surveys are invariably close to estimates based on ILO ISCO estimates from Canadian census data.[13] I assume that these Canadian surveys, combined with re-analysis of the 1982 Clement and Myles survey, provide the most accurate currently available profiles of the changing employment class structure of production relations in this country, and also in connection with further related studies of class consciousness. The summary profiles of this changing class structure in Canada offer benchmarks for more current estimates of the changing employment class structure in other advanced capitalist countries.

The Changing Employment Structure in Canada, 1982–2016

The 1982–2016 series of national surveys in Canada permit estimation of trends in the distribution of employment classes generally. Table 4.2 summarizes continuity and change in the general class structure of the employed labour force from 1982 to 2016.

As ever in a capitalist economy driven by inter-firm competition, capital-labour negotiations and pursuit of more productive technologies, there has been continual fluctuation of production relations and employment class structure. The most important points to register about continuity and change in this employment class structure in Canada in this period are as follows.

Owners, including tiny numbers of corporate capitalists and large employers, small numbers of small employers and larger numbers of self-employed, all of whom control their own businesses, have continued to make up around 15 percent of the employed labour force. The numbers of corporate capitalists and large employers are too small for accurate estimates of change with these samples; even if the cut-off limit is as low as 10 employees, they are likely to remain at less than 1 percent of the labour force. These findings are consistent with mounting international evidence that more national capital assets are being consolidated in fewer hands (Serfati 2014).

The survey evidence does indicate that small employers have remained a consistently small percentage of the labour force. Small em-

Table 4.2 Employment Class Distribution, Employed Labour Force, Canada, 1982–2016 (%)

General Class Location	Employment Class	1982	1998	2004	2010	2016
Owners						
	Corporate capitalist/large employer	>1	>1	>1	>1	>1
	Small employer	3	6	6	5	4
	Self-employed	13	10	13	12	10
	All owners	16	16	19	17	14
Managerial						
	Upper manager	1	1	2	2	2
	Mid/low manager	4	7	10	10	13
	Supervisor	4	6	6	6	5
	All managerial	9	14	18	18	20
Non-managerial						
	Professional employee	12	17	18	24	23
	Service worker	33	26	22	23	25
	Industrial worker	30	27	23	18	18
	All non-managerial	75	70	63	65	66
	Employed N	1758	873	5570	1192	2881

Sources: Canada Work Learning Surveys 1998–2016.

ployers continue to generate significant numbers of new jobs but often with limited security for either their employees or themselves. The self-employed have continued to be a more substantial portion of the labour force, around 10 percent, albeit highly prone to bankruptcy and downward mobility into hired labour posts or unemployment and with limited prospects of becoming successful enough to hire others and become small employers. Virtually all self-employed remain highly dependent on their own labour, whether in independent enterprises or subcontracting to larger firms.

Among non-managerial employees, there has been a reduction of employment of industrial workers in private goods producing sectors to less than 20 percent of the employed labour force. This decline in manufacturing jobs during this period is a major consequence of automation and export of less skilled manual jobs to less developed countries.

A relative growth of service workers, or "white collar proletarians," through most of the twentieth century was grounded in increasing recognition by capital of the service sector as the "new frontier" for commodification, as well as the initial difficulty of mechanizing the growing array of discrete clerical recording and personal sales tasks involved in realizing the profits on the burgeoning numbers of material goods. Growth of public service workers was also related to processing general population entitlements for health, education and other state benefits. But, more recently, automation and routinization have also led to the rapid rise of self-service (think of the declines of bank tellers, secretarial pools, travel agents and toll booth collectors) and the export of portable service jobs. Clerical, sales and service workers have therefore declined somewhat since the 1980s although still making up around a quarter of the employed labour force.

The proportion of professional employees roughly doubled, to over 20 percent of the employed labour force, consistent with a multitude of predictions about the centrality of "knowledge workers" in the "new economy." Professional employees may be a larger part of the employed labour force than the declining numbers of industrial workers.

An absolute growth of managerial positions has been generally predicted in terms of the need to coordinate and control an increasingly capital- and technology-intensive labor process (Kenney 1997). The number of managerial employees grew almost continually through this period, making up about 20 percent of the labour force. Upper managers, who control a plant, branch or division of an entire organization, still make up only 2 percent of the labour force. Most of the relative increase has been in middle management, "back office" administrative functions regulating non-managerial workers and accounting for production output. Direct supervisors and forepersons still make up about the same proportion of the overall labour force as previously, so a smaller proportion of management per se is devoted to direct supervision. As the managerial hierarchy has expanded, more managers themselves are managed. In 1982, around a third of all managers had no manager above them to whom they were required to report; by 2010, the proportion had declined to around 5 percent (Livingstone, Pollock and Raykov 2016). This change is mainly reflective of the general inflation of the numbers of middle managers subordinated to upper managers. It should be noted here that there has been a pervasive assumption that all levels of managers generally share similar orientations. However, given their different coordinating and controlling roles, significant polarization of their powers has been found (Livingstone 2021).

So, overall, there have been three substantial changes in employment class structure during this period. The traditional working class of industrial workers and service workers, who mainly provide their labour without specialized requirements, has declined from a majority to a minority of the entire employed labour force. Second, professional employees with their more specialized knowledge requirements have become a much larger part of the non-managerial labour force. Third, middle managers are playing a larger role in regulating production processes.

Other empirical research on general occupational change in Canada has found grosser comparable trends in the growth of professional and managerial *occupations*. Using national level census data, both Baldwin and Beckstead (2003) and Lavoie, Roy and Therrien (2003) concluded that "knowledge work" is increasing significantly in Canada. It may well be that there has been some inflation of managerial job titles as well semi-professional occupational designations during this period. But the three major changes in class structure found here are consistent with general summaries of roughly comparable empirical studies in other countries. While their class labels vary, the leading empirical researchers of class structure from Weberian perspectives now agree that the proportion of traditional working-class or "routine" workers has continued to decline and that of professional employees or the "salariat" has continued to grow in recent decades in most of these other countries, as well as Canada (e.g., Goldthorpe 2016; Oesch 2006).

In summary, the surveys indicate that between 1982 and 2016 in Canada, managerial functions grew significantly, mainly through the increase of middle managers. The proportion of non-managerial employees declined from almost three-quarters to around 60 percent of the employed labour force, with a growing portion in professional-employee class positions. The trends for non-managerial workers generally and professional employees particularly, as well as owners, are basically consistent with 1992 to 2016 ILO KILM occupational data for the G7 and Nordic countries. The only real inconsistency is the smaller and fairly stable proportion of managers in the ILO KILM data, most likely because substantial numbers of lower managers remain hidden in the general non-managerial KILM5 occupational categories. The more accurate Canadian survey data are consistent with the generally accepted notion of an emerging knowledge economy with increasing proportions of both professional and managerial occupations — but without conflating them.

Comparative Employment Class Structure, G7 and Nordic Countries

The extent to which these trends in employment class distribution apply beyond Canada to other G7 and Nordic countries, as well as more broadly to advanced capitalism, remains to be determined. Approximations can be made using the ILO data sets for the 1992–2016 period. This involves using KILM3 status in employment figures in conjunction with the proportions of managers, professional employees, service workers and industrial workers in KILM5 occupational data. These manager and non-managerial employee numbers are expressed as proportions of the residual when proportions for employers and self-employed are discounted from KILM5 occupational data, as was done for Canada in 1998 in Figure 4.4. Aside from some underestimation of the numbers of managers and converse overestimation of the numbers of professional employees inherent in the KILM5 ISCO occupational categories, these are probably the best current estimates of the general class structure of the employed labour force available for these countries. Table 4.3 summarizes these class distributions for 1992 and 2016.

As previously noted, according to ILO KILM3 data, employers and self-employed owners together make up 15 percent or less of the labour force in most of these countries, with Italy still somewhat more reliant on independent small commodity producers. With proportionate reductions of these owners, from KILM5 occupational data, the traditional working class of industrial and service workers is still found to constitute around half of the employed labour force in most of these countries. But numbers of industrial workers are declining everywhere, while those of professional employees have increased significantly in all countries, constituting the largest class grouping in many. Managers appear to make up 10 percent or less of the labour force in all countries, with various fluctuations. However, once more, it is likely that substantial numbers of at least lower managers are actually counted as professional employees, service workers or industrial workers in KILM5 occupational data. As summarized in Table 4.2, there is clear evidence in the Canadian surveys of increasing size of the managerial hierarchy between the early 1980s and 2016; there are also indications of increasing polarization between upper managers and lower managers in working conditions and attitudes (Livingstone, Adams and Sawchuk 2021). All that we can be sure of from Table 4.3 is that the numbers for managers in all countries rep-

Table 4.3 Employment Class Structure, G7 and Nordic Countries
(% of Employed Labour Force in (1992/2016)

Country	Employers	Self-employed	Managers	Professional Employees	Service Workers	Industrial Workers
Canada	6 / 5	8 / 11	9 / 7	23 / 31	25 / 23	28 / 24
Denmark	4 / 3	5 / 5	4 / 6	29 / 40	27 / 26	31 / 24
Finland	4 / 4	12 / 10	4 / 3	22 / 37	30 / 22	28 / 24
France	5 / 4	8 / 7	6 / 6	27 / 34	26 / 21	29 / 27
Germany	5 / 4	4 / 6	4 / 4	28 / 36	25 / 25	34 / 25
Italy	8 / 7	19 / 16	2 / 3	18 / 25	21 / 23	33 / 26
Japan	4 / 2	11 / 6	3 / 2	18 / 24	37 / 39	27 / 27
Norway	4 / 2	6 / 5	13 / 7	21 / 42	27 / 25	30 / 20
Sweden	4 / 4	8 / 6	4 / 5	30 / 42	25 / 23	29 / 20
UK	4 / 2	9 / 13	9 / 9	30 / 32	24 / 24	25 / 20
US	4 / 2	5 / 4	8 / 10	29 / 34	28 / 27	26 / 23

Source: ILO KILM Report 2015.

resent those whose occupations are unambiguously managerial and that others beyond these numbers likely play at least some formal managerial roles.

The foregoing estimates of current patterns and recent trends in the employment class structure of major advanced capitalist countries provide the general profiles for the further analyses of class and class consciousness in this book.

Professional Employees as a "New Working Class"

In the wake of protest movements in France in the 1960s, a "new working class" was heralded as emerging among technical workers with scientific knowledge and significantly changed roles in more highly automated industrial sectors (Mallet 1975). Empirical researchers in other countries could find few intimations of challenges to capitalism among such workers (Gallie 1978). The evidence in this chapter suggests that the major change in the employment class structure of advanced capitalist countries since then has been the growth of non-managerial professional employees, including a continuum of long-established professions, as well as semi-professions and technical workers whose specialized knowledge has become increasingly pivotal to production relations in emergent "knowledge economies." As previously noted, all these professional employees have specialized post-secondary education job requirements. There continue to be many analysts who conflate professional employees conceptually with other professional classes (i.e., professional employers, self-employed professionals and professional managers) or confound them with managers more generally in a "professional-managerial class" amalgam. As we have seen, most official employment surveys have made distinguishing professional employees from both business owners and managers difficult. But there should be little doubt that professional employees have become one of the largest and most strategically important employment classes in advanced capitalism for continuing profitability of private capital as well as for public sector effectiveness. Arguments for the centrality of professional employees in "knowledge economies" are reminiscent of the earlier "new working class" thesis focused on technicians in automated industries — but now applied more broadly to professional employees across the entire labour force.

At least in some respects, professional employees can be seen as the skilled trades of the emergent twenty-first-century "knowledge economy." They are the most highly formally qualified part of the labour force. Second, they have been losing control of the end products of their labour, a process identified as "ideological proletarianization" (Derber 1983) and documented in my Canadian surveys and a few other longitudinal surveys distinguishing professional employees in terms of declining job control and other worsening working conditions in recent decades (Livingstone, Adams and Sawchuk 2021).[14] Third, professional employees have become the most highly organized part of the labour force, if we consider their memberships in both labour unions and professional associations within their own fields (Raykov and Livingstone 2014).

While traditional skilled trades are declining as a portion of the labour force, they were the most highly qualified members of the hired labour force in the late nineteenth century. In the craft guilds that preceded the rise of corporate capitalism, master craftspeople had been owners of their enterprises, with overarching control over hiring, training, discipline and sale of their products. These powers were gradually appropriated by mercantile capitalists. Craftspeople were then reduced to skilled tradespeople, and they ultimately became leaders in the formation of the twentieth-century labour movement. It is well-documented in the research literature on the primary self-regulating professions (such as physicians, lawyers, architects, dentists) that their work is becoming increasingly constrained by corporate organization, state intervention and client knowledge demands (e.g., Krause 1996; Livingstone, Adams and Sawchuk 2021). It is at least arguable that self-regulating professions are engaged in a similar proletarianization process to earlier craft guilds. While professional employees make up the majority of members of most professional associations, it remains to be seen in what direction current professional employers and self-employed professionals will go as corporate capital continues to appropriate more of their power. The labour movement contains increasing numbers of explicitly professional unions (e.g., Canadian Labour Congress 2020), but a basic question is now faced by many professional associations of predominantly professional employees mixed with managers with professional training and typically much smaller numbers of self-employed professionals and professional employers. Should they continue to aspire to increasingly remote self-regulating status or join other hired workers in the fight for collective labour rights, better working conditions, more training opportunities and recognition of opportunities for all workers in a sustainable economy?

I do not intend to exaggerate the coherence of professional employees` current conditions or minimize the obstacles to their effective mobilization, but it is just possible that professional employees could become a "new working class" to contribute to leading the labour movement in the twenty-first century. They therefore deserve more critical attention. Later analyses in this book offer comparative insights about the potential of professional employees and other non-managerial workers to contribute to social transformation.

Employment Class Structure and Other Social Connections

The foregoing general structural profiles tell us little about the other specific social and working conditions of people in these employment class locations in these countries. I address some of these below. I should also note here the general limits of survey data to provide insights into social processes. A series of cross-sectional surveys offers at best static snapshots of isolated individuals and can say little about workers' lived collective experience in specific sociohistorical contexts (see Fantasia 1995). Survey data offer merely rough approximations of general locations in and sentiments about class relations among employment-based aggregates that can only be of suggestive relevance in predicting the actions of more fully constituted particular class groups. But these data do offer guides for further investigation of employment classes and their life conditions and orientations in advanced capitalism. The starting point is the recognition of the tripartite character of current employment classes grounded in ownership, delegated managerial authority and non-managerial hired employment, and the best available evidence to distinguish patterns and trends in these terms in advanced capitalist countries. At least, it should be clear that owners need to be distinguished from hired employees and that managers need to be distinguished from non-managerial employees. It is also clear that sufficient data on both employment status and occupational groups have been gathered in official national surveys in all these countries to enable more accurate preliminary development of relevant employment class profiles — if it were made publicly available. For whatever political or technical reasons, combining these gathered data has not been permitted. Allowing retroactive access to the ILO data back to the early 1990s could lead to insightful documentation of further differences and trends in various benefits between employers, self-employed, higher managers and other non-managerial workers, differences only hinted at in analyses restricted to occupational profiles with underlying employment statuses suppressed or denied.

Perhaps more to the point, there is no good reason that further official government and independent sample surveys should not include and make easily available sufficient data to enable fuller comparative understanding of these basic employment classes in all these countries. In any case, the primary assumption of this inquiry going forward is that one's location within this basic employment class structure is associated with different class interests in the continuation of advanced capitalism. Larger employers are posited to have a strong interest in the expanded production of this system. Organized non-managerial workers are posited as the most likely to oppose the system. As we will see in Chapters 6 and 7, there is sufficient empirical evidence from some of these countries to conduct preliminary employment class analyses of connections with political attitudes and class consciousness, to generate some insights about the continuing relevance of these connections and to suggest the high relevance of further comparative studies.

There have also been significant changes connected with the employment class structure with regard to demographics, working conditions, mobility and wealth distribution that need to be considered. These are noted here with greater reliance on evidence from the Canadian case, with the most accurate employment class distinctions to date.

Employment Class Structure and Demographics
Along with the shifting employment class structure, there have been significant changes in demographic profiles of those in different class positions during this period.[15] In terms of sex ratios, by nearly every measure, women continued their century-long march into paid labour. For example, an increasing labour force participation rate among those aged 25 to 64 in recent decades has been fully attributable to women. In the early 1980s, at least small majorities of these women were employed in most advanced capitalist countries; by 2018, over three-quarters of these women were employed. Participation rates for men in these prime earning years remained at around 90 percent through this period with some recent declines. This paid-work gap has been closing faster than differences in unpaid work, where even men in fully employed dual earner families still do much less domestic labour (e.g., Garcia and Tomlinson 2021). The notable exception once more is Italy, where only 40 percent of women were in paid employment in the early 1980s; this increased to over 60 percent by 2018, with many other women continuing to contribute unpaid labour to family businesses. More generally, women outside paid employment have continued to be "hidden in the household," devoting most of their time to child care and housework.

According to my Canadian surveys, men have continued to dominate most ownership and upper-managerial class positions, but women have increased their presence. Virtually all large employers were male in 1982, but women made up about 20 percent in 2016. Men were over 80 percent of upper managers in 1982, but that proportion declined to around two-thirds in 2016. However, women's participation in management has continued to be limited largely to managing other women, and they remain virtually excluded from chief executive officer positions (Livingstone, Pollock and Raykov 2016). In terms of non-managerial class positions, men have continued to make up around 80 percent of the dwindling numbers of industrial workers. Women were three-quarters of all service workers in 1982 and still were over two-thirds in 2016.

Household and family forms have continued to shift throughout this period, with growing numbers living in common-law unions, increasing numbers of single-parent households, increasing numbers of non-family and multi-generational households, and a general decline in traditional nuclear families of co-resident couples with children (Moyser 2017). Large employers and upper managers have remained most likely to live in these traditional nuclear forms (over 80 percent). Service workers, most of whom are women, have continued to be more likely (over one-third) to be living alone or as single parents. Households in which there are co-resident couples still made up about 60 percent of all households in 2016. Post-World War II economic expansion increasingly drew married women into the active labour force. Between 1950 and 2003, the proportion of married women who were in the labour force rose from about 10 percent to over 60 percent (Statistics Canada 2011). Among the growing numbers of co-resident households in which women as well as men are employed, over 60 percent of non-managerial workers have non-managerial partners; smaller majorities of owners have partners who are also owners. However, in dual-earner households generally, there are substantial numbers of cross-class partners in this basic sense. For example, about a quarter of industrial workers have partners who are either owners or managerial employees, and most managerial employees have partners who are non-managerial workers. Only corporate capitalists appear to have more exclusive class households. Overall, there are diminishing numbers of co-resident households with a sole male "breadwinner" and growing numbers of co-resident households with partners in different employment classes. Increasingly, in these households, the positions of the partners in both production relations and domestic labour need to be considered to better understand the material conditions of the household and the attitudes of the partners (see Livingstone and Asner 1996).

The general population in all advanced capitalist countries is aging fast, a reflection of increasing longevity and lower general birth rates. As a consequence, the dependency ratio of those over 65 to those of standard working age, 15 to 64, has also been increasing. The most dramatic case is Japan, where this dependency ratio increased from less than 15 percent in the early 1980s to around 45 percent recently. But all these countries face major challenges in providing established health care, pensions and other benefits to growing numbers of seniors. The employed labour force per se is aging mainly because of later entry with more advanced formal education, complemented by increasing numbers of seniors remaining in the employed labour force because of economic need. In 1982, about a quarter of the employed Canadian labour force was over 45 years of age; by 2016 this proportion was over 40 percent. Large majorities of corporate capitalists and large employers are over 45, considering the time it often takes to climb the corporate ladder or build up a business. However, in general, people have been entering regular employment later and women especially are staying employed longer to make ends meet.

With the continued global expansion of capitalist production, all these advanced economies have significantly increased their international trade in goods and services since the early 1980s, as well as increasing international migration. In light of their aging domestic labour forces, governments in most of these countries have increasingly encouraged immigration from younger, less economically developed countries. Canada has continually been a leader in attracting mostly highly qualified immigrants; the foreign-born make up well over 20 percent of the general Canadian population. But the foreign-born have substantially increased in nearly all these countries during this period, perhaps most dramatically in Germany, with a recent net loss of total population and admission of a million Syrian war refugees. A major consequence of increased immigration has been increasing ethno-linguistic diversity of populations and labour forces. The general proportion of whites in Canada has decreased from over 90 percent to around 80 percent during this period; non-whites in the employed labour force increased from about 6 percent in 1982 to around 18 percent in 2016. Upper managers — who remain most likely to be selected by employers on ascriptive criteria related to profitability — remain over 90 percent white. Workers in the most precarious, poorly paid non-managerial class positions are increasingly non-white. The exception to this general trend to ethnic diversity is Japan, where well over 95 percent remain Japanese, but the rapidly aging population and labour force shortages have led to rapid recent increases in foreign guest workers. In all these countries, the increases in ethnic diversity is leading to both demands from increasingly qualified minorities for equitable treatment and anti-immigrant or racist sentiments among native-born who see their established way of life threatened. As Adolph Reed (2002) has observed, capitalism has never existed without regimes of racial stratification; current regimes are being actively challenged from all sides.

In all these advanced capitalist countries, there have been substantial increases in formal education attainment since the 1980s, with a doubling of those with post-secondary education completion. Majorities of those aged 25 to 64 in Canada and Japan have post-secondary degrees as have more than 40 percent in the UK, US and Nordic countries. More generally, the formal and informal learning attainments of the eligible labour force in these countries are at unprecedented high levels and have been increasing more rapidly than the education requirements to enter and perform available jobs (Livingstone 2009; 2010). The promise of economic salvation through higher education promoted since WWII is becoming less credible.

Finally in demographic terms, there is a growing "density divide" with continuing urbanization. All these countries besides Italy had populations that were over 70 percent urban in 1980 and all have increased significantly to over 80 percent recently (United Nations Population Division 2018). The basic pattern in most countries has been the clustering of increasingly ethnically diverse and generally more highly educated people in metropolitan zones, with more predominantly white people with less formal education remaining in more rural areas (Wilkinson 2019). In terms of employment classes, the increasing numbers of highly qualified professional employees have located mainly in more ethnically diverse metropolitan zones, which have been the major points of job growth. They represent the core of what has been celebrated more vaguely as the "creative class" (Florida 2014). The declining numbers of predominantly male industrial workers with lower qualifications are more likely to be white and less inclined to move from more rural areas. These are national-level tendencies with many local variants.

Employment Class Structure and Working Conditions

We know from multiple sources of evidence for all these advanced capitalist countries that growing majorities in the employed labour force have been witnessing various forms of organizational restructuring and instability.[16] Workloads are intensifying. Job tenures are becoming more precarious with increasing incidence of temporary, irregular jobs, especially among women and visible minority non-managerial employees.

Union membership has declined significantly in most countries. Deindustrialization has greatly reduced the proportion of heavily unionized, primarily male, private sector industrial worker jobs since the early

1980s. Predominantly female, public sector service worker jobs have managed to remain relatively highly unionized to date. The composition of union membership has therefore shifted from dominance by primarily private sector industries to roughly equal numbers of public and private sector members. Women union members have increased from a smaller minority in the early 1980s to near parity today in generally less unionized labour forces. The exception to declining unionization, as noted earlier, is the growing number of professional employees who have become members of professional unions during this period.

Trend analyses of the Canadian national surveys have documented significant changes in workplace authority and control. Professional employees have experienced declining job control in terms of both design autonomy and organizational decision power. There is also evidence that the managerial hierarchy is becoming more polarized, with upper managers gaining added organizational power versus lower managers (Livingstone, Adams and Sawchuk 2021). Temporary status prevails in newly created jobs (Katz and Krueger 2016), and it is now just as common among professional employees as other non-managerial occupations (Barley and Kunda 2004).

The compositional shift to greater proportions of professional employees and declining proportions of industrial and service workers suggests that the number of class positions with specialized knowledge qualifications is increasing. Accordingly, the Canadian surveys find that the proportion of Canadian wage and salary earners who required a post-secondary credential to get their jobs increased from around a quarter in 1982 to over half by 2016. Formal education requirements are a limited proxy for labour process requirements and may involve significant credential inflation compared to the specialized knowledge and skill actually needed to perform particular jobs. In any case, hired labourers have kept well ahead of these increasing job requirements. In terms of the general match between workers' formal education attainment and the credential required to get their jobs, about 30 percent of employed Canadian workers were underemployed in 1998 while over 20 percent were underqualified for their jobs. By 2016, underemployment of credentials increased to around 40 percent of all workers while the underqualified decreased to around 10 percent. In most of these countries, increasing numbers in most employment classes are becoming underemployed in terms of having greater education qualifications than their jobs require (e.g., Green and Henseke 2016). In Canada, nearly half of service workers, 40 percent of industrial workers and 30 percent of professional employees are now underemployed (Livingstone 2019a). The point here is that virtually all remaining industrial and service workers as well as the increasing numbers of professional employees are becoming much more highly educated and much more underemployed. As these non-managerial workers converge in their perceived working conditions, a reserve army of highly qualified unemployed and underemployed labour becomes increasingly available in advanced capitalism for alternative uses of their time and energy.

These general trends in working conditions should be kept in mind when considering the more specific relations between employment classes and political attitudes later in the book, particularly in Chapters 7 and 8.

Employment Class Structure and Intergenerational Mobility

Movement between positions in the class structure of advanced capitalism is continual. In contrast to slavery and feudalism, people born into lower classes are no longer tied to the land while inheritance of proprietorial status has also become less guaranteed. With inter-firm competition over commodity markets and class struggles between employers and wage laborers as driving forces, reliance on ascriptive criteria for assigning employment class positions has diminished as capitalist production systems have expanded. Labour market exchanges relying on formal criteria such as education credentials have become increasing determinants of adult employment class position. Serious class biases and inequities, as well as racial and gender biases, persist as public education has expanded. Children from lower-class and racialized origins are still being relegated disproportionately to dead-end jobs and unemployment. But there has been a significant increase in education opportunities for these children (Curtis, Livingstone and Smaller 1992; Clandfield et al. 2014).

Expanded production in advanced capitalist economies historically generated new openings in the upper portions of the class hierarchy because the owner classes were unable to produce sufficient numbers of offspring as the capitalist mode of production took over prior modes of production. Additional entrants to these positions were drawn from domestic lower classes and from immigrant labour. The transitional period from land-based small commodity production to industrial capitalism witnessed extensive class mobility. For example, during the industrialization of Sweden in the 1880s, there was about 60 percent mobility out of class of origin, with decreasing property inheritance, population growth and migration and increasing importance of formal education (Maas and van Leeuwen 2002). In Canada, the "settler economy" first supplanted Indigenous societies, then continued to expand into additional spaces well into the twentieth century as European immigrants took up small landholding and provided most of the wage labour for the development of a capitalist production system. Small commodity production in agriculture and other extractive industries then experienced rapid post-World War II decline with the growth of larger corporate enterprises and state sector employment. Continuing expansion of capitalist manufacturing and service industries came to rely increasingly on immigrant labour from the Global South. Throughout most of the history of modern Canada, many immigrants regarded Canada as a way station to the US, which has further limited intergenerational reproduction of the class structure.

As we have seen, intensified production in advanced capitalism has more recently been associated with decline of traditional working-class positions and growth of both specialized professional employment and middle management. The prospect of being thrown into unemployment is also a continuing threat.

With these structural changes, the chances of young people assuming the class positions of their parents has decreased. Canada, with its relatively new settler capitalist economy, recent economic dependence on the US and relative openness to highly skilled immigrants, appears by some criteria to have one of the highest rates of intergenerational class mobility of all advanced capitalist societies. Measures of intergenerational income variations indicate that only about 20 percent of the relative income difference between parents is generally being passed on to their children in Canada. This figure is comparable to the figures for Sweden and Finland, but much lower than the figures for the United States and the United Kingdom, where between 40 and 60 percent of the difference has been passed on (Corak 2001: 279–280). John Goldthorpe (2016), in a summation of one of the most extensive time series of surveys of intergenerational occupational class mobility in the UK, concludes that the overall mobility rate for men was remarkably stable during much of the twentieth century, at around 50 percent, albeit with increasing upward mobility and decreasing downward mobility related to the growth of a "salariat" of professional and managerial occupations and the decline of manual workers in manufacturing and extractive industries. Goldthorpe also notes a disturbing lack of positive association between increasing formal education and upward mobility in employment (i.e., underemployment) and intimates the need for more progressive economic policies — a growing point of agreement between people of diverse political stripes that I address in the final chapter.

My estimates of intergenerational class mobility in Canada are based on my own surveys and are more concerned than Goldthorpe to distinguish owners (including large employers, small employers, self-employed) from employees, as well as distinguishing managerial from non-managerial employees (including professional employees as well as service workers and industrial workers). I focus here on intergenerational mobility between owner, manager and non-managerial class positions. Respondents to my largest 2004 survey were asked to identify the class position of the main income earner in their family while they were growing up. Basic intergenerational mobility rates in 2004 are summarized in Figure 4.5.

A small majority of owners come from owner class family origins (52 percent). A larger majority of non-managerial class employees come from non-managerial family class origins (62 percent). Most managers also come from non-managerial family class origins (55 percent). These patterns are similar for the total sample, as well as for males and females under and over 45 years of age. So, on the one hand, those born into either owner class families or non-managerial class families are most likely to remain in these basic class positions; this includes movement between employer and self-employment positions for owners, as well as movement from industrial worker to service worker and professional employee positions for non-managerial employees. On the other hand, there has been substantial movement out of class of origin. Nearly half of all owners come from non-owner origins, many of these from non-managerial employee backgrounds. Nearly 40 percent of non-managerial employees come from owner or managerial backgrounds, most of these from self-employed family origins.

With regard to the growing numbers of professional and managerial employee class positions in emerging "knowledge economies," nei-

Figure 4.5 Intergenerational Class Mobility, Employed Labour Force, Canada, 2004 (%)

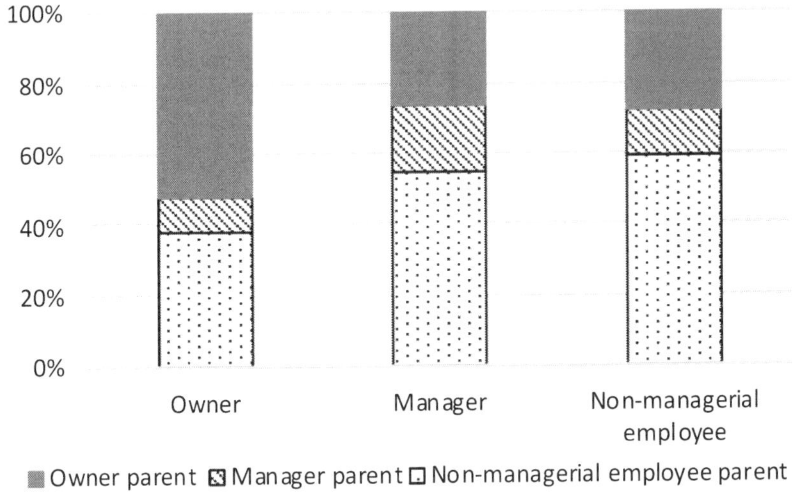

■ Owner parent ☒ Manager parent ☐ Non-managerial employee parent

Source: Canada Work Learning Surveys 1998–2016, WALL I 2004 (N=9,063).

ther show signs yet of being able to reproduce internally. The growing numbers of managers are much more likely to come from non-managerial families, or from owner families, than from managerial ones. Professional employees under 45 are still most likely to come from traditional working-class origins. According to the 1982–2016 series of Canadian national surveys and related case studies, the vast majority of managers have continued to be appointed from non-professional occupations, only a small proportion of those from professional backgrounds take up managerial positions, and those who do often lose professional skills and commitment (Livingstone, Adams and Sawchuk 2021). The much heralded "professional-managerial class" remains mythical, and membership in both professional and managerial class groups continues to be largely dependent on personal specialized qualifications and employer delegated authority, respectively.

The employment classes in which large majorities retain the same adult class position as their class origin are most likely to be at the extremes. Corporate capitalists with huge wealth advantage continue to provide exclusive private schooling, "high-brow culture" exposure and social network support to ensure that most of their offspring can easily follow in their affluent footsteps (Clement 1974; Savage 2015). Those at the bottom end of the traditional working class of precarious service and industrial workers are unlikely to have sufficient material resources to enable their children to gain an advanced formal education or climb out of poverty (Procyk, Lewchuk and Shields 2017; Savage 2015). Again, in both instances, these groups are largely beyond the scope of normal survey techniques.[17]

Overall, the probability of remaining in the same basic employment class position as your class of origin appears to be around 50 percent in Canada in recent times for those who end up as either owners or non-managerial employees. This is similar to the rate found over several generations in the United Kingdom using somewhat different occupational distinctions. Those who end up as managers are more likely to come from non-managerial origins. Between the extremes of very rich corporate capitalists and the most impoverished "precariat," class mobility — either upward or downward — between owner and non-managerial employee classes may be almost as common as intergenerational class stability.

Employment Class Structure and Wealth

Increasing economic inequality is widely documented in all advanced capitalist economies. Many measures have been used to estimate the vast amount of wealth in the hands of a few, the very limited relative assets of most people and growing trends to even greater inequality (e.g., Piketty 2014). Wages and benefits that had generally improved since the Great Depression under the impetus of relatively strong industrial unions and responsive governments began to reverse with increasing neoliberal measures. By most measures, the US now has the most extreme wealth inequities. According to documentation amassed by Piketty and his team, in recent years the top 1 percent of the US population have held almost 40 percent of the net wealth, an almost unprecedented concentration of wealth. In the early 1980s, average CEO compensation was around twenty times as great as the compensation of the typical worker; this ratio exploded to around 300 times greater in 2020 (Economic Policy Institute 2020). Corporate capitalists' extreme wealth is increasing rapidly globally. In 2016, the average annual pay of the top hundred CEOs in Canada increased to over $10 million, while the average workers' pay lost to inflation and remained under $50,000, a ratio of around 200 to one. (Macdonald 2018: 5). A pivotal global example is Laurence Fink, chair and CEO of Blackrock Inc., often called the most powerful institution in the world financial system. In 2020, Fink's annual compensation was over $24 million and his net was wealth estimated at around a billion dollars (Laurence Fink Net Worth 2021). But these numbers pale in comparison with the annual compensation of a growing number of hedge fund managers raking in multi-*billions,* with recent annual increases of over 50 percent (Frank 2021). Even so, such publicly accessible figures take no account of massive private hiding and hoarding of profits in tax havens and such. A smaller and smaller number of mainly financial corporate capitalists are accumulating huge amounts of wealth that are far beyond any meaningful comparative scale and far beyond any possible justification in terms of their actual labour, entrepreneurial ingenuity or "luck." The corporate leader quoted in Chapter 2 on the danger that the rich "may" be getting richer is at very least a master of understatement!

Far below the corporate capitalist heights, the vast majority of large employers had net household assets (value of house, consumer durables and investments minus mortgage and other debts) of over a million dollars, according to our 2016 Canada survey. In stark contrast to large employers, less than 5 percent of all of those in the employed labour force had net household assets at this level, typically after a generation of dual-earner paid labour and mostly inflated house values. The majority of non-managerial employees had net household assets of under 100,000 dollars. This is true not only for service workers and industrial workers but also for professional employees and lower managerial employees. Growing numbers in most countries are living paycheque to paycheque, saving little and closer to poverty. This is especially true for younger workers, who face bleak prospects for owning homes and starting families. Since 1980, household debt in all these countries — including home mortgages, credit card loans, student loans and auto loans — has increased greatly. Again, the US is an extreme case. Over this period, according to the Federal Reserve (Federal Reserve System 2021), total consumer debt grew from around a trillion dollars to over $14 trillion. Much of this debt relates to high housing prices and mortgages but also indicates that growing numbers of non-managerial employees are unable to earn enough to keep themselves and their households above water without becoming effectively indentured to finance capital. In Canada, the amount that employed people owe relative to their income has hit record highs, with household credit market debt reaching over 170 percent as a proportion of household disposable income (Wong 2017). There are growing numbers of actively unemployed, discouraged workers and others excluded from employment--the "precariat"-- who have virtually no net assets and face increasingly desperate conditions to survive at all in such "advanced" societies (e.g., Standing 2011; Savage 2015). At a macro level, the combination of consumer debt and government debt had reached unprecedented levels prior to the COVID-19 pandemic, while conventional government fiscal and monetary policies in most of these countries had little room left for economic stimulus. Major subsequent increases in government funding to cope with the pandemic have served to increase public indebtedness to financial capital with little room to "build back better" without economic transformation, an issue I rejoin in the final chapter.

As noted at the beginning of this chapter, value chains in global capitalist networks have become quite complex, but such complexities cannot hide the gigantic inequities between different locations in the employment class structure. Small numbers of financial corporate capitalists with control over massive global capital assets have become obscenely rich. Increasing numbers of non-managerial employees are sinking into greater insecurity and debt, in spite of having greater job qualifications and no less motivation to work than earlier generations of workers. Marx's labour theory of surplus value should be as relevant now as ever to those whose increasingly productive labour is generating unprecedented profits while they become increasingly more disadvantaged. The bottom line is that virtually everybody is now witness to and affected in some way by these unprecedented, inhuman, unjustifiable accumulations of wealth, while most non-managerial employees and the unemployed are experiencing at least serious relative deprivation of benefits compared to prior generations. When will these grotesque inequities reach the tipping point?

Employment Class Structure and Health

The tipping point for an established way of life often comes when inequities become intolerable for health and survival of a large part of the potential labour force. One of the most profound instances was the Black Death, the bubonic plague pandemic that was the most fatal to date in human history, occurring initially in the mid-1300s in Afro-Eurasia.[18] The plague may have killed around half the population of Europe. It devastated the feudal serf population in particular and provoked remaining peasants into desperate actions to fight for wages and freedoms that led to the end of feudalism. I do not draw a parallel between the Black Death–end of feudalism and COVID-19–end of advanced capitalism. Longevity and basic medical provision are much greater now as is general health knowledge, but class inequities in incidence of sickness and in heath provisions, as well as systematic efforts to increase such inequities, may be even greater . There have been relatively few empirical research efforts to document these inequities in terms of the sorts of employment class distinctions identified here (Scambler 2018; Muntaner et al. 2010) and many studies that either obscure or truncate them. The studies that have looked have found extreme differentials between corporate capitalists and non-managerial employees as well as precarious workers in terms of sickness incidence and provision of health services. The systematic efforts noted here refer to concerted corporate capitalist campaigns since the 1980s to strangle "good health asset flows" through governments to people in need (see Scambler 2019). These health inequities are most evident in the US, with the most technologically advanced and costly medical system in the world — available to the rich while tens of millions are excluded from virtually any care. The escapist and profiteering responses of many corporate capitalists to the COVID-19 pandemic while many of their essential workers remain unprotected, fall ill and even die will be a sickening and lingering legacy (Kazan 2020).

Concluding Remarks

While capitalism is arguably the most rapidly changing mode of production the world has ever known, the employment class structure of advanced capitalism retains a greater stability than the many advocates of post-industrialism and knowledge economies or seers of the end of work under the impact of automation have any inkling. Yes, concentration and centralization of production increase in sphere after sphere and much previously central manual labour has been moved offshore. But smaller employers and self-employed entrepreneurs continue to generate more mainly service commodity forms for possible profits and thereby create paid wage jobs for a still growing proportion of the population, mainly women, seeking them. Standardization and automation have increased productivity and reduced numbers of direct producers of saleable commodities while increasing capital`s need for managerial control. The composition of direct producers has clearly shifted somewhat from manual labour to more specialized professional knowledge work. Most paid employment is becoming more insecure with worsening working conditions and with employment benefits under sustained attack. Intergenerational mobility between classes is substantial, but the basic employment class distribution between owners of the means of production and non-managerial workers has otherwise changed only gradually over the past few generations in most of these advanced capitalist countries.

The continuing socialization of forces of production (e.g., the internet) means that there is increasing access to production-related information and knowledge for the potential labour force of advanced capitalism at the same time as popular demand for formal education continues to expand. The increasingly capital-intensive production process requires increasingly active engagement of the minds of many of the remaining non-managerial workers in these emergent "knowledge economies." Use of tactics of responsible technical autonomy and shifts in local decision-making in the capitalist labour process — as reflected in some perceived recent increases in relative discretion for industrial and service workers in Canadian, UK and Nordic surveys — is indicative of continuing revision of production relations. Along with the gross and blatant inequities of wealth and poverty, underemployment is chronic and a highly qualified reserve army of labour of unemployed and marginalized people is growing rapidly. It has been clear for some time that advanced capitalist countries are now "knowledge societies" with much larger proportions of well-qualified people than their narrow "knowledge economies" are able to utilize (Livingstone 2009).

The employment classes generated in production relations are at the heart of advanced capitalism. Greater efforts should be made to detect the changing contours of these classes through both new research studies and secondary analyses of existing sources of evidence, but the question of how these employment classes resonate with broader class and social movements is equally important. The following chapters begin to address this question of the translation of class into class consciousness. Chapter 5 outlines the transition from feudal modes of thought to the bourgeois capitalist mode of thought that in some sense encapsulates us all. Chapter 6 explores general expressions of different levels of class consciousness. Chapter 7 provides an acid test of the extent to which these employment classes connect with levels of class consciousness.

Notes

A previous version of early portions of this chapter was published in Livingstone and Scholtz (2016).

1. For continuing assertions of the significance of versions of this purported class, see, for example, Burnham (1941); Bell (1976); Ehrenreich and Ehrenreich (1977); Castells (2000); Duménil and Lévy (2018).
2. This cutoff number is somewhat arbitrary to ensure sufficient numbers of "large employers" for at least some empirical analyses.
3. See Livingstone (2014) and Livingstone, Adams and Sawchuk (2021) for further discussion and empirical analysis distinguishing professional employees from professional owners, self-employed professionals and professional managers. Professional employees are found throughout private and public industrial and service sectors.
4. Wright's (1978) initial class model with contradictory class locations was based on positions in relations of production per se and relied on survey respondents' self-reports to determine class locations. These surveys also gathered specific occupational information and then faced conundrums, for example, over how to treat janitors who reported high levels of authority and autonomy within the labour process. Controversies about forms of job autonomy and mental labour as class criteria have led to complex models of professional and managerial class positions (e.g., Kivinen 1989). My model is based on ownership status *and* relations of authority and specialized knowledge *limited by* types of occupations.
5. See Johnson (1977) for one of the earliest efforts to recognize professionals in the class structure of advanced capitalism.
6. For a related body of research based on class relations in paid employment and unpaid household labour, with a primary focus on steelwork families, see Livingstone and Mangan (1996a) and Corman and Luxton (2001). For another related body of research addressing class relations in paid employment, unpaid household labour and community volunteer work, as well as formal and informal learning, see Livingstone (2010).
7. For an insightful account of the historical development of different characterizations of class positions between orthodox capital and labour in the production process, see Carter (1985).
8. The design and detailed findings of these surveys may be found at Canada Work Learning Surveys 1998–2016, "Corporate Executive Surveys 1980–2000."
9. For an overview and access to the available survey data for some of these countries, see CSCC (1980s) at <https://www.icpsr.umich.edu/web/ICPSR/series/115>.
10. KILM Report data projections for employment by status and employment by occupation are also available for more recent years, but the most recent comparable national survey of employment class structure is 2016.
11. For further details on the ISCO-08, see <http://www.ilo.org/public/english/bureau/stat/isco/isco08/>.
12. Use of these occupational concordances for Canadian occupational changes is a fairly straightforward process including CCDO to NOC and NOC to ISCO. See Canada, Employment and Immigration, Occupational and Career Information Branch n.d. and Statistics Canada 2011.
13. As discussed in Appendix 1, my estimates for 1982 are close to estimates with Wright's initial criteria, with the exception of his overestimation of managers, and

— particularly with his later suggested near disappearance of professional employees — more plausible than Wright's revised estimates.
14. See also Mustosmaki, Oinas, and Anttila (2016); Green, Felstead, Gallie, and Henseke (2016); and Häusermann, Kurer, and Schwander (2015).
15. Unless otherwise specified, the evidence referred to in this and the following sections of this chapter is drawn from the Comparative Political Economy Data Base (CPEDB).
16. All non-Canadian data mentioned in this section, unless otherwise specified, are drawn from the Comparative Political Economy Data Base (CPEDB).
17. Analyses from the rare series of surveys of current corporate executives that we conducted in Ontario between 1980 and 2000 (see Canada Work Learning Surveys 1998–2016, "Corporate Executive Surveys 1980–2000.") confirm that the majority of current corporate executives come from proprietorial families. However, since corporate executives are such a small fraction of the general population (i.e., much less than 1 percent), it has not been possible to generate from these general surveys the reliable random sample of prior generation corporate executives that is required to estimate intergenerational reproduction of this class fraction.
18. For an accessible overview with extensive references, see Wikipedia, "Black Death."

5

Advanced Capitalist Mode of Thought

Bourgeois Ideology

In class-based societies, those who manage to gain control of surplus production have generally tried to ensure their continuing control. The means may include bribing some with a bit of the surplus and forcing others through imprisonment or exile. However, at least in more complex societies, maintaining this control almost always involves trying to convince many others that current controllers really deserve the surplus because of their particular qualities. From the vantage point of a jail cell in fascist Italy, Antonio Gramsci (1971) generated one of the most deeply insightful accounts of how this ideological process was constructed by organic intellectuals of the rising bourgeoisie in the emergence of industrial capitalism. In this chapter, I look briefly at general modes of thought that serve to shape peoples' views of social reality, compare feudal and capitalist modes of thought and dominant ideas, and point to some of the dominant and contesting political ideas that may be guiding class consciousness today.

Modes of Thought and Classes

We make our history through our own immediate thoughts and actions, but we do so within the circumstances of existing modes of production and modes of thought. It is obvious that our thoughts are conditioned by the historical material conditions in which we live. Marx's (1970 [1859], 67) most explicit comment on the relation between modes of production and modes of thought was made in reaction to a strong idealist bias in the dominant forms of thought in his era:

> The mode of production of material life conditions the general process of social, political and intellectual life. It is not the con-

sciousness of men that determines their existence, but their social existence that determines their consciousness. In studying [eras of social revolution] it is always necessary to distinguish between the material transformation of the economic conditions of production, which can be determined with the precision of natural science, and the legal, political, religious, artistic or philosophic — in short, ideological forms in which men [sic] become conscious of this conflict and fight it out.

This orthodox Marxist notion that material conditions determine consciousness is too simplistic to comprehend this relationship. A defensible version of this thesis might claim that "the context-specific views of most people who come to occupy similar positions in an organization will tend to converge over time" (Seccombe and Livingstone 1999, 23). However, several further revisions are needed to proceed effectively with analyses of modes of thought and expressions of social consciousness. First, greater reciprocity needs to be recognized: solidarity and struggle by those with shared beliefs in alternate values can modify material conditions. Second, material circumstances do not dictate specific courses of action; there are typically multiple constraints on and options for conceivable actions. Third, the hopeful orthodox Marxist notion that worsening material conditions necessarily lead to oppositional consciousness and then to activism by oppressed groups ignores complex mediations grounded in racialization and gender as well as class dimensions of inequality and the contradictory contingencies they often present.[1] Fourth, and most important for the current analysis, the capitalist class dominates national economies via the prevailing social relations of production and exchange, as outlined in Chapter 3. The capitalist class does not rule in the sense of presenting a highly unified worldview to any nation-state's people. This dominant class is divided by virtue of its competitive corporate form into many capitals driven to maximize their firms' profits and their own incomes. Nation-state political regimes can serve to unify capitalist interests through private property laws and friendly regulations while also offering some response to popular democratic demands. But the capitalist class does not, cannot, think, act or rule as a collective entity. The competitive drive for profits with different market and sector agendas continually undermines efforts at uniformity within the realm of ideas. The deeply shared material interest in profit maximizing provokes periodic ideological disputes among capitalist factions and also offers openings for more progressive forms of thought to "fight it out."

All advanced species continually process information from their material conditions in order to cope with their environments. Homo sapiens are distinctive in the complexity of both the modes of production and the modes of thought we have constructed in this survival process. In this chapter, I take as context the discussion in Chapter 3 of the basic characteristics and tendencies of capitalism as a mode of production that continue to animate the structuring and change of relations between capital and labour. As outlined in Chapter 3, the capitalist mode of production has rarely if ever appeared in pure form. The dominant labour form, hired wage labour, has typically been combined with pre-capitalist forms of labour in any given social formation or nation-state. Similarly, dominant forms of thought have usually been combined with pre-capitalist forms in any given social formation. My focus here is on ideological forms expressing central ideas of capital and labour rights, which I presume to be understandable across all current advanced capitalist countries.

This comparative analysis of the capitalist mode of thought is necessarily more schematic, selective and exploratory compared to the richer body of prior analyses of the capitalist mode of production. This account remains generic, ignoring many historical variations in ways of thinking about class relations. Gender- and race-based ideologies of exclusion are not addressed (Smith 1975; Doane 2017), but I assume that class-based modes of thought are generally as consequential as modes of production to understanding different historical societies and therefore at least need to be addressed generically in this inquiry. Critical attention to the currently dominant mode of thought is a necessary condition to understanding contemporary class consciousness. The modes of thought in which we become conscious of material conditions and "make our own history" also mediate our actions and deserve careful attention as conditioning specific thoughts and actions.

There are several levels of relationship between modes of thought and modes of production. At a most general level, some scholars have suggested that the development of abstract philosophical thought and pure mathematics in Western societies was a consequence of the extension of commodity exchange markets and the invention of coinage systems in seventh century BCE Greece (Thomson 1955). It has similarly been suggested that the development of modern science was inherently connected with the rise of modern capitalism. Sohn-Rethel (1978, 111–135) has argued that, during the fifteenth and sixteenth centuries in western Europe, as labour control was removed from artisans, the transition from feudal to large-scale commercial production needed more socialized logic of mathematical thought; hence, the emergence of architects, engineers and "experimenting masters." In particular, Sohn-Rethel claimed that the rise of modern science occurred around 1600 with Galileo's application of mathematics to the calculation of natural phenomena of motion, notably the ballistics of cannonballs. Such arguments have been criticized as Eurocentric, reductionist and overly linear (e.g., Goody 2006; Cardoso Machado 2013). Even largely Eurocentric perspectives on the increasing mechanized views of nature and knowledge making in this period now recognize many more practical and political disputes than earlier idealized accounts of the Scientific Revolution (e.g., Shapin 1996). In any event, there is fairly convincing twentieth-century empirical evidence, from rural Russian peasants' experience in the transition from feudal conditions to Soviet industrialization, of significant related shifts from concrete to more abstract modes of thought (e.g., Luria 1976). I leave aside further debate at this general level except to note that modes of thought are historically conditioned just as modes of production are.

There are also multiple substantive levels at which we can study modes of thought (e.g., Fikentscher 1995). If one is interested in specifying group differences in forms of thought, the most evident focus would be on *ideologies*. Most generally, as Stuart Hall (1986, 29) observed, ideologies denote "the mental frameworks — the languages, the concepts, categories, imagery of thought, and the systems of representation — which different classes and social groups deploy in order to make sense of, define, figure out and render intelligible the way society works." My focus here is limited to more explicit ideological forms, general clusters of ideas and beliefs adhered to and promoted by major class groupings as reflective of their worldviews and notions of reality and through which conscious social actors make sense of their political worlds (cf. Eagleton 1991).

Dominant class ideologies are clusters of ideas and beliefs professed by controlling classes in their own interests. In all class societies, as noted in Chapter 1, organic intellectuals have promoted such ideas intended to serve the leadership and authority of dominant classes. In my view, preliminary critical study of class-based ideologies in capitalism can be traced to the 1840s consolidation of industrial capitalists and the emergence of hired industrial workers as an opposing collective force. Most significantly, particularly after the failure of the revolutions of 1848, Karl Marx (1970 [1859]) developed a systematic exposé of the exploitative character of bourgeois civil society through a detailed critique of its most advanced form of thought, political economy. Marx first identified conflicts between productive forces and relations of production. He then suggested ways in which various forms of political, legal and other ideologies expressed these class conflicts. The systematic study of ideological class struggle has had modest development since that point.[2]

The conflict between optimal profit margins and tolerable working conditions in global capitalism regularly inspires renewed efforts among capitalist leaders and aligned intellectuals to revise the dominant ideological narrative, often in ways that are internally inconsistent, as we will see. Conversely, the contrast between the relative impoverishment of the masses and the gross overconsumption of the bourgeoisie frequently undermines general capitalist claims of universal freedom and equality. This contradiction provokes both negative resistance to capitalist ideology and positive ideological creativity within the labouring classes (e.g., Prakesh and Esteva 1998; Livingstone and Sawchuk 2000). The rare recognition that these labouring class activities constitute a proletarian public sphere in contemporary societies (see Negt and Kluge 1993 should stimulate further development of theory and practice of ideological class struggle by progressive forces.

The acceptance of dominant class ideas either actively or at least passively by subordinate classes is now recognized as a condition of "ideological hegemony" (Gramsci 1971; Livingstone 1976). Just as modes of production involve continuing negotiation between classes, so is ideological hegemony often renegotiated. In the capitalist era, there have been few systematic studies of ideological forms in and of themselves, and of the classes and alliances creating and modifying them. Gramsci's (1971) studies from the confines of his prison cell is one of few. The rarity of such analyses is itself symptomatic of scholarly acceptance of capitalist hegemony in recent times. The extent of popular acceptance of such dominant ideas has even more rarely been systematically assessed empirically. The inquiry into levels of class consciousness in the following two chapters addresses this question.

General thematic forms of ideological thought of historical civilizations have typically addressed basic questions such as the character of our relations with our natural environment, with other human beings, to time and territory, and to sources of knowledge. Some modern scholars have attempted to construct trans-historical models and inventories of basic "value orientations." Kluckhohn and Strodtbeck (1961) suggest that these issues generally include conceptions of the following: human relations with the animate and inanimate environment; human relationships including the bases of superiority and subordination, the relative significance of the individual and the collectivity, and territorial relations between peoples; human nature per se, including its rational or instinctual character and the importance of mind versus matter; and human destiny or purpose, including the extent of freedom and determinism and the location of such purposes in time.[3]

In this chapter, I offer general profiles of the basic value orientations and central ideas of the dominant class in capitalism, the "bourgeoisie." I compare these ideas with those of dominant elites in pre-capitalist feudal modes of thought, as well as with opposing ideas expressed by subordinate class leaders in advanced capitalism. The term bourgeoisie originally referred to inhabitants of the towns that grew in medieval times as centres for longer-distance trade; these town enclaves were dominated by merchants who made their living by buying goods from local tradespeople and selling them more widely for monetary gain and accumulating wealth. By the end of the eighteenth century, bourgeoisie referred primarily to the class that owned most of society's wealth. Today, "bourgeois" is often used as a diffuse pejorative to refer to a broad middle class seen to be fixated on materialistic values. But, as used in this book, the term refers to the capitalist class who own the major means of production in advanced capitalism.

The Feudal Mode of Thought and Elite Omniscience

In pre-capitalist tribute-paying modes of production generally and feudalism in particular, most people were in labouring classes tied to the land. Royal elites tended to hold hereditary domination over larger regions. Lords and nobles exercised control over local areas. Lords required allegiance from those allocated smaller parcels, including preparedness to fight to defend their lord's claims. The labouring classes of serfs and peasants of various designations spent their lives producing their own subsistence on the lord's estate and devoted whatever additional time and energy they had to labour for their lord. Religious elites intermingled with royalty tended to promote modes of ideological thought that stressed the superiority of the rulers, collective obedience to rituals, reliance on spiritual revelation as truth and the virtue of constant repetition of established historical practices to ensure social stability. Dominant ideas of the divine right of kings coupled with the infallibility of priestly guidance promoted the absolute power of kings and popes over significant economic and political matters. But, in most regions of medieval Europe, there were continual, often bloody conflicts and changing alliances between kings, priests, lords and knights, as well as cruel or indifferent treatment of labouring classes. Romantic idealization of the Middle Ages has been common, but it is probably a mistake to presume that these ideas were ever widely consciously accepted by serfs.

In any case, this medieval mode of thought was modified significantly over the centuries, initially in terms of questions raised by internal contradictions within ideas of divine right and infallibility (e.g., Abelard 1976 [1121].) and increasingly in terms of challenges of relations between spiritual and temporal power (e.g., Canning 1996), particularly as wider struggles over property emerged. In feudal societies, loyalty to the crown and church were promoted regularly through performance of rituals aimed to underline the constant certainty of the established economic and political order. The principles of divine right and infallibility asserted the superiority and omniscience of royal and religious elites with profound expectation of loyalty and obedience from their subjects. Widespread promotion of these ideas served continuing extraction of surplus from the labouring classes (such as tithing by serfs tied to the land) to support the conspicuous consumption needs of dominant classes (castles, treasures...). In such tribute-paying modes of production focused on local land-based labour, there was little demand for dominant classes to expand their means of production beyond their land holdings. Making gains through monetary speculation was widely condemned, and loans were often strictly regulated by church and state. As late as the mid-1700s, Pope Benedict XIV's (1745) encyclical *Vix Pervenit*, in response to increasing frequency of moneylending, pronounced: "A loan contract … demands, by its very nature, that one return to another only as much as he has received. The sin [of usury] rests on the fact that sometimes the creditor desires more than he has given ..., but any gain which exceeds the amount he gave is illicit and usurious."

But such edicts increasingly ran in the face of demands from feudal nobles for greater political rights vis-à-vis the crown and church, particularly lower taxes and more freedom to use their lands for their own gain. In addition, there were demands for greater political rights from the merchants exchanging an expanding array of goods related to their growing independent property values. With the development over several centuries of towns as independent production centres for long-distance trade, the bourgeoisie had won legal charters establishing their status within the feudal hierarchy and more importantly a status "based upon buying and selling ... inconsistent with the fundamental feudal notion of ties of fealty" (Tigar and Levy 1977, 112). The idea of private property rights gained validity for those who had any significant amount of property outside of dominant royal and religious circles, including craft guild owners. At the same time, greater availability of labour freed from feudal obligations on the land to sell their labour to different employers also led to popular notions of wider workers' rights, as exemplified by the Diggers movement in the 1650s for freedom to use common and waste land for their own benefit. The challenges to dominant feudal ideas of divine right and infallibility became as incessant as the ritual practices that were increasingly seen as invalid by many.

Against dominant claims that God had made all people naturally subject to a monarch's infallible edicts, writers such as John Locke (1632–1704) argued that men are by nature free and equal and that each had a natural right to defend his life, health, liberty and possessions. Declarations of the rights of male citizens with freehold property and of free men in general became more widely proclaimed from the late 1700s onward in western Europe. For example, the French Revolution of 1789 abolished feudalism and the absolute monarchy. Shortly after the first French Republic was established, the Declaration of the Rights of Man and of the Citizen was adopted by a national assembly. The Declaration proclaimed that all citizens were to be guaranteed the rights of property, liberty, security and resistance to oppression based on the natural rights of each person. Popular writing and political movements stressed the right to independent ownership and productive use of property as well as a growing array of other human rights. Similar claims have been repeated in most rights declarations ever since. The Universal Declaration of Human Rights adopted by the United Nations General Assembly in 1948 began with assertion of the general principle that all human beings are born free and equal in dignity and rights. It goes on to affirm that everyone has the right to their own property without arbitrary dispossession, and that everyone has the right to work, with just conditions and the right to form and join associations to protect their interests.

In contrast to a general prohibition in feudal societies against speculative gains from loans, the right to profit through ownership and accumulation of diverse assets became a central dominant idea in emerging capitalist economies.

Bourgeois Thought and Dominant Ideas

The general mode of ideological thought that emerged in the Renaissance coincided roughly with the rise of industrial capitalism in western Europe. From the sixteenth century to the 1880s this mode of thought became increasingly pervasive (see McNeill 1963, 565–793) at the same time as owners of property capital became increasingly powerful. The dominant bourgeois form can be schematically summarized as stressing the following value orientations on basic ideological issues (counterposed to prior dominant feudal beliefs):

- individualism — capacity and dignity of the individual (versus medieval collectivism);

- nationalism — the nation-state as the main referent for human political allegiances (versus fealty to local lords and tribute to more remote kings)[4];

- mastery over nature — people as distinct from natural environment and capable of dominating it (versus necessity to respond to acts of nature);

- rationalism — applied reason discovering laws of existence (versus spiritual revelation and intuition);

- materialism —satisfaction of increasing material wants bringing the greatest good (versus virtue and spirit of restraint to ensure meeting of well-established needs); and

- secular progress — continual improvement of human society and economic growth (versus stable secure reproducibility).

Several leading ideas have become central within this dominant ideology. The most central has been the right to acquire private property for one's own purposes and the freedom to use such property as one chooses for personal gain. This belief, in opposition to absolutist powers, was frequently asserted as leading to the greatest good for greatest numbers. Private property rights have been promoted not only for individuals but for large private corporations as legal persons. The centrality of private property rights pervades civil society, with the widespread belief that all should have the freedom to buy any commodity they desire, subject only to sufficient funds, a condition that Macpherson (1962) aptly terms "possessive individualism."[5]

A second dominant idea has been the separation of economic and political powers. This idea emerged initially in terms of the reduction of absolutist monarchs' executive power through development of legislative and judicial decision-making to be exercised by independent bodies representing other property owners. With the development of the capitalist mode of production, owners of capital increasingly asserted private property rights to run their own businesses in free markets with minimal state interference, while also acceding that state decision-making powers should be accessible to all citizens. The notion that the economy should run basically on liberal market laws of supply and demand while the state should operate on democratic grounds became an essential feature of bourgeois ideology — however intimately political and economic power were actually linked in capitalist societies.

Third, with virtually every technological advance, the notion that the application of rational scientific thought is improving general material welfare and guarantees continuing economic growth became a more common article of faith. Fourth and most pervasively, an ethos of economic materialism infused everyday thought with a dominant tendency for everything to be viewed in terms of commodity value. A persistent message has been that the most meaningful aspects of life are the goods and services we should be aspiring to acquire; we should see such commodities as the primary measure of ourselves. These dominant ideas, continually promoted by bourgeois intellectuals and allies and hammered home through mass media, coalesced in multiple dynamic ways. They are at the core of contemporary capitalist ideology.

A further supportive idea has been that the human social rights of previously oppressed people can be effectively addressed within capitalism. Various social groups, from labour unions to many civil rights activists, feminists, Indigenous peoples, environmentalists and others have organized effectively to demand greater recognition and justice. The dominant ideology has been modified, at least symbolically, to legitimate these social rights and re-establish capitalist ideological hegemony. Since the 1880s, the social movements for labour rights, gender rights and civil rights for racially oppressed, disabled and other marginalized people, as well as protection of the natural environment against further degradation have cumulatively increased pressure on the dominant capitalist ideology for concessions.

While these bourgeois ideas became dominant in the general mode of thought that developed with the capitalist mode of production, they never became universal in the sense of being the only publicly acknowledged ways of thinking. In a world driven by competitive pursuit of profits in market exchange, there are continual sources of emergent ideas, as discussed in a following section. There are also residual forms originating in prior modes of thought that continue to exert influence. A prominent instance is the organized religions that prevailed in European feudalism. Christian religions have continued to play a large role in the ideological forms of most advanced capitalist societies and to co-exist in a delicate dance with the growing influence of rational scientific thought. The ideological dominance of any set of central ideas in capitalism is continually subject to renegotiation with both pre-existing and emergent forms.

Since the 1880s, there have been persistent challenges to this dominant capitalist mode of thought. With regard to prevalent general value orientations, according to Wagar (1972, 9–10): "The only discernible common theme in Western intellectual and cultural history is disintegration…. Everything fragments." Virtually all the dominant bourgeois value orientations have been questioned. In particular, the presumptions of mastery over nature, unlimited pursuit of material desires and irreversible progress are all seriously undermined by growing awareness of environmental crises — many human-made. But such modifications in general value orientations do not necessarily translate into serious challenges to capitalist ideological hegemony.

There has been divergence between two dominant currents of ideological thought within advanced capitalism: "technocratic" ideology and "liberal democratic" ideology. *Technocratic ideology* applies principles of technocratic rationality to all areas of life, with individual rights becoming entirely secondary. As Quinney (1974, 12–13) put it:

> The modern institutional order finds its legitimation in an ideology that stresses the rationality of science and technology. A generalized belief in the importance of controlled scientific technical progress gives legitimacy to a particular class — the one that utilizes science and technology. The extent to which this ideology pervades the whole culture limits the possibility of emancipation, limits even the perception of the need for liberation.

Hence, economic activities are most efficiently performed under the ministrations of scientific experts, political issues are best left to the neutral mediation of the state's bureaucratic administration, and a host of "inalienable" human rights and liberties are treated as secondary issues. Heralds of the "knowledge economy" exemplify this perspective.

Conversely, *liberal democratic ideology* expounds on the merits of individualism in all human endeavours. The essential features are most evident in the "American Creed," which Myrdal (1945, 4) described like this:

> These ideas of the essential dignity of the individual human being, of the fundamental equality of all men [sic], and of certain inalienable rights to freedom, justice, and a fair opportunity represent to the American people the essential meaning of the nation's early struggle for independence.

The individual's free expression of their own self-interest in all venues — the market place, leisure pursuits and especially the forums of popular sovereignty such as parliamentary democracy and public opinion — is seen as inherently yielding "the greatest good for the greatest number." Advocates of neoliberalism offer the most extreme expressions.

Any extensive effort to describe the dominant ideological forms of advanced capitalism finds both of these currents in an ambiguous coexistence (e.g., Campbell et al.1974, 64). This tension has perhaps been most evident in corporate business ideology, with contending classical liberal and regulated, managerial themes (Sutton et al. 1956; cf. Moskvichov 1974, 152–161; Seider 1974). As discussed in the following section, the ascendance of neoliberal ideology since the 1970s to celebrate free markets and individual choice represents a concerted effort to adapt the dominant form to changing social conditions — but without resolving its internal ambiguities and continually prone to competitive revisions by capitalist factions.

Such ideological tensions are not a sufficient basis to conclude that dominant bourgeois ideas have shifted definitively from those that were prominent a century ago. Short of societal extinction, dominant ideological forms have not been transformed entirely and abruptly any more than modes of production and other material structures have been. Every historical period has seen the co-existence of numerous systems and currents of thought, and even the most dominant ideological worldviews have usually contained many ideas from earlier eras and cultures (cf. Gramsci 1971, 321–343; McNeill 1963). The familiarity of the mass populace with a general cluster of dominant ideas, and the absence of any other coherent worldview to make collective sense of the world, is probably as important for the continuing hegemony of any dominant class as is its physical control of economic and political institutions. While many general value orientations may be changing and fragmenting, the central ideas cited above have continued to be widely asserted by bourgeois intellectuals and presumed to be widely accepted throughout the advanced capitalist world.

Gramsci (1971, 245–246) saw the separation of political and economic powers as the crucial tenet of the liberal ideology of competitive capitalism. Apologists for the capitalist state assert the separation of executive, legislative and judicial powers and suggest that their independent operation provides checks and balances on each other and fairness for all. More pertinently, the powers of owners of capital to use it as they please continue to be widely asserted as superordinate rights in production relations, subject only to occasional limits of rights abuses by state regulators. The dominant notion has been that all people have equal political rights and freedoms before the law in a democracy, while economic matters are most fairly and efficiently decided by free and equal market exchanges beyond the political power of the state. Pursuit of profit remains the most sacred property right, its centrality re-asserted in neoliberalism while its pervasiveness is rarely publicly recognized and more rarely directly challenged.

At the same time, the belief that a widening array of social rights can and should be recognized through political action directed largely at state powers also continues to be widely asserted. For example, the Universal Declaration of Human Rights (United Nations 1948) devoted most of its attention to a long list of social rights. In addition to property rights and labour rights, the UDHR includes the following:

- right to equal protection of the law without any discrimination;
- freedom from arbitrary arrest, detention or exile;
- right to the protection of the law against arbitrary interference in privacy or attacks upon reputation;
- right to freedom of movement and residence within the borders of each state;
- right to a nationality;
- right to marry freely and to found a family;
- right to freedom of thought, conscience and religion;
- right to freedom of peaceful assembly and association;
- right to take part in the government of one's country;
- right to social security necessary for the free development of one's personality;
- right to rest and leisure;
- right to a standard of living adequate for well-being;
- right to education;
- right freely to participate in the cultural life of the community.

All these rights and freedoms are declared to be exercised with due recognition and respect for the rights and freedoms of others and the general welfare in a democratic society.

Even if many of these social rights would require action by prerogative of capitalist owners of the means of production for significant implementation within capitalism and even though state actions are generally regarded as indirect, most popular expectations and actions continue to be focused on the state. This is another indicator of continuing acceptance of the notion of the separation of powers. The fact that this widening array of social rights finds some recognition within views expressed by some bourgeois intellectual leaders, with little concern for their impact on profit maximization or managerial workplace prerogative, is indicative of how separate and insulated capitalist economic power remains from political power. From the popular demands by landless labour in transition from feudalism to the many movements that now call for general social rights, such rights have generally found only marginal address within bourgeois ideologies. Nevertheless, their continuing expression has helped to keep the notions of progressive reforms within and alternatives to capitalism alive.

Profit Squeeze and Neoliberal Offensive

The dominant ideology of most relevance for current analysis of class consciousness in advanced capitalism is neoliberalism. Many critical observers have identified the leading ideas and related economic and political policies that crystalized in the 1970s in response to declining profits and increasing public protests. The central idea was the reassertion of the rights of individual entrepreneurs in competitive markets to pursuit of profits unimpeded by state regulation (e.g., Harvey 2005; Klein 2007). The origins of this form of thought can be traced to early twentieth-century Austrian economist-philosophers who were highly concerned with the emergence of centralized (communist, socialist or fascist) state planning as a threat to market efficiencies. During and after WWII, state regime leadership was generally regarded as necessary for effective production and distribution, as reflected in capital-labour accords and Keynesian economic policies. The following "Golden Age" was one of sustained economic growth with both increasing profits and increasing wages and benefits for workers in advanced capitalism. The capitalist economy was expanding globally and well-organized workers won unprecedented wage gains to make up for the deprivations of the Great Depression and WWII. General social gains included various state-provided social welfare benefits (e.g., unemployment insurance, health insurance, public education, pensions, poverty reduction measures). By 1970, unionization rates were at their highest ever, organized workers were continuing to press their wage demands and social protests for greater economic and civil rights were widespread. As profits began to decline and protests continued, some capitalist leaders expressed real concern about survival of the system.

A declaration often used to exemplify this rising concern was by Lewis Powell (1971, 1) corporate lawyer, board member and future US Supreme Court Justice to the US Chamber of Commerce:

> The American economic system is under broad attack ... the assault on the enterprise system is broadly based and consistently pursued ... from the college campus, the pulpit, the media, the intellectual and literary journals, the arts and sciences, and from politicians.... The time has come — indeed, it is long overdue — for the wisdom, ingenuity, and resources of American business to be marshaled against those who would destroy it.

Many American corporate leaders answered the call (Volscho 2017). There is scarcely a corporate capitalist then or now who would seriously doubt the centrality of private property rights. Some would give secondary priority to labour and social demands, but advocacy of liberalizing markets to save the system became more concerted. While the timing and coherence of a liberalizing offensive in advanced capitalist countries and the global system differed widely, they became increasingly prevalent. As Connell and Dados (2014, 117) observe: "Neoliberal power and market-dominated society have become practical reality for much of the world's population. Policy agendas that combine tax cuts, deregulation, privatization, trade liberalization, insecure labor, and the squeezing of welfare, education, and health spending have gained immense influence since the 1970s." The essence of neoliberalism as both an ideology and policy agenda has been to reduce the weight of social needs relative to corporate demands in order to re-establish profits. In terms of weakening labour and social demands, it appeared to fare well in advanced capitalism until the Great Recession of 2007–08.

However, neoliberalism has two increasingly evident internal contradictions that undermine its continued dominance: first, inherent austerity pressures on social demand and consumer purchasing capacity diminish economic growth and sustained profits, while liberal credit provisions lead to speculative financial hoarding and reduce real production (see O'Connor 2010). Second, a fixation on money market profits willfully ignores ecological limits to growth of capital (Allen 2018). Ideologies can persist with various contradictions, and there are efforts to craft greener versions of neoliberal ideology and related policies, such as a "net zero economy." But the array of contradictions with the lived experience of recent times makes it unlikely that revised neoliberalism can constitute an effective new capitalist ideological hegemony (e.g., Sitaraman 2019; Matutinovic 2020).

Emerging Post-Capitalist Rights and Visions

The capitalist mode of production and the bourgeois mode of thought emerged interactively through infiltration of prior modes of production and thought. As noted in Chapter 3, the emergence came initially through enclave towns involved in long-distance trade on the peripheries of feudal/tribute-paying modes of production, enclaves that served as incubators for alternative forms of production and thought. I consider in the concluding chapter the extent to which comparable progressive "enclaves" may now exist in advanced capitalism.

In any case, substantial alternative sorts of working ideologies continue to exist in advanced capitalism. In addition to the dominant bourgeois ideology, two generic alternative types of meaning systems have been identified as operating in contemporary capitalist societies, as well as in most historical societies (see Parkin 1971): *subordinate ideologies*, which promote various deferential positions, and *radical ideologies*, which present an oppositional view of the existing social structure and alternatives to it.

Subordinate ideologies derive from the everyday lives of people who, in today's terms, are clearly located beneath the dominant bourgeois class. The leading ideas of the dominant ideology, complete with logical inconsistencies, tend to be reworked as a general value context. However, as Sennett and Cobb's (1972) analysis of working-class "badges of ability" graphically illustrated, such ideals are interpreted and accepted pragmatically in terms mostly limited to localized issues (see Mann 1970).

Radical ideologies involve the explicit rejection of some of the major ideas promulgated by dominant institutions. Since the Enlightenment, many counter-ideologies have emerged to take issue with the dominant bourgeois ideological form, usually with only one or two of the fundamental value dimensions at a time (e.g., egalitarian collectivist, anti-progress or growth, naturalist, anti-materialist, anti-rationalist or anti-nationalist ideological currents). Many of these oppositional ideologies have asserted the rights of other social groups either explicitly or implicitly versus the right of capital to profit. From the outset, organized labour groups have continued to counterpose the right to strike for decent wages and working conditions against capitalist profits and have negotiated wherever feasible for more equitable terms to improve lives and avoid impoverishment. Expression of and mobilization to demand recognition of rights based on gender, racialization, age and imputed disabilities and increasingly on environmental rights to life have also strengthened. Social movements based on each of these sets of social rights are active in all advanced capitalist countries, with growing awareness of both their common interests and the fomenting opposition against them.

Beyond utopian literature and experiments, there have been very few systematic efforts yet to compare bourgeois ideology with *inclusive* emergent alternative radical ideologies — for the simple reason that no such ideologies are yet widely perceived to exist.[6] It is arguable that the worldviews of Indigenous Peoples, which have been suppressed throughout the history of capitalism, and the often-ridiculed anarchist tradition of thought represent legitimate alternatives. But I know of no systematic comparative analyses yet.

Karl Mannheim's (1936) *Ideology and Utopia* did suggest a framework for critical comparative ideological inquiries that has been taken up to some extent in subsequent sociology of knowledge research. Ernst Bloch (1989 [1959]) later produced an impressive inventory of the wishful images expressed in popular culture, their articulation in multiple fields of formal thought and suggestions for realizing their latent potentialities. But partial radical counter-ideologies to bourgeois ideology continue to emerge, often inspired by socialist traditions of thought.

My narrower objective in this chapter is to establish some specific terms of reference for estimating the extent of acceptance of general bourgeois ideas and both contradictory subordinate and radical alternatives among classes in contemporary advanced capitalist formations. Through most of the past century the capitalist bourgeoisie had control of the major mass means of mental production (most notably, books and newspapers, radio and television), thereby enabling pervasive promotion of its array of dominant ideas. The relatively recent rapid expansion of formal education and more recent explosion of personal computers, the internet and social media have made wider forms of knowledge and dissemination of alternative ideas available to a much larger part of the population of advanced capitalist societies. Capitalism has continued to provide diverse goods and services commodities to many people in advanced capitalist societies, but, as noted above, the economic inequities generated between owners of capital and hired labour have provoked thinking about and actions to create alternative ways of life. The major radical intellectual tradition contending in our times with bourgeois ideology may be broadly termed socialist thought. Early socialist thinkers tended to be utopians, moved by their revolutionary distaste for capitalist disorder to attempt to develop pictures of how the world ought to be.[7] Marx and Engels recognized a debt to these thinkers but tended to dismiss their visions as pure fantasies, as did many later leaders in the international communist movement. The lack of a theory of a desirable socialist society long remained a serious shortcoming of Marxist praxis. Most of the socialist visions of preferred futures over the past century have been generated by non-orthodox socialists, mainly by people engaged in either anarchist, syndicalist or religious socialist movements.[8]

Both visionary literary works and material efforts to establish alternative communities have continued to be part of the cultural and political histories of most advanced capitalist countries (e.g., Brick 2019). In the wake of the social protests of the 1960s, there was a steady stream of anti-capitalist thought and actions in most of these countries (e.g., Tormey 2004). However, since the Great Recession, the extreme wealth of elites on the one hand and the precariousness of most peoples' lives and the relative poverty of many others on the other hand are becoming much harder for the knowledgeable to ignore, as exemplified by the Occupy movement "for the 99 percent against the one percent." The burgeoning global movement against climate change speaks even more loudly to awareness of the threats of profit-driven production to a sustainable environment. It is arguable that there have been more concerted efforts to formulate, promote and implement alternative ideologies to capitalism since the Great Recession than at any other time since the emergence of corporate capitalism in the 1880s (e.g., Speth and Courrier 2020). We may be approaching a time comparable to the ideological transition from feudalism to capitalism in western Europe when, as noted above, the claimed omniscience of monarchs and popes was challenged to tipping point by dissident feudal lords, merchant capitalists and guild owners who needed political recognition of their property rights.

With the development of capitalism, large private property owners' political rights became dominant, enshrined in both law and cultural norms. As MacPherson (1942, 408) observed in the depths of WWII, the right to the unrestricted use of private property, which was once the chief object of democrats to secure — because it was regarded as a right without which the free and equal individual could not attain their full stature — has become incompatible with most individuals' attainment of that stature. Now the central political struggle is between this dominant bourgeoisie, with its increasing concentration of private corporate ownership, and the growing numbers *without* substantial private property ownership rights, whose demands for their social rights mount as their knowledge of threats grows.

Those with a little private property justifiably want to protect it to enable their survival and prospect for a decent life. A pivotal issue becomes whether, in conjunction with protecting their valued small pieces of private property, they accede to the now established priority of a social order based on massive accumulation of private property for a few beyond decency, or support growing demands of others for fairer social entitlements. In addition to a growing articulation of human rights in social movements and popular discourse, strong philosophical arguments are being made for giving priority to basic human rights and treating property rights as contingent (e.g., Hayward 2013). That is, if a property right serves to exclude a person from access to the means to life and is not necessary to enable the owner's decent life chances, property rights should yield to human rights. Similar claims and arguments are promoted in terms of environmental rights versus property rights (e.g., Bromley 1991). It should be stressed again here that the property rights at issue are those beyond enabling decent life chances. The effective argument does not support depriving anyone of fair personal property rights or justify wholesale collectivization of private property by the state. While institutionalized practices and dominant capitalist ideology still generally presume unconditional individual private property rights and the sanctity of the profit motive, this central dominant idea is being challenged as it more evidently incurs on basic human rights and environmental issues.[9]

Most of the opposition to dominant bourgeois ideology has been preoccupied with articulating and fighting for specific legislative rights on the terrain of capitalist-oriented state systems. Each of these brave efforts contains at least an implicit sense of an alternative world, whether specific rights are to be realized through reform of advanced capitalism or transformation. But, as noted in previous chapters, there is at least one potentially transformative alternative to capitalism that has existed from the outset both in practical settings and a traceable intellectual tradition: economic democracy.

A distinguishing feature of economic democracy as an alternative is democratic control of investment for socially useful sustainable production as opposed to profit-driven production controlled by capitalist owners. In contrast to corporate owners benefitting at the expense of workers and consumers, all producers and consumers in an organization or community are eligible to participate in resource allocation for the greatest good for the greatest number. Workers control their own labour power through self-management of work organizations. This contrasts with the exercise of managerial prerogative, which prevails in all private capitalist organizations where small numbers of owners either dominate personally or delegate such authority to a managerial hierarchy. So, two distinct features of economic democracy are socially useful sustainable production instead of profit-driven production, and self-managed work instead of managerial prerogative. Both features are discernible in many of the alternative intellectual visions posed by socialist and anarchist thinkers in reaction to the rise of industrial capitalism in the early nineteenth century. But with growing disillusion over the excesses of global corporate capitalism, and in the wake of the failures of state communist regimes and the fall of the Soviet Union, economic democracy has increasingly emerged as an explicit alternative vision and political project (see Wright 2010; Malleson 2014). These key features of economic democracy are increasingly evident in the alternatives posed since the Great Recession and pervasive awareness of climate crisis (e.g., Speth and Courrier 2020).

MacPherson (1942) underlined the basic democratic considerations: democracy has always been a protest against the class privilege which prevents some people, by reason of their position, from having equal access with others to the means of self-development; a limit is likely reached at the point where the expectations of some classes cannot be met with established forms of production. Democracy, like any other form of government, is a matter of giving up some individual liberties in order to ensure other individual liberties which we think are more important. Also, given existing asymmetries of private corporate power, recognition of collective rights of diverse social groups is essential to any considerable degree of economic democracy.

In terms of basic class-based opposed rights ideologies in advanced capitalism, I see on one hand a dominant bourgeois ideology asserting the right to optimal profit taking and against labour's right to strike. On the other hand, there is an enduring labour counter-ideology that opposes the right to unlimited profits and asserts retaining the right to strike. With regard to alternative ideological visions, the dominant bourgeois view presumes and promotes the necessity of the profit drive for societal survival and an inherent managerial prerogative for efficient production. Labour-based economic democracy sees profit maximization as a profound threat to survival and promotes genuine participatory democratic decisions as necessary to ensure socially useful sustainable production. Of course, there are many other important features of dominant, subordinate and radical ideologies, but these are the dimensions of rights and visions that I focus on in making empirical assessments of higher levels of class consciousness in the following chapters.

Whether current ideological class struggle leads to re-incorporation within capitalist hegemony or movement toward a new mode of thought and mode of production is still an open question, contingent on the social forces that come into play. However, we are in a historical moment beyond straightforward reproduction of capitalist ideological hegemony. Current social movements focused on economic inequities in and environmental destruction by capitalism may or may not presage a wholesale overturn of the capitalist mode of thought. But they do exemplify the most concerted ideological and practical challenges to date, as discussed in the final chapter.

As long as the founding idea of liberal democracy remains an active part of dominant bourgeois capitalist ideology, partial alternative worldviews remain open to those who directly experience undermining of their social rights. There are troubling signs that democratic political institutions are under serious threat from autocratic forces in some advanced capitalist countries (e.g., Alizada et al. 2021). When corporate capitalists such as Donald Trump gain official political office and attempt to exercise unilateral privilege, the notion of separation of powers becomes increasingly difficult to maintain. Where the ostensible insulation of the economy and the polity diminishes such that questions of economic organization cannot assume a separate "non-political" appearance, the attraction of radical alternative ideologies is also likely to increase. In any event, the dominant ideology is continually changing in advanced capitalist societies. There is a tense co-existence of neoliberal assertions of private property rights and heightening concentration of capitalist ownership versus expansive versions of civil and social rights demanded by a growing array of knowledgeable social groups for decent living conditions, dignity and survival. This at least presents difficult challenges for re-establishing capitalist ideological hegemony (see Hayward 2013).

In any case, no dominant ideological form is ever capable of totally negating the experience of the majority. In this respect, the durability and general importance of the worldviews emerging from the cumulative experience of common people should neither be denied because they have always been largely unrecorded nor simply identified with the prominent intellectual formulations of any period. Indeed, the success of the ideological efforts of both bourgeois and revolutionary agents should be understood in terms of their actual resonance with notions that are already implicit in general human activity (Gramsci 1971, 335; Bloch 1989 [1959]). I begin to assess this resonance in the following chapters.

Admittedly, I am only scratching the surface of the advanced capitalist mode of thought and its dominant ideas. In the empirical analysis, I focus on indicators of oppositional political rights as well as preferences for bourgeois and revolutionary visions of the future. This investigation is limited in terms of assessment of the extent of current dominance of bourgeois ideas. But at least it brings together a systematic profile of the current class-based ideological context with expressions of the subjective class consciousness of those acting within this context.

Profit Maximization and the Right to Strike

Histories of political ideas from ancient as well as feudal times have been traced in terms of changing forms of property rights and other social rights as pivotal features of dominant ideologies (Ishay 2008). Popular notions and legal articulations of human rights, as well as the extent to which various rights are widely assumed to be immutable, have frequently been modified in relation to contests between different social groups in capitalist societies (e.g., Tushnet 1992). The pivotal issue in adapting bourgeois ideology in advanced capitalism is reconciling increasingly concentrated capitalist ownership and profit accumulation with increasing dispossession from and demand for restoration of the social rights of others.

I focus on the key dominant capitalist idea of the right to profit maximization from private property in the means of production, as well as the basic social right of labour, the right to strike. I take these to be the central rights of capital and labour, respectively. In the next chapter, I argue that different combinations of views on these rights issues are associated with different forms and levels of class consciousness. Here, I take the ways in which views on these rights issues are expressed by contemporary class leaders to be indicative of the range of prominent bourgeois and radical labour ideologies in advanced capitalism today. I consider the views on these central ideas articulated in the current period by prominent leaders of capital and labour: corporate executives and trade union leaders. The illustrative quotes that follow are from transcripts of interviews I conducted with select leaders in Canada and Australia in 1990 and 2016. All respondents were guaranteed anonymity to ensure most candid expression.

Profit Maximization

To repeat it one more time, the most fundamental imperative of capitalism is profit maximization. Contemporary expressions of the right to profit maximization by corporate leaders I interviewed in 1990 offer some insight into the depth of and differing rationales for this central dominant idea as well as its continuing modification:

> Private corporations should be able to invest their earnings wherever they can make the greatest profit. I don't see any argument for restricting [Australian] investment abroad and I think the internationalization of business has gone too far to try to impose any restrictions…. The profit motive is essential, and one only has to look at Russia and China to see the truth of that. After years of trying to remove a profit motive, they are trying to put it back because the economy doesn't work effectively without a proper motive, without the discipline that's imposed by the need to make a profit.

> In order to be competitive on a worldwide basis, you must allow for the free flow of capital. For example, for a domestic operation you may need component parts that are available in a distant land where the rates are cheaper. I would much prefer to have the operation in the foreign country owned by Canadian

capital so that at least we have a piece of the action. That said, we should concentrate on businesses here where we do have comparative advantages for profits, knowledge industries and our very strong natural resource base.

More recently, in 2016, some more far-sighted corporate leaders recognized that negative impacts of profit maximization need to be dealt with to ensure survival of the system.

> Fair profits are very important to economic success. The profit motive makes a lot of good things happen. But excessive greed is becoming a real problem. The inequity of some CEO's gross rewards is becoming ridiculous while workers fall further behind. Corporate business has forced more government regulation upon itself through financial screw-ups, absurd levels of top compensation and indifference to environmental impacts. There is a sense of public outrage that we have to become increasingly concerned about.

But none of the corporate leaders I interviewed expressed the slightest doubt that the profit motive should remain central to the organization of any economy. Conversely, all the labour leaders I interviewed offered strong arguments for limiting the flow of profits to enable working people to lead decent lives:

> We shouldn't have a society that encourages extreme exploitation by playing off workers in one country against others. It's wise and sound to have some control on the flow of capital to make it more responsible. I would love to have a world where hired labour and the unemployed are treated properly…. With the uncontrolled profits and uncontrolled rape of the economy that we have now, many workers are getting their asses kicked all over the world.

More recently, in 2016, labour leaders expressed an increasing sense that profit maximizing has become highly counter-productive and intolerable:

> I oppose unregulated profit taking wholeheartedly. All the information that's come out recently about all the profits that are

being stashed in off-shore accounts by wealthy bosses.... If profits are being made in this country, they should be reinvested in this country. It never should be all about shareholder profits. The bastards have already effectively written all the fucking laws in the land. They started de-regulating markets years ago, now they're talking about more de-regulation. What do they want us to do — bleed into a bucket for them!

Right to Strike

The most basic right of hired workers in capitalist economies is the capacity to withhold their labour to negotiate for more tolerable working conditions. The right to strike has been as central to the sustainability of labour as profit maximization has been to the reproduction of capital. This basic right has been asserted by hired labourers whenever even small numbers have felt it was opportune to negotiate with employers for more tolerable working conditions. The Canadian labour leaders I interviewed supported this principle unreservedly:

> The only way for workers to balance their economic powers is to have the right to collectively withdraw their labour against the massive powers of management. From a moral point of view, I'm given the right to withdraw my labour. Not having a ban on "scabs" is giving the right to steal my job, to diminish my only real economic power. If you come to the plant to legally picket and there is some guy going in there to take your job, it's like he was coming out of your house with your TV and VCR, but he is stealing something far more valuable.... All workers should have the right to strike to get the best circumstances they can for their work. They only have their labour to sell and the only way to get a fair deal is to threaten collectively to withdraw it.

Australian labour leaders were even more vehement about the right to strike, given a national context in which strikes were illegal, in contravention of widely recognized international standards:

> Any worker should have the right to withdraw their labour as a defence for the encroachments of employers. I think it's an inherent right of all people who work. Strike-breaking is very immoral, it's just very abhorrent!

By 2016, with organized labour under continuing onslaught from neoliberal actions, labour leaders were even more strident in defence of the right to strike:

> Every worker must retain the right to organize, be part of a union and have the right to strike! I know all the increasing claims about essential services. But in an antagonistic system like ours, you just cannot deny workers the right to strike mainly because employers want to bully them into getting even less decent working conditions. Lives would have to be immediately at risk to deny any worker this essential right now.

Corporate leaders have tended to recognize workers' rights to organize, to negotiate working conditions with their employers under *some* circumstances and to tolerate the existence of trade unions as a necessary evil. Even in the extreme case of Australia, where strikes are legally banned, unions have been grudgingly tolerated along with dispute mechanisms to mitigate conflict without jeopardizing productivity:

> We don't recognize a legal right to strike in this country. Workers and trade unions have the benefits of a compulsory conciliation and arbitration system, so they forego the right to strike. We have an independent tribunal that can make decisions in favour of the employee and enforce those decisions against the employer.... But trade unions are here to stay because some workers think they are necessary to defend their interests. It may be possible for employers to deal with workers as individuals in some circumstances, but there will still be collective effort by workers to improve their conditions.

> The only ultimate weapon that any organized labour group has is the possible threat to down tools and go on strike. But there should be dispute mechanisms to resolve differences by unbiased arbitration. There should be legislative restraints that impose upon employers and unions duties to bargain in good faith. But if [Canadian] workers have the right to strike, then employers should have the complementary right to hire replacement workers, even if it exacerbates an already difficult situation.

In 2016, some corporate leaders expressed somewhat more support for the right to strike as a counterbalance to irresponsible actions of their colleagues that jeopardize sustainability of the system:

> Workers need the right to strike as a balancing act against unilateral managerial prerogative. I've had very mixed experience with trade unions. But their collective power is certainly needed and important to contend against arbitrary corporate action and especially recent gross rewards of some CEOs.

The view of corporate executives is consistently strong support for profit maximization but with increasing recognition by some that more care is needed in limiting excesses to avoid public outrage. Union leaders universally plead for profit controls to limit the damage to workers. In addition, union leaders universally and strongly support the right to strike as essential to workers' chances for decent lives. Some corporate leaders concede that workers may need some sort of collective representation for good faith bargaining but none would concede an unconditional right to strike.

Basically, pro-capital rights ideologies as expressed by corporate leaders continue to assert the profit motive as beneficial for all and to minimize workers' bargaining rights that could jeopardize profits. Pro-labour rights ideologies of union leaders stress workers' right to strike as their essential defence against profit-taking exploitation by employers. Support for the right to profit and resistance to the right to strike are central to pro-capital oppositional consciousness. Support for the right to strike and resistance to profit taking define pro-labour oppositional consciousness. We see in the next two chapters how widespread these clearly opposed views are in advanced capitalism generally and in specific employment classes.

In addition to formulations of opposed class-based rights, capital- and labour-oriented ideologies expressed by class leaders also at least implicitly tend to contain contrasting preferred capital and labour rights-based visions of the future. Capitalist ideologies typically take for granted pursuit of profit as the driving force of any conceivable economy along with necessary guidance by their managerial prerogative, with no consideration whatsoever of any possible future alternative. Pro-labour future ideologies give credibility to greater worker involvement in workplace management and more rarely intimate legitimate prospects of socially useful production through critiques of wasteful profits. These are dimensions of hegemonic capitalist and revolutionary labour visions of society that I take to distinguish the worldviews of the most class conscious leaders of capital and labour respectively, and potentially to animate the political actions of class forces more generally. However, at least among the class leaders I interviewed, there was a decided reluctance to speak much about future visions. For the corporate leaders, there was no feasible alternative to capitalism. For the labour leaders, there was understandable preoccupation with defending diminishing current rights. The relevance of these dimensions of class-based ideologies in the consciousness of the labour forces of advanced capitalism are assessed in the following two chapters.

Concluding Remarks

Writing in the depths of the Great Depression from a conservative aristocratic standpoint, Ludovici (1932, 30–31) observed:

> In the comparatively recent system called *capitalism*, in which the irresponsible administration of wealth, combined with large accumulations of it in a few hands, is accompanied by the existence of a vast multitude of disinherited or destitute people, we find the recurrence of abuses and errors, which are leading to a fresh crisis, in the anticipation of which the masses are again being taught both by doctrinaires and circumstances, to call the institution of private property into question.

Nearly a century later, the institution of private property is still largely intact. More generally, it is difficult for anyone living within a dominant mode of thought to think outside it, to become critically conscious of its limiting dimensions. Paradigm shifts in scientific research may occur under the weight of cumulative empirical evidence (e.g., Kuhn 1962), but dominant modes of ideological thought are more unwieldy forms. They may continue to envelop us even as we contest their most central dominant ideas. All we can be sure of at this point is that some of the dominant bourgeois ideas of advanced capitalism are under concerted challenge. The right to use private property in the means of production for maximum profit is still firmly adhered to by corporate capitalists and perhaps by their most faithful allies. But challenges are mounting in terms of making the right to profit contingent on not endangering other basic rights. Basic human rights and environmental rights are increasingly being asserted as overriding priorities by dissident intellectuals and increasingly knowledgeable citizenries alike. The contexts for critical analyses of both dominant capitalist ideas and emergent oppositional alternatives are becoming more transparent as challenges mount. At least we can begin to see the actual shape of the dominant bourgeois ideology somewhat more clearly. I offer empirical assessments of the extent of popular acceptance of some of the central ideas in capitalist ideology as well as receptivity to alternative pro-labour views in the following two chapters.

Notes

1. See Seccombe and Livingstone (1999) for fuller development of this perspective and a case study with steelworker families.
2. A brief historical account of positive and negative aspects of such ideological class struggles, complicated by Stalinist communism and Western Marxism, can be found in Livingstone (2003).
3. Kluckhohn and Strodtbeck (1961) identified five basic "value orientations": human nature, man-nature, time, activity and relational orientations; then they tested them in several different communities in the US, and others have conducted similar empirical investigations. Such research has been subject to withering criticism as overly abstract and ad hoc, but with recognition that the issue of different value orientations or modes of thought is worthy of further grounded investigations (Spates 1983).
4. It is also fairly clear that competing capitalist empires became the leading global political forms after 1500. Their inter-imperialist state rivalries and transnational corporations have dominated world events ever since.
5. The ideological emphasis remains on the individual right to possess private property. But the actual right is sometimes superseded by the capitalist state directly or on behalf of large private corporations overriding individual property rights.
6. Throughout the history of the state of the Soviet Union, an alternative communist ideology was asserted. But aside from official egalitarian collectivist principles, it was largely indistinguishable from bourgeois ideology on the other basic dimensions of the dominant bourgeois mode of thought.
7. See, for example, Wittke (1950).
8. For a brief account of the historical development of preferred socialist and bourgeois visions of the future, see Livingstone and Lake (1977).
9. Discussion of property rights in Western societies has almost invariably presumed the incompatibility of individual and social property. Their possible coexistence is at least suggested by the Chinese household responsibility system and the "fuzzy" regime of land ownership that it instituted (see Ireland and Meng 2017).

6

Class Consciousness in Advanced Capitalism

General Forms and Recent Trends

How people think of themselves in terms of class relations and the extent to which they are disposed to act in support of their perceived class interests are central concerns of this book. How people identify themselves in particular classes merely offers a snapshot, or a series of snapshots, of where they choose to locate themselves in models of class structure (see Chapter 2). More important questions about class consciousness for social practice are how people see the ongoing relations of their own perceived class with other classes and what they are inclined to consider doing either to maintain or to change these relations. This chapter offers profiles of general patterns and trends in all these levels and forms of class consciousness since the early 1980s. The chapter concludes by tracking association between the highest forms of class consciousness and attitudes about poverty and global warming.

Class consciousness per se is only one aspect of social consciousness, just as class position is one aspect of objective material being. Gender consciousness, ethno-racial consciousness, age consciousness, as well as consciousness of disability for instance, are also all irreducible parts of our perceptions of social reality and are much in need of critical inquiry in their own right as well as in relation to class consciousness.[1] Oppression on grounds of racialization, gender, age and disability all are systemic and should be challenged and overcome. But I consider these factors here and in the following chapter only to the extent that their effects are found to modify relations between class and class consciousness grounded in paid workplaces.

The prior chapter outlined the centrality of individual private property rights and profit maximization as dominant ideas in the capitalist mode of thought, the challenges mounted to these ideas by assertion of other social rights and the possible emergence of post-capitalist modes of thought. The focus in this chapter is limited to the responses of anonymous individuals to national surveys in several advanced capitalist countries and on a few replicated questions about levels of class consciousness. The intent is to make rough estimates of general variations and trends. The findings may be suggestive of dispositions to social action. The following chapter examines connections between class positions in production relations and these expressions of class consciousness.

Levels and Forms of Class Consciousness

At least three basic levels have been distinguished in contemporary analyses of class consciousness:

- class identity, which is awareness of classes and extent of affiliation with a particular class;

- oppositional class consciousness, which is recognition of conflict of interest with another class or classes; and

- hegemonic (or revolutionary) class consciousness, which is recognition of a vision of society consistent with a class interest and commitment to maintain (or realize) this vision.[2]

In other words, do you think of yourself as being in a distinct class position, do you think that the rights of your class conflict with those of other classes, and do you have a view of the future that defends now dominant rights or a transformative view that aspires to achieve unrealized rights? From my standpoint, historical subjects' individual and collective sense of opposed class interests is pivotal for the development of effective class consciousness. However intensely a subjective class identity may be held, it is unlikely to be of much positive effect in mediating more specific political attitudes or political action. Classic examples are "deferential workers," who celebrate a subordinate working-class identity while expressing profound loyalty to their boss (e.g., McKenzie and Silver 1968). Similarly, preferences for alternative economic futures may not be of much political efficacy if they are unconnected to oppositional consciousness.

In terms of logical possibilities, the following seven forms of class consciousness can be distinguished in advanced capitalist economies:

- hegemonic capitalist class consciousness;
- oppositional capitalist class consciousness;
- capitalist sympathizer;
- contradictory class consciousness;
- labour sympathizer;
- oppositional labour class consciousness; and
- revolutionary labour class consciousness.

These different forms are based on combinations of class identity, oppositional consciousness and hegemonic (or revolutionary) consciousness. Among those with a coherent sense of the opposed class interests of capital and labour, three forms of class consciousness may be distinguished on each side.

In schematic terms and in line with my prior discussion of the advanced capitalist mode of thought, some people have dominant (i.e., upper or upper-middle) class identities, unreservedly support a corporate right to profits and oppose labour's unconditional right to strike, and also express a clear preference for maintaining a profit-driven economy with clear managerial control. Such people can be said to have a "hegemonic capitalist consciousness," seeing themselves as privileged by a system that naturally serves and will continue to serve their interests as universal interest. Some of these will be organic capitalist intellectuals. Those with "oppositional capitalist consciousness" see themselves as part of the dominant classes and also support corporate profits and oppose labour's unconditional right to strike, but with a more diffuse vision of the essential features of capitalism to be protected. "Capitalist sympathizers" express support for corporate profit rights and opposition to labour's rights but assign themselves subordinate class identities or decline to identify themselves in class terms; they also hold more diffuse attitudes about the essential features of capitalism. These are deferential or class-blind supporters of capitalism.

Conversely, three forms of labour consciousness may also be distinguished. At the other extreme to hegemonic capitalist consciousness, there are those who have subordinate (i.e., lower, working or lower-middle) class identities, express support for the rights of labour and opposition to corporate profit rights, and also hold a clear preference for a non-profit economy with worker control as central features of a transformed system. Such people hold a "revolutionary labour consciousness," views consistent with prospective action to build alternatives to capitalism. Those with "oppositional labour consciousness" see themselves as part of the subordinate classes and display a similar sense of coherent labour class interests, but without a necessary sense of a clear alternative to extant capitalism. "Labour sympathizers" express support for the rights of labour and opposition to corporate profit rights but either assign themselves upper or upper middle-class identities or decline to identify themselves in class terms, again without a necessary sense of an alternative to capitalism. These people are class-blind supporters of labour.

In addition to these forms of coherent oppositional capitalist and labour class consciousness, there are those who express inconsistent or non-committed views on the opposed interests of capital and labour. The rights of capital and labour are fundamentally opposed and reflect ultimately irreconcilable class interests. It is, of course, possible for workers hired by a corporation to situationally support profit maximizing tactics by their companies to stay in business at the same time as they might support the right to strike to secure their own jobs. Such people may declare various class identities or decline to do so. But the logical inconsistency of supporting basic interests of both capital and labour inhibits the development of any form of coherent disposition to oppositional class consciousness (or effective connection with either hegemonic capitalist or revolutionary labour consciousness). So, in logical terms, all those who express support for the basic rights of *both* capital and labour — however immediately practical that might seem to them — are considered in this perspective to be exhibiting "contradictory class consciousness."

These are all merely logical possibilities. These options suggest the range of forms and levels of class consciousness that might be found in advanced capitalist settings. The actual array of views that emerge and shift in any given population should be subjected to extensive continuing empirical investigation. So far, there has not been a lot of attention to either oppositional or hegemonic/revolutionary levels of class consciousness.

Overview of General Class Consciousness Studies

There has been a lot more investigation of the views of the masses by agents of elites than there has been of the views of elites by agents of the masses. The more powerful have tended to control the instruments of knowledge gathering as well as dissemination. This previously self-evident fact may become somewhat less true with the expansion of social media, but it is still largely the case. There have been multitudes of celebratory accounts of the views of captains of corporate capitalism, from J.P. Morgan to Bill Gates, but there have been few critical inquiries into their views or comparisons with other people. Max Weber (1894, 70) observed of the landed noble in late nineteenth century Germany: "The absence of reflection was of course one of his most essential virtues of domination" (cited in Smith [1998, 46] from Kasler [1998]).

The economically powerful still rarely expose themselves to critical scrutiny by others.

Conversely, the masses are continually probed for their attitudes on everything from electoral preferences to dishwasher soap, primarily to assess and even shape consumption behaviour.[3] Weber himself served as an agent of the German bourgeoisie in attempting to read the previously unknown attitudes of wage workers "from the point of view of profitability" (Smith 1998, 48). Karl Marx, on the other hand, at the request of emergent working-class organizations, constructed surveys — that were never published — to be administered to clarify the thoughts of the workers themselves on their situation and its causes (Marx 1938).

There has also been a tendency among progressive intellectuals to dismiss the inherent potential for development of class consciousness of the "dispossessed" because they have not measured up to theoretical expectations. Or, they have proven passive or reactionary in various situations and therefore been denigrated as holding false or deluded consciousness. During the rise of industrial capitalism in mid-nineteenth-century Europe, the greatest opposition to capitalism emerged from the growing collectivities of factory workers organized in unions and political movements, such as the Chartists in England. From their inception, trade unions were preoccupied with contesting profit-maximizing working conditions with heavy reliance on strike threats. In Marx's view, these initiatives were invaluable but were seriously limited by "trade union consciousness" focused on concessions from capital (Marx 1947 [1865], 55). This view prevailed among progressive intellectuals until the Russian revolution in 1917. Lenin (1963 [1902]), the most influential leader, developed the view that small organized vanguards were needed to mobilize more revolutionary visions among dispossessed workers and peasants.[4]

In the aftermath of this revolution, with the failure of a "proletcult" movement in Russia and of incipient social political movements elsewhere, progressive intellectuals emphasized transformations of subjectivity with increasing commodification as barriers to development of working-class revolutionary consciousness (Lukács 1971 [1923]). There continued to be relatively little empirical attention to actual representative expressions of class consciousness outside of mobilizing union actions.

The growth of trade unions through the Great Depression led to Fordist bargains with capitalist employers which were associated with an unprecedented period of post-WWII economic expansion, with wage and benefit gains for working people until the mid-1960s. By that time, the "false promises" of Fordism were becoming more apparent in alienated work (Aronowitz 1973), as expressed most strongly in student and worker protests of 1968–69 in France and Italy. Such protests led to some critical investigations into the existence of revolutionary working-class consciousness (e.g., Leggett 1968). One of the most influential inquiries was the work of Michael Mann (1973), who distinguished the three levels noted above (i.e., class identity; class opposition and vision of alternative society). He also identified an intermediate level above class opposition that he termed "totality," signifying a stage when workers perceive their socioeconomic situation and the entire construction of society in class terms. In Mann's view, true "revolutionary consciousness" occurs when the combination of all four of these levels is present among the working class. Mann (1973, 13) asserted: "Marxism provides a theory of escalation of consciousness from the first to the fourth (stage). Consciousness grows as the worker links his [sic] own concrete experience to an analysis of wider structures and then to alternative structures." While admirable in aiming to investigate multiple levels of class consciousness in historical context, Mann's (1973, 73) research ultimately constructed another set of abstract criteria and once again found that the dispossessed failed to measure up. He concluded: "It seems rather unlikely that the proletariat [aka working class] carries *in itself* the power to be a class *for itself*" [emphasis in original].

From the 1970s onward, capitalist-class responses to emergent protests included corporatist accords with established trade unions and then global restructuring of material production by moving it out of advanced core centres, which served to reduce established trade union membership. This was followed by mounting neoliberal austerity, inequality and precarity of employment. The Great Recession of 2007–08 was followed by the most concerted protests, such as Occupy, among students and workers since the 1960s. Further protest movements led by Black Lives Matter, Idle No More and others increasingly link social justice and environmental issues.[5] The COVID-19 pandemic has raised these protests to a wider, more intense level. There have been few large-scale empirical inquiries into the existence of oppositional or revolutionary class consciousness since the early 1970s. It is time for more. In the following investigation here and in the next chapter, I present the data on patterns and trends for relevant class issues according to the direct responses of people from diverse economic backgrounds as they gave them over the 1980–2016 period and in a few more recent surveys.

A few caveats. First, regardless of how well elaborated measures of levels and forms of class consciousness may be, no questionnaire survey can capture the full variety and fluidity of the phenomenon. In particular, questionnaire replies may completely miss the responses embedded in the social practices of class cultures, such as worker cultures of resistance (see Cohen 1980; Fantasia 1995). Further, most of the surveys used here were conducted primarily for wider purposes rather than focused on class consciousness issues per se. The continuing series of surveys since the 1990s in Canada were done at regular intervals not closely related to major economic and political change conditions — excepting the 2010 survey, done in the aftermath of the Great Recession. The questions used to estimate class consciousness were drawn from the unique set of cross-national surveys conducted by the Class Structure and Class Consciousness (CSCC) project led by Erik Olin Wright in the 1980s (discussed in Chapter 4 and more fully in the following section on oppositional consciousness) and replicated in my later surveys for trend estimation. These are the best available questions rather than the best possible questions to read recent levels and forms of class consciousness and make some estimates of trends. Also note that questions to estimate all these aspects of class consciousness are only available in some of the post-1980s surveys.

Second, no neat linear progression of levels of class consciousness should necessarily be expected in subjective responses to survey questionnaire items. As Mann (1973, 69) correctly observed, the different elements of class consciousness are "separable in reality and can occur, in varying degrees, without the others." For example, in contrast to Mann,

I argue that oppositional labour consciousness could develop without a standard working-class identity as many non-managerial workers take up the notions of "working middle class" identity, discussed in Chapter 2. Further, a fairly widespread sense of an alternative society could be gestating in emergent modes of thought, popular consciousness and even organized social movements somewhat disconnected from widely shared common class identity or oppositional labour consciousness. Conversely, even strong oppositional labour consciousness can be diverted from serious consideration of alternatives by capitalist ideology and commodity "fetishism," even if grounded in solidary material conditions. It is a hallmark of dominant class ideology that many in subordinate classes are presumed to accept tacitly the existing form of society even when they have a deep sense of opposed class interests. We should pay attention to expressions of class consciousness at all three levels without assuming any natural progression.

Finally, I reassert — along with a few others who have tried to empirically assess higher levels of class consciousness in this century — that oppositional class consciousness is likely pivotal in that a coherent sense of opposed class interests is basic to any concerted action to change (or maintain) current class relations.[6] So, let's take a look at the approximations of class consciousness available from contemporary national surveys.

Levels of Class Consciousness: Empirical Profiles 1980–2016

As Marx appreciated, there is nothing inherently capitalist about sample surveys. In fact, representative sample surveys can be invaluable, relatively economical ways to assess the conditions and needs of large populations quite quickly. Many organized groups, including trade unions and progressive political parties and movements, could make much greater use of sample surveys to understand the range and intensity of attitudes of present and potential members on major policy issues, rather than presuming them or relying on mainstream surveys designed to address narrow and often trivial issues more superficially. This potential is especially relevant today with nearly universal access to social media and readily available researchers with sound training in survey methods in all advanced capitalist countries.

My presentation of available survey findings on levels and forms of class consciousness deals first with class identity, next oppositional class consciousness, then hegemonic or revolutionary class consciousness, followed by a summation of the full range of class consciousness. The basic questions used in the initial 1980s surveys and replicated in most later surveys are presented in Table 6.1. Each of the seven forms of class consciousness outlined above has been estimated in terms of combinations of responses to the questions in the table. These combinations are fully summarized in Appendix 2. But it is probably best to look at each of the three levels first, plus some interactions between them, and then proceed to assess the full range of class consciousness.

The findings for class identity, oppositional consciousness and hegemonic/revolutionary consciousness are presented for all the countries for which relevant data are available in the 1980s, followed for each level by more recent patterns and trends for Canada. Reference is also made to other partially relevant recent empirical studies in selected countries.

Class Identity

The few studies that have ever compared relative pertinence of social identification in terms of racialization, sex and age as well as class have found that strongest identifications on all dimensions tend to be among those with the most subordinated statuses.[7] The oppressed are typically more sensitive to their systemic discrimination than their oppressors are to their privileges. As noted in Chapter 2, class identity is not likely seen by most people most of the time as the primary feature of their existence when there are many other more visible features in everyday life. In contrast to these other characteristics with more indelible markings (however much we may try to disguise them), class is a condition that is more continually produced and modified through relations with others. The lack of indelible markings makes it easier to deny or ignore the relevance of class. It is often in the interest of those in dominant classes, as in other dominant social groups, to encourage those in other classes to deny the relevance of their subordinate statuses. From a perspective of power relations, I suggest that the most basic class distinction is between those who identify as dominant class, see themselves in subordinate classes or deny the relevance of classes. Do you see yourself as above the most common classes, as a member of the common classes or are you unable or unwilling to identify yourself in class terms? Much of the research on class identity treats it as a status continuum, ignoring or evading power relations.

Table 6.1 Class Consciousness Items and Response Codes, 1980–2016

Item	Question Wording	Response Codes
Class identity	IF YOU HAD TO CHOOSE one of the following names for your social class, which one would you say you belong to: upper class, upper middle class, lower middle class, working class or lower class?	1 Upper class
		2 Upper middle class
		3 Middle class
		4 Lower middle class
		5 Working class
		6 Lower class
		7 I don't think of myself as part of any class (specify)_____
		98 I don't know
		99 I prefer not to answer
Opposed Class Interests		
Replacement workers	During a strike, management should be prohibited by law from hiring workers to take the place of strikers. Do you strongly agree, somewhat agree, neither agree nor disagree, somewhat disagree, or strongly disagree?	1 Strongly agree
		2 Somewhat agree
		3 Neither
		4 Somewhat disagree
		5 Strongly disagree
		98 I don't know
		99 I prefer not to answer
Corporate owners gain	Owners of corporations make gains at the expense of their workers. Do you strongly agree, somewhat agree, neither agree nor disagree, somewhat disagree, or strongly disagree?	1 Strongly agree 2 Somewhat agree 3 Neither 4 Somewhat disagree 5 Strongly disagree 98 I don't know 99 I prefer not to answer
Preferred Future		
Non-profit economy	It is possible for a modern economy to run effectively without the profit motive? Do you strongly agree, somewhat agree, neither agree nor disagree, somewhat disagree, or strongly disagree?	1 Strongly agree
		2 Somewhat agree
		3 Neither
		4 Somewhat disagree
		5 Strongly disagree
		98 I don't know
		99 I prefer not to answer

Item	Question Wording	Response Codes
Worker self-management	Non-management could run things without bosses. Do you strongly agree, somewhat agree, neither agree nor disagree, somewhat disagree, or strongly disagree?	1 Strongly agree
		2 Somewhat agree
		3 Neither
		4 Somewhat disagree
		5 Strongly disagree
		98 I don't know
		99 I prefer not to answer

Researchers continue to debate both the historical and current pertinence of class identification in both individual and collective terms (e.g., Archer and Orr 2011), but when the question of classes is posed in terms of their existence, the vast majority of people recognize that classes do exist, as documented in Chapter 2. If people are asked to locate themselves in terms of standard class labels, most will readily do so. As a current illustration, take the results of a recent World Values Survey of the general population in a wide array of around fifty countries, selectively summarized in Table 6.2.

When asked directly whether they would describe themselves as belonging to the classes listed here, nearly all respondents in nearly all countries chose one, and very few declined to do so. Tiny numbers in any country declare an upper-class identity. Those who opt for an upper-middle-class identity, suggestive of some aspect of dominance or superiority, are a minority everywhere. The vast majority in all countries see themselves in more subordinated lower middle, working or lower classes. Surveys with different standard categories generate different results. In particular, surveys that offer "middle class" as an option along with "upper middle class" always find lesser numbers distinguishing themselves as "upper middle class." In any case, the general pattern in all advanced capitalist countries is minorities opting for dominant class identities, majorities taking more subordinated middling working-class identities, and few declining to declare class identity.

However, by the end of the 1970s, various inquiries into popular images of class structure in advanced capitalist societies had concluded that such images were becoming increasingly fragmented and inconsistent. For example, in concluding a case study of British manual and clerical workers, Howard Davis (1979, 188) stated: "It is likely that inconsistencies in and between workers' accounts of their experience and social relationships is evidence of the growing difficulty of constructing a coherent social consciousness [aka class identity] in a world of work in which the technical and social division of labour has become unimaginably complex." In retrospect, as documented in Chapter 4, the major class structure changes that have occurred from the 1960s onward have been largely sectoral shifts of employment from material production to a growing array of services, while the basic class structure of employers, self-employed and hired labourers has remained largely intact. Presumptions about declining subjective "working class" identity in lived experience may have been at least partly a reflection of researchers' inferences based on diminishing manual labour content and proliferation of varieties of "white collar" work in emergent "knowledge economies."

Since the 1930s, empirical social scientists have produced a massive amount of evidence indicating that people believe that classes exist and that they can readily identify themselves in class terms. For example, all the surveys cited in Figure 2.1 in Chapter 2 found that around 90 percent of Canadian respondents agreed that classes exist. Various surveys have found that quite a few respondents say that they do not typically tend to think of themselves in class terms, but one can have a strong affective sense of belonging to a class without having high cognitive clarity about either class structure or formal class labels. Across all the advanced capitalist countries, most studies that have bothered to ask have found that

Table 6.2 Standard Class Identity, World Values Survey, 2017–2020 (%)

Country	Upper	Upper Middle	Lower Middle	Working	Lower	Decline	N
Australia	1	29	32	31	4	2	1813
Germany	1	36	41	17	2	3	1528
Greece	<1	11	33	41	13	3	1200
Hong Kong	1	16	43	27	13	<1	2075
Japan	2	15	42	26	10	5	1353
New Zealand	1	30	27	25	3	14	1057
US	1	29	36	25	7	1	2596
Total	2	18	38	27	13	1	70867

Note: Question asked: People sometimes describe themselves as belonging to the working class, the middle class or the upper or lower class. Would you describe yourself as belonging to one of them? Source: EVS/WVS (2020).

over 90 percent of respondents believe that social classes exist. Similar proportions, as in the recent World Values Survey in Table 6.2, continue to be willing to identify themselves in class terms.[8] In the US — often claimed to have the lowest levels of class consciousness — surveys that have asked directly have found that the vast majority of people have definite feelings about belonging to a class, understood in terms of differing economic power and resources (e.g., Centers 1949; Jackman and Jackman 1983; Vanneman and Cannon 1987, 21). In short, subjective class identification remains a recognized social fact in all these countries, however pertinent it may be in people's everyday thoughts.

In the nineteenth and much of the twentieth centuries, many labour leaders and leftist scholars invoked or presumed the "working class" identity of the core of non-managerial hired workers. It has often been assumed that a clearly working-class identity is fundamental for the development of oppositional labour consciousness or revolutionary consciousness. This article of faith persists in diminished forms. Several decades ago, in a generally insightful and constructive critique of prior scholarship on US workers' perceptions of class, Vanneman and Cannon (1987) centred their attention on the distinction between "working class" and "middle class" identities. Relying largely on general surveys in the US and UK and comparable standard class identity questions, they designated respondents as working class by imputing their lack of the economic, political and ideological control exercised by a presumed "middle class." Vanneman and Cannon (1987, 61) asserted: "To be middle class in America is to own productive property, or to have supervisory authority, or to perform mental labor at the expense of manual workers." They thereby conflate corporate capitalists and other owners, as well as those at various managerial levels, with professionals in various classes; they exclude non-managerial professional employees (and some other service workers) from legitimately seeing themselves as exploited or subordinated workers. Their empirical analysis convincingly showed that there was little difference between the workers they designated as working class in both countries in their inclination to subjectively identify as "working class." They attributed a lower general incidence of working-class identity in the US primarily to an overweening power of American capitalists and weak accommodating forms of the US labour movement and political party structures. Hence, goodbye to "American exceptionalism" in terms of class consciousness.

But we know from review of popular notions of class in Chapter 2 that many employed people in advanced capitalist societies now hold perceptions of themselves as part of a "working middle class" — subordinated to others in their jobs and sharing common lifestyles and distinct from the increasingly affluent above them, and also concerned not to fall into the increasingly visible destitute below them. We saw that this common perception is widely shared, for example, by steelworkers — long regarded by left scholars as at the core of the working class. Seeing yourself in the middle of the class structure does not necessarily disqualify you from being dominated by superiors or from developing a form of pro-labour consciousness. The forms of class consciousness outlined in Appendix 2 suggest this possibility among those in "the middle" who — just as those who identify as "working" or "lower" class — see themselves as subordinated to others above them. Those who identify as "upper" or "upper middle" class are not excluded from possible pro-labour views, but the chances of such class blindness are typically more remote.

We also know from Chapter 4 that industrial workers have made up a declining part of the class structure in advanced capitalism since at least the 1980s while non-managerial professional employees have made up a growing part. There is compelling evidence that these professional employees are experiencing worsening working conditions, equivalent to other non-managerial workers (see Livingstone 2019b; Livingstone, Adams and Sawchuk 2021). Such workers are excluded from the working class by many scholars, including Vanneman and Cannon. But they are being "proletarianized" — and thereby prone to developing higher levels of oppositional labour consciousness.

There is no necessary correspondence between objective class position and subjective class consciousness. The failure to find much revolutionary labour consciousness among industrial workers has frustrated many left intellectuals for a long time, to the extent that many have given up looking for it and rationalized or presumed its absence. However, to insist that a standard working-class identity is a necessary prerequisite for higher levels of oppositional labour consciousness is highly restrictive. We should investigate higher levels of class consciousness, as well as their relations with class identity, in their own terms, rather than dismissing their possibility because of either restrictive criteria of objective class positions or diminishing standard "working class" perceptions.

The Class Structure and Class Consciousness (CSCC 1980s) surveys in the early 1980s asked respondents to identify themselves in terms of standard class labels (i.e., working class, middle class or upper middle class).[9] Figure 6.1 summarizes the responses.

Variations in these class identities could be expected given particular class structures and different economic and political histories. But the basic pattern in most of these countries in the 1980s surveys showed majorities or near majorities with general middle-class identities, lesser numbers opting for working-class identities and relatively few choosing an upper-middle-class identity. More people at that time in most countries saw themselves in the middle class than in the working class, and few saw themselves above a common middle.

Only in the UK was there a majority (56 percent) claiming a working-class identity, while in Japan there was an even division between those with middle class (48 percent) and working class (47 percent) identities. It is beyond the scope of the current analysis to address national differences in any depth, but with regard to these exceptions, the UK was the

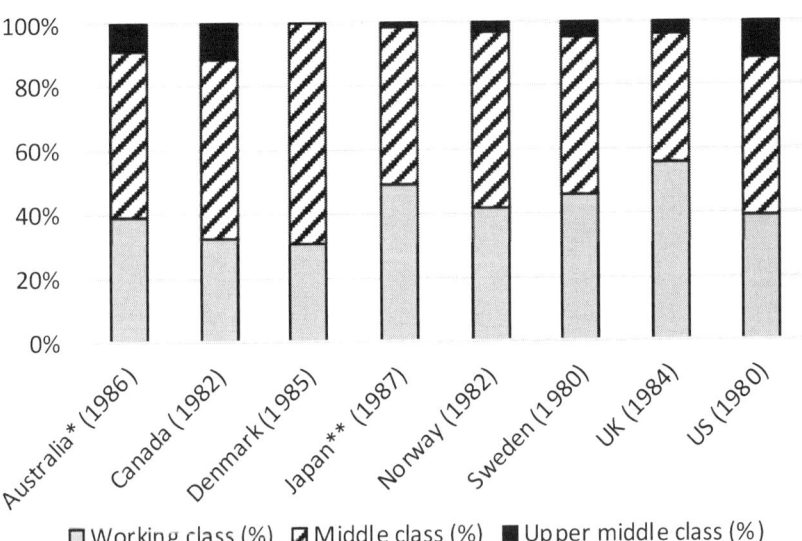

Figure 6.1 Standard Class Identities, Advanced Capitalist Countries, 1980s

☐ Working class (%) ▨ Middle class (%) ■ Upper middle class (%)

Australia 1986 (N=563*); Canada 1982 (N=807); Denmark 1986 (N=498); Japan 1987 (N=515**); Norway 1982 (N=1174); Sweden 1980 (N=640); UK 1984 (N=1204); US 1980 (N=902).
*Includes 37 "no classes" responses
**Includes 32 "other" responses
Sources: CSCC (1980s) Data archive; Canada Work Learning Surveys 1998–2016. 1982 CCS National Dataset.

first capitalist economy with large concentrations of industrial workers, established relatively strong working-class institutions and post-WWII Labour governments declaring support for the working class. In addition, in 1980, the UK had one of the highest trade union densities in Europe, with 50 percent of all workers and particularly industrial workers in unions (Visser 2006). Nevertheless, even in the UK, 40 percent opted for a middle-class identity in the early 1980s. As documented in Chapter 4, Japan has been distinctive among these advanced capitalist countries in retaining a higher proportion of industrial workers in the labour force. At least until the 1990s, there was a strong shared tradition in many large Japanese corporations of the "salaryman" starting at the bottom in collaborative lifelong work regimes, with relatively little mobility to higher professional status beyond. But in the more recent survey cited in Table 6.2, only a quarter of Japanese respondents identified as "working class" while upper-middle-class identifiers increased to 15 percent.

Longer trends in standard class identities in Canada have already been discussed in Chapter 2 (Figure 2.4). Findings for the 1982–2016 period are summarized in Figure 6.2.

The major trends in Canada from 1982 until 2016 are a decline in working-class identity, continued growth in middle-class identity and an increase in the still small numbers of those with upper-middle-class identities. Working-class identity declined from 32 percent in 1982 to 16 percent in 2016. Middle-class identity grew from 55 percent in 1982 to 60 percent in 2016. Upper-middle-class identity almost doubled, from 11 percent to 18 percent, over this period. The main expressed change in class identity since the early 1980s in Canada has been the declining numbers who see themselves as working class. This is likely related to the decline of the traditional core of the working class in industrial work and related trade unions, as documented in Chapter 4. The increase in recent decades in the proportion who see themselves as upper middle class is likely related to the increasing proportions of professional and managerial "white collar" jobs with relatively higher incomes and consumption capacities.

A wide array of surveys in the US from the 1960s to the present also suggest a slow growth in general middle-class identity and decline in working-class identity over this period.[10] Table 6.2 and Figure 6.2 suggest that, at least in some countries, there now may be about as many em-

Figure 6.2 Standard Class Identities, Canada 1982–2016 (%)

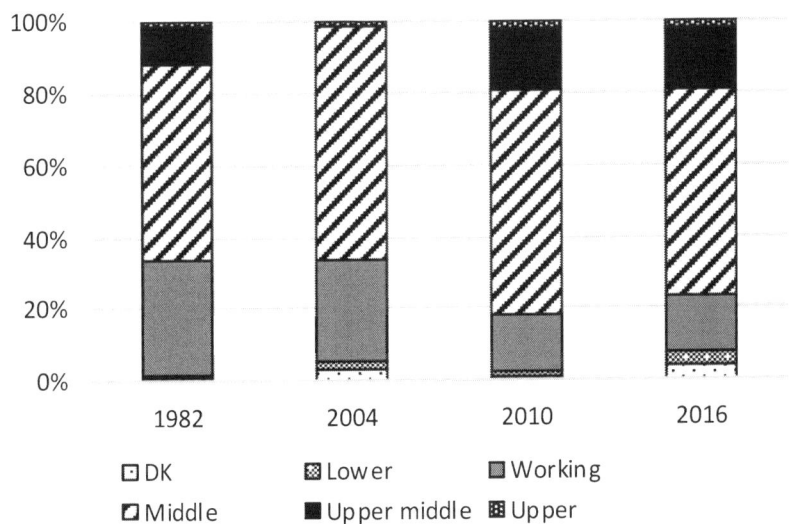

Sources: 1982 Clement and Myles (1994); Canada Work Learning Surveys. 1998–2016.

ployed people who see themselves as upper middle class as the declining numbers who hold clear working-class identities. However, the overall tendency so far — in the context of the widening of common consumption patterns concerning housing, clothing, food, entertainment, education, transport and information technology dimensions of lifestyle described in Chapter 2 — has been for most people to think of themselves as in the middle of whatever image of class structure they might hold.

No fully comparable surveys are available for all advanced capitalist countries since the 1980s, but the array of somewhat comparable studies is consistent with continuing recent trends of decreasing working-class identity and increasing middle-class identities. Explanations typically refer to some combination of the decline of organized industrial workers and widening consumption patterns. Both the survey profiles in Chapter 2 and more open-ended studies revealed a wider variety of views about the actual number and composition of classes in advanced capitalist societies (e.g., Willener 1970; Lopreato and Hazelrigg 1972), but, in fact, most people tended to give themselves some sort of middle-working identity. This suggests a degree of correspondence between subjective class identity and objective class situation that has rarely been pointed out by empirical researchers. However, in Charles Anderson's (1974, 137) judgement:

This middling, working identity *is* objectively rather accurate. For despite a [wide range of incomes], this income inequality is of secondary importance compared to the *similarity* of interests of the underlying masses concerning job security, inflationary squeezes, peace, rising personal tax burdens, public school quality, food and housing costs, medicine, consumer rights, clean air and water, street safety, and dozens of other matters which concern the [controlling class] only insofar as they threaten to disrupt their system of power and wealth. The [controlling class] in their personal lives are either profiting by these large-scale problems and/or remain largely unaffected by their existence — typically both.

This tendency toward a common middling, working identity and disaffection for those more favoured is confirmed by the most recent and widely reported Great British Class Survey. Savage (2015, 369, 388) summarizes:

> [All the classes] tend most to identify subjectively with being somewhere "in the middle".... While most people in Britain might not directly identify with a particular class, the extent of inequality, and the way it shapes people's life chance unequally, means that class is still deeply felt in people's identities.... Many people drew distinct and aggressive class boundaries.

It may be reasonable to assume that those who still identify clearly as "working class" are defining themselves as relatively subordinated to others in employment or relatively deprived in living conditions, as distinct from others who see themselves as in a middling class because of relatively greater income or job qualifications. Such "working class" numbers appear to have continued to decline in recent decades. The number of those who are evidently situated in the middle may have grown compared to the numbers of those who exhibit privilege above them and to those who suffer serious impoverishment below them. However, if we look further back at all the post-1945 survey results for the US, where such studies were most extensive, more cyclical patterns in the distribution of middle- and working-class identities, rather than simple linear trends, are found.[11] Given the contradictory imperatives underlying class relations generally and the actual changes in class composition documented in Chapter 4, it would be surprising if there were not substantial historical fluctuations in perceived subjective class identities. Continuation of recently growing middle-class identities is hardly inevitable — if more people are relegated to precarious employment and impoverishment, for example.

People who deny the relevance of any basic identifying features for themselves may still hold definite views about such features of others. They may have definite views about class relations more generally — and also be prepared to express them. We have seen that nearly everybody can locate themselves in standard class categories — if given the chance. Denial of the relevance of class identity is not sufficient reason to exclude consideration of views on other levels of class consciousness. The logically possible forms of class consciousness outlined at the beginning of this chapter and in Appendix 2 include options for those who deny their own class identity but have views on other aspects of class consciousness. Most pertinently, those who decline to offer a particular class of belonging may have definite views on oppositional class interest issues. Whether specific class identity is diverted, suppressed or repressed, people in advanced capitalist societies still develop views that relate to their material conditions on issues such as profits and strikes. Those who hold coherent oppositional class views without consistent class identities may be either "capitalist sympathizers" or "labour sympathizers." Fortunately, the surveys drawn upon here asked those without consistent class identities for their views on these other class issues.

So, the next questions are what patterns are found in oppositional class consciousness and how do these relate to these recent changes in class identity?

Oppositional Class Consciousness

Oppositional consciousness generally involves a sense of conflict between the interests of an affinity group and interests of one or more other groups. Most of the research on oppositional consciousness has understandably focused on oppressed groups' contention with systems of domination (e.g., Mansbridge and Morris 2001). In recent generations, feminist movements have challenged patriarchal male privilege in many forms. Many women with various sexual identities, as well as some men, have developed greater feminist oppositional consciousness in support of women's rights and rejected presumed male prerogatives.

Conversely, some men especially have reacted to feminist challenges with more vigorous assertions of established male rights. Oppositional gender consciousness, both in support of feminist interests and in defence of male privilege, is arguably greater than ever in advanced capitalism. Similar claims could be made about oppositional race consciousness, with mounting demands to address the rights of Black and Indigenous Peoples in many countries. Conversely, whites who presume their own racial identity may also hold a strong sense of oppositional racial consciousness. More generally, social identities can be associated with diverse forms of oppositional social consciousness.

With regard to oppositional *class* consciousness in capitalist societies, the most basic conflict is between capital and labour. The central issue is the rights of capital to profits versus the rights of labour to withhold it and the extent to which support for one of these rights is associated with disapproval for the other. As with class identity, aspects of oppositional class consciousness may not always be top of mind. They may be better regarded as attitudinal predispositions that are activated and change situationally. Many people appear to be more willing to express their opinions on issues related to racialization, sex, age and class than to think of themselves in terms of these identities. Such sentiments are not necessarily congruent with actions, but they can serve as indicators of prospects for action on issues when situations emerge. The stronger the sense of oppositional consciousness, the more likely one is to be mobilized in support of shared interests.

But, again, there have been few studies of higher levels of class consciousness since the 1970s. The previously mentioned Class Structure and Class Consciousness (CSCC 1980s) project in the 1980s, led by Erik Olin Wright (1997), is one of the few more recent cross-national empirical studies focused on oppositional class consciousness. This research network eventually included researchers and national surveys in ten advanced capitalist countries: United States (1980), Sweden (1980), Finland (1981), Norway (1982), Canada (1982), United Kingdom (1984), West Germany (1985), Denmark (1985), Australia (1986) and Japan (1987).[12] Most of these surveys included items related to class identity, oppositional consciousness and hegemonic (or revolutionary) consciousness, as summarized in Table 6.1 and Appendix 2. This was a project of unprecedented scope, and it remains a singular benchmark source for cross-national comparisons of levels of class consciousness.

But there has been very little comparative analysis of these data on class consciousness since the surveys were completed. These surveys are used in Chapter 4 to aid in 1980s analyses of class structure and in Figure 6.1 to compare standard class identities. The further national surveys I conducted in Canada in 1998, 2004, 2010 and 2016 replicated the same class consciousness items. Unfortunately, the cscc project was discontinued. The rare comparable data from more recent national surveys in other countries are cited where available.

Wright (1997, 410) relied on an index of five political attitudes tapping working-class or capitalist oppositional class interests, aggregated into "a fairly simple, transparent class consciousness scale." His empirical assessment was based mainly on the 1980s national surveys in the US, Sweden and Japan. His conclusions related mainly to patterns of the relationship between class location and class consciousness and are discussed in Chapter 7. Wright was aware of many of the limitations of these surveys and indicated that his model and measure of class consciousness in particular were merely part of a framework for defining an exploratory agenda of problems for empirical research in class analysis and class consciousness. Wright's "anti-capitalist index" has been criticized on several grounds, including the finding that the five attitudes do not appear to organize most people's attitudes in a consistent way (Savage 2000, 38–41). In contrast to the current logic outlined in Appendix 2, the Wright index also conflates at least one question about visions of future alternatives with several about oppositional class interests.[13] But very few subsequent assessments of class and class consciousness include such potentially valuable data for attitudes on both capital and labour rights. Wright was conceptually aware of the distinction between levels of oppositional and revolutionary working-class consciousness. His judgement was that, given the limitations of survey research methods, he would not stretch the data to operationalize different levels of class consciousness. However, Wright's survey data do offer the rarest of evidence to distinguish both oppositional and hegemonic/revolutionary class consciousness in the 1980s, and I use it for cross-national comparisons. Both Wright's data and mine are available for any who wish to do further comparative analyses.

It is remarkable how few studies of oppositional class consciousness there have been since the 1980s and particularly since the Great Recession. One of the few, inspired by both Mann (1973) and Wright, was an investigation of class consciousness in Indiana in 1998. Wallace and Junisbai (2003, 417) concluded: "Our results provide evidence that opposition to capitalists is alive and well in the new economy.... There is evidence for a broad, subterranean discontent targeted against capitalists and business executives." The authors' appeal for the revival of studies of oppositional class consciousness in the fertile ground of the "new economy" fell largely on deaf ears.

In the wake of the Great Recession of 2007–08, increasing economic inequality has stimulated a few further inquiries into psychological differences between classes that have touched on aspects of oppositional class consciousness (e.g., Keefer, Goode and Van Berkel 2015; Sawyer and Gampa 2020). Such well-intentioned studies, based on mixed sets of attitudes and class structures with unrepresentative samples, offer little more than the conclusion that indicators of alienation are significantly related to indicators of class consciousness. The continuing dearth of conceptually clear, empirically grounded studies of higher levels of class consciousness is at least partially an indictment of the lack of interest among mature scholars with access to research funding.

So, I proceed to look further at the CSCC surveys. In terms of empirical indicators of the central opposed class interests of capital and labour, the same two questions were asked in all of the 1980s CSCC surveys to estimate attitudes toward capitalist profit maximization and workers' right to strike. Many of those who declined to respond to a voluntary class identity question readily offered their views on these issues.

For capital's right to profit, the question was: Owners of corporations make gains at the expense of their workers. Do you strongly agree, somewhat agree, neither agree nor disagree, somewhat disagree, or strongly disagree?

For workers' right to strike the question was: During a strike, management should be prohibited by law from hiring workers to take the place of strikers. Do you strongly agree, somewhat agree, neither agree nor disagree, somewhat disagree, or strongly disagree?

Ideally, one might prefer questions that asked more directly about capitalists' right to profit maximization and hired workers' right to strike, but this was not possible. I should note that prior empirical studies I conducted in Ontario, Canada, during the 1980s with such direct items did find similar patterns to those summarized here (Livingstone 1987). The basic response patterns on these two questions for all countries with fully comparable data in the 1980s CSCC surveys are summarized in Table 6.3.

Table 6.3 Support for Right to Profit and Right to Strike, Advanced Capitalist Countries, 1980s (%)

Country	Owners Benefit		Right to Strike	
	Agree	Disagree	Agree	Disagree
Sweden	63	37	78	22
Japan	65	35	78	22
Canada	67	33	61	39
US	58	42	51	49
Norway	47	53	49	51
Australia	54	46	32	68

Sources: CSCC (1980s) Data Archive; Canada Work Learning Surveys 1998–2016; 1982 CCS National Dataset for Canada 1982.

Majorities in nearly all countries agreed that owners of corporations make gains at the expense of their workers, with somewhat stronger opposition in Canada, Japan and Sweden. Norway was the exception, with slightly more than half indicating more supportive views of corporate owners. This may reflect the strong historical ownership role of the Norwegian state in commercial corporations, especially in the exploitation of natural resources, including hydro-electric power, aluminum and then oil and gas (Kallevig 2005). Later, in 1990, a large sovereign wealth fund, Norges, was established. However, in contrast to Sweden, where labour organization initiatives had moved toward worker-ownership of private corporations, the Norwegian wealth fund was designed to participate in private corporate profit maximization and has become one of the major private equity owners on many of the largest private stock markets in most advanced capitalist countries. Profits are used to finance Norwegian pensions while employees in many countries are indirectly deprived of benefits (Rugemer 2019, 39). In most of these other countries, there was significantly more opposition to private corporate owners benefitting, but there was also disagreement that corporate owners benefitted unfairly by at least a third of respondents.

With regard to the right to strike, views were more mixed. Strong majorities supported the right to strike in Sweden, Japan and Canada, while views were split in Norway and the US. There was strong opposition to the right to strike in Australia. Australia's highly restrictive laws against industrial action have long been in breach of international law and are without peer among advanced capitalist economies in virtually denying the right to strike as a civil liberty (McCrystal 2010). Prior to the Australian survey in 1986, a Labour government with a 1983 landslide victory implemented the Prices and Incomes Accord, through which unions further agreed to restrict wage demands. A later related Australian national survey in 1995 (Western 1999) similarly found relatively wide opposition to unions and strikes as well as relatively strong support for private ownership of industry.

Since the 1980s, general sentiment on these rights issues has been challenged by private corporate neoliberal initiatives to enhance profits and to weaken the right to strike. The right to strike has been under attack at virtually every level across the world through measures of exclusion and repression, with union membership declining widely (Xhafa 2016). However, the evidence suggests that support for labour unions and strike rights have recently increased in response to attacks in some of these countries (e.g., Jones 2019). Similarly, the numbers who think that business corporations make too much profit may also have increased since the early 1990s (e.g., Pew Research Center 2017). The most recent US surveys find increasing antipathy to big business since the early 2000s and sharp increases in affinity for organized labour over the past decade (DiVito and Sojourner 2021).

Since the 1980s, only the Canadian national surveys have provided comparable trend information on these questions of corporate benefits and right to strike. The basic patterns are summarized in Table 6.4 for available years.

In spite of later private corporate offensives, the strong agreement that corporate owners benefitted at the expense of workers, which was found in Canada in 1982, continued in the later surveys, with about two-thirds indicating this view in all later surveys. Support for the right strike also continued to be supported by over 60 percent of respondents in all later surveys. There is some suggestion of possible general increase in both opposition to corporate owners benefitting and support for the right to strike in the most recent 2016 survey. But overall, general popular sentiments on both issues remained strong during this period, with clear majority support for the right to strike and opposition to corporate benefits. This pattern is in a context of small declines in Canadian union membership, mostly in the 1990s, followed by relatively resilient

Table 6.4 Support for Right to Profit and Right to Strike, Canada, 1982–2016 (%)

Year	Owners Benefit		Right to Strike	
	Agree	Disagree	Agree	Disagree
1982	67	33	61	39
2004	69	31	62	38
2010	65	35	64	36
2016	72	28	68	32

Source: Canada Work Learning Surveys 1998–2016.

membership levels more recently compared to most industrial countries (Stanford 2020).

A summary measure of general oppositional class consciousness is constructed by combining responses to both items. Those who deny that corporate owners gain at the expense of workers and also support hiring replacement workers to break strikes are seen as having a "pro-capital oppositional class consciousness." Conversely, those who agree that corporate owners gain over workers and oppose hiring replacement workers express "pro-labour oppositional consciousness." Those with inconsistent views or uncertainty on these items are considered to have "contradictory oppositional consciousness."[14] Figure 6.3 summarizes the 1980s findings for all available countries in the CSCC surveys when responses to both the corporate owners' gain and replacement workers items are combined.

Once again, both economic and political histories and recent organizational capacities of capital and labour may be related to varied expressions of oppositional class consciousness in these countries. However, the survey findings do suggest some general tendencies. Contradictory oppositional consciousness tended to be substantial (i.e., held by over a third of the labour force) everywhere. A tendency to pragmatic acceptance of *both* profit maximization and workers' right to strike as normatively tolerable — although logically inconsistent — is likely at the heart of this perspective.[15] Contradictory views were relatively more prevalent in countries where both pro-capital and pro-labour oppositional views were fairly evenly present. In Australia, Norway and the US, with both pro-capital and pro-labour views held by over 20 percent, contradictory views were more common than either oppositional view. In Japan and Canada, where pro-labour views were much more common than pro-capital ones, contradictory views were nearly as widespread as pro-

Figure 6.3 Oppositional Class Consciousness, Advanced Capitalist Countries, 1980s (%)

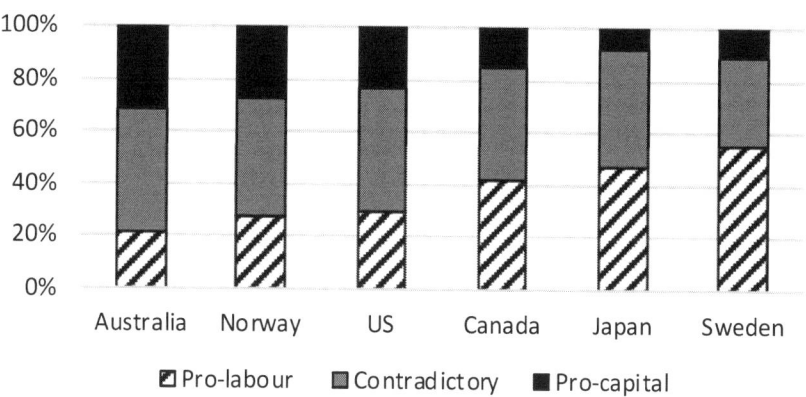

Sources: CSCC (1980s) Data Archive; Canada Work Learning Surveys 1998–2016; 1982 CCS National Dataset.

labour ones. In Sweden, where a majority held pro-labour oppositional views, contradictory views were notably less common, but they were still held by about a third.

One might expect a general correlation between pro-labour consciousness and trade union membership. The official union membership rates in these countries in 1980 were: Sweden 78 percent; Norway 58 percent; Australia 50 percent; Canada 35 percent; Japan 31 percent; US 20 percent (Visser 2006). The finding that Sweden had the highest pro-labour consciousness is consistent with having one of the highest rates of union membership and strongest labour organizations in the world, as well as a supportive social democratic regime at the time. But Norway and Australia also had majority unionization, and in their labour forces, pro-capital views were at least as widespread as pro-labour ones in relation to their institutions and legislation. The additional finding that Japan, Canada and even perhaps the US, with relatively weak union movements, had more widespread expressions of pro-labour oppositional consciousness than some other countries with majority union memberships may point to the limits of trade union organizations that Marx suggested around their origins. In particular, pro-labour views were much higher than pro-capital views in Japan. The prevalence there of relatively weak enterprise-based unions shaped by the postwar US occupation and strong corporate governance of workplaces in a coordinated-economy model may suggest that Japanese workers — in spite of relatively common "working class" identities — were relatively restricted in expressing their class interests within these organizations.

Overall, the most important finding on general oppositional class consciousness in the 1980s is probably that in nearly all these advanced capitalist countries — where both the mode of production and mode of thought had long been dominated by elite class forces (including corporate leaders as well as political, cultural and media allies) — pro-labour oppositional class consciousness was usually at least as widespread as pro-capital consciousness and often much more so. Contradictory class consciousness among "the masses" generally serves dominant class control. Pro-labour oppositional consciousness represents a continuing challenge to capitalist ideological dominance, and plenty of this was found in many of these countries. Recent estimates on this general oppositional class consciousness composite are only available from the Canadian national surveys. The findings for the entire 1982–2016 period for Canada are summarized in Figure 6.4.

The findings for this series of Canadian surveys suggest a high degree of general continuity in these elements of oppositional class consciousness over the 1982–2016 period. In all available surveys, at least a plurality (44 to 54 percent) expressed contradictory oppositional consciousness. But in all surveys, oppositional labour consciousness (33 to 42 percent) was around three times as great as oppositional capitalist consciousness (10 to 15 percent). Throughout this period, as Table 6.4

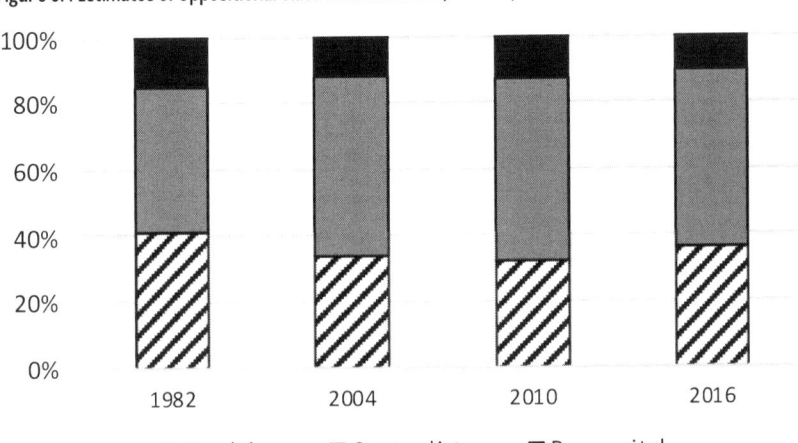

Figure 6.4 Estimates of Oppositional Class Consciousness, Canada, 1982–2016

Sources: Canada Work Learning Surveys 1998–2016 (includes 1982 CCS National Dataset).

documents, general popular sentiments opposing corporate profit-taking at the expense of workers (and consumers) as well as support for workers' right to strike to protect their jobs were each expressed by clear majorities of the employed labour force. Many people likely shared general concerns about their own job insecurities and cost of living pressures related to housing and education costs, along with anger or envy at the privileged benefits of the very rich. So, pro-labour sentiments were much more common than pro-capital ones, but views of labour rights were often inconsistently held in combination with capital rights. This is a classic condition of capitalist ideological dominance, depending at least as much on a mixed and contradictory sense of interests among the "dispossessed" as on as pro-capital consciousness among supporters.

My tentative conclusion, on the basis of the available evidence in these advanced capitalist countries, is that pro-labour oppositional class consciousness has continued to be much greater that pro-capital oppositional consciousness and that pro-capital oppositional consciousness may have diminished somewhat in some countries in recent decades. None of the few prior direct studies of oppositional class consciousness recognized the extent of general oppositional labour consciousness in these countries — which according to the available indicators has ranged upward from at least 20 percent of the employed labour force. But pragmatic acceptance of both the opposed rights of capital and labour by much of the labour force — as well as probable limited association with a clear sense of an alternative way forward by many with coherent oppositional labour consciousness — have continued to enable the reproduction of capitalist dominance of economic and political conditions. In the absence of comparable trend evidence for most advanced capitalist countries, I can only urge further studies of relevant indicators.

Oppositional Class Consciousness by Class Identity

Assuming these patterns of oppositional class consciousness have some validity, what relation, if any, do they have with subjective class identity? Table 6.5 summarizes the proportions of those in the employed labour force with different standard class identities who expressed pro-labour oppositional views in the 1980s CSCC surveys.

Table 6.5 Proportion with Pro-Labour Oppositional Consciousness (%) by Standard Class Identity, Advanced Capitalist Countries, 1980s (%)

Country	Upper Middle Class	Middle Class	Working Class	No Valid Class ID
Sweden	29	43	62	61
Canada	36	41	42	43
US	14	28	37	30
Japan	14	28	36	30
Norway	16	20	35	32
Australia	12	21	22	23

Sources: CSCC (1980s) Data Archive; Canada Work Learning Surveys 1998–2016; 1982 CCS National Dataset.

Keeping in mind that pro-labour oppositional views were generally expressed by minorities in nearly all countries, there was a greater tendency for those with working-class identities to have pro-labour views than those with upper-middle-class identities. Those who saw themselves as a cut above were less likely to be sympathetic with labour versus capital interests.

In Australia and Norway, with the highest general levels of pro-capital oppositional consciousness, the majority with upper-middle-class identities exhibited pro-capital oppositional views. In countries with less pro-capital oppositional consciousness, many of those with upper-middle-class identities had more contradictory oppositional views.

There was generally little difference between those with working-class identity and general middle-class identity in the proportions expressing pro-labour views. The greatest difference was in Sweden, the only country where a general majority held pro-labour views. But, as Figure 6.1 shows, just as many Swedes considered themselves to be generally middle class as working class. Many Swedes with pro-labour views thought of themselves as middle class. This was more likely the case in Australia, Canada and the US, where general middle-class identities were even more common. The basic point to make here is that identifying oneself in the middle of a class structure between the very rich and the poor does not prevent the development of pro-labour oppositional class consciousness.

It should also be registered that many respondents to some of the CSCC 1980s surveys were not given a chance to identify themselves in terms of standard class identities. This included many who would have readily done so as well as a few who would have declined. The responses to the class rights questions for those without voluntary class identities are also summarized in Table 6.5. The oppositional consciousness response patterns among those who did not provide class identities were similar to the common general patterns in the respective countries. Around 60 percent of Swedes who did not provide a class identity expressed pro-labour views, compared to only around 20 percent of Australians. Again, not readily volunteering a specific class identity does not disqualify one from holding views on opposed class interests.

Once more, trend assessment of relations between class identity and oppositional consciousness can only be made for the Canadian case. The basic patterns for 1982, 2004, 2010 and 2016 are summarized in Table 6.6.

Table 6.6 Proportion with Pro-Labour Oppositional Consciousness by Standard Class Identity, Canada, 1982–2016 (%)

	Upper Middle Class	Middle Class	Working Class	No Valid Class ID
1982	36	41	42	43
2004	34	34	35	26
2010	31	35	31	20
2016	32	37	43	17

Sources: Canada Work Learning Surveys 1998–2016 (includes 1982 CCS National Dataset).

As Table 6.5 showed, differences in pro-labour oppositional consciousness by class identity were relatively small in Canada in the 1982 survey. Around 40 percent of respondents with each of these different class identities all expressed pro-labour views. There was a slightly greater tendency for those with upper middle-class identities to hold pro-capital views. But both pro-labour and contradictory views were more common than pro-capital views among all class identities. These patterns continued in more recent surveys. The most significant change in post-1982 surveys is the reduced numbers with pro-labour views among those with no valid class identity. However, this is largely attributable to the fact that in later surveys in Canada this group is reduced to the extremely small numbers who refuse to respond to the standard class identity question; these people also have exceptionally high inconsistent or non-response to the class interest questions (around 75 percent). Overall, both working-class and general middle-class identities have been about equally likely to be associated with oppositional labour consciousness. Those with upper-middle-class identities have differed mainly in the declining minority (dropping from 27 percent in 1982 to 13 percent in 2016) associated with pro-capital views. Among the increasing minority with upper-middle-class identities, diminishing numbers are inclined to defend the interests of capital.

Pro-labour views have been much more common than pro-capital views at all these class identity levels in Canada, still somewhat less so for those with upper middle-class identities. But holding a general middle-class identity — or even an upper-middle-class identity — has not prohibited expression of pro-labour oppositional consciousness; in fact, given the increased tendency toward general middle-class identity, a numerical majority of those who express pro-labour oppositional consciousness have middle-class identities themselves. I'll say that again. A general middle-class subjective class identity is the most common one associated with pro-labour oppositional class consciousness — even if similar numbers of these middle-class identifiers express contradictory oppositional class consciousness. At minimum, the varied patterns found in the available 1980s cross-national surveys coupled with the time series findings for Canada suggest a contingent and somewhat fluid relation between class identity and oppositional class consciousness.

Hegemonic versus Revolutionary Class Consciousness

The highest or most fully developed level of class consciousness explored here involves combining oppositional consciousness with clear visions of a preferred future. Those with "hegemonic capitalist consciousness" not only have consistent pro-capital oppositional interests but have a clear vision of essential conditions for continuance; conversely, those with a "revolutionary labour consciousness" not only have coherent pro-labour oppositional interests but have a vision of alternative organization of society.

To be more specific, "hegemonic capitalist consciousness" is characterized by an upper- or upper-middle-class identity and coherent support for strike breaking and denial of the notion of corporate exploitation of workers, combined with defence of a profit-driven economy and managerial prerogative. At the other extreme, "revolutionary labour consciousness" is marked by a subordinate (lower-middle, working or lower) class identity and coherent opposition to strike breaking and recognition of corporate exploitation of workers, combined with preference for a non-profit economy and worker self-management.

But once more, these are merely logical possibilities. The extent to which these most fully developed forms actually exist is a matter for empirical investigation. Hegemonic and revolutionary class consciousness are the forms of class consciousness most likely related to the defence of capitalism or its transformation, respectively. Up to this point, there has been almost no large-scale investigation of this level of class consciousness. The few studies that touched on the issue — Mann (1973) and Wallace and Junisbai (2003), for example —typically dismissed the possibility of revolutionary labour consciousness. Mann's (1973) inquiry — focused on issues of "macro control" — found no expression of revolutionary class consciousness even among the "new working class" in highly automated French factories. Wallace and Junisbai (2003, 417) more recently merely assumed that the prospects are "dim."

My own earlier studies based on a series of surveys between 1978 and 1984 in Ontario with direct measures comparable to those used here (Livingstone 1985, 56) found that "only very small proportions of the population had hegemonic capitalist or revolutionary labour levels of class consciousness.... Revolutionary class consciousness currently appears to be highly limited even in the core of the Ontario industrial working class." The "very small proportions" referred to were a few percentage points in the overall population and labour force, quite tiny indeed. I noted at that time that earlier local studies in some countries had found indications of revolutionary consciousness ranging as high as 15 percent in particular non-managerial employment classes in different times and places. I stressed that further sensitive general inquiries were much needed. This remains true. I return to relations between class and class consciousness in the next chapter.

The two questions initially used in the 1980s CSCC survey series to estimate alternative visions of society refer to an alternative to a profit-driven economy and an alternative to capitalist control of the labour process. To my knowledge, these data have remained largely unexamined by other researchers.

The question on alternative modes of production asks about an economy without the profit motive: It is possible for a modern economy to run effectively without the profit motive. Do you strongly agree, somewhat agree, neither agree nor disagree, somewhat disagree, or strongly disagree?

The question on alternative labour process asks about worker control: Non-management could run things without bosses. Do you strongly agree, somewhat agree, neither agree nor disagree, somewhat disagree, or strongly disagree?

Once again, more direct questions about preferences for capitalist and post-capitalist alternatives might be preferred, but this is the hand I was dealt. The basic responses to these questions on the 1980s surveys in the countries with comparable data are summarized in Table 6.7.

Table 6.7 Support for Non-Profit and Worker-Control Alternatives, Advanced Capitalist Countries, 1980s (%)

	Non-Profit Economy		Worker Control	
Country	Agree	Disagree	Agree	Disagree
Norway	68	32	44	56
Sweden	42	58	47	53
Canada	34	66	39	61
US	30	70	45	55
Australia	25	75	42	58

Sources: cscc (1980s) Data Archive; Canada Work Learning Surveys 1998–2016; 1982 ccs National Dataset.

Dominant themes in bourgeois ideology incessantly promote private profit maximization and naturalize managerial prerogative in paid workplaces. On these grounds, one might expect to find little popular support in the employed labour force for either a non-profit economy or worker self-management in most countries. On the contrary, there was substantial minority support for both a non-profit economy and worker self-management in all these countries. Indeed, in Norway, with a long tradition of state ownership of commercial corporations benefitting Norwegians, there was majority support for a non-profit economy.[16] Support for both a non-profit economy and worker self-management were expressed by at least a quarter of respondents in all countries. Demand for worker self-management was generally relatively greater than support for a non-profit economy. In these countries with highly qualified labour forces, many had made considerable investment in their "human capital" but with more limited recognition in their jobs.

Excepting the nationalizing twist of Norway, private profit maximizing remained widely preferred to non-profit, especially in the US and Australia, where organized labour was weakest or most compromised.

Trends on these questions can only be assessed for the Canadian case. The basic 1982, 2010 and 2016 patterns are summarized in Table 6.8.

Table 6.8 Support for Non-Profit and Worker-Control Alternatives, Canada, 1982–2016 (%)

Year	Non-Profit Economy		Worker Control	
	Agree	Disagree	Agree	Disagree
1982	34	66	39	61
2010	45	55	—	—
2016	46	54	44	56

Sources: Canada Work Learning Surveys 1998–2016 (includes 1982 CCS National Dataset).

Canadian support for a non-profit economy increased over this period (from 34 percent to 46 percent) and support for worker control may have increased somewhat (from 39 percent to 44 percent), too. But the growing support for a non-profit economy as an alternative to a capitalist economy coupled with the growing opposition to corporate owners' profit taking is most notable and should be tracked in any further studies.

Alternative Visions: Potential Defenders versus Transformers

An even more pertinent question for potential social change is the extent to which these notions of the role of profit and workplace control might combine in people's minds to constitute alternative visions of the future. On the one hand, those who support profit maximization and managerial prerogative in paid workplaces have clear pro-capitalist visions and may be considered potential advocates or "defenders" of the capitalist system. On the other hand, those who support the possibility of an alternative economy based on worker control and not driven by profits are potential "transformers." The general extent to which these alternative tendencies have existed in these countries are estimated in Table 6.9, which also includes the proportions of the labour force with more inconsistent or contradictory images of the future in these terms.

Table 6.9 General Defenders versus Transformers of Capitalism, Advanced Capitalist Countries, 1980s (%)

Country	Defenders	Uncertain	Transformers
Australia (1986)	50	35	15
Norway (1982)	20	47	33
Sweden (1980)	33	36	31
US (1980)	44	41	15
Canada (1982)	41	41	18
Canada (2016)	37	36	27

Sources: CSCC (1980s) Data Archive; Canada Work Learning Surveys 1998–2016 (includes 1982 CCS National Dataset).

In the 1980s, the strongest combined defence for the profit motive and managerial prerogative, in both absolute terms and relative to transformers, was found in the countries with the weakest labour movements: Australia (50 percent versus 15 percent) and the US (44 percent versus 15 percent). In all countries, those with contradictory views on these issues made up over a third of the labour force. For most of the employed labour force, a possible alternative to capitalism seems to have been out of sight and out of mind.

In terms of general support for a transformed non-profit economy with worker self-management, in the 1980s this ranged from 15 percent in both Australia and the US and 18 percent in Canada, to over 30 percent in Norway and Sweden, the countries with the strongest labour movements.

The more recent, 2016, data available for Canada, also summarized in Table 6.9, suggest that the hegemonic view of no real alternative to a profit-driven economy controlled by a managerial hierarchy has continued to be accepted by a plurality (41 percent in 1982 and 37 percent in 2016). A similar, slightly declining proportion in 2016 still express uncertain preferences. However, combined support for both a non-profit economy and worker control appears to have increased from 18 percent to 27 percent — which suggests *a growing predisposition to post-capitalist alternatives* in the general labour force. Since the onset of the COVID 19 pandemic, receptivity to such major economic system change has probably increased substantially, with relevant surveys in some advanced capitalist countries finding majorities in favour of either complete reform or major system changes (e.g., Devlin, Schumacher and Moncus 2021).

The Full Range of Class Consciousness

The central issue is how such visions of society in advanced capitalist countries have combined with other levels of class consciousness to constitute the full range of forms of class consciousness, including both hegemonic capitalist consciousness and revolutionary labour consciousness. Table 6.10 provides a summary for all available countries from the 1980s CSCC surveys. (Again, the logic for all seven forms of class consciousness is provided in Appendix 2).

Table 6.10 Full Range of Consciousness, Advanced Capitalist Countries, 1980s (%)

	Australia	Canada	Norway	Sweden	US
Hegemonic capitalist consciousness	1	1	1	1	1
Oppositional capitalist consciousness	1	1	1	1	1
Capitalist sympathizer	29	13	27	10	32
Contradictory class consciousness	47	44	44	34	47
Labour sympathizer	13	25	11	28	15
Oppositional labour consciousness	6	13	11	18	12
Revolutionary labour consciousness	4	4	7	11	3

Effective employed sample sizes: Australia N=1167; Canada N=1758; Norway N=1691; Sweden N=1137; US N=1700.
Sources: CSCC Data Archive; Canada Work Learning Surveys 1998–2016; 1982 CCS National Dataset.

Contradictory class consciousness was the most common form in all countries, ranging from 34 percent to 47 percent of all respondents. Again, this partly reflects a pragmatic normative acceptance of both profit maximization and workers' right to strike. From either a hegemonic capitalist perspective or a revolutionary labour perspective, these two rights are ultimately irreconcilable. But dominant ideological messages presume the sanctity and necessity of profits and stress the practical imperative for workers to worry about their job security. Nevertheless, in all available countries, the combination of oppositional and revolutionary labour consciousness far outnumbered those with oppositional and hegemonic capitalist consciousness by a ratio of at least five to one. *Everywhere, oppositional and revolutionary labour consciousness were much more widespread than oppositional and hegemonic capitalist consciousness.*

When those with clear visions of alternatives are distinguished from more diffuse oppositional views, the proportions who held hegemonic capitalist visions of society with upper-middle-class identities were only around 1 percent of the labour force in all countries. Those who held revolutionary labour views with subordinate class identities were also small but were at least 3 percent in all countries and several times greater than hegemonic capitalist proportions everywhere. The greatest disproportions were in Nordic countries, with over 10 percent expressing revolutionary labour consciousness in Sweden and somewhat less in Norway. The existence of larger numbers with more developed revolutionary labour consciousness in these countries is consistent with their larger labour movements and sympathetic social democratic governments. However, the finding that in all instances those with revolutionary labour consciousness far outnumbered those with hegemonic capitalist consciousness should be a point of reference for further studies.

Once more, I can draw on the later Canadian national surveys to estimate more recent changes in the full distribution of class consciousness. The findings are summarized in Table 6.11.

Table 6.11 Full Range of Class Consciousness, Canada, 1982–2016 (%)

	1982	2004*	2010*	2016
Hegemonic capitalist consciousness	1	—	—	2
Oppositional capitalist consciousness	1	5	3	1
Capitalist sympathizer	13	8	11	8
Contradictory class consciousness	44	54	55	54
Labour sympathizer	25	12	7	7
Oppositional labour consciousness	13	22	26	21
Revolutionary labour consciousness	4	—	—	8

*Alternative vision questions to distinguish hegemonic from oppositional consciousness omitted in 2004 and 2010 surveys.
Sources: Canada Work Learning Surveys 1998–2016 (includes 1982 CCS National Dataset).
Effective employed sample sizes: 1982 N=1758; 2004 N=2865; 2010 N=1256; 2016 N=2979.

Contradictory class consciousness appears to have continued to be the most common form throughout this period in Canada, with around half expressing views that mix support for capital and labour rights, and with many of these also having inconsistent preferences for capitalist and post-capitalist visions of society. Such contradictory class consciousness may have ranged from about 44 to 55 percent of the entire employed labour force. The tendency for pragmatic acceptance of both profit maximization and workers' right to strike as normative has remained at the heart of this perspective. Such pragmatic acceptance of profit maximizing at least partially explains why around a quarter of all Canadians voted for economically conservative free market parties in recent elections. But, as noted previously, pro-labour oppositional consciousness has been much more common than pro-capital oppositional consciousness throughout this period. Those with subordinate class identity and pro-labour oppositional views in 2016 represented nearly 30 percent of respondents compared to 3 percent with dominant class identity and pro-capital oppositional consciousness: a ratio of 10 to 1. There may have been a significant increase in those with oppositional labour consciousness since 1982. The proportion with revolutionary labour consciousness may also have increased significantly, from about 4 percent to 8 percent. Conversely, those with upper-middle-class identities and either oppositional capitalist or hegemonic capitalist consciousness have remained at a few percentage points. This possible increase in revolutionary labour consciousness remains limited to a relatively small proportion of the labour force. But any absolute or relative increases in revolutionary consciousness compared to hegemonic capitalist consciousness warrant careful scrutiny going forward. With their highly developed class consciousness and definite visions of the future, respondents with revolutionary labour consciousness — or hegemonic capitalist consciousness — may represent those with the greatest potential to lead transformation — or defence — of the capitalist system, respectively.

These possible absolute and relative increases in the proportions with revolutionary labour consciousness in Canada should be considered in relation to the levels of class consciousness over this period in other countries. It is notable that in the 1980s CSCC surveys summarized in Table 6.10, similar levels of revolutionary labour consciousness (3 to 4 percent) were found in Australia and the US as well as Canada. The possible increase in revolutionary consciousness in Canada indicated in the 2016 survey would bring it closer to that found in Sweden in the early 1980s. However, as preconditions for such development, both Sweden and Canada in the 1980s had greater absolute levels of general oppositional labour consciousness and such levels relative to pro-capital oppositional consciousness than the other countries in these samples. As summarized in Figure 6.3, Sweden in that period was 56 percent pro-labour versus 11 percent pro-capital, and Canada was 42 percent pro-labour versus 15 percent pro-capital. Oppositional views in other countries were closer. The US was 30 percent pro-labour versus 23 percent pro-capital; in Norway, pro-labour and pro-capital levels were about equal (28 percent versus 28 percent); and in Australia, pro-capital oppositional consciousness (32 percent) exceeded pro-labour consciousness (22 percent). In the early 1980s, Sweden and Canada had corporatist economic reform programs underway and social democratic parties suggesting economic alternatives. Sweden had a stronger progressive labour movement and a responsive social democratic government that had begun to implement profit controls and workplace democratization measures. Arguably, these measures "came closer to the ideal of a classless society than any other country" (Meidner 1993, 226), but popular sentiments in favour of pro-labour measures were relatively stronger in Canada than in these other countries besides Sweden at the time, enabling further growth. Subsequent union membership has also been relatively resilient in Canada (Stanford 2020). What has happened to higher levels of class consciousness in all these countries more recently remains largely a matter of speculation, with further inquiry much needed.

None of these observations are offered to explain these distributions of committed supporters and opponents of capitalism, merely as contextual information. Both defensive reproduction of the capitalist system and any transformative movement are likely to be dependent on at least tacit support of substantial numbers beyond the small core numbers with hegemonic and revolutionary class consciousness. The available evidence at least suggests that the prospects for transformation may be growing in some places.

Class Consciousness and Support for the Poor and Climate Change

If expressed levels of class consciousness are to have implications for human action, they should be associated with views on more specific social issues. The two issues examined here are support for the poor and concern with the existential threat of global warming to human life.

Class Consciousness and Support for the Poor

How has class consciousness related to the persistent social problem of human poverty? All the CSCC country surveys providing class consciousness data in Table 6.10 also asked the question "Many in [your country] get less income than they deserve." Agreement with this statement may be taken to indicate preparedness to support redistributive measures to improve the material conditions of poor people and provide more equal opportunities for living decent lives. This issue has historically been a highly divisive one in many advanced capitalist countries, with the more affluent tending to see the poverty of others as their own individual responsibility and the less well-to-do pointing to general economic conditions (e.g., Howard, Freeman, Wilson and Brown 2017). But in recent decades, with increasingly conspicuous wealth and visible impoverishment, there has been a general increase in sentiments of support for poverty reduction in many countries (Barrientos and Neff 2010; Hall, Leary and Greevy 2014). The relations between general forms of class consciousness and such sentiments of support for the poor in the 1980s are summarized in Table 6.12.

Table 6.12 Support for the Poor by Class Consciousness, Advanced Capitalist Countries, 1980s (% agree)

Class Consciousness Level	Australia	Canada	Norway	Sweden	US
Hegemonic capitalist	27	37	*	38	37
Oppositional capitalist	20	53	46	*	68
Capitalist sympathizer	27	48	52	50	52
Contradictory	53	68	66	68	73
Labour sympathizer	69	75	86	87	83
Oppositional labour	72	73	73	81	83
Revolutionary labour	82	81	88	88	88
Total labour force %	48	68	67	76	71
Total N	1020	1723	1660	1062	1552

*Less than five cases.
Sources: CSCC (1980s) Data Archive; Canada Work Learning Surveys 1998–2016; 1982 CCS National Dataset.

In nearly all these countries in the 1980s, those with hegemonic capitalist consciousness were distinctive in their majority disagreement with this poverty statement. In stark contrast, the vast majority of those with both revolutionary and oppositional labour consciousness agreed with the statement. Generally, those who saw themselves at the upper level of the class structure, with a clear sense of its profit-centred essence, were loath to support measures that might diminish competition among potential hired labour. Conversely, those with any oppositional labour consciousness strongly supported measures that could enhance decent living conditions.

The 2016 Canadian survey repeated the same question about support for the poor. The comparative 1982 and 2016 findings are summarized in Table 6.13.

Table 6.13 Support for the Poor by Class Consciousness, Canada, 1982 and 2016 (% agree)

Class Consciousness Level	1982	2016
Hegemonic capitalist	37	31
Oppositional capitalist	53	51
Capitalist sympathizer	48	58
Contradictory	68	83
Labour sympathizer	75	88
Oppositional labour	73	94
Revolutionary labour	81	97
Total labour force %	68	84

Sources: Canada Work Learning Surveys 1998–2016 (includes 1982 CCS National Dataset).

The main point to observe is that general agreement on poverty support measures in Canada increased over this period from two-thirds to 84 percent. Support increased across the board — except for those with hegemonic and oppositional capitalist consciousness. As in all countries in the 1980s, the majority of those with a hegemonic capitalist mentality continued to refuse concessions. In this period, support for poverty reduction increased to near total unanimity among the larger numbers with pro-labour consciousness — but state austerity measures prevailed, consistent with the influence of tiny numbers that held hegemonic capitalist views.

Class Consciousness and Climate Change

One of the most pressing current issues is the effects of climate change. As noted in the Introduction, the accumulating scientific evience indicates that global warming is rapidly approaching a tipping point that would lead to irreversible catastrophic damage to the ecosystem and life on earth. In the wake of demonstrable increases in average temperatures, storms, fires and droughts, as well as virtually unanimous scientific consensus, widespread documentation on social media and strong advocacy by diverse political interest groups, there has been a substantial increase in public concern about climate change. Surveys in the first decade of this century in the US found only around a third of respondents felt that global warming was a threat to human life (Nisbet and Myers 2007). By 2020, two-thirds of US respondents believe we are facing a climate emergency, with even higher proportions who believe this in most other advanced capitalist countries (United Nations Development Program 2021). Table 6.14 summarizes the findings of the 2016 national survey in Canada on the linkage between class consciousness and views on whether global warming is a threat to human life.

Table 6.14 Threat of Global Warming to Human Life by Class Consciousness, Canada, 2016 (% agree/disagree)

Class Consciousness Level	% Agree	% Disagree
Hegemonic capitalist	45	55
Oppositional capitalist	70	30
Capitalist sympathizer	69	31
Contradictory	81	19
Labour sympathizer	90	10
Oppositional labour	85	15
Revolutionary labour	94	6
Total labour force %	82	18

Sources: Canada Work Learning Surveys 1998–2016. CWKE 2016 Total N=2509.

In 2016, a strong majority of all Canadians in the employed labour force (82 percent) agreed that global warming is a threat to human life.[17] A clear majority of those at most levels of class consciousness now accept this view. The strongest support is among those with revolutionary labour consciousness and others with pro-labour oppositional consciousness. In striking contrast, a majority (55 percent) of those with hegemonic capitalist class consciousness are almost the only ones in denial about the threat of global warming. That is, only people who consistently hold pro-capital views and also consider themselves to be in the upper classes in capitalist society are mostly inclined to refuse to accept the magnitude of the threat to life in general — and to their perceived privileged status within this system. This is a classic elite class mentality — to deny civilizational threats even as many others do not have the wherewithal to avoid threats happening in their everyday lives. On the other hand, those with pro-labour labour consciousness appear to have the most coherent set of views that could lead to concerted action for serious alternatives to address climate change.

Concluding Remarks

What we have here is a working hypothesis building on accepted conceptions of three levels of class consciousness (i.e., class identity, oppositional and hegemonic) and an exploration of limited available data to address the extent of seven forms of class consciousness in advanced capitalism. While there have been numerous empirical studies of class consciousness in advanced capitalist societies, the vast majority of these have been concerned with aspects of class awareness (images of class structure or subjective class identity) or specific political attitudes. There has been little empirical effort to study the three basic levels of expressed class consciousness simultaneously.[18] The systematic exploration of these three basic levels of class consciousness here with use of the rare available cross-national national survey data has generated some novel findings about forms and trends that require further critical inquiry to confirm validity. However, I suggest the following tentative conclusions at this point:

- The increasing incidence of middle-class identities found by many studies in the late twentieth century appears to have continued. While many studies explained this trend in terms of common consumption patterns or dominant ideology, it is perfectly sensible for most of those in the employed labour force to see themselves in the middle between affluent capitalist owners of the means of production on the one hand and those evidently excluded from decent employment on the other.

- Oppositional class consciousness, the extent to which people recognize opposition of interest with another class or classes, has been subjected to much less study. Contradictory oppositional class consciousness has continued to be the most common perspective during this period, generally held by around half of the employed labour force. The core of the contradiction has been a tendency to pragmatic acceptance of two ultimately irreconcilable rights, both profit maximization and the right to strike, as normative.

- Oppositional labour consciousness has been more common than oppositional capitalist consciousness in most of these countries. At least 20 percent of the employed labour force have consistently expressed support for the right to strike *and* opposition to profit maximization, and in most countries the proportions have been much higher.

- Middle-class identifiers are increasingly associated with pro-labour oppositional consciousness and represent the most current potential for fuller development of oppositional and revolutionary labour consciousness.

- Hegemonic *capitalist* consciousness appears to have remained limited to small numbers (around 1 percent of the labour force). Revolutionary *labour* consciousness in Canada may have increased between the early 1980s and 2016, from about 4 percent to 8 percent. Such numbers elsewhere are open to speculation, but these numbers indicating fully developed hegemonic — or revolutionary — class consciousness represent the most likely potential leaders of actual economic and political change ultimately defending — or transforming — the capitalist system.

- Nordic country surveys in the 1980s found the highest yet detected popular support for a transformative post-capitalist vision (around one-third of the employed) but the most recent Canadian survey approaches these levels — and other countries could as well.

- Oppositional and hegemonic levels of class consciousness are associated with attitudes on important social policy issues and these relations are worthy of much further study. This includes both the strong support of those with revolutionary labour consciousness for addressing issues of poverty and global warming — and the strong opposition of those with hegemonic capitalist consciousness on these same issues.

The worldviews emerging from the cumulative experience of "common" people should neither be denied because they have always been largely unrecorded, nor should they be identified simply with the dominant intellectual formulations of modes of thought of any period. The class interests expressed in these surveys suggest contending conceptions that are implicit in general human activity (Gramsci 1971: 335). The ideological efforts of both pro-capital and pro-labour agents to direct and shape these views along the lines drawn in Chapter 5 are just one mediating factor.

The general profiles of class consciousness here might suggest to some a sufficiently widespread contradictory consciousness to enable reproduction of capitalist relations of production with relatively small numbers of solid supporters, far less than a majority of all citizens or potential voters. Conversely, the much greater pro-labour oppositional consciousness than pro-capital consciousness, and the higher incidence of revolutionary labour consciousness than hegemonic capitalist consciousness, suggest much greater potential for mobilizing such dispositions for alternatives to capitalism. The surveys in this chapter found that in recent times over 10 percent of the labour force of several advanced capitalist countries have been coherently supportive of capital's rights over workers' rights. But much higher proportions have been consistently supportive of workers' rights over capital's rights. It is arguable that with mounting evidence of economic inequities and ecological disasters pro-labour anti-capitalist views are becoming more coherent and widespread. Certainly, there is evidence of widespread popular sentiments for action on issues such as poverty reduction and global warming, including virtual unanimity among those with pro-labour class consciousness. So, the next question is what are the connections between the class structure of advanced capitalism and intentions to defend capitalism or transform it?

In the 1980s and 90s, I was involved in a research project that partnered with the United Steelworkers of America (USWA) Local 1005, at the time one of the largest industrial unions in Canada with over 14,000 members at Hilton Works in Hamilton, Ontario, Canada's "steeltown" (Seccombe and Livingstone 1999; Livingstone, Smith and Smith 2011). Local 1005 was renowned for its progressive role in the development of industrial relations in Canada. The project involved listening to a representative sample of steelworkers and their household partners with questionnaire surveys and more in-depth interviews on many aspects of coping with life in the wake of the first mass layoffs in the history of the Canadian steel industry. Our research found few signs of developed revolutionary consciousness but strong oppositional labour consciousness and many heartfelt expressions of aspirations for a better future. A veteran steelworker I interviewed in the mid-1990s put it like this: "I want my kids to grow up in a world with a fair chance of a decent job with a fair wage. Is that too much to ask?" In the wake of slightly earlier mass layoffs in the US steel industry, a veteran millhand with time to be more reflective (Spencer 1977, 242) was also more hopeful:

> It is often easy to misjudge the early signs of social change. It is easy to be silent about the blue-collar workers, who are far down at the bottom of the social heap. And, for those whose profession it is to govern the state, the temptations have always been to be concerned only with its top surface layers, the rich, the educated, the powerful. But sooner or later the world will shift.

In the following chapter, I look more closely at the extent to which both expressed levels of class consciousness and views on global threats issues are connected with potential agents in class relations.

Notes

1. Resource materials on these aspects of social consciousness include Gurin, Miller and Gurin (1980); Livingstone and Luxton (1989); Fredrickson (1988); Coulthard (2014); Chudacoff (1992); and Aries (1962). Those labelled as "disabled" may often experience the most extreme forms of discrimination. There have been few careful or comparative studies of their social identities to date.
2. For representative studies including the higher levels of class consciousness, mainly in the late 1960s and 1970s, see: Touraine (1966); Leggett (1968); Ollman (1972); Hazelrigg (1973); and Moorhouse (1976). For earlier presentations of my own approach and more extensive literature review, see Livingstone (1976; 1985; 1987).
3. For the depth of current probes led by Google, Facebook, Apple, Microsoft and other global digital corporations, see Zuboff (2019).
4. Lenin's view was arguably a departure from the Russian social democratic tradition, which gave more scope to development of revolutionary consciousness within the working class (see Mayer 1997).
5. On the pivotal role of the Occupy movement and related activities, see Levitin (2015).
6. For a variant of the argument for the centrality of oppositional class consciousness, see Wallace and Junisbai (2003).
7. Gurin, Miller and Gurin (1980) conducted one of the earliest and most suggestive of these still rare empirical inquiries.
8. As an earlier example, see Reid (1981), 23–31.
9. In the CSCC (1980s) surveys, respondents were initially asked whether they belonged to a social class. Then they were asked the standard class identity question.

Unfortunately, the results for these two questions are not fully comparable because in some country surveys (i.e., Australia, Canada, Denmark) those who did not respond to the "belong" question were not asked the standard identity question.

10. This US trend is documented in Livingstone (1983b).
11. These earlier cyclical patterns in class identity are reviewed for the US case in Livingstone (1983b).
12. For further information on the CSCC (1980s) project data, and access to the database, interested researchers can contact the Institute for Social Research at the University of Michigan, citing: Erik Olin Wright, Comparative Project on Class Structure and Class Consciousness: Core and Country-Specific Files [distributor], 1992-02-17 <https://doi.org/10.3886/ICPSR09323.v1>.
13. One of the items in Wright's (1997, 410) final class consciousness scale was "Non-management could run things without bosses," which is used in the current analysis as an indicator of alternative visions of the future and to distinguish the extent of revolutionary versus hegemonic capitalist consciousness. The other four items on Wright's oppositional scale include the "corporations benefit owners" and "opposition to strike breakers," used in the present study as key indicators of oppositional class consciousness.
14. I should note here that the 1980s surveys generally did not include a "don't know" option for attitude questions. Later surveys did and found around 10 percent of respondents generally chose this option. For comparability with 1980s surveys, findings are presented here omitting the "don't know" respondents in later surveys. Comparisons of the later surveys including the "don't know" respondents produce similar results, albeit with somewhat higher contradictory class consciousness.
15. See Mann (1970) for a thought-provoking account of the limited extent of general value consensus in the liberal democracies of Britain and the US; a lack of general value commitment and a pragmatic acceptance by subordinate classes are suggested. As in Mann's (1973) later related work, I find this analysis was inattentive to the full variation in core issues of class interest, especially the extent of oppositional labour consciousness.
16. As previously noted, the state-owned Norges assets fund has subsequently been invested in international private profit stocks.
17. As on the prior poverty issue, about 10 percent expressed uncertain views. They have been omitted for general comparability. Other recent general surveys including an uncertain option have found around 75 percent agreement regarding global warming.
18. The most notable exception in North America was the case study research of John Leggett (1968; 1979). These interview studies focused on employed and unemployed manual workers. Leggatt distinguished male workers with low class awareness (varying degrees of verbalization of general social issues in terms of class) from those with "skeptical" working-class consciousness (in terms of knowledge about the actual distribution of wealth) and "militant" working-class consciousness (in terms of predisposition to aggressive class action and support for equal distribution of wealth).

7

Connecting Class and Class Consciousness

The Acid Test

> Regardless of time or place — exploited communities always seem capable of reversing, negating, or ridiculing what elites want them to believe.... The human imagination is, thankfully, a hard thing to snuff out. (Day 2019, 3)

If class existence in the production relations of paid workplaces is to have progressive political effect in advanced capitalism, there have to be discernible connections between exploited peoples' location in these relations and their awareness of their exploitation. This chapter searches for these connections. More specifically, there should be detectable associations between non-managerial employee classes and expressions of both pro-labour oppositional and revolutionary class consciousness. Conversely, there should also be detectable associations of corporate capitalists, larger employers and upper managers with pro-capital oppositional and hegemonic class consciousness. Those in more intermediate class positions — small employers and the self-employed, as well as lower managers — should express more mixed variants of these forms of class consciousness. The primary focus in this chapter is on connections of employment class with these oppositional and hegemonic/revolutionary forms of class consciousness.[1]

After some introductory comments, I briefly review prior empirical research related to class and class consciousness in advanced capitalism. Next, I present my findings on class by class consciousness based primarily on the data sources used in the prior chapters. This includes connections between class and class identity, followed by class and oppositional consciousness, and class by revolutionary or hegemonic consciousness. Then I assess the extent to which strategic class groups with highly developed class consciousness hold distinctive attitudes on pivotal issues (ending poverty and recognizing the threat of global warming). The conclusion puts discovered connections in the general context of prospects for social change and leads to more specific discussion of prospects in the final chapter.

The following are the main headlines:

- identifying as middle class has not prevented development of pro-labour oppositional class consciousness among non-managerial workers;
- pro-labour oppositional and revolutionary consciousness are more widespread among non-managerial workers than previously recognized and may be increasing; and
- excepting corporate capitalists, pro-capital oppositional consciousness is much less widespread and may be decreasing in most classes.

Three points to start. First, as noted in the prior chapter, there are many other forms of awareness of oppression and domination in capitalism inside and outside paid workplaces, such as on grounds of racialization, gender, age and disability. I do not claim that class consciousness should be more pertinent than these other aspects of lived experience, but "identity politics" that stress one or more of these more visible forms of oppression at the expense of ignoring class exploitation can be counterproductive for human liberation in and from capitalism.

Second, a focus on class location in production relations cannot generate a full profile of class existence in the varied social formations of advanced capitalism. Classes in themselves cannot be reduced to positions in the labour process. They are also constituted in household and community spheres and by an array of circumstances (e.g., Seccombe and Livingstone 1999). However, in contrast to the now fashionable descriptions of current class situations fixated on market exchange and cultural consumption patterns, a focus on production relations allows direct exploration of connections between employment classes and subjective expressions of class consciousness.

Third, I assume that these possible connections are at least somewhat more accessible to independent investigation in advanced capitalist settings than they were in prior times when there were more overwhelming powers of domination, few independent investigators and less means of independent expression by subordinated workers. James C. Scott (1990, 198–199) suggestively illustrated how disguised, undisclosed forms of resistance — which he termed *"infrapolitics"* — have been vital to the lives of highly subjugated slaves and peasants, as well as the working class in the West. But he also recognizes the lower risks and difficulties, so far, of political expression in contemporary liberal democracies. This is not to suggest that many non-managerial employees will not be guarded in speaking to the more powerful today, but under a cloak of anonymity, such as a random-selection sample survey, many may be more likely to speak their minds than in more public forums or earlier times.

The obscene wealth of a few capitalists is blatantly obvious, while the wage share of hired non-managerial labour declines and job insecurity increases. If class positions in the production process are to mean anything for contemporary political change, they should at least show some association with aspects of oppositional class consciousness. But there is nothing inevitable about class consciousness. We make our choices about class identity, class interests and preferred futures based on both our material circumstances and our sense of possibilities. This chapter tracks these connections with the aid of the national surveys data on general patterns of class consciousness documented in the previous chapter. Connections that are found guide the discussion of prospects for change in the following final chapter.

Whether you are an owner of a large private firm or a hired labourer in such a business will generally push you in one direction or the other in support for capital or labour rights. Owners are driven by competition to maximize profits to stay in business. Hired labourers are driven by employers' profit-making demands to assert the right to strike to defend their working conditions and wages. But it is seldom that simple. Owners may have long-time secure markets, permitting more generous conditions for workers, or they may have complex labour requirements that demand greater concessions. Even if we discount the power of bourgeois ideology, workers may have long tenure in a job and enough vested interest in it that they reject the right to strike for themselves as well as other workers. In any case, the primary focus here is on the relation between basic class positions and dimensions of class consciousness in advanced capitalist countries and how this has changed since the 1980s.

The general operating assumption that there are likely to be significant associations between class positions and higher levels of class consciousness may be seen by some as obvious. But many analysts deny it, particularly for non-managerial manual workers. As noted in Chapter 6, various Marxist intellectuals and others have claimed for more than a century that the traditional working class of industrial workers has suffered from "false consciousness" by underestimating the extent of their own economic inequality and exploitation. More recent denials offer more subtle dismissals. They criticize this posited association as "economic reductionism," which sees attitudes and values simplistically as a reflex of class location; little evidence is claimed to have been found of significant relations between changing class positions and developed class consciousness (e.g., Savage 2000, 37–41). More generally, many scholars have inferred from a post-1960s lack of mass revolutionary action by organized workers and a pro-corporate business shift of some progressive political parties that those in subordinated jobs are politically disengaged or disinterested. More broadly, from perspectives encapsulated within the dominant bourgeois mode of thought, even critical analysts discount connection between materially disadvantaged class positions and oppositional or revolutionary labour consciousness (e.g., Fisher 2009). In contrast to these presumptions, I believe that we have sufficient direct evidence here on both class positions and levels of class consciousness to make a valid preliminary acid test of these connections.

In addition to looking at basic class by class consciousness relations, I analyze some of the other possible moderating factors[2] that can influence the development of class consciousness and for which there are available data: gender, age, racialization and ethnic background, as well as union membership, formal education attainment and specific working conditions — including being in a large or small private profit-making firm or public sector workplace. The basic objective is to gain some clues about class and other situating conditions that have moved people's consciousness either toward acceptance or rejection of capitalism.

The main working assumption of this chapter is that differences in expressions of class consciousness are related to exploitation in production relations. Exploitation is treating others unfairly in order to benefit from their labour. Such appropriation of benefit is largely determined by capitalist ownership control over labour power and the means of production. Exploitation implies domination of workers by capitalists and their agents and persists as long as capitalism exists.[3] In the period of the emergence of industrial capitalism, Marx's labour theory of value saw exploitation primarily in terms of the extraction of unpaid labour from hired workers, profits stolen from wages — a fundamental relation that continues to be denied or dismissed by many analysts. Some prior empirical studies in both advanced capitalist and global settings have found significant relations between rates of exploitation of manufacturing workers' compensation and their protest actions (Cuneo 1984; Boswell and Dixon 1993). However, there has been little recent interest in exploring such connections between hired workers' relative wages and benefits and more subjective aspects of class existence.

There is growing recognition of the extent of capitalist exploitation of other biophysical (energy, materials and land) resources beyond labour power (Hornborg 2016). The process of labour exploitation has been lengthened and complicated. As noted in Chapter 4, there is mounting dispute over which workers actually have unpaid labour extracted from them or do "productive labour," as well as the relevance of the labour theory of value and the distinction of productive labour per se.[4] We can probably all agree that a large amount of surplus is generated in advanced capitalist production in the form of profits, some of which has been used to enhance conditions of modern life. But the fact is well documented that profits have soared while wages have stagnated in recent decades.[5] We have seen in the last chapter a widespread and growing general sense of being "ripped off" by corporate owners. Effective distribution and use of this surplus is the pivotal issue of our times: profit maximization versus sustainable reproduction of the ecosystem and life on Earth.

The extraction of unpaid labour (surplus value) from hired workers for profit by enterprise owners continues to be a basic driving force in advanced capitalism. Otherwise, substantially more of the profits generated would be used to address pressing survival issues. Most value theorists would agree that manual production workers in private goods-producing industries (i.e., resource extraction, manufacturing and construction, in this book usually called "industrial workers") are direct producers of surplus value. Workers who produce material goods might still often have a somewhat better vantage point to see where profits originate, where the value they produce goes and how it is realized as profits in which they do not share. I explore the possibility that more direct and visible conditions of conversion of production value from these workers into sale price and profit may also dispose them to greater oppositional labour consciousness. I also consider whether non-managerial professional employees involved in producing private goods are similarly affected. In an advanced capitalist economy, many other non-managerial employees involved in creating diverse services for private sale may also be exploited in this sense and be part of the "collective worker" (Carchedi 1977). For purposes of this analysis, I initially distinguish non-managerial employees who are direct producers in private goods industries from those non-managerial employees involved in the creation, distribution and sale of private services (i.e., clerical, sales and service workers, here usually called "service workers").

It is arguable that any worker subjugated to capitalist social relations and performing alienated, imposed abstract labour is producing value for capital and therefore exploited (Harvie 2005). Hired labourers who are not direct producers of private goods or services commodities may be less clearly exploited in value terms, but they may also experience subordinated working conditions and hold negative views about them. An accounts clerk in a city hall, for example, may be extremely subordinated while technically not highly exploited in terms of commodity production. I also explore the extent to which non-managerial service workers, professional employees and industrial workers in the public sector share subjective class consciousness with private sector workers.

In any case, this book does not offer any precise measures of the differential exploitation of hired employees. It merely explores possible differences in class consciousness between those in private sector material goods production and other workers as well as such differences with those in other, more dominant class positions.

A New Working Class?

As suggested in Chapter 4, the spread of automation in leading industries in the 1960s was associated with celebration of the significance of scientific and technical workers for efficient production in advanced capitalist "knowledge economies." Some analysts, notably American ones, heralded these workers as part of the vanguard of a "professional-managerial class" or "technostructure" in a "post-industrial society" in which they would take over from corporate owners the pivotal leadership of a more bountiful maturing capitalism (e.g., Bell 1976; Galbraith 1967). Others, notably French analysts, foresaw the same workers as a "new working class," prepared to use their increasing centrality in highly interdependent production processes to lead other hired labour to gain greater worker control and begin to transform capitalism toward socialism (e.g., Mallet 1975). In previous analyses in this book and elsewhere (Livingstone, Adams and Sawchuk 2021), I documented the profound current differences between professional employees and managers in organizational power. I pointed out the equally profound error of conflating these two class positions. Further, professional employees have been found increasingly to share working conditions with other non-managerial employees, what I call the "proletarianization" of professional employees. The question remains, as it was in the 1960s, to what extent do professional employees in general or professional employees in private goods producing firms in particular share oppositional class consciousness with other hired workers? A central issue for the further development of advanced capitalist "knowledge economies" is whether the growing numbers of professional employees give their effective allegiances narrowly to their specialized fields while aspiring to managerial positions within established work organizations. Or do these professional employees recognize their diminishing relative advantage over other non-managerial hired workers, grasp their common interest with them and play a more strategic role in the mobilization of a labour movement for more sustainable economic alternatives in the current century? One of the contributions of this chapter is to address this question more closely with the aid of the class consciousness data presented more generally in the previous chapter.

Overview of Recent Class and Class Consciousness Studies

As discussed in Chapter 6, the different levels of class identity, opposed class interests and alternative visions of society were recognized aspects of class consciousness by some progressive researchers around the protests of the 1960s. In the decade or so after the student and worker rebellions of the late 1960s, there were a number of empirical studies of the capacity of various Marxist and Weberian-based class schemes to distinguish expressions of levels of class consciousness by different classes. For example, using survey data from around 1970 for the US, UK and/or Australia, several researchers concluded that both Marxist and Weber's original class divisions had statistically significant links with both class identity and selected political attitudes (e.g., Robinson and Kelley 1979). Drawing on a 1972 US national election survey, Goertzel (1979) found that a dichotomous capital–labour class model was limited for differentiating class identities and political attitudes and that the distinctive views of professional and managerial workers should be more fully recognized. In addition to the predicted polarity between the bourgeoisie and working class, other intermediate class groups and the traditional petty bourgeoisie of self-employed were sometimes found to express distinctive political attitudes (Johnston and Ornstein 1985). Generally, neo-Weberian occupational status scales were found to be better than either Marxist class schemes or Weber's original social class divisions at predicting subjective class identity, which has tended to be a fairly diffuse, consumption-related perception. Marxist class schemes based on property divisions and incorporating power relations within the labour process were generally better at predicting aspects of oppositional class consciousness than either simple owner/non-owner dichotomies or occupational status scales that confound basic property-based class divisions with moderating factors such as education, income and prestige.

Livingstone and Mangan (1996b) later used a survey conducted in a Canadian city in the mid-1980s to compare Marx's original model, several neo-Marxist schemes, including Erik Olin Wright's later twelve-class model, Weber's original model and several derived stratification scales, including Pierre Bourdieu's. We evaluated the various schemes both in terms of their structural correspondence and each model's ability to predict expressions of class consciousness. We found significant associations between employed men's current locations in the employment class structure and their expressions of class consciousness using most of these (highly correlated) Marxist and Weberian class schemes.[6]

As noted in the previous chapter, most prior surveys of general levels of class consciousness have been one-time cross-sectional studies, few have been conducted since the 1980s and very few have addressed higher levels of class consciousness. The comparative surveys of the class structure and class consciousness (cscc) project conducted under the leadership of Erik Olin Wright in the early 1980s do provide rare benchmarks going forward. As noted in Chapter 6, Wright's (1997, 387, 410) own cross-national analysis of the association of class position with oppositional class consciousness in the US, Sweden and Japan in the 1980s was based on an index of five political attitudes tapping opposed working-class and capitalist-class interests. His main conclusions were that the basic patterns of the relationship between class location and class consciousness were broadly consistent with the generation of people's subjectivity by experiences and interests within employment positions, with polarization between non-managerial hired workers and large employers and that there were some notable variations in associations between class location and class consciousness between countries. A criticism that the five attitude items in Wright's anti-capitalist index do not add up (Savage 2000, 38–41) is probably true. The items Wright chose have varying relevance to capital-labour relations. As seen in Chapter 6, oppositional class consciousness is not linear, and many people do hold contradictory views. But few subsequent assessments of class and class consciousness include data for a full range of class positions, including employers, as well as for attitudes on both capital and labour rights. As discussed in Chapter 6, the data in the CSCC project do contain sufficient information to conduct secondary analyses to generate fuller general profiles of class consciousness for several countries in the 1980s. The CSCC 1980s data also offer the empirical basis to conduct the further cross-national analyses of relations between class positions and different levels of class consciousness later in this chapter.

In one of the few more recent comparable studies, John Western (1999) conducted an analysis of a 1995 Australian survey that identified class positions similar to Wright's later schemes (discussed in Chapter 4) and used the private sector "working class" (i.e., non-managerial industrial and service workers) as the main reference group for comparisons with other class groupings. He found that people's views on class-based economic issues reflect their own class circumstances, particularly polarization between the private sector working class and private employers, and that there was greater difference of working-class positions from managers and professional employees in the private sector than in the public sector. Such sector differences are suggestive for further comparative attention to effects of exploitation in the private sphere where saleable commodities are produced.

Over the past three decades, there has been little research attention to connections between class and class consciousness per se. Studies of recent protests such as the Occupy movement, for example, have offered few insights into either their class composition or higher forms of class consciousness. However, in the wake of a bevy of dismissals of the relevance of class to life in a postmodern world, a continuing array of empirical studies document and confirm the robust significance of relations between employment-based class positions and contemporary attitudes on a wide diversity of political, economic and social topics. Some of the most substantial studies are noted here.

One of the most extensive of these inquiries has been the research of Stefan Svallfors (2006). Svallfors worked with a variant of the widely used Erikson-Goldthorpe (1992) class model that relied on reported occupations to distinguish service classes with salaried contracts — the "salariat" — from "routine non-manuals" and skilled and unskilled wage labourers, as well as the self-employed. He canvassed a wide diversity of attitudinal domains dealing not only with paid work but market distribution, state redistribution and family reproduction. The main comparative data source was the International Social Survey Programme (ISSP), with a focus on surveys done between 1992 and 2002 in Sweden, Britain, Germany and the US. This was complemented by a more thorough series of Swedish surveys from 1986 to 2002. Svallfors' basic conclusion was: "The class differences found, taken as a whole, are considerable, stable, and interpretable. Class has, so to speak, a wide reach in its power to shape people's beliefs and the society in which they operate" (165).

Some of these recent studies of class and attitudes have further distinguished positions within the "salariat" between "technocrats" and "cultural specialists" (e.g., Ares 2020), comparable to the distinction between managers and professional employees in my class model. Some report substantial attitude differences between these classes, with the "new class" of social and cultural specialists found to be much more progressive in its political orientation (Güveli, Need and de Graaf 2007). Others using similar class distinctions found growing unanimity among most hired employees on general welfare priorities (i.e., health, education and pensions), as well as possibly greater social investment preferences for a dichotomized "middle class" of managers and specialists compared to "working class" production workers, clerks and service workers (Häusermann, Pingerra, Ares and Enggistt 2019). Still others found that similar class schemas, including "higher and lower salariats" along with class identification and other working conditions, are all related to left-right ideological orientations (Bengtsson, Bergland and Oskarson 2013). One of the most recent extensive general reviews of relations between class and attitudes is by Lindh and McCall (2020, 433). While neatly sidestepping debates over class structure in advanced capitalism, they canvass a wide array of current research on links with economic, sociocultural and political issues and, similar to Svallfors before them, conclude: "At the forefront of political research today, there is clear recognition of the continued significance of class in shaping political opinion. Yet the analytical framework for understanding the role of class has expanded substantially from what was in place even a decade ago."

Wallace and Junisbai (2003) conducted one of the few surveys of class relations with class consciousness from a Marxist perspective in recent decades. They began with one of Wright's class schemes, an array of possible moderating factors in the "new economy" and a focus on oppositional class consciousness. Their survey was conducted in Indiana in 1998. Their class variable was dichotomized into "proletariat" and "non-proletariat".[7] Their oppositional consciousness variable included a number of items counterposing workers' interests with owners and bosses. Their basic findings were that oppositional labour consciousness was fairly high among Indiana workers and that class has significant direct effects also moderated by sociodemographic and employment factors. They concluded: "All told, there is substantial evidence of class's impact in how it shapes the perceptions of workers about various experiences at work and in the sociopolitical realm. Our results provide evidence that opposition to capitalists is alive and well in the new economy" (417).

Most recently, Sawyer and Gampa (2020) used a Marxist class scheme distinguishing "workers" and "freelancers" from "self-employed professionals," "middle managers" and "small business owners"; they dichotomized these into "working class" and "middle class" for further analysis. They relied on a multidimensional class consciousness scale (Keefer, Goode and Van Berkel 2015) as well as Wright's (1997) oppositional class consciousness scale; they combined these two scales into a single composite variable. They also included other socioeconomic status measures, work factors and indicators of alienation and activism. They conducted a small online survey and a larger representative sample survey in the US circa 2018. Their major findings were that their objective Marxist measure of social class was the only consistently significant predictor of alienation and that there was a link between alienation and class consciousness for working class participants.[8]

Other recent studies conversant with Marxist class and consciousness concepts focused on whether there are differences in class consciousness between the industrial workers, previously seen as the "core" of the working class, and others. For example, Ikeler and Crocker (2021) probe the frequent claim that workers who provide interactive services to customers, clients or patients have less oppositional working-class consciousness than manufacturing, construction and transport workers. Using a measure of the intensity and duration of job-based service interaction and a composite measure of class consciousness based on Mann's (1973) different levels, they conducted a small random sample in a New York county in 2015–16. They found that non-managerial status and union membership, as well as workplace pain and job insecurity, were all significantly related to greater oppositional working-class consciousness, but that service work was no less related than industrial work.

These recent studies serve to confirm significant influence of employment class structure on diverse political and social attitudes and the import of various moderating factors. But they suffer from two basic limitations. First, while many tend to refer conceptually to many of the class positions distinguished in Chapter 4, virtually all studies conflate them in their empirical analyses. Some simply dichotomize "workers" and "non-workers"; others conflate managers and supervisors with non-managerial workers; most continue to combine managers with professionals; nearly all lump professionals who are managers with those who are professional employees. Virtually none of these inquiries permit comparative interrogation of those who are owners of the means of production (i.e., corporate capitalists, large employers, small employers, self-employed) and those who are clearly parts of hired collective labour (i.e., industrial workers, service workers and professional employees), nor do they clearly distinguish the managerial employees who must mediate between capital and labour. In my view, these conflations vitiate the findings on class and class consciousness of even the otherwise most rigorously designed of these studies.

Second, few of these general studies of relations between class and attitudes deal directly with capital versus labour interests and rights. Svallfors (2006, 20) at least touches on the concept of class interests but choses to circumvent it in his extensive empirical inquiries. The now almost universal support across classes for effective distribution of the benefits of the modern welfare state is often observed (e.g., Güveli et al. 2007; Häusermann et al. 2019), but there is little counterposing of social and labour rights to ownership rights of capital. Those studies that drew explicitly on Marxist concepts of oppositional class consciousness typically folded them into composites that conflate class identity and/or revolutionary levels. Some of these studies followed Mann's (1973) conception of different levels of class consciousness but paid little heed to his observation that they need to be examined separately.

The presentation of findings in this chapter include evidence on all the owner, manager and non-managerial class positions identified in Chapter 4 and deal with connections with class identity, oppositional consciousness and hegemonic/revolutionary consciousness. The CSCC data files contain sufficient data for the 1980s to conduct secondary analyses to generate benchmarks for several of the countries involved regarding relations between class positions and different levels of class consciousness. Most of the following 1980s comparisons are based on available data for the US, Sweden, Norway, Japan and Canada. (Data for the other CSCC countries are less complete). In addition to the 1982 Canada survey with Wright's network, my 2004, 2010 and 2016 Canadian surveys offer measures of class identity, oppositional consciousness and alternative visions that permit inferences about trends in and current relations between class positions and levels of class consciousness in advanced capitalism.

I summarize these findings in terms of the basic relations between class positions and each of the three levels of class consciousness (class identity, opposed class interests, alternative visions) as well the effects of available moderating factors (sex, age and racialization, as well as union membership, education attainment, private or public sector and other working conditions). At each step, I look first at the earlier evidence for all available countries, then at more recent data only available for Canada. Then some basic summary patterns are suggested.

Before presenting the findings, I should note that the strength of connections between measures of class and class consciousness is estimated by ordinal statistical measures of association of class position (ordered from large employers to industrial workers)[9] with binary measures of differences in class consciousness (e.g., working-class/upper-middle-class identity). Most associations mentioned later in the chapter are significant at least at the 95 percent level of confidence on Kendall tau-b or c ordinal correlations.[10]

Corporate Capitalists' Privileged Views

There is a serious gap rarely acknowledged in much empirical class analysis: the absence of corporate capitalists. As noted in the prior chapter on class consciousness in general, the most powerful people in class societies seldom permit candid access to themselves. The most powerful persons in advanced capitalism are corporate capitalists. This includes the chief executive officers (CEOs) of transnational private corporations and controllers of large pools of investment capital, such as holding company and hedge fund leaders. Their numbers are tiny, far less than 1 percent of the employed labour force. They have been employed almost exclusively in profit-maximizing activities. From the limited available evidence, their class consciousness is unique.

In conjunction with other public attitude surveys, I was able to conduct biennial surveys of the attitudes of corporate executives of large transnational corporations with head offices in Ontario, the financial centre of Canada, between 1980 and 2000 (see Canada Work Learning Surveys 1998–2016. Corporate Executive Surveys (1980–2000). The basic relevant findings, noted in the following tables, were that throughout this period the vast majority of CEOs held upper-class or upper-middle-class identities and expressed strong pro-capital oppositional consciousness. In my few interviews with CEOs outlined in Chapters 2 and 5, they also revealed much more developed hegemonic class consciousness than any of the other major class groups I examine. Since that time, I know of only one other roughly comparable study, an intensive survey of the very wealthy in metropolitan Chicago in 2011 (Page, Bartels and Seawright 2013); it found that such people were much more politically active, much more conservative and much less supportive of social welfare programs than other Americans. We know that both corporate financial concentration (e.g., Vitali et al. 2011; Rugemer 2019) and personal wealth concentration (e.g., Piketty 2014) have increased in recent decades. It is clear that some of the wealthiest corporate capitalists, such as Bill Gates and Warren Buffett, have begun to respond to some negative effects of unconditional profit making. Public declarations of dominant corporate alliances have also been shifting recently from assertion of shareholder privilege to versions of "stakeholder capitalism" (e.g., Business Roundtable 2019). Other corporate leaders continue to assert more the unconditional rights of ownership in "free markets." But I think it is safe to assume that virtually all corporate capitalists adhere to an essence of hegemonic capitalist class consciousness — including the profit imperative and rejection of worker self-management — whatever reforms they might concede to save the system. The more accessible empirical question addressed here is the extent to which the class consciousness of other class groups serves to either defend or begin to transform this system.

Class and Class Identity: Working Class versus Upper-Middle Class Links

Most research on class consciousness has continued to focus on class identity. Such studies regularly confirm significant connections of various class and status position variables with subjective class identity and also often register a "middle-class identity bias" (e.g., Curtis 2013), consistent with the common consumption patterns discussed in Chapter 2. As documented in Chapter 6, it has been increasingly common in recent generations for many of those in the employed labour force to identify as "middle class." Some who see themselves in the middle of a standardized class structure now call themselves "working middle class," referencing their own hired labour conditions while seeing rich above and poor beneath them. People who continue to identify more simply as working class may see themselves as more subordinated to others in employment and also distinct from those in a higher class because of relatively less wealth, income and/or job qualifications. But more people also see themselves as "upper middle class" on the basis of their greater wealth or higher qualifications. The main conventional distinction between class positions has long been in the proportion who identify themselves as "working class." But the proportions who identify as "upper middle class" should also be assessed where data are available.

Table 7.1 summarizes the proportions in each class position in each of six available countries in the cscc data files who opted in the early 1980s for either a standard upper-middle-class identity or a working-class identity. Nearly all others opted for "middle class." Where the first figure in a cell in Table 7.1 is bolded, those with upper-middle-class identities were significantly greater than those with working-class identities. Where the second figure in a cell is bolded, those with working-class identities were significantly greater than those with upper-middle-class identities.

Table 7.1 Standard Class Identity by Class, Advanced Capitalist Countries, 1980s
(% Upper-Middle-Class Identity / % Working-Class Identity)

Class	US	Canada	Norway	Sweden	Japan	U.K.
Corporate capitalists	n/a	88/0*	n/a	n/a	n/a	n/a
Large employer	25/0	29/0	25/12	0/0	0/13	—
Upper manager	35/9	38/0	19/21	17/22	—	9/11
Small employer	18/42	18/12	4/42	10/42	3/44	—
Middle manager	20/35	20/17	0/31	10/20	0/24**	16/31
Lower manager	10/36	7/26	1/42	8/42	0/80	3/54
Self employed	13/37	16/29	4/35	0/50	2/52	5/41***
Professional employee	11/27	20/13	2/31	7/25	0/59	4/39
Service worker	10/45	8/33	1/42	1/44	1/43	2/58
Industrial worker	8/45	3/51	0/62	1/72	0/77	1/78
Total	11/39	11/33	3/42	5/46	1/51	4/56
N	902	806	1161	640	462	1204

*Corporate executive surveys 1980–2000 for 1982
**Includes upper managers
***includes employers as well as self-employed
Sources: CSCC (1980). Canada Work Learning Surveys 1998–2016; 1982 CCS National Dataset.

The evidence confirms that the vast majority of corporate capitalists held upper/upper-middle-class identities while the vast majority of industrial workers in the early 1980s held working-class identities. In the UK, Japan and Sweden, over 70 percent of industrial workers indicated they were "working class"; only in the US was there less than a majority (45 percent). Service workers were typically less likely to identify as working class, but over 40 percent did so in most countries; most service workers identified as middle class. Professional employees, the other non-managerial worker group, were generally less likely to identify as working class but over a quarter did so in most countries; again most identified as middle class. The partial exception was Canada, with the highest proportions of professional employees who had post-secondary education credentials and more identified as upper middle class (20 percent) than working class (13 percent), but most still identified as middle class. However, relatively few non-managerial workers anywhere identified as upper middle class.

The most distinctive comparative finding may be the extreme reluctance of Japanese, including large employers, to identify as upper middle class. This was probably related to the long-term "salaryman" tradition of entry into higher level employment class positions from lower level non-managerial ones within the same firm and an emphasis on cooperative "kaizan" production processes. The majority of all employed Japanese and of those in most class positions apparently identified themselves as working-class team members. The most notable exceptions were large employers and probably higher-level managers.[11]

Among owners besides corporate capitalists, large employers tended to see themselves in the middle class with some variations, and few claimed to be working class. However, among small employers and the self-employed, significantly higher proportions claimed to be working class than upper middle class, probably reflecting recognition that their direct labour was essential to the viability of their businesses. This was true both for the self-employed working for themselves and for small employers working beside their employees.

Managers were most likely to see themselves as they are: in the middle of the employment class structure. Upper managers, closest to the top of the hierarchy, were more likely than lower managers to think of themselves as upper middle class, especially in the US and Canada. But managers beneath them were more inclined to identify as working class, especially lower level managers, who were as likely as non-managerial workers to see themselves as working class. Japanese lower managers were exceptional in expressing a high working-class identity, given a higher likelihood of "salaryman" emergence from and continuing close engagement with service and industrial worker positions.

In all cases, there were large differences between the small proportions of large employers and upper managers prepared to call themselves working class and the large proportions of industrial workers prepared to do so. Patterns were more mixed in other class positions, but usually with substantial minorities prepared to say they were working class. Upper-middle-class identities remained in relatively small proportions for those beneath large-employer and upper-manager class positions.

The bottom line is that there were stark differences in class identity between those capitalists at the very top of the ownership classes and the industrial workers most directly subordinated in material goods production relations in the 1980s. In most other class positions, combinations of consumption patterns and working conditions encouraged most of the employed labour force to think of themselves as in the middle class.

In addition to class position, in these 1980s surveys there were a few other fairly consistent moderating factors on class identity. In nearly all these countries, union membership was associated with majority levels of working-class identity compared to minorities for non-union members. In Canada, with relatively low union membership (around 30 percent), there was little difference, and non-unionized industrial workers were even more likely (57 percent) than unionized industrial workers (44 percent) to express working-class identity.

In all countries, completion of higher formal schooling was related to lower levels of working-class identity; the majority of those with less than high school education saw themselves as working class, compared to small minorities of graduates from higher education. Greater formal education encouraged a more middle-class identity while union membership tended to encourage working-class solidarity. Data on racial differences were only available for the US and Canada. Compared to white people, much larger majorities of Black people were in non-managerial employee-class positions; majorities of Black people but only minorities of white people in non-managerial positions identified as working class. Reliable income data were only available for Canada; the majority of those with the lowest personal and family incomes identified as working class, in contrast to virtually none of those with the highest incomes. No consistent class-identity effects were found for gender, age or by private versus public sector. In terms of relative effects of class position and other moderating variables on class identity, class effects were generally stronger. But higher education attainment also reduced working-class identity among all Swedish and Norwegian employee classes. In the US, Black professional employees had much higher working-class identities than white professional employees. Overall, in the 1980s, while general middle-class identity was becoming more common, working-class identity continued to be significantly associated with industrial and service worker class positions, and class position in general was significantly associated with class identity.

For purposes of assessing more recent relations between class position and different levels of class consciousness, I rely mostly on my continuing series of Canadian national surveys, in 2004, 2010 and 2016. Table 7.2 summarizes relations between class position and class identity from 1982 to 2016, again focusing on the proportion in each class who have continued to identify themselves as part of the working class and those who identify as upper middle class. Once again, where the first figure in a cell in Table 7.2 is bolded, those with upper middle-class identities were significantly greater than those with working class identities. Where the second figure in a cell is bolded, those with working-class identities were significantly greater than those with upper middle-class identities.

Table 7.2 Class Identity by Class, Canada, 1982–2016 (% Upper Middle Class / % Working Class)

Class	1982	2004	2010	2016
Corporate capitalist*	**88**/0	**92**/0	n/a	n/a
Large employer	29/0	**67**/6	**100**/0	**61**/17
Upper manager	**38**/0	**66**/11	**31**/11	**40**/5
Small employer	18/12	**44**/18	24/8	30/17
Middle manager	20/17	**45**/20	24/9	26/12
Lower manager	7/**26**	28/36	15/21	16/25
Self employed	16/29	29/34	18/19	22/19
Professional employee	20/13	**38**/23	21/7	25/10
Service worker	8/**33**	24/**39**	11/**23**	11/**28**
Industrial worker	3/**51**	21/**42**	13/**29**	12/**28**
Total %	11/**33**	31/32	18/17	20/20
Total N	806	5572	1192	2884

*Corporate executive surveys 1980–2000 data for 1982 and 2000.
Sources: Canada Work Learning Surveys 1998–2016 (including Corporate executive surveys 1980–2000).

In the latest available Canadian surveys, corporate capitalists continued to be virtually unanimous in their upper/upper-middle-class identities. The majority of large employers have come to see themselves as upper middle class. Upper managers are also more likely to see themselves as upper middle class, and few identify as working class. These are the only class positions where majorities or near majorities say they are upper middle class.

As documented in Chapter 4, the major changes in the class composition in advanced capitalism probably have been the decline in the numbers of industrial workers and the growth of professional employee and managerial classes. Consequently, there has been a declining traditional working-class identity in the employed Canadian labour force. The proportion of the entire employed labour force that identifies as working class declined from a third in 1982 to around 20 percent in 2016. Among industrial workers themselves, working-class identity dropped from about half to around a quarter. No other changes in class identity have been this substantial. The decreasing numbers of industrial workers are increasingly likely to see themselves in the middle of the class structure — above the poor and beneath the affluent — but this tendency to middle-class identity is longstanding. As the residuals for Table 7.2 suggest, 59 percent of service workers in 1982 (i.e., 100-[8+33]) identified as middle class, and 61 percent in 2016 (i.e., 100-[11+28]); but for industrial workers, there was an increase from 46 percent in 1982 (i.e., 100-[3+51]) to 60 percent in 2016 (i.e., 100-[12+28]) identifying as middle class.

Professional employees in Canada have not taken on a more working-class identity as their numbers among non-managerial workers have grown. The growing numbers of these highly educated workers have remained more reluctant to think of themselves as working class than in the other countries surveyed in the 1980s. About a quarter persist in seeing themselves as upper middle class, reflecting relatively high qualifications, even as they experience increasing subordination in job control and declining material benefits. But most continue to see themselves as middle class.

Small employers and self-employed have continued to identify themselves in more mixed terms, with some seeing themselves as upper middle class based on their ownership privileges while similar numbers identify as working class based on their own direct labour contributions. Managers below upper managers continue to see themselves in the middle; the lower the manager, the more likely to see themselves as working class.

In sum, most industrial workers, service workers and professional employees as well as majorities in most other class positions — besides corporate capitalists, large employers and upper managers — tend to see themselves in the middle of the class structure — dependent on their own labour and sharing common consumption patterns. Indeed, the basic divide in class identity in advanced capitalism may now be between those in the "working middle" and those who see themselves as in a more dominant upper middle class. Since the 1980s, increases in proportions with upper-middle-class identity in Canada have occurred mostly in association with large employer and upper manager class positions.

I suggest that such increases in upper-middle-class identity and closer links with large employer and upper manager classes are likely occurring in most other advanced capitalist countries, including Japan in spite of such earlier reluctance.[12] The declining numbers of industrial workers in these countries also now probably share "working-middle-class" identities with other non-managerial workers more greatly than they did in most of the 1980s surveys. Dominant discourse also commonly conflates "middle class" with "working people." Once again, further studies are needed to confirm these claims across countries. However, as outlined in Appendix 2, the distinction between upper- and upper-middle-class identities versus general middle-class and working-class identities are the primary division in class identities for further analyses here.

In addition to the significant association of class position and class identity in the 2004, 2010 and 2016 Canadian surveys, education attainment, racialization and income all had significant effects. Those who did not complete high school, racialize people and those with the lowest incomes all were more likely to identify as working class. Again, no consistent effects were found for gender, age or by private versus public sector. When class position and other moderating factors are assessed in relation to class identity, even with declining working-class identities, class position prevails. Overall, the relation between class position in production relations and class identity remains significant with available evidence.

The dominant trend to increasing general middle-class identity in most class positions may well have been associated with increasing levels of mass consumption, as discussed in Chapter 2. It is also associated with increasing school completion. Particularly in Canada, with among the highest post-secondary completion rates in the world, most of the employed labour force now have a university or college degree and see themselves as well qualified for good "middle-class" jobs. Skilled unionized industrial workers with relatively high incomes and increasing education tend to regard themselves in the middle of their own class schemes between the rich and the poor — but with growing awareness that good jobs in the middle of the class structure have been declining (Seccombe and Livingstone 1999). At the other extreme of the class structure, the increase in upper-middle-class identities since the 1980s is found mainly among large employers and managers with the greatest workplace authority. Whatever other moderating factors are considered, the most striking differences in class identity are between the large proportions of corporate capitalists, large employers and upper managers who say they are upper middle class and the very large proportions of industrial and service workers who say they are not.

We know from the last chapter that the long-presumed general connection between working-class identity and pro-labour oppositional consciousness also appears to be shifting. Identifying oneself as "middle class" may be increasingly accurate for many hired employees in advanced capitalist countries, in the sense that they see themselves between the extremely wealthy and the growing numbers of marginalized and impoverished at home and abroad. Identifying oneself as middle class has not prevented the increasing development of pro-labour oppositional class consciousness among those who exist beyond narrow scholarly definitions of the working class. Non-managerial workers (i.e., industrial workers, service workers and professional employees) are all posited here as exploited and most see themselves with subordinate class identities (i.e., working class, lower middle class or lower class) rather than in more dominant upper- or upper-middle-class statuses. We also know from the last chapter that substantial numbers of those with pro-labour oppositional consciousness have held views favouring the transformation of capitalism. Where are these people located in the class structure? The next question is the extent to which dominant and subordinate class positions are connected with different forms of oppositional class consciousness.

Class and Oppositional Class Consciousness

Pro-capital oppositional consciousness is indicated in all the available surveys by support for corporate owners' profit taking and opposition to the right to strike. Conversely, pro-labour oppositional consciousness is indicated by opposition to corporate profit taking and support for the right to strike.[13] In most of these countries, contradictory oppositional class consciousness was the single most common form in the early 1980s (as summarized in Figure 6.3). That is to say, many people had either mixed views on ownership rights to profit and the right to strike or expressed uncertainty on one or both of these issues. Table 7.3 summarizes the most basic differences by class position in the 1980s, which were in the respective proportions with definite pro-capital versus pro-labour views. The other responses expressed forms of contradictory consciousness. Where the first figure in a cell is bolded, pro-capital views were significantly greater than pro-labour views; where the second figure is bolded, pro-labour views were greater than pro-capital views.

Table 7.3 Oppositional Class Consciousness by Class, Advanced Capitalist Countries, 1980s (% Pro-Capital / % Pro-Labour)

Class	US	Norway	Canada	Japan	Sweden
Corporate capitalist*	n/a	n/a	80/0	n/a	n/a
Large employer	**50**/8	**43**/17	**55**/9	**38**/25	**100**/0
Upper manager	**46**/15	**47**/14	**53**/6	**	32/26
Small employer	**30**/15	**44**/12	**39**/11	13/20	36/21
Lower manager	24/30	31/27	19/**37**	10/**50**	10/**54**
Self employed	25/35	31/26	21/25	2/**52**	20/33
Professional employee	22/36	27/26	14/**48**	9/**49**	12/**52**
Service worker	17/30	25/29	13/**41**	5/**50**	7/**59**
Industrial worker	13/**40**	16/**39**	8/**54**	9/**51**	3/**71**
Total %	23/30	28/28	15/**42**	8/**46**	11/**55**
Total N	1697	1676	1758	547	1137

*Corporate executive surveys 1980–2000 for 1982
Sources: CSCC (1980s) data files. Canada Work Learning Surveys 1998–2016; 1982 CCS National Dataset.

In nearly all countries, the greatest differences in oppositional consciousness in the 1980s were between corporate capitalists and large employers versus industrial workers. I take this to be consistent with the prediction that manual production workers in goods-producing industries (i.e., "industrial workers") who experience fairly direct conversion of their labour power into profit may also have been more disposed to oppositional labour consciousness than other workers. Proportions ranging from large pluralities to strong majorities of industrial workers held pro-labour views in all countries, varying from around 40 percent in the US and Norway to over 70 percent in Sweden.

Nearly all corporate capitalists and at very least pluralities of large employers expressed a pro-capital oppositional consciousness, as expected. At least pluralities of upper managers and small employers in the US, Norway and Canada also held pro-capital views. The picture among these classes was different in Sweden and Japan. In Sweden, large employers — under threat from Meidner Plan initiatives — had strong pro-capital views, but upper managers and small employers were quite divided, with those in the more highly unionized public sector more inclined to pro-labour views. In Japan, the strong general pro-labour sentiment at the time was also reflected in significant pro-labour support among higher-level managers, small employers and even large employers. This is consistent with a relatively strong commitment to internal promotion and long-term careers within Japanese transnational corporations and also reflected in more limited compensation for corporate executives (Pan and Zhou 2018).

Middle managers were more likely to have pro-capital views in the US and Norway, with more mixed pro-capital and pro-labour views in Canada, Japan and Sweden; conversely, lower level managers were more likely to hold pro-labour views in these three countries and have more mixed views in the US and Norway. The self-employed had mixed views in all countries except Japan, where they shared strong pro-labour views with most other classes. Professional employees and service workers in all countries showed similar patterns as lower managers. In the US and Norway, both professional employees and service workers had mixed views, while in Canada, Japan and Sweden they were almost as likely to express pro-labour views as industrial workers were.

So overall, the US, with its internationally dominant corporate capitalist class, and Norway, with its distinctive corporate profit-driven public investment funds, had the strongest pro-capital support from all levels of employers and both upper and middle managers, as well as the lowest pro-labour views in other classes. In the other countries, lower managers as well as professional employees and service workers had majority or at least plurality pro-labour views very close to those of industrial workers in their countries.

The polarization between majorities or at least pluralities of large employers holding pro-capital oppositional class consciousness and pluralities to large majorities of industrial workers holding pro-labour oppositional class consciousness was the most pronounced finding, consistent with their actual opposed class interests. This finding is at odds with the "dominant ideology thesis" — common at the time — that presumed little working-class oppositional consciousness against capitalism (see Abercrombie, Hill and Turner 1980; Therborn 1980).

In addition to class position, union membership, level of formal education and racialization were significant moderating factors in oppositional class consciousness in the 1980s. Given that unions were founded as major advocates of labour rights, one might expect most members to express oppositional consciousness. This was the case for the majority in Sweden, Canada and the US, with slighter differences in Norway from non-members. No union differences were found in Japan, again suggesting the political limits of trade unions then and there. Conversely, formal education had a conservative effect. The more highly educated expressed lower oppositional labour consciousness in Sweden, the US and Norway. This conservative effect was most notable in Sweden, where there was the highest general oppositional labour consciousness. Most of those with less than high school in all countries held an oppositional labour consciousness compared to a third of college graduates. The number of college graduates has increased rapidly since then in all these countries, including Sweden. In Canada and Japan, with the highest college completion rates and most highly educated labour forces, this education-based difference in oppositional consciousness seemed to have disappeared by the 1980s. There were only sufficient data by racialization for the US. These indicate that Black people, who were predominantly in non-managerial industrial and service worker positions, were much more likely to hold oppositional labour consciousness.[14] No consistent effects were found for gender, age or by private versus public sector.

In terms of relative effects, class position generally had stronger effects than other moderating factors on oppositional consciousness, with the notable exception of union effects for professional employees in the US and Canada. There were relatively few unionized professional employees in the early 1980s. Those professional employees who were unionized were much more likely in both the US (71 percent) and Canada (60 percent) to express oppositional labour consciousness than non-unionized professional employees (US 27 percent; Canada 35 percent). I will return to this finding in light of the later growth of unionized professional employees.

For estimates of trends in relations between class position and oppositional consciousness since the 1980s, I have to rely on the Canadian national surveys. The findings are summarized in Table 7.4, again focusing on the proportion in each class position holding pro-capital and pro-labour views. Again, a bolded first figure in a cell indicates pro-capital views are significantly greater than pro-labour views; a bolded second figure indicates pro-labour views are greater than pro-capital views.

Table 7.4 Oppositional Class Consciousness, by Class, Canada, 1982–2016 (% Pro-Capital / % Pro-Labour)

Class	1982	2004	2010	2016
Corporate capitalist*	80/0	64/2	n/a	n/a
Large employer	55/9	37/11	25/0	17/11
Upper manager	53/6	33/23	28/14	23/17
Small employer	39/11	29/21	14/25	29/14
Middle manager	28/25	19/30	21/21	16/28
Lower manager	19/37	3/28	17/41	13/34
Self employed	21/25	14/30	9/36	13/29
Professional employee	14/48	10/38	8/40	8/41
Service worker	13/41	9/39	13/27	7/37
Industrial worker	8/54	11/41	14/37	6/49
Total %	15/42	13/35	13/33	10/37
Total N	1758	2776	1193	2883

*Corporate executive surveys 1980–2000 for 1982 and 2000 figures.
Sources: Canada Work Learning Surveys 1998–2016 (includes 1982 CCS National Dataset).

The largest class difference in oppositional consciousness over the 1982–2016 period continues to be corporate capitalists' strong pro-capital views versus industrial workers' pro-labour views. But, at least in the Canadian case, other non-managerial workers (i.e., service workers and professional employees) were almost as likely as industrial workers to express pro-labour views throughout this period. The most notable changes in oppositional consciousness appear to be among both large employers and upper managers, with reductions from majority pro-capital views in the 1980s to majorities expressing contradictory oppositional consciousness more recently. This suggests a weakening of supportive sentiments among corporate capital's closest allies.

Further insight into these notable reductions in pro-capital oppositional consciousness among corporate capital's closest allies is provided by more detailed inspection of the critical component, defence of corporate profits (see Figure 7.1).

As the discussion in Chapter 6 documents and Figure 7.1 specifies, there has been a general consensus throughout this period that private corporations benefit their owners at the expense of workers and consumers, but there appears to have been a major loss of confidence by large employers and upper managers, in particular around the Great Recession of 2007–08. Their majority support until early in this century dropped to a minority of defenders of corporate profit taking after the

Figure 7.1 Corporations Benefit Owners at the Expense of Workers and Consumers by Class Position, Canada, 1982–2016 (% agree)

■ Large employer   ▦ Upper manager
▩ Industrial worker   ▨ Total labour force

Ns for respective years (large employers: 11/25/5/17; upper managers: 18/35/22/51; industrial workers: 510/506/197/424)
Sources: Canada Work Learning Surveys 1998–2016 (includes 1982 CCS National Dataset).

government bailouts of many firms "too big to fail" and has not bounced back. This is a pivotal indicator that strength of support for the profit imperative may have weakened among corporate capital's closest allies.

Referring back to Table 7.4, middle managers have expressed mixed oppositional views throughout this period, in keeping with their position right in the middle between capital and labour. Lower managers are consistently more likely to express pro-labour views. While upper managers' pro-capital views may have weakened, they continue to be less likely than lower managers to have pro-labour views. These findings contrast with a prevalent assumption in management literature of a widely shared pro-capital consensus among managers generally.[15]

As in most countries in the earlier 1980s surveys, the self-employed continued to express mixed oppositional views in keeping with their distinctive condition of providing the direct labour for their own-account businesses. They might be doing well for themselves in some special niches but are increasingly likely to be reduced to serving as hired labour subcontractors to larger corporations.

Professional employees in Canada, and in at least some other countries, have been most likely to express pro-labour views throughout this period, much more likely than most managers. The small number of empirical studies that have distinguished non-managerial professional employees from managers generally have begun to recognize political differences between them (e.g., Johnston and Ornstein 1985; Güveli et al. 2007). As I argued elsewhere (Livingstone et al. 2021), it is time to bury the misleading notion of a "professional-managerial class."

In Canada, besides class position, the most significant moderating factor on oppositional class consciousness in recent times has been union membership. Trade unions have retained more stable memberships (i.e., around 30 percent of the labour force) than in most other advanced capitalist countries experiencing significant declines (Stanford 2020), and they have managed to extend their reach among professional employees in particular. As in the early 1980s, a majority of union members generally express oppositional labour consciousness, compared to around a quarter of non-members. With regard to racialization, the pattern was inconsistent in earlier years, but in 2016 a majority of Black people expressed oppositional labour consciousness compared to a minority of white people. As noted earlier, no significant differences in oppositional consciousness have been found in Canada by formal education attainment — which has been relatively high since the 1980s. Income and wealth differences are clearly linked at the extremes, with pro-capital views for the rich and pro-labour views for the lowest income groups. Once again, no consistent effects are found for gender, age or by private versus public sector.

In terms of the relative effects of class and other factors, Black industrial workers are now more likely (74 percent) to have pro-labour oppositional consciousness than white industrial workers (50 percent). Low income is linked to greater pro-labour views among industrial workers (61 percent). Greater accumulated wealth is linked with lower pro-labour views among the self-employed (14 percent). The most important moderating effect is unionization among both industrial workers and professional employees. Both among the growing numbers of professional employees and declining numbers of industrial workers, majorities of unionized workers express oppositional labour consciousness; together they may represent the leading core of the current organized labor movement. Overall, class position has remained the most significant effect on oppositional class consciousness, and large employers and industrial workers have remained the most opposed classes.

There are many people who continue to express mixed views about their support for capital and labour in advanced capitalist societies. This contradictory consciousness includes increasing proportions of large employers and upper managers opposed to corporate profit taking. Their sample numbers in Figure 7.1 are small and further confirming studies are much needed. However, if we consider the apparent decline in pro-capital oppositional consciousness among large employers (from 55 percent to 17 percent) and upper managers (from 54 percent to 23 percent) between 1982 and 2016, along with the decline among corporate capitalists themselves between 1982 and 2000 (from 80 percent to 64 percent), it appears that pro-capital oppositional consciousness has been waning and contradictory consciousness growing among the dominant classes.

However, in contrast to pervasively promoted notions of contradictory, confused or ambivalent consciousness among the masses, patterns of pro-labour oppositional consciousness are linked, strongly in some cases, to non-managerial class position. Compared to the decline in pro-capital consciousness among dominant classes, pluralities of all non-managerial workers (professional employees, service workers and industrial workers) have continued to hold clear pro-labour oppositional views. It should come as no large surprise that pro-labour oppositional consciousness has generally been much more common among non-managerial workers than pro-capital consciousness. But the magnitude of these differences should also be recognized. In the 1980s, the differences for industrial workers between pro-labour and pro-capital views were: (Norway: 39 percent vs 16 percent; US: 40 percent vs 13 percent; Japan: 51 percent vs 9 percent; Canada: 55 percent vs 8 percent; and Sweden: 71 percent vs 3 percent). In Canada in 2016, the difference was 49 percent vs 6 percent. In all instances, there were more industrial workers with coherent oppositional labour consciousness than contradictory consciousness, and pro-labour consciousness prevailed over pro-capital views by a large ratio. In Sweden, Japan and Canada in the 1980s, the oppositional consciousness patterns were similar for both professional employees and service workers. The same was true for Canada in the later surveys. While Sweden in the 1980s registered the highest national levels of pro-labour oppositional consciousness so far documented, the recent levels of pro-labour views among non-managerial workers in Canada are not far behind.

The polarization between the large proportion of large employers holding pro-capital oppositional class consciousness and the large proportions of industrial workers as well as professional employees and service workers holding pro-labour oppositional class consciousness is the most consistent finding in all these surveys. This finding has rarely been addressed in empirical research and should be in further studies. But there has been even less attention to how these oppositional views are linked with alternative visions for society among these classes.

Class and the Highest Levels of Class Consciousness

Beyond oppositional class consciousness there are two central issues: the extent to which alternative views of the future are held by different classes, and the extent to which these views combine with class identity and oppositional consciousness to express the highest forms of hegemonic and revolutionary consciousness among those in different class positions.[16] First, I look at the general connections between class and generally preferred possible futures defending or transforming capitalism. Then I estimate the extent to which different classes have combined class identity, oppositional consciousness and future preferences into hegemonic capitalist versus revolutionary labour forms of class consciousness, which more dispose to action to either defend or transform advanced capitalism. As Chapter 6 demonstrated, we are dealing here with relatively small proportions of the entire employed labour force who express clear preferred visions of the future linked to class interests.

Class and Potential Defenders versus Transformers

So, to what extent do different classes hold views serving to defend capitalism versus views to transform this system? I assume that those who believe in the necessity of a profit-driven economy as well as retention of managerial prerogative are potentially strong defenders of existing capitalist systems. Conversely, those who support visions of an alternative non-profit economy based on worker control are potentially committed transformers of capitalism. As a first step, I look at all those who express preferences as either defenders or transformers, regardless of their class identities and levels of oppositional consciousness.

Table 7.5 provides estimates of these general proportions of defenders and transformers of capitalism from the available surveys in the early 1980s. The first figure in each cell in this table includes those in respective class positions who held pro-capitalist visions of a profit-driven economy with managerial prerogative, considered here to be likely defenders. The second figure refers to those who held alternative visions of worker control and a non-profit economy, potential transformers. Those not included in these two proportions held more mixed or uncertain preferences about the future, whatever their class identities and interests. Once more, a bolded first figure in a cell denotes class positions where defenders are significantly greater than transformers; bolded second figures indicate transformers greater than defenders.

Table 7.5 Defending versus Transforming Class Consciousness by Class, Advanced Capitalist Countries, 1980s (% Defender / % Transformer)

Class	US	Norway	Canada	Sweden
Corporate capitalist	n/a	n/a	n/a	n/a
Large employer	**26**/0	8/0	**55**/0	**100**/0
Upper manager	**32**/2	**19**/7	**53**/0	19/10
Small employer	**21**/3	**21**/3	**31**/3	**18**/0
Middle manager	**28**/3	**13**/3	**24**/3	**22**/8
Lower manager	14/5	7/13	11/4	7/**17**
Self employed	14/11	8/11	14/7	6/7
Professional employee	12/6	8/14	10/9	7/**23**
Service worker	8/7	8/11	5/11	5/**25**
Industrial worker	5/10	4/**16**	5/**16**	2/**36**
Total %	13/6	4/11	9/11	7/**23**
Total N	1697	1676	1758	1137

Source: CSCC (1980) data files; Canada Work Learning Surveys 1998–2016 (includes 1982 CCS National Dataset).

The relatively small numbers in this table should be scrutinized with some caution, but they do provide some distinctive and plausible patterns. Clear defenders of capitalism in the 1980s were most prominent among large and small employers as well as upper and middle managers in most countries. In Sweden and Canada, the majority of large employers were defenders of capitalism, but this was less so in the US and Norway. The lesser enthusiasm of large employers in the US could be related to greater dominance of corporate profits over theirs, and in Norway to the distinctive public corporate investment model. In all cases, large employers completely opposed anti-capitalist alternatives. Defenders also far outnumbered transformers among small employers everywhere. Upper managers were among the most likely to defend the system in all countries, most strongly in Canada (53 percent) but with much less support in Sweden and Norway (19 percent) along with some transformers (7 to 10 percent) mainly in the public sector. Smaller proportions of clearly committed defenders were found among lower managers and the self-employed, as well as in all non-managerial class positions. But in the early 1980s, there were discernible numbers of defenders of capitalism in nearly all class positions.

The self-employed and lower managers were both more evenly divided between committed defenders and transformers in all countries, as befits their marginal class positions between capital and non-managerial labour, and least likely to be strongly committed to either. Among industrial workers, transformers outnumbered defenders in all countries. The highest proportions were found among Swedish industrial workers (36 percent), with significant support among both service workers (25 percent) and professional employees (23 percent). In all other countries, industrial workers were also the more likely to be transformers, outnumbering defenders by at least two to one everywhere, but in other countries the numbers of transformers among industrial workers did not exceed 16 percent.

There were more mixed patterns among service workers and professional employees. Service workers may have been slightly more likely to be transformers than defenders in countries besides Sweden but in smaller proportions (around 10 percent or less). Professional employees had similarly small proportions and in the US may have been more likely to be defenders (12 percent) than transformers (6 percent). Sweden was distinctive in the extent to which transformers clearly outnumbered defenders among all non-managerial workers, and most greatly among industrial workers (36 percent versus 2 percent).

Overall, the class distribution indicated by these figures suggests that Sweden had the highest levels of potential transformational consciousness among all non-managerial classes (well over 25 percent of these workers), heavily outnumbering non-managerial workers who might defend capitalism (less than 5 percent). In the US, on the other hand, industrial workers were also somewhat more likely to be transformers than defenders (10 percent versus 5 percent) but they had relatively few potential allies even among other non-managerial workers. Sweden and the US may have represented the extremes of revolutionary potential versus defence of capitalism in the early 1980s.

The most significant moderating factor in the 1980s was union membership. In Sweden, the US and Canada, union members were about twice as likely to be transformers as other workers — going beyond the presumed limits of trade union consciousness. To give some idea of the relative extent of organized transformers in all these countries in the early 1980s, about 20 percent of US workers were unionized and 15 percent of unionized workers held visions of an alternative economy. This amounted to about 3 percent of the total employed labour force. In Sweden, about 78 percent were unionized and 23 percent indicated transformer views, about 18 percent of the labour force — six times as many transformers as in the US. There was some indication in the US that Black people were more likely to be transformers than white people. No other differences by age, sex, education or private/public sector were found.

Overall, class disposition to defend capitalism in the 1980s may have been relatively strongest and most widely distributed among classes in the US (13 percent of the labour force). But disposition to defend capitalism was most concentrated in Sweden among the small numbers of large employers. It was there that capitalism faced the greatest challenge from potential transformers, almost a quarter of the labour force. The unanimity of Swedish large employers with corporate capitalists suggests their strong solidarity to contest concerted social democratic wage reforms that had challenged "excess profits." They did so effectively over the following decade, including withdrawal of the employers' confederation (SAF) from centralized wage negotiations in the early 1980s and major movement of large Swedish companies to international settings. Swedish capital's offensive coupled with the large labour organization's division over continuing wage compression policies and wage earner fund use led to decline of the Swedish initiative that was clearly one of the greatest actual threats to the sanctity of private capitalist profits to date (Meidner 1993, 226).[17]

Once again, Canada provides the only available trend data for more recent times and only for 2016. Table 7.6 summarizes the proportions of defenders and transformers in each class position in both 1982 and 2016. Once more, the bolded first figure denotes class positions where defenders are significantly greater than transformers; bolded second figures indicate transformers greater than defenders.

Table 7.6 Defending versus Transforming Class Consciousness by Class, Canada, 1982–2016 (% Defender / % Transformer)

Class	1982	2016
Corporate capitalist	n/a	n/a
Large employer	55/0	11/0
Upper manager	53/0	17/2
Small employer	31/3	19/6
Middle manager	24/3	9/6
Lower manager	11/4	8/10
Self employed	14/7	7/9
Professional employee	10/9	4/11
Service worker	5/11	3/12
Industrial worker	5/16	3/12
Total %	9/11	6/12
Total N	1758	2882

Source: Canada Work Learning Surveys 1998–2016 (includes 1982 ccs National Dataset).

The main change that appears to have occurred during this period is declining relative commitment in dominant classes to a profit-driven economic vision. We have previously seen that supporters of current corporate benefits among both large employers and upper managers dropped from majorities to small minorities. Clear support for future profit maximization with managerial prerogative has also declined both among large employers and upper managers from majorities to small minorities, along with smaller declines to similar minorities among small employers and middle managers. Recall the Canadian corporate leader quoted in Chapter 2 who said: "There is a sense of public outrage [about excessive corporate greed] that we have to become increasingly concerned about." Corporate defenders and their allies are becoming more reserved about both present and future profit advocacy.

In addition to declining defenders among large employers and upper managers, there are suggestive — if not statistically significant — declines in all non-managerial classes in the minority proportions of system defenders. Among professional employees, system defenders may have declined from 10 percent to 4 percent, but, among all three classes of non-managerial workers (professional employees, service workers and industrial workers) transformers now outnumber defenders by about four to one. Professional employees and service workers are as likely as industrial workers to be transformers, more so than in the early 1980s.

Potential system transformers in 2016 in Canada were still concentrated among non-managerial employees as they had been in the early 1980s, both in proportionate terms and much more so in their larger absolute numbers. About 12 percent of professional employees and service workers as well as industrial workers support system transformation, similar to the overall non-managerial proportion of transformers in the early 1980s. Potential transformational consciousness may have increased somewhat in some other classes in Canada — except corporate capitalists and large employers. Among the self-employed and lower managers, the proportions of potential transformers — although still in very small proportions — may exceed the proportions of those disposed to defend the system.

Union membership is still a significant moderating factor in disposition to transformation in Canada, with union members among non-managerial workers about twice as likely to favour transforming the system. In addition, Black people are much more likely than white people to favour transforming the system. The recent income and wealth data confirm that the more well-to-do are least likely to be interested in transforming capitalism. No differences by age, sex, education or private/public sector appear.

Class and Hegemonic versus Revolutionary Consciousness

The relationship between class position and hegemonic or revolutionary class consciousness needs to be approached surgically. Here we are talking about the members of a class who have developed a sufficiently clear sense of the opposed interests of their class and other classes as well as a coherent vision of society to have the capacity to lead that class in either defending society or transforming it. At most times, it is likely that only small minorities of most classes will have developed such high levels of class consciousness. The central issue is the relative commitment to these contending forms of consciousness to defend the existing system and to transform it. What proportions of the members of a dominant class and its allies maintain hegemonic capitalist consciousness and, conversely, to what extent are subordinate classes developing revolutionary labour consciousness?

So, the ultimate question is the extent to which those in different classes with clear alternative visions of potential futures combine these views with either dominant or subordinate class identities and oppositional consciousness, thereby increasing their capacity to act to defend their established class interests or to transform current conditions. The foregoing analysis of preferred futures by class position offers some clues, but preferred futures may not mean much unless they are seen as connected to class interests you see as your own.

I have confirmed from my surveys of corporate executives with key corporate leaders in Canada what should be obvious. The vast majority of corporate capitalists have clearly identified as upper or upper middle class and have virtually unanimous pro-capital oppositional views (i.e., support profit taking and oppose the unconditional right to strike). In my interviews with corporate capitalists in Canada and Australia, all respondents also affirmed the necessity of the profit motive and rejected any prospect of workers taking control of businesses. This tiny group have predominantly hegemonic capitalist consciousness and hold extraordinary power, but they are far too small in number to exercise this power alone. To what extent do their key class allies share hegemonic class consciousness?

We also know from the prior analyses that industrial workers have had the highest levels of working class and general subordinate class identity, have had the highest oppositional labour consciousness and have been the most likely to hold transformative visions. So, industrial workers probably have the highest revolutionary labour consciousness. But what is the relative strength of such revolutionary consciousness and how widely has it been shared among non-managerial workers generally and other potential class allies?

The basic distributions of class by hegemonic versus revolutionary class consciousness in the 1980s for all available countries (i.e., US, Sweden, Norway and Canada) are summarized in Table 7.7. The first figure in each cell refers to the proportion with hegemonic capitalist consciousness; the second figure refers to those with revolutionary labour consciousness.

The proportions are very small and, especially for respondents in smaller classes, should be treated only as roughly indicative of strategic trace elements. Rarely and only in larger classes have differences in consciousness at this magnitude reached normal statistical significance (only in 1980 among Swedish industrial workers, at 17 percent in these surveys). But the percentages are at least suggestive of the proportions in

Table 7.7 Highest Class Consciousness by Class, Advanced Capitalist Countries, 1980s (% Hegemonic / % Revolutionary)

Class	US	Canada	Norway	Sweden
Corporate capitalist	n/a	n/a	n/a	n/a
Large employer	0/0	10/0	8/0	0/0
Upper manager	5/0	6/0	5/4	7/7
Small employer	4/2	3/0	0/3	0/0
Middle manager	4/2	3/0	0/3	8/0
Lower manager	1/3	1/0	0/8	0/8
Self employed	0/5	1/1	0/9	0/2
Professional employee	0/1	1/4	0/8	2/11
Service worker	1/4	1/4	0/8	0/11
Industrial worker	1/6	0/6	0/9	0/17
Total %	1/3	1/4	1/7	1/11
Total N	1697	1676	1758	1137

Source: CSCC data files.

different class positions with fully developed hegemonic or revolutionary consciousness grounded in clear class identities and class interests, and therefore more likely to play leading roles in class-based actions.

The first point to notice is that, beyond corporate capitalists, few in other classes exhibited hegemonic capitalist consciousness. Even among large employers in some countries, such views were negligible, and below middle managers they were virtually nonexistent. This finding is consistent with the argument that — beyond an enduring pro-capital oppositional consciousness among most employers and higher managers — the system has not recently had a deep hegemonic leadership to reproduce itself. This condition suggests *substantial political vulnerability of advanced capitalism to transformative tipping points.*

Second, revolutionary consciousness was discernible in virtually all non-managerial classes while hegemonic capitalist consciousness was negligible in all these classes. The only exception in 1980 was professional employees in the US, where revolutionary and hegemonic consciousness were both negligible. But in all countries in the 1980s, there were discernible proportions of both industrial workers and service workers (i.e., 4 percent or greater) with revolutionary labour consciousness. In most countries, they were joined by professional employees. Once again, Sweden was the leading case, with over 10 percent of service workers and professional employees, as well as some managers, joining industrial workers with revolutionary consciousness. As with transformative visions of the future generally, revolutionary labour consciousness was more discernible than hegemonic capitalist consciousness in nearly all classes in these countries in these 1980s surveys.

More recent estimates of the incidence of hegemonic capitalist versus revolutionary labour consciousness by class position are only available from the 2016 Canada national survey. The basic findings are summarized in comparison to 1982 findings in Table 7.8.

Table 7.8 Higher Class Consciousness by Class, Canada, 1982–2016 (% Hegemonic / % Revolutionary)

Class	1982	2016
Corporate capitalist	n/a	n/a
Large employer	10/0	6/0
Upper manager	6/0	10/0
Small employer	3/0	2/6
Middle manager	3/0	3/5
Lower manager	1/0	1/8
Self employed	1/1	2/6
Professional employee	1/4	1/10
Service worker	1/4	1/10
Industrial worker	0/6	0/11
Total %	1/4	2/8
Total N	1758	2878

Sources: Canada Work Learning Surveys 1998–2016 (includes 1982 CCS National Dataset).

Prior caveats about small numbers and trace elements apply, but a few interesting changes are suggested. First, the incidence of revolutionary consciousness among Canadian non-managerial workers (professional employees, service workers and industrial workers) may have increased, in aggregate from around 5 percent to around 10 percent. This is comparable to the aggregate level of revolutionary consciousness expressed by all Swedish non-managerial workers in the 1980s survey. Second, discernible expressions of revolutionary labour consciousness (around 5 percent) may be found among middle and lower managerial classes as well as smaller employer and self-employed classes, where there was virtually none in the early 1980s. Third, large employers and upper managers, typically the closest practical class allies of corporate capitalists, are still the most likely other class groups to express hegemonic capitalist consciousness in Canada. But their numbers and proportions are small at the same time as pro-capital oppositional consciousness and vision of a profit-driven economy have weakened considerably among both groups. The main change at this highest level of class consciousness in Canada was *that revolutionary labour consciousness was more discernible in 2016 than in 1982 and more widely detectable across the class structure.*

These "strategic trace elements" are all too small for reliable relative analyses of most other possible moderating factors, but among these shifting proportions, union members and visible minorities are generally overrepresented with revolutionary consciousness; the wealthy are conspicuously absent.

In sum, the basic findings regarding class and this highest level of class consciousness are as follows:

- In all countries, industrial workers were the most likely to have revolutionary labour consciousness.

- In all countries, non-managerial workers (including industrial workers, service workers and professional employees) comprised most of those with revolutionary labour consciousness, possibly in increasing proportions if Canada is indicative.

- Large employers and upper managers were generally the most likely allied classes to have hegemonic capitalist class consciousness but only in very small minorities in both class positions, compared to virtually all corporate capitalists.

- Corporate capitalist dominance has depended much more on contradictory class consciousness among non-managerial classes than on possibly declining oppositional capitalist consciousness among other employer and managerial classes.

Many of these estimations of class connections with higher levels of class consciousness involve small numbers subject to qualifications. On the basis of this evidence, some might say that we are still in a classic situation of ideological hegemony (see Livingstone 1976), where the leading corporate capitalist fraction of the dominant class consistently believes in and acts to realize its class interests while other subordinate classes generally express more mixed or contradictory views and are vulnerable to alliances and actions against their class interests. But we have previously seen that pro-labour oppositional consciousness is much more widespread than pro-capital oppositional consciousness, and we see here that revolutionary labour class consciousness is more concentrated among non-managerial workers and may have increased in proportions compared to the more negligible proportions in most classes with hegemonic capitalist consciousness. In any case, these proportions should be attended to as reflective of the most committed defenders of existing capitalism and its most committed visionary transformers. Some among them are likely to play respectively pivotal roles in directing the next stage toward tipping points.

Strategic Class Groups, Hegemonic or Revolutionary Consciousness and Public Policy

We saw in the last chapter that revolutionary labour consciousness in general was strongly associated with support for poverty reduction and concern about global warming. Conversely, hegemonic capitalist consciousness in general was strongly associated with opposition to poverty reduction as well as denial of the threat of global warming. I can now connect these policy views with class positions to get a somewhat better grasp of the class agents who might play strategic roles in public policies for defending or transforming advanced capitalism.

First, I look at connections of class and class consciousness with poverty reduction views in the countries with available data in the 1980s and Canada in 2016. Then I look at views on global warming in Canada in 2016. Finally, I offer a few tentative conclusions about discernible connections of class and class consciousness with actual policy change based on the available evidence.

The focus here is on the strategic class groups (besides the most privileged and inaccessible corporate capitalists) with the most opposed objective class interests and in which hegemonic capitalist consciousness or revolutionary labour consciousness have been most frequently detected: large and small employers and upper managers versus non-managerial employees, respectively. Both the critical mass and relative concentration of these two groups should be considered. In the early 1980s, employers and upper managers with hegemonic capitalist consciousness represented fewer than 1 percent of the total employed la-

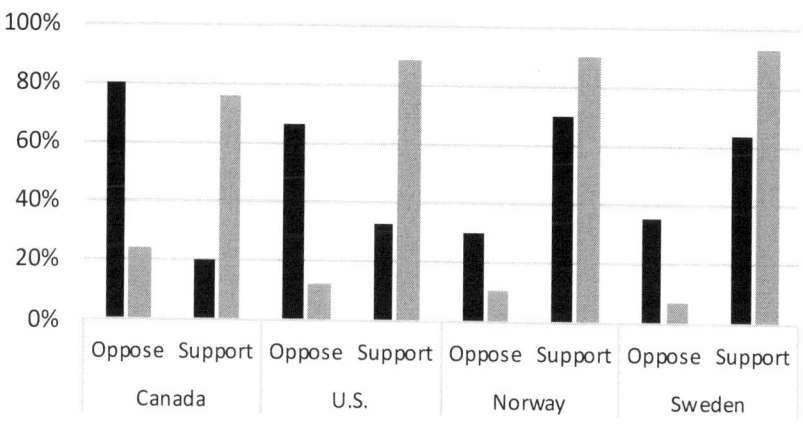

Figure 7.2 Support for the Poor by Strategic Class Groups, Hegemonic or Revolutionary Class Consciousness, Canada, US, Sweden, Norway, 1980s (% Oppose / % Support)

- Employers, upper managers with hegemonic consciousness
- Non-managerial employees with revolutionary consciousness

Source: CSCC (1980) data files.

bour force in all these countries. The proportions for non-managerial workers with revolutionary consciousness were larger and more varied. In Norway, Canada and the US, the proportions were between 3 and 4 percent of the labour force. In Sweden, non-managerial workers with revolutionary consciousness made up about 9 percent of the total labour force. Once again, Sweden exhibited the most revolutionary potential. However, in all cases, hegemonic consciousness was likely highly concentrated among corporate capitalists themselves while revolutionary consciousness was expressed by minorities among the non-managerial classes, including fewer than 20 percent of Swedish industrial workers.

Figure 7.2 summarizes the attitudes of these strategic class conscious groups on support for the poor in all available countries in the 1980s. While both strategic groups are small, the attitude differences between them are large.

The first point to note is that in all four countries there was strong unanimity among highly class conscious non-managerial workers on the need for increasing support for the poor. Majorities of class conscious employers and upper managers in Canada and the US opposed such support measures, consistent with a dominant free market ideology. In both Sweden and Norway, where social democratic regimes had been long established, class conscious business leaders tended to

Figure 7.3 Support for the Poor by Strategic Class Groups, Hegemonic or Revolutionary Class Consciousness, Canada, 1982, 2016 (%)

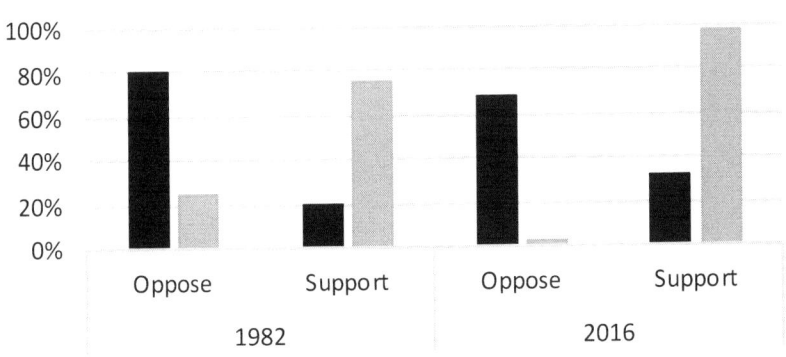

■ Employers, upper managers with hegemonic consciousness
▨ Non-managerial employees with revolutionary consciousness

Sources: CCS (1980) Data archive 1982; Canada Work Learning Surveys 1998–2016.

support such measures, but less so than non-managerial workers. This Nordic policy consensus is probably related to the institutionalization of more substantial anti-poverty measures in these countries (see Marx, Nolan and Olivera 2014).

Some insight into possible changes in such poverty policy preferences is offered by comparison of the Canadian survey findings on the same question in 1982 and 2016, as summarized in Figure 7.3.

First, it should be noted that Canadian non-managerial workers with revolutionary consciousness increased in aggregate from 3 percent of the labour force to over 6 percent by 2016, closer to the earlier Swedish level. Employers and upper managers with hegemonic consciousness remained at less than 1 percent of the labour force. Consistent with their US colleagues in 1982, these class conscious Canadian business leaders continued in 2016 to oppose anti-poverty measures as interfering with needed free market discipline of the labour force. These views may have softened somewhat but most of these business leaders were still opposed. Conversely, class conscious non-managerial workers who were strongly supportive of anti-poverty measures in 1982 were virtually unanimously so in 2016 as poverty became more evident. These are strikingly and consistently opposed policy attitudes. Over this period, the general labour force consensus supporting anti-poverty measures did increase significantly (from 67 percent to 84 percent of the total employed labour force). The support of growing proportions of class conscious workers — over-represented in labour unions and other anti-poverty movements — may well have contributed to this increase. But the slow pace of actual anti-poverty initiatives may have had more to do with continued political opposition of corporate capitalists and their closest allies among other employers and upper managers.

With regard to global warming as a threat to human survival, the basic recent attitude differences by class are shown in Figure 7.4.

Class conscious non-managerial workers are now virtually unanimous in support of action to address the threat of global warming to human survival. There is consensual support among about three-quarters of the employed labour force, but it is among these most class conscious workers that the most concerted class force for environmental change is concentrated. There are more mixed views among class conscious business class leaders — trying to accommodate climate change reduction initiatives with profit maximizing pro-growth priorities in such notions as a "net zero economy" (Pacthod and Pinner 2021).

More generally, the evidence presented here suggests that highly class conscious workers may have held strongly coherent views on a number of matters of progressive public policy since the 1980s. The most class conscious in more dominant class groups have been most resistant to

Figure 7.4 Threat of Global Warming by, Strategic Class Groups, Hegemonic or Revolutionary Class Consciousness, Canada, 2016 (%)

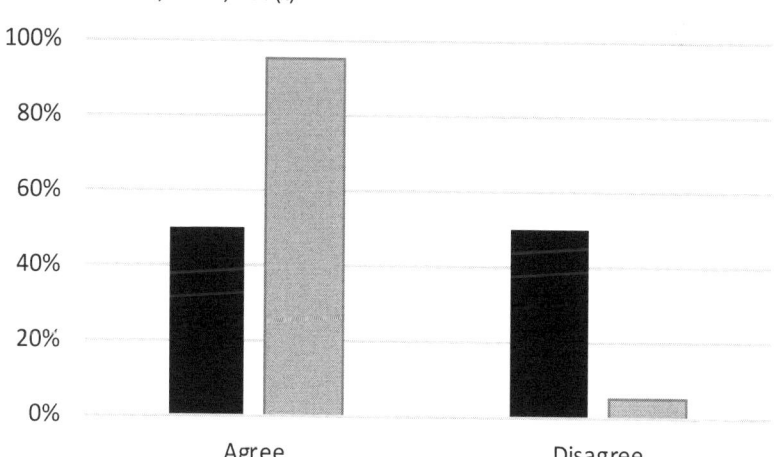

Source: Canada Work Learning Surveys 1998–2016.

these increasingly popular progressive policy options. These class patterns are consistent with the few recent cross-national surveys that have found major attitude differences between large employers, who reject welfare and climate policies, and professional employees, who show the highest rates of acceptance of both welfare and climate policies (Fritz and Koch 2019). If these increasingly progressive views have not yet been translated into many actual policies, this should not be used to deny the existence of highly class conscious workers or their potential to influence future social movements and public policies.

Concluding Remarks: Tipping Points for Transformation

Recent class-blind research on the historical effectiveness of social change action has suggested that non-violent change movements have often been more effective at social policy and regime change than violent ones (Chenoweth and Stephan 2012). However accurate this claim may prove to be (see Anisin 2020), the sustained commitment of a small portion of the populace has frequently led greater numbers to act to address the gap between institutionalized practices and popular conceptions of social justice. Key factors appear to be participation in protest actions by diverse groups, continuation of varied campaigns beyond protests and shifting loyalties among elites and security forces when they sense that popular sentiments are moving against them. Based on a review of hundreds of change campaigns in the twentieth century, Chenoweth (2013) suggested that when somewhat over 3 percent of the population engage in systematic campaigns of noncooperation over a sustained period, non-violent campaigns for social justice have most often been successful. More speculative studies suggest that when 10 percent of the population holds an "unshakable" belief, their belief will almost certainly be adopted by the majority of the society (Xie et al. 2011). The latter studies used primarily computational and analytical methods to discover tipping points where a minority belief becomes the majority opinion. These researchers cite the women's suffrage movement early in the twentieth century as well as the civil rights movement that bore some fruit in the US shortly after African-Americans became 10 percent of the US population. Such simple rules pay little attention to counter-strategies of established powers, but they do register the potential of small committed social justice movements that have been able to resonate with popular sentiments and beliefs in social rights.

The surveys in this chapter found that only tiny proportions in any class outside corporate capitalists attest full commitment to defending advanced capitalism. Much greater proportions of non-managerial workers and other classes have expressed clear support for alternative futures. In the available surveys, only in 1980 Sweden has (just barely) over 10 percent of the employed labour force actually been found to be clearly class conscious supporters of transforming capitalism. Even in this most advanced case, this sentiment was not sufficient to prevent pro-capital reversals of progressive policies from the 1980s onward. The 2016 Canadian survey found that over 10 percent of non-managerial workers and over 8 percent of the entire employed labour force had revolutionary class consciousness and that these people have become almost unanimous in their support for anti-poverty measures and preparedness to fight global warming. There is also more recent evidence of growing public concern about the threats of global warming and increases in income inequality both in "rich countries" and across the world.[18] It is highly probable that pro-labour anti-capitalist views are becoming more coherent and widespread across classes in many countries with mounting evidence of economic inequities and ecological disasters. Growing popular support appears to be animating more sustained related social movements for significant economic and ecological policy changes. At very least, there are substantial signs of growing protest actions at all levels of civil society (e.g., Chenoweth, Pinckney and Lewis 2018) in advanced capitalism on many issues of social justice.

Tipping points *are* increasingly probable, but we are also witnessing strategic reassertions of capital's profit drive. This is a truly deadly struggle led by increasingly desperate corporate capitalist forces' strategies to divide progressive forces. Labour and social movements face major challenges to build and maintain alliances in this struggle, while also dealing with the changing class composition of the labour force, with fewer industrial workers, more professional employees and more socially diverse workers. Corporate capitalists cannot continue to defend the existing system without both active pro-capital support from members of allied classes, as well as contradictory consciousness of many others. There are signs of weakening loyalties among corporate class allies. However, it is also likely that highly class conscious non-managerial workers will need substantial support from other sympathetic workers and other class allies for sustained social change action to realize more transformative goals.

The analysis of relations of class consciousness with class positions in this chapter has found vital connections, especially the persistence and possible growth of revolutionary class consciousness among non-managerial workers. This inquiry is an initial step. More comprehensive comparative studies are much needed, including inquiry into the class consciousness of workers in unorganized sectors witnessing new unionizing drives. In addition to well-informed collective practice by progressive activists, creation of more humane, liberating futures depends on continuing efforts to interpret social reality accurately.

Critics may rightly say that these macro-level profiles provide little insight into the experiential realities of class relations lived through racialization, gender and generational dimensions as well as in household and community spheres in particular countries or social formations. Such survey data offer merely rough approximations of expressions of class consciousness among employment aggregates, but these profiles do suggest general dispositions for alliances and actions among employment class groups.

The supplementary analyses here of the effects of moderating factors on connections between class and class consciousness have found significant effects of unionization, racialization, income and education. Perhaps most notably, racial minority status (of Black and Indigenous peoples) among non-managerial workers is now associated with greater pro-labour oppositional consciousness. This suggests that class exploitation and racial oppression can have strong combined effects on development of progressive class consciousness in advanced capitalism. Few significant effects by gender or generation have been found on these measured forms of class consciousness, although there are discernible tendencies for both women and younger people to hold more progressive views; potential combined effects of both gender and age-based oppression on class consciousness require much more in-depth study. Finally, contrary to the initially posited possible greater exploitation of private goods direct producers, there was a general absence of public/private sector differences per se in class consciousness. This suggests that the shared subordination of non-managerial workers in both private and public spheres is having common effects on their class consciousness.

This analysis sheds new light on the class consciousness of professional employees. We have seen that, since the 1980s, non-managerial professional employees have been the fastest growing employment class in all advanced capitalist societies. While sharing initial training disciplines, non-managerial professional employees should be distinguished from professional employers, self-employed professionals and professional managers with other class interests. During this period, professional employees have faced declining job control and increasing underemployment of their advanced training. They have come to express similar levels of oppositional labour and revolutionary class consciousness to the declining numbers of industrial workers. Professional employees in general are now the most highly organized employee class group, with the majority being members of unions and/or associations (Raykov and Livingstone 2014; Livingstone et al. 2021). Their worsening conditions of work and learning are placing them in comparable situations to the skilled trades workers of the late nineteenth century. Strategic numbers of those crafts workers responded by joining and leading the labour movements of the twentieth century, while those who had been owners of their own firms largely disappeared. Will it be different this time as we face unprecedented tipping points?

More generally, the increasingly capital-intensive and automated production processes of advanced capitalism require increasing active engagement of the minds of many of the remaining hired workers in all spheres, while there are fewer decent jobs for workers. The popular demand for more formal education and qualifications continues to grow, as does the underemployment gap. Will continuing revisions within the capitalist labour process and government economic and environment policies defuse pro-labour oppositional and revolutionary consciousness? The answer so far in this century is the opposite.

Gross inequities of reward are blatant, underemployment is increasingly chronic, and a highly qualified reserve army of labour of unemployed and marginalized people is growing. Indeed, as I have argued elsewhere, advanced capitalist countries have become "knowledge societies" with much larger proportions of well-qualified people than their narrow "knowledge economies" are able to utilize (Livingstone 2009). In this context, the class consciousness of those who are most exploited in "knowledge economies" — including industrial workers, service workers and professional employees — is of critical importance.

Social protests against the inequities and excesses of capitalism continually erupt. In the wake of the Great Recession of 2007–08, speculation abounded about future prospects for capitalism (Mann 2013; Streeck 2016), and leftist scholars reflected soberly about class fractions with the potential to lead offensives challenging capitalist hegemony (Therborn 2014). The present analysis suggests that the hegemonic class consciousness of the corporate core of the capitalist class may remain quite solid but with weakening class alliances. In most advanced capitalist countries, mixed class consciousness may have continued to prevail among many employment class positions. But disaffection and skepticism with corporate capital's domination over labour and sustainable life is widespread among many class positions and show signs of growing and consolidating. General sentiments of resistance among classes based in paid workplaces — the "residual" industrial working class, precarious service workers, underemployed professional employees and others — indicate fertile ground for progressive change movements. Sustainable progressive change will surely involve alliances between activists in relatively secure and more precarious employment class positions as well as the "relative surplus population" in both "rich countries" and the Global South (Neilson and Stubbs 2011).

Production relations in the capitalist labour process reproduce and change classes every day. These class relations animate central parts of our lives. Continuing analysis of connections between employment classes and their class consciousness and policy sentiments is needed to comprehend the resonance and potential alliances of these classes with broader social movements. The COVID-19 pandemic offers another critical moment for possible transformation. The final chapter addresses more fully the current prospects for activism.

Notes

1. The general forms of class consciousness and measures used to estimate them are defined at the beginning of Chapter 6 and in Appendix 2.
2. Class origins, history and aspirations may also be significantly related to differences in aspects of class consciousness. Comparable evidence on these dimensions is beyond the scope of the current inquiry.
3. For logical and substantive clarifications of the relationship between exploitation and domination, see Vrousalis (2013) and Terray and Serrano (2020).
4. For some indication of the continuing development of distinctions between productive and unproductive labour in advanced capitalism, see Roberts (2014); Fuchs and Fisher (2015); Moraitis and Copley (2017); and Huws (2019).

5. See, for example, Stone et al. (2020) and Stansbury and Summers (2020).
6. As discussed in the Livingstone and Mangan (1996a; 1996b) chapter and the related book, much of the analysis of employment classes has been sex blind. We began by comparing these schemes through their own terms of reference and limited to male respondents. An analysis of household classes (Livingstone and Asner 1996) was also conducted using the same Hamilton survey data. The current chapter has insufficient comparative data on spousal employment. Only simple possible gender effects on class by class consciousness are considered.
7. In terms of the class model used in this book, this "proletariat" included industrial workers and service workers; the "non-proletariat" lumped together corporate capitalists, large employers, small employers, self-employed, upper, middle and lower managers and professional employees — quite a mishmash!
8. This study defined alienation as a psychological estrangement or disconnect that involves a negative emotional and cognitive separation from work; it was measured by an eight-item scale.
9. The assumed order of class positions (excluding the tiny numbers of corporate capitalists) for these measures is: 1 large employers; 2 upper managers; 3 small employers; 4 middle managers; 5 lower managers; 6 self-employed; 7 professional employees; 8 service workers; 9 industrial workers. This order is assumed to reflect the combined power of ownership and control over labour as discussed in Chapter 4. The specific order may vary according to circumstances, but large employers and upper managers are at the top of the class hierarchy and industrial and service workers at the bottom in virtually all advanced capitalist production settings.
10. The exceptions are hegemonic capitalist and revolutionary labour consciousness, where the incidence has typically been too small to reach conventional statistical significance.
11. As noted in Table 7.1, upper managers are not distinguishable from middle managers in this Japanese sample.
12. In Table 7.1, only 1 percent of Japanese in 1987 opted for an upper-middle-class identity, compared to 17 percent opting for upper (2 percent) or upper-middle-class (15 percent) identity in 2017, as per Table 6.2.
13. Once again, the general forms of class consciousness and measures used to estimate them are defined at the beginning of Chapter 6 and in Appendix 2.
14. Wright's (1997, 446–451) similar findings of significantly higher scores for the black than white working class on his anti-capitalism index in the U.S in 1980 might be noted here.
15. For a critical review of the management literature and further documentation of differences between managerial levels, see Livingstone et al. (2021).
16. It should be noted that Japan is omitted from this stage of the analysis of the 1980s surveys because items on preferred futures were excluded from the survey questionnaire.
17. For a useful retrospective account, see Viktorsson and Gowan (2017).
18. See, for example, United Nations Development Program (2021); Gornick and Johnson (2020).

8

Tipping Point for Advanced Capitalism

This Time Is Different

> The deepest shadow that hangs over us is neither terror, environmental collapse, nor global recession. It is the internalized fatalism that holds there is no possible alternative to capital's world order. (Kovel and Lowy 2001, 1)

We are living in a pivotal moment in the history of capitalism. Building on the prior analysis, in this chapter I underline the distinctive features of these times and suggest the means of progressive transformation.

Capitalism is killing us all. This prolific mode of production served to liberate many from slavery and serfdom tied to the land. However, in the deepest irony, most of us are free to choose among increasingly insecure, uncertain and underemployed hired labours controlled by tiny numbers of incredibly wealthy corporate capitalists and their top managers. Meanwhile, the land and the entire ecosystem are devastated by this still expanding system of profit-driven production and consumption. Much of the time, many still choose to preoccupy ourselves with the attractions of this system. Many try to ignore, forget and deny the consequent devastation that diminishes our chances for sustainable lives. But the devastation gets harder to ignore. We are reaching the tipping point for advanced capitalism.

The capitalist system that now spans the globe took over from the feudal mode of production in western Europe gradually by infiltration through trading city enclaves and more rapidly through conquest of tribute-paying modes of production and civilizations elsewhere. In both instances, the transitions were uneven, marked by uncertainties and fears of the unknown. There are diverse enclaves at many levels throughout the world infiltrating the neoliberal variant of advanced capitalism in response to popular democratic demands. Their potential to lead a durable transition to a more sustainable and equitable way of life, as illustrated here, is significantly greater than most people realize.

This analysis has documented continuity and change in the class structure since the early 1980s, most notably the growth of non-managerial professional employees who are widely regarded as strategic knowledge workers. I provide one of the few comparative profiles of higher levels of class consciousness during this period, finding much greater pro-labour class consciousness than pro-capital class consciousness generally among employed labour forces. I also found much greater incidence of oppositional and revolutionary labour consciousness among non-managerial workers and declining support for the system among corporate capitalists' closest allies. Finally, I found that highly class conscious non-managerial workers are virtually unanimous in supporting ending poverty and seeing the threat of global warming, while the most class conscious capitalist forces are much more divided on such issues. These findings suggest that the pro-labour class forces for leading progressive change are now much greater than most analysts presume. Their success hinges on activating the shared sympathies of wider mass movements.

Capitalism is the most dynamic economic system ever devised. It is marked by continual change of techniques of production driven by competition between business owners to reduce costs to gain profits. For hundreds of years, from the widespread enclosures of common land in feudal England to the consolidation of peasant plots in China in the past generation, more efficient farming techniques have served to release subsistence labour from the land to seek hired employment in whatever factory or street it could be found. This process has represented a form of liberation. Some with entrepreneurial ambition have flourished. Some with specialized work skills or collective bargaining strength have obtained relatively secure employment and greater personal freedom. The possibilities for mainly upward intergenerational mobility did expand as capitalism increased its global reach. But land enclosures have always generated major threats to subsistence and resource access, and these remain overwhelming for many people today as globalizing capital continually moves on, industrializing the countryside and deindustrializing established urban zones in pursuit of profit margins.

Apologists for advanced capitalism frequently refer to the billions lifted out of poverty. An oft-quoted report from the Brookings Institution

(Kharas and Hamel 2018, 3) declares: "For the first time since agriculture-based civilization began 10,000 years ago, the majority of humankind is no longer poor or vulnerable to falling into poverty." It is true that production techniques under capitalism have generated a vast array of goods and services, commodities that have made material life more comfortable for many with a secure wage, most recently in the case of China. But this claim is patently false in terms of vulnerability. The vast majority of the many millions of workers who have gone from subsistence on the land to seek to sell their labour elsewhere in recent decades have gone into a precarious existence, often in urban slums (e.g., Davis 2005) and generally in jobs of temporary tenure. It is undoubtedly true that growing numbers are increasingly dependent on a monetary wage — even though over half the work we do remains unpaid household and community labour (Livingstone 2010). But these wages are becoming more inequitable and insecure as are the inequalities in many other human rights needed for a fulfilling life today (e.g., access to formal education, health care, secure jobs, political decisions).[1] Capitalist apologists have typically ignored such subsistence threats and inequities or discounted them as side effects of meritocratic opportunity. Even a dissident millionaire at Davos (Hooker 2022, 1) is moved to exclaim: "I know how skewed our economy is…. We have hit the end of the line when another quarter of a billion people will be pushed into extreme poverty this year." But, more blatantly, these apologists never admit the depth of the ecological threat of capitalist dynamics to human survival. This tipping point is scientifically established as imminent[2] while capitalist apologists celebrate or call for short-term monetary material gains for a fraction of humanity.

A Different Time

There has been an extraordinary amount written about tipping points for advanced capitalism in the wake of the Great Recession of 2007–08, and there will be much more in the aftermath of the COVID-19 pandemic (e.g., Independent Panel for Pandemic Preparedness and Response 2021). Whether or not capitalism is blamed for climate change, the most recent opinion surveys across advanced capitalist countries find widespread and increasing public concern about climate change as well as majority willingness to change how they live and work to reduce its effects (Bell et al. 2021). Economic inequalities exceed those of the Great Depression in relative terms.[3] A nuclear winter is at least as likely as during the Cold War,[4] heightened by the Russia-Ukraine war. Popular political demands specified in this chapter are reaching unprecedented levels. Sensibilities about all these tipping points are amplifying each other, in both progressive and regressive ways. This is not the first epoch-threatening crisis faced by capitalism and it may not be the last. But it is distinctive.

This possible transition from advanced capitalism to whatever succeeds it will likely be different in several respects from the transition to capitalism:

1. First and foremost, the transition will be more definite. Geopolitical conflicts and the attendant nuclear threat continually undermine cooperative international efforts regarding climate change. Regardless, the multiple threats of global warming, environmental pollutants and critical natural resource exhaustion will destroy the capitalist way of life if it is not transformed. At least nine of the fifteen known environmental elements that regulate the state of the planet, including losses of several polar ice sheets, rain forest droughts and coral reef die-offs, have already been activated, and there is clear scientific support to declare a state of planetary emergency for the existential threat to civilization (Steffen et al. 2018; Wallace-Wells 2019).

2. The transition in whatever form will likely be global. No prior mode of production has had such a wide expanse. No part of the Earth is going to be able to isolate itself from consequences of this transition.

3. We know the basic timeline for reversibility, really a matter of a decade or so (IPCC 2022), in contrast to prior civilizations that tended to presume their own continuity until some combination of economic, political and ecological circumstances often brought their rapid collapse.[5]

4. The neoliberal era of globalization has left capitalist state economic toolchests relatively bare. Interest rates were held at relatively low levels for decades and combined government and consumer debt are still at historic highs in the wake of the Great Recession. With dominant financial capital focused on enhancing share value rather than productive investment while wage levels stagnate, there are few

standard options for capital-oriented governments besides further increasing debt. Post-capitalist alternatives stand a better chance versus such state reforms.

5. The COVID-19 pandemic has had an exceptionally rapid global impact in disrupting economies, reducing employment and reshaping daily life while graphically demonstrating the limits of conventional measures in current capitalist economies to cope with current and probable future health, environmental and economic crises. There are few greater indictments of advanced capitalism than the refusal of large private pharmaceutical corporations to reduce profits to permit mass production of vaccines in poor countries while millions died.

6. We know what many of the actions are that are needed to ensure survival, including more equitable distribution of resources to meet pressing needs and gearing production to social use and sustainability rather than continuing to produce anything that can make a profit while further polluting the Earth. As illustrated below, there are many working alternative societal models among us;[6] they need to be developed more rapidly.

7. We have a more knowledgeable population and more productive tools than ever before to accomplish a sustainable transition from capitalism. Much of this most highly qualified labour force languishes in burgeoning underemployment, bouncing between precarious jobs and unemployment with diminished expectations about their possibilities in capitalist society. The most highly qualified reserve army of labour in history has unprecedented potential for creative work and fulfilling lives.[7]

8. Finally, the culture of protest in recent years over inequity and environmental issues has had growing popular resonance for social change, as exemplified by widespread demonstrations and campaigns. Beyond "stakeholder" rhetoric, the dominant global capital response has been to evade or try to block any regulations, taxes or other measures to reduce inequality or environmental degradation that might diminish profits. But the shift from shareholder to stakeholder rhetoric shows how discredited the neoliberal model of capitalism has become.

In sum, we have an unprecedented chance to create a better world and precious little time to do it. Most effective major social change processes contain at least three basic ingredients: critique and protest; an alternative model; and strategic agency. In this chapter I address all three in relation to the prior analyses and the current imminent tipping point.

Critique and Protest

Through human history, major social transformations have involved not only inspirational revolutionary leadership but mass protests by many fed up with worsening social conditions. An instructive example is the end of slavery in the US. Abraham Lincoln is widely celebrated for signing the abolition proclamation, but the hundreds of thousands of slaves who fled southern plantations and the many more who gave subtle and tacit resistance while remaining on them are most often forgotten (see Roediger 2014). We are in the midst of an even more profound transformation for life itself. There are highly visible inspirational leaders of climate change action, from Gretta Thunberg to Bill McKibben, but without the sustained effort of those in mass movements such leadership would be almost useless. (See Camfield 2022 for a compelling case).

Tigar and Levy (1977) traced a jurisprudence of insurgency in relation to emergence of the merchant bourgeoisie and private property rights from the constraints of European feudalism. Tigar later also provocatively suggests that a similar insurgency has been occurring in advanced capitalism as lawyers allied with labour, civil rights and other social rights movements have used the courts in liberal democracies to establish, solidify and defend social rights, often against private property rights (Tigar 2002). This has probably been true at least in a general cumulative sense over the past century, but such legal gains are only sustainable with widespread popular democratic demand for fuller social rights. There are many signs of such support.

The numbers of mass social protests have generally increased globally since the end of World War II, and recent years may have seen the largest wave of non-violent mass movements in world history (Chenoweth et al. 2019). The protests of unprecedented scale and sustained intensity that have rocked advanced capitalist societies in recent years have had two basic sorts of objectives: stopping environmental degradation and overcoming economic, racial and sexual discrimination. Prominent examples include climate marches, protests against fossil fuel construction and/or spills, women's rights marches, mass mobilizations in support of strikes by teachers and nurses and anti-racism demonstrations highlighted by the Black Lives Matter global protests in the summer of 2020. Critical concerns about economic, racial and sexual inequalities have been increasingly mixed with fears about environmental threats, along with a sense that governments have been ineffectual in addressing either. The COVID-19 pandemic limited street protests but did not diminish interacting popular concerns. In contrast, the right-wing protests to restore individual freedoms that have drawn so much media coverage and faced less repressive police treatment reflect the views of tiny minorities.

An OECD (2018) survey conducted in twenty-one countries just before the pandemic found a widespread sense of dissatisfaction and injustice in all countries. A US respondent said: "If I were to lose my job, I would lose everything.... I have no savings ... no retirement set aside for the future, and massive credit card debt" (11). Of course, there were differences by social background and by national levels of benefit provisions, but there was pervasive concern about difficulties of making ends meet and majority support in all countries for taxing the rich more to support the poor. An earlier *Financial Times*/Harris Poll in the US and the five largest European countries just before the Great Recession found little enthusiasm for free-market capitalism and majority agreement in all countries that multinational corporations have too much power. There was general pessimism about countries' future and strong support for the important role of trade unions in today's work environment (Harris Poll 2007). In a more recent Canadian survey, a majority agreed that the COVID-19 pandemic shows that we need to radically transform our economy to work differently in the future (Innovative Research Group 2020). Popular criticisms of the neoliberal variant of advanced capitalism from different standpoints are coming to a shared conclusion. This economic system based on unlimited inequitable accumulation of capital, profits and commodities — while generating environmental destruction and societal breakdown — cannot be sustained much longer. Cumulative popular support for major social change continues to grow.

The science behind global warming has been broadly known for over a century in scientific circles,[8] and the central role of fossil fuels has been well understood for generations — even as the fossil fuel industry has tried to suppress this knowledge.[9] The environmental effects are so widely experienced and the major sources so well documented that mounting popular awareness, protests and demands for change have led to some government policies and private corporate gestures to address the issue. The Paris Climate Agreement of 2015 was a significant formal step, but even after the United Nations Climate Change Conference in Glasgow in late 2021, few nations had yet taken effective measures to meet their commitments. The central criteria of climate justice remained undefined. Fossil fuel companies remained among the major sponsors "in the henhouse," the baselines for action were ambiguous, and the formal commitments have been increasingly recognized as woefully inadequate both in their extent and mechanisms of accountability.[10] The protests for both serious reforms and more revolutionary change continue to mount.

Concern about the economic inequities generated by capital accumulation has also become increasingly evident. In 1953, when the CEO of General Motors was nominated by President Eisenhower to be his secretary of defence, Charles Wilson confidently declared that what was good for GM was good for America.[11] Such corporate claims may have had some plausibility then, but they have virtually none today. During the COVID-19 pandemic, as unemployment soared, evictions climbed and repressive police actions increased, stock markets surged right alongside. Since the 1970s, the neoliberal deregulation of markets in favour of profit motive "magic" has led to the privatization of many public functions and the rise of financial capital and private equity firms to decisive roles. A mainstream article early in the COVID-19 pandemic (Baradaran 2020, 44) accurately summarized the dominant recent tendency of corporate capital:

> Private equity firms use money provided by institutional investors like pension funds and university endowments to take over and restructure companies or industries…. In pursuit of maximum returns, such firms have squeezed businesses for every last drop of profit, cutting jobs, pensions and salaries where possible. The debt-laden buyouts privatize gains when they work, and socialize losses when they don't, driving previously healthy firms to bankruptcy and leaving many others permanently hobbled.

As documented in the Chapter 7, a growing sense of being ripped off has greatly reduced support for maximizing corporate profits even among large employers and upper managers. The increasing gap between profit maximizing and general economic benefits is grossly displayed in the growing rate of corporate executive pay compared to median employee packages. In the most extreme case in the US, CEO benefits increased over 900 percent between 1978 and 2019, the typical worker's wage by around 10 percent after adjusting for inflation.[12] The experiential gap between the liberal democratic promise of equal opportunities and the incidence of systemic discrimination, particularly against working people of colour, becomes increasingly evident in light of such conspicuous inequities. High tech billionaires such as Jeff Bezos and Elon Musk devote some of their massive profits to space travel while the most exploited and oppressed struggle to make ends meet here on Earth. But the record profits of Bezos's Amazon, one of the largest private corporations in the world, are being strongly resisted by organizing campaigns of its low-paid workers on every continent. The protests of the summer of 2020 are a more widespread expression of this cumulative sense of injustice.

Several surveys indicate that the Black Lives Matter protests, which peaked in June 2020, were the largest in US history,[13] involving between 6 and 10 percent of the entire adult population, and dwarfing the depth and breadth of numbers involved in civil rights protests in the 1960s. The Black Lives Matter network provided materials, and many activists shared protest details through social media to a wide array of participants, including unprecedented numbers of white protesters in many parts of the US. Being exposed to a video of George Floyd's killing while captive to the pandemic and under the adversarial stance of Trump's presidency, was clearly moving and catalytic.[14] The strength of these protests quickly began to produce some immediate progressive changes in police forces (banning of choke holds, access to disciplinary records, funding reforms) after generations of increased militarization.[15] Whether these unprecedented protests will lead to more substantial changes in use of force remains an open question.

However widespread critical sentiments may be, the numbers involved in popular protests do not guarantee success even if they truly reflect general public opinion. One of the clearest recent historical examples of this was the Japanese protests against the presence of US military bases in Okinawa in 1959–60, one of the largest mobilizations in human history. About 30 million people, or a third of the population, and including a popular front of hundreds of organizations, took part in demonstrations against the "Anpo" security treaty, which had granted the US military bases there in exchange for the end of American occupation. There was little doubt that the vast majority of the remaining population opposed the renewal of this treaty, but in the end the treaty was renewed by the governing Liberal Democratic Party (LDP), which forced through votes in the Diet parliament surrounded by riot police. Protests continued for a while but soon dissipated in the wake of concessionary economic policies that have been key measures in keeping the LDP in power ever since (see Kapur 2018). This case points to the limits of any simplistic rules of protest participation in relation to success, such as the much cited "3.5 percent rule" as a population threshold for success of non-violent protest campaigns.[16]

In the Japanese Anpo case, as in the recent extensive Hong Kong pro-democracy protests centred on China's proposed extradition measure and subsequent new security law, population base criteria are further complicated by the potential coercive force of an external occupying power, the US and China, respectively. In both cases, beyond widespread unanimity of opposition to proposed deals, protest effects also appear to have been limited by lack of agreement on shared objectives beyond sheer deal rejection as well as by diverse and weakly allied political organizations and leaders.

In a recent reflection, Erica Chenoweth (2020, 2–3), the original formulator of the 3.5 percent rule, concedes that committed strategic leadership and innovative tactics are at least as important as short-term mobilization for protest movements. She recognizes that wider tacit popular support is needed to sustain such movements:

> The historical record suggests that large-scale participation is usually the tip of the iceberg, and there is usually much broader public support for the movement than the people who are active in the streets. But unlike active participation in a mass movement, there is no way to calculate how much popular support is needed for a movement to succeed without comprehensive opinion polling.

A popular sentiment for justice and reform often grows as a response to a deteriorating situation. The opinion surveys analyzed in the prior chapters and several more recent surveys offer some indications. Most clearly, on environmental issues, opinion surveys have found that there is support for action on global warming by the vast majority, as well as virtual unanimity among nearly 10 percent of the population who express a revolutionary class consciousness. On capitalist inequities, support for anti-poverty action has gained increased majority support and also unanimity among those with revolutionary class consciousness. The national surveys summarized in Chapter 6 found that majorities of the labour force in Sweden, Japan, Canada and the US in the 1980s believed that corporate owners were benefitting at their expense; by 2016 this sentiment had increased in Canada and very likely in most other countries. In Sweden, Japan and Canada over 40 percent of the labour force expressed a pro-labour oppositional class consciousness in the 1980s. That is, they both consistently supported the right to strike and opposed corporate profit taking at workers' expense. Pro-labour consciousness was at least as strong in 2016 and continued to be the most common form of class consciousness, with most others holding more mixed views and few coherent supporters of capital. In all these instances there was sufficient popular support for more substantial social change than actually occurred. In addition, the popular sense of economic inequality has probably broadened from focus on wages and profits to more widespread opposition to monetary inequality in many contributing forms: financial gains via capital concentration and resulting oligopolies, mergers and acquisitions, investment income, real estate, inheritance, costs of university education and resulting student debt, and reduction of taxes on the rich.

A growing number of national and international surveys are finding increasing popular sentiment against excesses of capitalism and particularly big business. According to a recent international survey (Legatum Institute Foundation 2015, 2), there is an almost universal belief in the US, Britain, Germany and several other countries that "the world's biggest businesses have cheated and polluted their way to success — with barely ten per cent of respondents in all seven countries surveyed thinking big businesses are 'clean.'" Another recent international survey (*Financial Times*/Harris Poll 2019) finds growing opposition to free market capitalism in several advanced capitalist countries.

A national survey I conducted in Canada in the midst of the pandemic asked about the extent of agreement with the statement "Canada's capitalist economy is based on maximizing profits for the rich."[17] The findings are summarized by class position in Figure 8.1.

Figure 8.1 "Canada's capitalist economy is based on maximizing profits for the rich" by Class, Canada, 2020 (%)

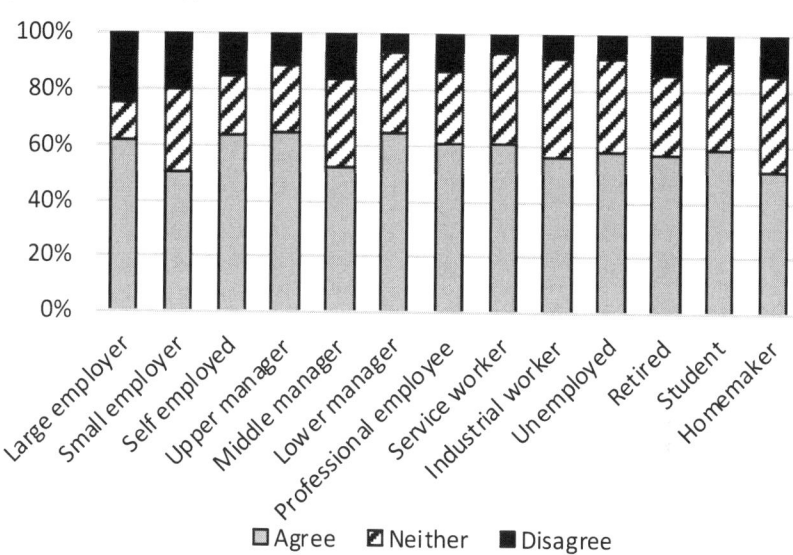

Source: Canada Work Learning Surveys 1998–2016. Leger 2020. N = 3177.

There is widespread recognition that profit maximization for the rich has been the driving force of the Canadian economy, including by majorities in all class positions. This includes admission by majorities of increasingly disenchanted large employers and upper managers. Once again, corporate capitalists escape scrutiny, and many of them likely still advocate "trickle down" benefits. But there are few in most employment class positions or out of the employed labour force who believe in such wider distribution of benefits (about 10 percent overall). Critiques and growing doubts about the systemic limits of advanced capitalism to deliver the goods have become pervasive across the class structure.

More empirical research is certainly needed to deepen many of the findings presented in this study. Similar comparative studies could quickly be conducted in many countries with current survey technologies through partnerships of progressive labour and social movements with qualified sympathetic researchers. Such studies are infinitely easier now than when the elderly Marx tried in 1880 with French workers (Marx 1938).

The powers and strategies of dominant capitalist forces should never be underestimated. Gestural reforms proposed by corporate leaders and allied governing parties in attempts to marginally reduce economic inequities or delay environmental destruction could have short-term placating effects. The scale and momentum of both ecological and economic crises certainly seriously reduce corporate capitalists' prospects. More far-sighted corporate leaders register formal concern, as indicated by declarations of social responsibility to stakeholders and the environment, and they even refer to tipping points for capitalism (e.g., Business Roundtable 2019; Dimon 2020). Such declarations contrast sharply with the reality of the few private equity firms (i.e., Blackrock, Vanguard and State Street) increasingly dominating world financial markets with ruthless oligopolistic practices against workers and the population at large (Rugemer 2019; Ewart 2020).

Sustained mass protest movements are essential both to defend against persistent capitalist profit offensives and to support progressive environmental and economic change. As Klein (2016, 3) argues, "Climate change acts as an accelerant to many of our social ills — inequality, wars, racism — but it can also be an accelerant for the opposite, for the forces working for economic and social justice and against militarism." Organizing direct actions can be taken in many places, especially extra-parliamentary settings, including paid workplaces and local communities. However, in spite of widespread popular sentiments favouring progressive mass action, there are still relatively few dynamic organized mass movements in advanced capitalist countries today. I share Camfield's (2022, 30) response to this situation. In short, as an essential urgent condition for transformation, we should do everything we can to build progressive organizations and mass action campaigns. Second, such protests and struggles as mentioned above suggest that more sustained mass social movements are very possible. Third, in Camfield's (2022, 30) words: "The terrible path that capitalism has us on will create conditions in society out of which larger social movements are more likely to erupt in the years ahead, in ways we can't predict." As I said at the outset of this study, I have no crystal ball. But I am sure that without the continuation of democratically constituted protest actions against mounting risks we are unlikely to have a future that most will find tolerable.

In any case, unless popular protest movements develop practical alternatives with clear shared objectives, coupled with capable strategic agencies to navigate forward, even the most widespread protests can dissipate. So, what are the most promising alternatives and where are the strategic agencies?

Alternatives: Economic Democracy

The contradictions between obsessive profit taking and sustaining benefits for most of humanity, coupled with rapidly mounting ecological crises make basic changes in ways of making future general economic and political decisions imperative. By their nature, protests are emotional expressions of collective felt needs to end very problematic conditions. They sometimes lead to reform of specific policies or practices. Protests have rarely articulated general systemic alternatives to existing conditions. But a close observer of the Black Lives Matter (BLM) protests in the US (Joseph 2020) sees more:

> Many seem to recognize that the criminal justice system is just one part of a panorama of structures of oppression across this country, from the criminalization of the poor to widespread, unequal access to housing, nutritious food, employment, environmental safety, health care, clean air, water and citizenship. Organizations from BLM to prison abolitionists have come to the table with more than just outrage; they have sharp, clear-eyed, radical proposals to defund the criminal justice system and redirect resources that currently are spent punishing, incarcerating and killing black communities into investments that will allow these neighborhoods to thrive.

In all societies for which there is intelligible evidence of the aspirations of oppressed people, there has most often been expression of a sense of needed alternatives. As Geoghegan (2008, 9) put it: "There is nothing like being at the sharp end of oppression on a daily basis to generate insight and the desire to introduce a better reality." Contemporary intellectuals continue to produce abstract models of alternatives, but unless they translate into popular activism, they just gather dust.

I suggest economic democracy as the most preferable and practical general alternative to neoliberal advanced capitalism. Economic democracy can be most easily understood as the organization of work in a society so that all who contribute have a voice and a vote in how and why it is done. The first principle is worker self-management. All workers are permitted involvement in decisions. The second principle is cooperative sustainable production. The greatest lasting good for the greatest number comes through mutual respect and collaboration. Individual rights are respected and nurtured up to the point where they infringe on others' rights. Genuinely democratic decisions aim to enable maximum consideration and selection of options to ensure human fulfillment and environmental sustainability.

Serious widening practical assessment of economic democracy is happening. One indicator is the extent to which different working models are compared critically. There is growing recognition of the relative merits of models combining universal worker control with sustainable forms of equitable public ownership that avoid creation of a labour aristocracy, or "epitocracy" (see Vrousalis 2020). To go from a capitalist oligarchy to a technocracy dominated by specialize knowledge workers would not be much better in terms of economic justice. But the available evidence in this book and elsewhere suggests that class conscious professional employees as the core knowledge workers are most likely — regardless of their income levels — to share class interests and seek alliances with other non-managerial workers for economic transformation (Livingstone 2023).

An indication of the varied extent of general movement in this direction in advanced capitalist countries is offered by an economic democracy index (EDI) developed by Andrew Cumbers and colleagues (Cumbers 2018). The EDI is constructed using a number of established international databases and includes four components: workplace and employment rights; degree of associational economic democracy; distribution of economic decision-making powers; and transparency and democratic engagement in macroeconomic decision-making.[18] Figure 8.2 summarizes the relative development of economic democracy in these terms in the G7 and Nordic countries.

The long-established social democratic regimes in Sweden, Denmark, Finland and Norway all have relatively high scores on this index while the Anglo-American countries of the UK, Canada and the US as well as Japan all have fairly low scores. Cumbers' team found strong correlations in OECD countries between the EDI and the Gini index, which measures the general distribution of income across the population. For example, in 2020 the bivariate correlation for the countries in Figure 8.1 is -.75 (.001); higher levels of economic democracy tend to reduce economic inequality. This team found that higher EDI levels are also associated with greater labour productivity. But they also found that there has been a general decline in levels of economic democracy since the

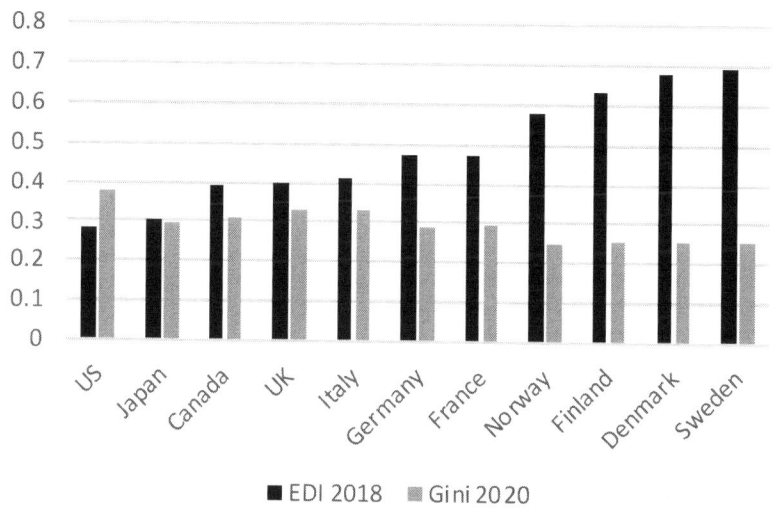

Figure 8.2 Economic Democracy Index and Gini Index, G7 and Nordic Countries, circa 2020

Source: Cumbers 2018.

financial crisis of 2008. Cumbers (2018, 6) concludes: "These findings challenge much of the conventional policy wisdom of the 1990s onwards regarding the perceived benefits of Anglo-American style flexible labour market policies, employment and financial deregulation, and macro-economic management, suggesting such approaches may contribute to poverty and inequality." None of these findings should be taken to suggest that life in Nordic countries is massively better than elsewhere in advanced capitalism. The same basic tipping point faces us all. It is just that countries that are somewhat more advanced toward economic democracy can offer some guides to the merits of its further development and the limits of neoliberalism.

There have been many initiatives to form social movements and establish communities and programs under the banner of economic democracy.[19] Specific designs, inclusiveness and success have varied greatly. Some current working examples are drawn on here. The basic point is that economic democracy is an alternative that increasingly responds to the needs and capacities of the current general population of advanced capitalism. It should be obvious that such social movements are most sustainable when popular involvement is nurtured and protected — whether the immediate concerns are with environmental sustainability, class exploitation or forms of oppression such as systemic racism and sexism or, increasingly, with their intersection. Four basic issues are con-

Figure 8.3 "Canada's economy should be transformed into a more democratic system focusing on (a) the needs of all Canadians and (b) environmental stability" by Class, Canada, 2020 (%)

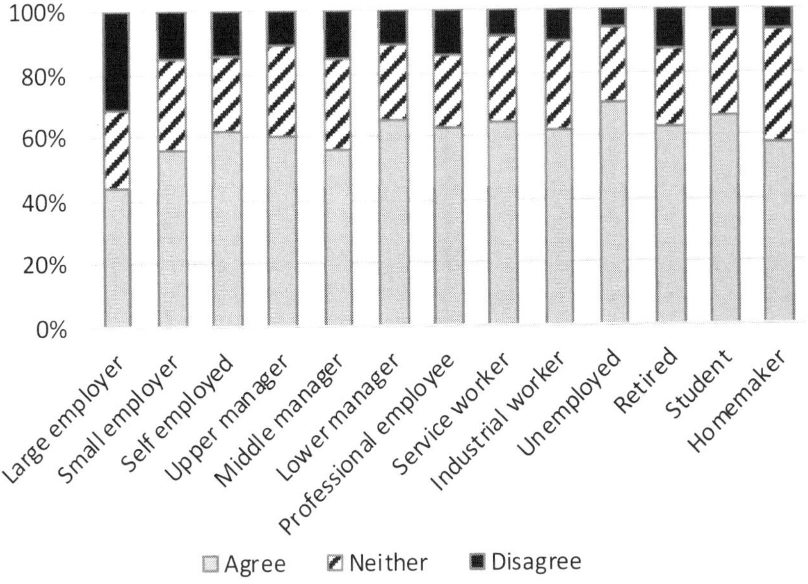

[Bar chart showing percentages of Agree / Neither / Disagree across class categories: Large employer, Small employer, Self employed, Upper manager, Middle manager, Lower manager, Professional employee, Service worker, Industrial worker, Unemployed, Retired, Student, Homemaker]

□ Agree   ▨ Neither   ■ Disagree

Source: Canada Work Learning Surveys 1998–2016. Leger 2020. N = 3177.

sidered here: general public receptivity to progressive alternatives; preferred organizational form; energy to sustain it; and feasible financing.

General Receptivity to Progressive Alternatives

In terms of systemic alternatives, we know from Chapter 6 that nearly half of the employed labour force in Canada in 2016 felt it was possible for a modern economy to run effectively without the profit motive and by worker self-management (see Table 6.8). The basic alternatives to advanced capitalism involve both a more democratic economic system and a sustainable environment. My 2020 Canada survey asked about basic support for transformation to such a system. Results are summarized in Figure 8.3.

Popular interest in more democratic alternatives to capitalism appears to be increasing. Majorities in nearly all class positions now express support for such a transition. The strongest support may be among the unemployed, including many abruptly losing jobs in the pandemic, but among large employers, and presumably corporate capitalists — major beneficiaries of the current system — there is only minority support. Otherwise, there appears to be little attitudinal opposition to seriously considering transition to an alternative system, at least when the proposition is posed in this way. It should also be noted that the strongest support in the employed labour force comes from those in the growing non-profit sector (69 percent).

Recent surveys in other countries that have posed questions about support for "capitalism" or "socialism" have found increasing support for socialism, especially among younger respondents. Back in 1942, a Gallup Survey in the US found that 25 percent thought socialism would be a good thing for the country; in 2019, support increased to 43 percent (Jones 2019).[20] As Alperovitz (2016, 3) concludes for the US case:

> The Sanders insurgency, the polling data, and the growing experimentation with a range of alternatives all suggest that we may be on the brink of a new era — an extended and difficult period in which a new economy is slowly forged. Such a system might perhaps be called a "pluralist commonwealth" to reflect its diverse forms of common ownership. But whatever we call it, it is time to start discussing this system more openly and to refine its practical elements.

Surveys have seldom gone beyond suggesting such general labels, but there is clearly popular support and an opening for fuller consideration of organizational alternatives to capitalism, including economic democracy.

Organizational Forms of Economic Democracy

"Socialism" and "communism" were dismissed in popular discourse in many advanced capitalist societies throughout the Cold War until the end of the Soviet Union in 1991. Over the past century, political movements using these ideological banners had sometimes managed to gain state power and to enable some material gains for masses of workers, often against stiff opposition by international capitalist forces. These regimes generally devolved into centralized state systems in which many aspects of life were controlled by authoritarian bureaucracies, in contrast to the formal freedoms of employment and civil rights claimed by the defenders of capitalism. Since the fall of the Soviet Union, China is widely seen as the major exemplar of "authoritarian communism." Since the 1970s, China has opened to investment from and integration with the global capitalist economy while the central state regime has retained control of much of the domestic economy and continues to espouse its own version of communist political ideology.[21] Whatever the material benefits to some, this model holds little attraction to those with democratic values in advanced capitalist countries.

In any case, in advanced capitalist countries, popular sentiment in opposition to capitalist organization of the economy has been increasing in recent decades, as indicated by numerous opinion polls (e.g., Wike et al. 2021) and continuing mass protests (e.g., Chenoweth, Pinckney and Lewis 2018). National political candidates and platforms have emerged urging transition to "democratic socialism" — notably Bernie Sanders in the US and Jeremy Corbyn in the UK. Associated networks of activists have mobilized in these regimes where "socialism" had previously been widely used as a term of derision. There is clearly an increasing openness to considering alternatives to capitalism in the public sphere. It is becoming easier to recognize the existence of organizational alternatives to capitalism within advanced capitalist societies that are attempting to address the problematic conditions that have brought us to this precipice. Some of these practical alternatives already have a substantial history.

As discussed in the chapters on modes of production (Chapter 3) and modes of thought (Chapter 5), organizational alternatives have co-existed with capitalism from the outset. There have been many variants of "socialism."[22] The most distinct feature of democratic socialism is *social ownership* rather than private ownership of the means of production, to be regulated by the community as a whole. Various models of more democratic political decision-making have been tried on some scale, ranging from elected councils to cybernetic networks at different levels. In terms of the labour process, one basic organizational alternative is worker-managed cooperatives. The worker cooperative movement has a long lineage, and cooperatives have a significant presence in all advanced capitalist economies.[23] Research overviews of organizational alternatives to capitalism often begin with worker co-ops.[24] Some worker co-ops, such as Mondragon in the Basque region of Spain, effectively compete with capitalist firms in various product markets while distributing benefits on bases of social needs to their members.

But the larger significance of co-ops is demonstrating that worker-managed organizations can be at least as productive as private firms within capitalist markets while also utilizing the talents of their workers more effectively (i.e., less underemployment) and generating more free time to be used for other socially useful pursuits.²⁵ The potential for wider generalization of worker self-management beyond current advanced capitalist economies for more equitable distribution of employment and life opportunities and for sustaining ecosystems should be obvious. Such worker co-ops and their benefits are literally under our noses in advanced capitalist countries. The fact that they are currently little known to wider publics that have strong majority preferences for alternative democratic organization of the economy is symptomatic of both capitalist media dominance and limited advocacy by the co-op movement.

Beyond the co-op movement there are many organizational initiatives responding to popular democratic demand at levels from small local communities to national associations to engage all members in forms of economic democracy to address a wide range of pressing social needs.²⁶ Some of these are noted in the following discussion.

Initiatives for deliberative democracy that are springing up have wide potential impact.²⁷ Deliberative democracy is a model for organizational decision-making that maximizes opportunities for members to gain relevant balanced information about issues, to debate choices and to contribute to reaching actionable majority decisions. This is a form of direct democracy that can include the articulation and aggregation of the breadth of views in even large populations — in extreme contrast to highly restrictive forms of elite political dominance that prevail in all liberal democracies.²⁸ With the aid of random sampling techniques, focus group explorations, representative opinion surveys and discussion forums, it is technically possible to achieve informed majority decisions about many social issues.²⁹ This model is well-suited for any organization or community where there is serious commitment to respecting the views of all members, a basic proviso of economic democracy — as long as the information generated in this process remains accessible to all participants for further cooperative use. Ironically, the most sustained applications to date have been within a few large capitalist corporations where variants appealing to subordinate employees have resulted in more secure corporate profits (see Adler 2019).

Sustaining Energies

Economic democracy requires two essential forms of energy. First, as in most effective organizations, it needs many fully engaged people. It is reasonably clear that where people have greater job control and autonomy in their work, they are both more productive and healthier.[30] Organizations run on principles of economic democracy should be optimal for ensuring the greatest control and autonomy for the greatest number of engaged members.

Second, an environmentally sustainable alternative mode of production demands transition to renewable energy. Producing all new energy from wind, water, solar and geothermal power has been technologically possible for over a decade, and replacing pre-existing fossil sources of energy by 2050 is technically feasible.[31] Rapid implementation of renewable energy systems could obviously contribute greatly to addressing the imminent threat of global warming. Fossil fuel shortages provoked by the Russia-Ukraine war have at least somewhat begun to accelerate some government moves in this direction. Distributed renewable energy sources and technologies, including community-owned solar and wind microgrids as basic elements, are also highly compatible with more democratic governance structures, such as worker self-managed firms. The main barriers are not technological but political. Climate mitigation requires an end to fossil fuel investments and subsidies, as well as related land use practices and consumption patterns, all of which remain strongly resisted by the fossil fuel industry and allies. While we continue to use fossil fuels in the short-term transition, private energy companies must be compelled by democratic mandates to pay for the negative externalities that their carbon-based fossil fuel extracts have been pouring into the atmosphere for free and heating up the planet for over a century — but this can only be a short-term measure. The Paris Accord with real teeth must replace empty promises and short-term bandaids.

The mounting numbers of fossil fuel protests and the development of democratically run renewable community systems are building popular political demand and energy capacity. But ultimately the major changes will have to involve national governments in cooperation at a scale at least comparable to the public hydropower projects of the Depression era. As Burke and Stephens (2018, 89) conclude their general assessment: "A democratic response to climate emergency requires immediate resistance to fossil fuels coupled with the deployment of renewable energy systems at a pace that sustains and can be sustained by democratic governance, lest projects of democratization collapse and renewable solutions rapidly transform into the next human catastrophe." Without the effective coupling of renewable energy development based on social need with democratic governance built from the community level, the prospects for avoiding climate catastrophe are bleak. Energy democracy has become an essential basis of a sustainable alternative.

While energy democracy is most urgent, the needs and benefits of more democratic control are broadly applicable to most sectors of the economy. In some instances, corporate capital has been willing to make short-term concessions to greater worker control in conjunction with productivity gains. The quintessential point is that the productive technological capacity available in all advanced capitalist economies could enable equitable and fair distribution of opportunities to fulfill social needs. When and if issues like shorter work weeks or greater worker say in hiring and firing are raised, most corporate capitalists have instinctively resisted threats to profit margins. Of course, there are many other social needs and rights that should be addressed in a more democratic alternative to capitalism. These include universal access to health care, formal education, food, shelter and transit, as well as social justice on grounds of racialization, gender, sexual orientation and so on in the quest to create a fairer society. Many of these social needs and rights have been called for in the platforms, manifestos and models of progressive movements for a long time.[32] Some of these demands have been addressed to varying extents in different advanced capitalist regimes, generally for the dual purposes of responding to organized workers' and citizens' demands and of reproducing a viable labour force. But the distribution of most such benefits has been highly inequitable even in the most progressive "social democratic" regimes.

Capitalism deserves due credit for stimulating the technological capacity now achieved, but it also deserves at least as much criticism for the fixation on profit maximization that deprives most people of many due benefits. There is no inherent reason that a democratically organized economy with current technological levels and a highly knowledgeable population cannot be energized to respond more effectively to current environmental and economic conditions than corporate executives can. More and more people are coming to this conclusion.

Feasible Financing
Whatever the specific features of the alternatives posed to capitalism, a sticking point for development has always been financing. Once again, there are working models: public banks. The state of North Dakota has had a public state-owned bank for a century and the most community

banks per capita in the US. In recent times, North Dakota was also the only US state with a major budget surplus, and it has had the lowest unemployment and default rates in the country. Since 1969, the Banco Popular y de Desarrollo Comunal cooperative bank has been democratically owned and managed by the workers of Costa Rica. In the UK, a recent national survey found that 50 percent wanted to bring the banking sector into public ownership, suggesting a ready audience for the Labour Party's proposals for a new "public banking ecosystem" (Berry and Macfarlane 2019). In the wake of the Great Recession and public disgust at "too big to fail" Wall Street bailouts, many other places in the US and beyond with heavy personal and government debt loads moved to establish publicly owned banks. Public banks are now widespread, with more than 900 worldwide, and with combined assets of around $49 trillion (Marois 2021). Such community-based ownership opens the door for more responsive financial resource allocation within the public spheres of states.

Shockingly, in the wake of the crushing COVID-19 pandemic in the US and with the collusion of leaders of both major political parties and the Federal Reserve, most of the government financial aid has again gone to large private financial and non-financial corporations.[33] As noted in the prior section, majorities in all advanced capitalist countries support increased taxes on the rich. During the neoliberal era, central governments in many countries have given tax cuts to wealthy households that have become much wealthier during the pandemic, with deepening inequality for most others. Recent detailed analyses indicate that very modest progressive taxes on the very wealthy could lift billions out of poverty, make enough vaccines for the whole world and deliver universal health care and social protection for all the citizens of low- and lower middle-income countries (Fight Inequality Alliance et al. 2022).

If and when these gross misallocations are widely recognized, there will be no plausible basis for refusing public funding for massive real social needs in post-COVID-19 recovery and to service related debt with new financing as in postwar recoveries. The basic attraction of public banks in this context is that social ownership encourages investment of discretionary funds in relation to the needs of the community rather than for more speculative profit seeking. Some credit unions with similar orientations have long histories and are also growing in many countries. With governments proposing wartime spending levels to deal with pandemic recovery, funding through the private capitalist banking system promises to send state and personal debt levels through the roof of inequity. The feasibility of public banks is undeniable and could be widely demonstrated to provide a more attractive alternative source of necessary funding, especially for decentralized community-based production. Whether the most pressing funding issue is extraordinary new spending to support pandemic recovery or making long-term investments to sustain community services, financing high priority needs through establishing and nurturing public banks is an eminently practical option.

The big private banks with their financial clout and political power will resist such growth firmly. The hyper-growth of global financial investment banks — such as Morgan Stanley, Goldman Sachs, Credit Suisse, JP Morgan, Deutsche Bank — has led to the displacement of many smaller private deposit banks serving residents and smaller businesses in local communities, with mounting riches for the "1 percent" and mounting personal debt levels for most workers. The contrast with the benefits of public banks could not be starker.

As noted in Chapter 1, both of my grandparent families were driven by debt. Consequently, my father took a safe civil service job, and my parents did everything they could to avoid going into chronic debt. I was fortunate enough to get scholarships and decent summer jobs and completed my doctoral studies debt free. But now nearly everyone is at least as driven by debt as my grandparents were.

The tipping point in this regard was the 1970s. From the earliest known civilizations, ruling elites in many class societies have used money markets, coinage and taxes to pay soldiers and subjugate labouring classes (Graeber 2011). Regardless of many claims of workers' ideological submission in the post-WWII expansionary era, workers' personal debt levels were already significant (see Day 2019). But until the 1970s, there were at least significant constraints on the interest rates and debt levels that could be imposed and options for most hired labourers to avoid chronic debt. At that point, both organized labour and organizations based on civil rights, gender rights and other social rights were making democratic demands that seriously threatened profits in advanced capitalist economies. Neoliberal reforms began to be introduced to undercut these demands and restore profit levels. Democratic demands were not diminished but they were diverted. The basic mechanism again was personal debt. US President Nixon led the world off the gold standard in 1971, opening the door for governments to inflate currencies and allow high prices of consumer goods while wage increases stayed low. At the same time, liberalized loan policies and pervasive commercial advertising encouraged all to buy whatever we desired: housing with low down payments, cars with low monthly payments, student loans to meet mounting tuition costs, and pretty much anything using rapidly spreading credit cards that soon allowed interest rates over 20 percent. The most qualified labour force in world history also quickly became one of the most indebted. At the end of the 1970s, Federal Reserve chair Volcker raised bank rates to 20 percent, goods producing industries had mass layoffs, and recession drove down inflation. With regressive tax rates, many government current accounts went into chronic deficit by the 1990s while personal debt levels soared. Many factors contributed to the diverting of democratic demands, but personal debt loads were pivotal.

Throughout the history of class societies, when debt levels have soared, the typical solution has been some form of debt forgiveness, or "jubilee" (Graeber 2011). The Great Recession of 2007–08 ended with bailouts to corporations deemed "too big to fail" while millions of workers lost their homes and secure jobs. Since then, wage levels have continued to stagnate and personal debt levels to increase while corporate profits have been restored and soared. With few conventional fiscal or monetary tools left and mounting pandemic levels of suffering with food, housing and employment hardships, governments have been increasingly compelled to offer forms of debt relief (e.g., housing vouchers, child tax credits, student loan holidays, emergency income replacement programs). Governments in these circumstances should at least not impede and might encourage worker and community initiatives based on workers' use of their own creative capacities and financial resources to make ends meet — including forms of economic democracy.

As noted above, at least half of all work done in advanced capitalist societies is unpaid household and community labour. Forgiveness of personal debt would provide time and incentives for many to engage in socially useful unpaid work as well as paid work to produce savings for further useful investment. The neoliberal argument that such debt forgiveness would increase government debt intolerably appears ridiculous in the wake of recent rounds of corporate bailouts and tax reductions as well as the precedent of comparable public debt levels coupled with regulated production systems in wartime. Most people at least recognize we are in a war to cope with climate change.

If democratically owned workplaces became more widespread, coupled with distributed renewable energy networks and public banks, then various other options often associated with democratic socialism would become much more practicable. These include shorter normal workweeks with further automation and universal basic incomes, which, even when successful, have generally been aborted under capitalist pressures to keep labour "available." Most moves in the direction of sustained worker ownership of the means of production in conjunction with such measures are likely to be strongly resisted by corporate capitalists.

This brings us to the Meidner Plan. As alluded to earlier, a worker-controlled wage-earner fund (WEF) was proposed by the Swedish Labour Organization (LO) in summer 1975 (Meidner 1981). This plan proposed requiring Swedish firms with over fifty employees to transfer a portion of the profits every year to the WEF as newly issued shares. At the recommended transfer rate of 20 percent, it would take around twenty to thirty-five years for the workers to attain majority ownership of Swedish capital. Coincidentally, under attack by capital to reduce union wage demands, the LO withdrew from a decades old bargaining agreement in 1976, and that year there were nearly 300 wildcat strikes, the most per year in Swedish history. The WEF was overwhelmingly endorsed by LO members at a congress in June 1976. In September, the Social Democratic Party (SAP), which had been strongly allied with the LO, lost government for the first time in forty years to a centre-right coalition. The WEF was subsequently diluted by the LO, faced intense countermobilization by Swedish capital and was abandoned by 1983. Post-mortems abound.[34]

A few points are most relevant here. As the 1980 national survey discussed in Chapters 6 and 7 documents, Swedish workers were among the most highly organized and class conscious in the world at that time. The initial WEF plan clearly targeted a significant fraction of privately held profits and evoked strong resistance from capitalists who saw the real threat. The failure of LO and SAP leaders to refine and promote the universal benefits of the plan and mobilize organized workers in this period was a fatal flaw at a moment of historic opportunity. The potential of share levies on corporate profits lives on and represents one of the most promising means of increasing social ownership within advanced capitalist economies. But the real lesson of the Meidner Plan is the need to move to direct social ownership of productive enterprises.

Since the 1980s, the value of private pension funds has multiplied massively. These deferred wages are invested in every industry and asset class, and pension funds have become strategic agents in globally integrated financial markets (see Skerrett et al. 2017). In effect, workers in these pension plans have much greater collective ownership claims on capital in general than ever before, even though direct wage benefits have suffered, and defined contribution plans make personal benefits more uncertain. Much more refined models than the Meidner Plan have been developed, and the scale of these funds gives them much greater relative power. Before the Great Recession, Blackburn (2006, 181) summarized the promise of the share levy model:

> The share levy robustly addresses the yawning crisis of pension provision. It could raise large sums at a time when the extra costs of an aging society, a knowledge-based economy, and ecological shocks will be immense. They could also help to subsidize free time and freely chosen work. There are few alternative proposals which can claim the same. Moreover, the interlinked proposals are all based on tendencies or practices already present in today's "gray capitalism,"[35] and their suggested rearrangement into a more coherent, democratic, and accountable schema is, I believe, consequently deserving of the name "real utopia."

These observations are even more relevant and resonant in the wake of the Great Recession of 2007–08 and the COVID-19 pandemic, as well as the resulting massive increases in wealth accruing to corporate capitalists. A major barrier has been orthodox financial rules for pension fund trustees that required general profit maximization, often at the expense of the needs of the communities where members live, and workers' firms are directly affected. This contradiction has become ever more evident as economic inequities and ecological shocks mount. Both worker representation and investment decision rules are becoming more responsive to community and environmental needs.[36] As Guinan (2019, 23) recently put it:

The core components of the Meidner proposal — the share levy and the impetus towards collective ownership of capital — are ripe for reconsideration and recovery given today's yawning inequality and widespread sense of the need for a very different pattern of political economy.... For a newly re-emergent left ... deep substantive engagement with the key models from recent history could produce valuable lessons and inform future designs and strategies. The Meidner Plan is one such model, illuminating a potential pathway forward towards economic democracy through collective capital ownership.

In sum, basic ingredients of a viable alternative to capitalism, including democratic community and workplace governance coupled with distributed renewable energy models and funded by public banks and worker-controlled pension funds, are more widely available than ever before. The remaining question is whether there are sufficient strategic agencies to effectively lead their implementation in the face of predictable capitalist resistance.

Strategic Agencies

The evidence in Chapters 6 and 7 confirms three vital points about current agencies for change: (1) there are now many more people with revolutionary class consciousness and pro-labour oppositional consciousness than those with hegemonic capitalist consciousness and pro-capital consciousness in advanced capitalism; (2) those with revolutionary class consciousness are virtually unanimous in wanting to fight against global warming and poverty; and (3) they tend to be most concentrated among industrial workers and professional employees who are most likely to be members of unions and associations. The aggregate potential among this core of people for active engagement in and leadership of progressive social movements may be greater than ever.

In virtually all major political regime changes in modern history, a small fraction of the population has been directly involved as active agents. The tacit and reactive support of much of the rest of the population has been a critical factor. The attitude survey results in this and prior chapters suggest that there may be majority tacit support for transformation from capitalism to a more democratic, environmentally stable economy. In one more example, respondents to my June 2020 survey were asked whether they would vote for a political candidate standing for such change. The results are summarized in Figure 8.4.

The majority indicate they would vote for such a candidate, including majorities in most class positions. The most notable exceptions are again large employers, especially those with high incomes (and undoubtedly corporate capitalists), who are most likely to oppose such transformation as against their class interests. Nowhere else is opposition above 20 percent, and in all other class positions there is at least plurality support for such change. There is strong majority support among all non-managerial employees (i.e., professional employees, industrial workers and service workers) but also among the self-employed and managers, as well as the unemployed and both students and retired people. There is stronger support among those who are union or professional association members and those who work in non-profits. The strongest support is found among Black and Muslim workers (nearly 90 percent), probably reflecting greater current discrimination against these racialized and religious minorities. There are slight tendencies for

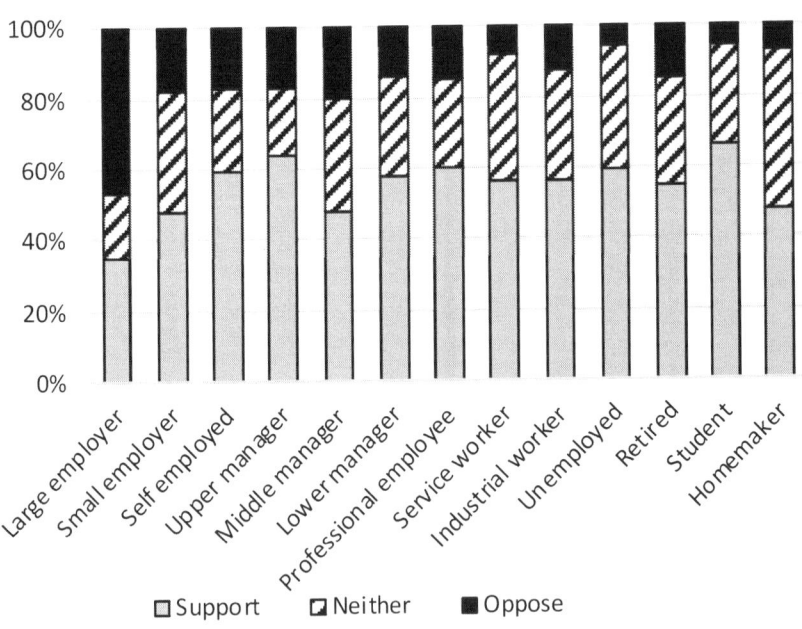

Figure 8.4 "I would vote for a political candidate who proposes to transform the Canadian economy to a more democratic system based on (a) the needs of all Canadians and (b) environmental stability" by Class, Canada, 2020 (%)

Source: Canada Work Learning Surveys 1998–2016. Leger 2020. N = 3177.

younger people and women to be more supportive of an alternative system candidate.

It should also be noted that unemployed rural white males with less than college education appear to be more uncertain and less supportive of transformation than other demographic groups, consistent with symptoms of despair recently detected in the older "white working class" in the US (Case and Deaton 2020). However, overall, the findings on voting preferences suggest that if they had a real choice, most working people and most others would vote for such an economic democracy or anti-capitalist alternative to the present capitalist system.

Two caveats here. First, voter turnout globally has declined significantly since the 1980s with growing skepticism, especially among younger people, and more voting with their feet, on the streets (International Institute for Democracy and Electoral Assistance 2021). Second, much of this skepticism can be attributed to a growing sense that many policies enacted by elected politicians correspond closely to the interests of economic elites while average citizens and mass-based interest groups have little or no independent influence. This condition is confirmed by extensive empirical research (Gilens and Page 2014).

How do we get to a condition where real democratic choices can be put to a representative electorate? To go beyond street protests, successful mass social movements need clear alternatives resonating with growing constituencies and creative leadership committed to fight for the alternative with all legitimate means. Economic democracy represents a valid and widely appealing alternative. Building the strategic agencies at different levels to move toward it is the immediate compelling challenge.

It is vital to register here what is already happening on the ground. One of the most promising changes is the development of ecological or earth charters. Recall that mercantile guilds gained town charters from feudal lords to expand their private property rights. Today many hundreds of cities and towns around the globe have democratically established their own charters to fight environmental challenges.[37] These are legal vehicles that can aid progressive community groupings to build sustainable networks of services in many areas of social need. Just as significantly, many hundreds of grassroots movements are taking back ownership of water, energy and other assets that were privatized during the height of neoliberalism.[38]

It is well established that, over the past century, democratic national transitions have been more likely to take place when opposition to the incumbent regime were led by industrial workers (Dahlum, Knutsen and Wig 2019). Whatever political alliances emerge to lead grassroots transition, one thing is certain. Representatives of non-managerial hired labour — Marx's proletariat — will be centrally involved. In current terms, this includes industrial workers, service workers and professional employees. As we have seen in prior chapters, the core of capitalism's "working class" has changed markedly since the Industrial Revolution. But these are the people who are most directly exploited by capital to generate the profits to reproduce this economic system. They have often been divided on bases of racial, gender, education and urban-rural grounds but they have remained consistently those with the most oppositional labour class consciousness and revolutionary consciousness required to lead transition.

From the Chartist movement through the International Workers of the World to radical caucuses in many modern trade unions, there have been networks among organized working people making the case for transcending capitalism. Major challenges have been getting sufficient rank-and-file union members and established union leaders to see and feel alternatives as legitimate and realizable. The popular sentiments expressed in the attitude surveys referred to in this book suggest that democratic alternatives to capitalism now have widespread legitimacy. These sentiments open the door for progressive change. There are unprecedented opportunities for inspired leaders to articulate programs that would appeal strongly to majorities in many advanced capitalist countries. In countries where there are unions with high memberships and social democratic political parties with a history of responsiveness to working people's needs (i.e., Nordic countries), voluntary voter participation in national elections has remained relatively high (i.e., generally over 80 percent). The abandoning of the Meidner Plan in Sweden in the 1980s in the context of a highly class conscious working class can now be seen as a failure of courage by avowedly progressive labour union and political party leaderships to confer effectively with and mobilize a highly receptive electorate for a major challenge to capitalist dominance. The Meidner Plan failure also occurred at a time of less widespread anti-capitalist sentiment and of wider options for global capital. The scale of the popular protests of 2020 against socio-economic inequities and climate change threat and the widening awareness of feasible alternatives represent unsurpassed chances for transition — if social movements involved can muster collective strategic agency.

The candidates for immediate strategic agencies in most countries generally include progressive trade unions and professional associations, environmental organizations, anti-racist groups, feminist groups and other sympathetic organizations. Different issues have appealed to these specific groups in different ways. Keys to cooperative action are the framing of issues in broad inclusive terms and the engagement of activists from each of these movements in leadership. Social forums bringing together leaders from these groups are occurring with increasing frequency and are using methods of deliberative democracy to create more public spaces for articulation of shared progressive policies at local, national and transnational levels.[39]

New communications technologies can aid both sustained dialogue and rapid mobilization among and beyond strategic agents. The internet, and all its public and private vehicles of communication, enables people with similar viewpoints and interests to communicate with others they have never met in person, people who live far apart and in different regions. The net is clearly an important new facilitator for developing social movements, a powerful two-way audio-visual tool of mass communication, for spreading both truth and lies. In the 2011 Middle East and Occupy Wall Street uprisings, cell phones and social media were instrumental. By 2020 actions, encrypted apps such as WhatsApp, AirDrop and Telegram had become more secure means of collective sharing of plans and priorities. The mass mobilizations around the murder of George Floyd were galvanized by the wide sharing of a young woman's cell phone video of Chauvin kneeling on Floyd's neck for nine minutes. But whatever the technical aids drawn on by strategic agencies, successful transition is likely to entail clear, widely shared anti-capitalist objectives and diverse nonviolent tactics that maintain tacit support of non-participants. Alliance activists will have to anticipate and resist reactionary regime pressures and capitalist seduction and misinformation using similar communications technologies.

The collective agencies most involved at the moment are indeed alliances of unions and professional associations, anti-racist and feminist groups and other sympathetic social justice organizations. The general Strike for Black Lives, which occurred on July 20, 2020, in dozens of US cities to protest systemic racism and economic inequality, illustrates such emergent alliances.[40] This strike was organized by partners including the Service Employees International Union, International Brotherhood of Teamsters, American Federation of Teachers, United Food and Commercial Workers, United Farm Workers, Fight for $15 and a Union, Coalition of Black Trade Unionists, Jobs with Justice, Youth Climate Strike Coalition, 350.org, Climate Justice Alliance, National Partnership for Women and Families and Union of Concerned Scientists, as well as dozens of other social justice groups. Actions ranged from moments of silence to full-day work stoppages. Demands included justice for Black communities, rewriting racist laws and corporate rules and allowing all workers to join unions. Many of the participants were unionized non-managerial workers who probably felt compelled to be counted in the face of severe recent injustices and to become more fully engaged in such alliances. The immediate provoking causes of such collective agencies may be racism, sexism or more general economic or environmental injustice. The effect is stronger collective agencies with sufficient organized infrastructure and discipline to continue pressing the case for alternatives. These strategic agencies are critical vehicles to articulate sustained political expression of civil rights demands of majorities of non-managerial workers and people generally for a more democratic economic and environmental system.

These strategic agencies will also be essential to aid resistance to repressive reactions by capitalist forces that attempt to undermine, discredit and otherwise weaken democratic demands. The disproportionate reaction of the Trump regime to largely peaceful domestic protests of summer 2020 by unilaterally calling in federal troops offended many local elected officials and even drew dissent from federal military leaders. Future reactions to democratic demands for alternatives may be similarly militaristic or in more legal-constitutional form. But strategic alliances of mass movements and responsive representatives within legitimate political parties will be needed to sustain the democratic demands now so widely held by many in most walks of life and most definitely held by most non-managerial workers of all "races" and sexual orientations.

This brings us to the actual roles of political parties. The recent re-emergence of activists with declared democratic socialist agendas in centre-left parties in several advanced capitalist states represents a critical springboard. As we have seen earlier in this book, Erik Olin Wright made many fertile conceptual and empirical contributions to understanding classes in advanced capitalist societies. In his last, posthumously published work, Wright (2019, 57) recognized the pivotal nature of links between mass social movements and political parties:

> For these various kinds of civil society based collective actors to have sustained efficacy in changing the rules of the game enforced by the state, they need to somehow be connected to progressive political parties capable of acting directly within the state. Ultimately, then, the strategy of eroding capitalism depends on the existence of a web of collective actors anchored in civil society and political parties committed to such a political project.

With characteristic taxonomic care, Wright laid out constituting dimensions of such collective actors in terms of identities, interests and values. Sadly, he died before he had the chance to apply this schema to the US or elsewhere.

In a critical appreciation of Wright's work, the late Leo Panitch (2020, 50) underlined the distinctiveness of recent centre-left party reorientations beyond Wright's analysis:

> It has much to do with the frustrations of two decades of episodic mass protests, isolated local community practices, and the marginality of those small revolutionary parties which provided little strategic perspective beyond direct action, all of them leaving to the side the matter of how to enter the state to change what it does, let alone to change what it is. At the same time, the emergence of the twenty-first century socialism which neither defines itself by the Bolshevik model nor abjectly shrinks from advancing a socialist project for fear of being tainted by it, is itself a historic development.

It is fair to say that the two major sorts of parties of the European left in the postwar period — "socialist" (social democratic) and "communist" (Stalinist) — both failed to provide an attractive and credible pathway to socialism. In the current moment, with popular opposition to the capitalist status quo increasing both in breadth and intensity, this double failure does make revival of a credible socialist alternative more difficult. This is not because of capitalism's attraction but due to socialism's abstraction. It is important to recognize the failure of both sorts of parties that were presented to the people of western Europe as alternative pathways to socialist transformation. The socialist parties often won elections and formed governments but made only modest reforms and disappointed their members who aspired to significant transformations. The communist parties were deliberately marginalized by reference to Communist Party dictatorship in the Soviet Union and Eastern Europe, and their working-class membership gradually declined. So, both pathways to socialism were discredited, not simply by bourgeois ideologues but by their own failures. Despite the orthodox Marxist belief that socialism naturally succeeds capitalism, in the actual history of the world, capitalism ended up outlasting the Soviet Union and its Eastern European states. The deadweight of this twin failure on socialist prospects today can be discouraging, despite the objectionable nature of modern capitalism.

On the other hand, neither the composition nor the programs of current established political parties are cast in stone. To take one current example, in France, voter turnout fell seriously from 78 percent in 1986 to 42 percent in 2017. The biggest drop was from the presidential election of 2012 (55 percent) to 2017. A former investment banker and political neophyte, Emmanuel Macron, resigned his post as minister of economy in Francois Hollande's Socialist government, founded his own En Marche centrist party, attracted endorsements from diverse political interests and won the presidency in 2017, clearly (66 percent) defeating right-wing populist Marine Le Pen in the second round. Macron's subsequent mix of policies pleased very few, provoked sustained protests by the yellow vests movement and established unions over threats to prices and benefits and led to new initiatives by various other current and emergent parties, leaving France in a state of political flux.[41] Macron's second defeat of Le Pen in May 2022 did little to stabilize conditions, but it did inspire progressive political parties to move toward popular front initiatives in the face of stronger popular sentiment and weaker capitalist forces than faced the Leon Blum coalition government of 1936 or other later coalitions. The point here is that the field of electoral politics is open to significant change. There are now major openings for strong alliances of progressive social movements to help fundamentally reshape the memberships and agendas of nominally progressive parties or to form their own parties to appeal to disenchanted electorates, reach democratic government and enact alternatives.

Elected governments in advanced capitalist countries have responded to pandemic conditions with substantial support for affected people, the financial scale of which had only previously been seen in the world wars of the prior century. The precedent has been set for expanded public funding of evident social needs, including health care, infrastructure, renewable energy, housing, education and food support. Nominally progressive political parties have major opportunities to put forward platforms to promote equitable, just and fair proposals to address these needs. Through the neoliberal era, many governing parties have been captive to corporate capitalist free market lobbies threatening to move investments to cheaper places and demanding deregulation. But the globe is getting smaller, and, with little apparent maneuverability, governing parties are beginning to try to re-regulate global capital with measures such as standard minimum corporate tax rates. The party re-compositions inspired by the likes of Corbyn and Sanders began to shake neoliberal policies and offer openings for more fundamental alternative policies and electoral platforms that will be needed for democratic transition. The re-composition of some established progressive political parties is the most straightforward route to democratic transition, and many activists inside and outside these parties continue to do what they can to aid more transformative democratic direction. Given the current probable tipping point, either already established political parties must be recomposed very soon and take up the agenda, or new parties linked to mass movements must be formed to present anti-capitalist alternatives to a democratic electorate.

This urgency is underlined by the recent rise of political forces with neofascist appeals in several countries. In the wake of the January 6, 2021, storming of the US Capital, numerous pundits speculate about unrepresentative small groups taking political power undemocratically. I do not add to such speculations, but I register a few relevant basic points. First, the weight of survey evidence presented in this book and other recent class-sensitive surveys in advanced capitalist countries indicate that professional employees generally are strongly supportive of progressive social policies and left-oriented political parties, while the much smaller numbers of large employers and upper managers are clearly inclined to right-oriented parties.[42] Unionized industrial workers and service workers have also tended to remain progressive politically.[43] But, particularly in countries with weaker union movements, at least small numbers of established non-managerial workers — as distinct from the most discriminated exploited workers — have recently been attracted by forces opposing immigration and ethnic diversity.[44] Second, radical right-wing parties and coercive actions have tended to be sponsored in early stages by the most reactionary elites and ideologues fomenting racist fears and to draw support from relatively well-to-do whites seeing relative loss of privilege. This is probably as true of the process reflected in the January 6 insurrection as it was in the rise of Nazism in Weimar Germany.[45] Third, the limited empirical evidence from a rare opinion survey in Weimar Germany suggests that the majority of employees and skilled workers did express a superficial acceptance of left ideology and absence of authoritarianism, but only a small minority of left party supporters among them indicated sufficient democratic commitment to resist Nazism (Brunner 1994). The big difference now is that in most advanced capitalist countries, the majority of non-managerial workers and particularly class conscious workers are more presumptive of their earned fundamental democratic rights and committed to defending them when seriously and obviously pushed — as they may well be in the near future.

Many progressive changes are actually happening at local and regional levels: workplaces, co-ops, communities, workers' pension funds, etc. Prospects for genuine progressive change through political parties, democratic elections and responsive governments are becoming thinkable and plausible. There has always been a debate among social activists over the relationship between community and political party actions and how they can be creatively combined. Community activists working on important local issues have often disdained those who spent time working in the established left parties, and those to the left of these parties have often failed to connect meaningfully with, and support, grassroots struggles.

It should now be obvious and compelling to all progressive change agents that the most effective and sustainable radical changes occur when activists oppose from outside the institutions needing to change and also have allies inside them who can fight for the reforms these activists advocate. Mutual support and alliance by those at local and wider levels, inside and outside established institutional practices, is now a strategic necessity for sustainable democratic transition.

This brings us a final time to the Meidner Plan. As Panitch notes, Wright dealt with this plan in his 2010 book *Envisioning Real Utopias*, largely in terms of the general logics of workers and capitalist class interests. Neither the high level of workers' revolutionary class consciousness (found by Wright's Swedish survey team in 1980 and documented here in Chapter 7) nor unionized workers' initial involvement in the wage earner fund development or their later exclusion from mobilization by both LO and SAP leaders were considered in Wright's account. These are precisely the vital connections recognized in his final work. I agree with Panitch that Wright's hopeful sense of inquiry will be greatly missed and that elaborating on such connections and developing them strategically are of pivotal importance. What is most clear moving forward is that, with the very large numbers now supporting transition to a more democratic economy and sustainable environment, activists in unions and mass social movements and political candidates need to find ways to work cooperatively to respond to these widespread wishes effectively and quickly.

The recent passage of a new climate action law in Denmark based on such cooperation offers one hopeful example.[46] This law commits Denmark to reducing emissions 70 percent by 2030, with targets to be tracked every year and subject to government confidence votes. This is precisely what the Paris Accord lacks — forms of accountability with legal consequences that exert pressure on governments and corporations for substantial change, year after year. Otherwise, promises of where we will be a decade or more are "feel good" gestures that can easily relax the pressure for change because people are pleased that their government's leaders have declared their support for it. This law is supported by nine parties representing 95 percent of voters. Among advanced capitalist countries, Denmark is relatively advanced on the road to economic democracy and to more equitable resource use (see Figure 8.1). It has one of the most highly organized non-managerial labour forces with among the highest proportions of professional employees (see Table 4.1). Many highly class conscious workers among them, particularly in professional unions, have been actively involved in the economic and political organizations throughout Danish society that pressed for meaningful climate action and elected the coalition government that quickly passed the 2020 Climate Change Act. Denmark is a small country with a long way to go to get beyond fossil fuel dependency (Menu 2021) and corporate economic dominance (e.g., Rathgeb 2019). But Danish actions on renewable energy agreements from local cooperatives to central government legislation do chart a path forward. This sort of law is currently less conceivable in the absence of the wide array of democratically owned community renewable energy projects and grassroots organizations that have articulated and aggregated Danish support for it. Similar actions in larger countries without proportional representation will be more challenging, but innovative forms of deliberative participation in state policy making are being created in many advanced capitalist countries (see OECD 2020). The same deliberative forms also provide pathways beyond established state policy forums for durable development of democratic transformative alternatives by progressive groups in the post-COVID-19 moment to avoid either diversion or co-optation into twenty-first-century variants of advanced capitalism

As the environmental effects of capitalist development quickly become more obviously devastating, it is imperative for governments at all levels to take serious remedial actions. Most established political parties in advanced capitalist economies, such as the G7 and Nordic countries, have proposed policies to combat climate change to some extent. The scope of these policies varies both in the extent of democratic participation and types of natural resources. However, the largely gestural efforts to date, such as "green new deals," will be widely recognized as failures. More serious sustained responses in such liberal democratic regimes are likely to continue to be severely constrained and much slower than needed because of established political practices favouring private capital. Competitive profit seeking generally trumps cooperative corporate social responsibility, and corporate profits will continue to be used to protect the right to profit at the expense of the environment and all other social rights. Green capitalism will never work effectively (see Tanuro 2014). Stronger mandates for environmental action will be proposed with relative success on some measures in more authoritarian political regimes — such as Cuba, in spite of the massive enduring burden of the US blockade, or China, where massive compulsory mobilizations have apparently been widely obeyed. The prospect of more autocratic regimes once again replacing more liberal democratic ones in advanced capitalist countries obviously cannot be discounted. But the basic argument in this chapter is that the historic struggle for democratic social and environmental rights in advanced capitalism has reached a level that moving from liberal democratic forms to more participatory democracy is much more likely than moving to more authoritarian systems. The shift to more participatory democracy requires going beyond electoralism to engage in and support grassroots progressive organizations devoted to the ongoing politics of multiracial class struggle (see McNally and Post 2021). Facing the tipping point, the final question remains. Can strategic agencies of class conscious workers and allied social activists effectively mobilize the grassroots majorities who now widely presume these environmental and democratic rights to defend these rights seriously now that they are under imminent threat?

Concluding Thoughts

At the end of this inquiry several things should be a bit clearer. First, in contrast to the many intellectuals who currently deny the relevance of class or portray it in terms of consumer tastes, we know that employment classes based in relations of ownership and control in production processes are fundamental to understanding differences in objective material existence and social consciousness in advanced capitalism. We have seen that the class structure of advanced capitalism continues to shift in many ways but distinctively in terms of the growth of professional employees. These are strategically central non-managerial workers with specialized knowledge whose diminishing job control and increasing precarity are quickly coming to resemble those of the declining numbers of industrial workers who previously made up the core of the working class in capitalist production settings. Professional employees now tend to be among the most highly organized non-managerial workers, increasingly share progressive class consciousness and are becoming more fully allied with the general labour movement and primed to contest democratic control of workplaces as well as other social causes.

Second, we know that, while excessive technologically aided capitalist material goods production has increased to the point of almost irreversibly polluting the planet, the unemployment, underemployment and misemployment of massive numbers of highly qualified workers represent a massive amount of wasted talent. Paid and unpaid work could be redesigned and redistributed in a democratic economy so that everyone's modest subsistence needs are addressed and all people have a minimum of decent socially useful work and significant free time to fulfill their potential. Marx saw a historical precursor of this contradictory condition in terms of the established private relations of production on feudal estates being "burst asunder" by forces of production such as the steam engine, allowing emergent capitalists to create private enterprises that turned serfs into wage labourers. He correctly grasped the contradictory and persistently crisis-prone nature of capitalism, but his hopeful projections about its demise in *The Communist Manifesto* and elsewhere were much too optimistic. At the same time, Marx was exceptionally prescient in recognizing the metabolic rift emerging between natural environmental processes and the scale and pace in industrial capitalism (Bellamy-Foster, Clark and York 2010). More people are becoming aware of this rift today and of the need for an alternative mode of production beyond capitalism as essential for human survival.

Third, we know that transition to a more democratic, environmentally sustainable system is both preferable and practical. The environmental case for responding profoundly to global warming is now indisputable to all but the dimmest or richest narcissists. Financial affordability should not be an issue. Levels of emergency funding during the COVID-19 pandemic have demonstrated government capacity to allocate money far beyond prior claimed austerity limits. Public banks can and should be developed to ensure that savings can be effectively applied to address recovery needs. Pension funds should be committed to social ownership in post-Meidner plans that apply profits to socially useful production activities. The excess profits in recent times and the decreases in labour share of produced value are far greater than the conditions in the late 1970s that inspired the initial Swedish plan. In the wake of the massive real economic and social disruptions of the pandemic, there is a grotesque double spectacle. The US federal government and Federal Reserve give bailouts and almost interest-free loans to private corporations that make 2008 look piddling. At the same time, most of the wealthiest US corporations have made extraordinary profits during the pandemic and distributed virtually all of them to shareholders. A 2020 Oxfam report's call for a wartime-like excess-profits tax would now have almost unanimous public support — except among corporate capitalists and their declining minions. Coupled with increased social ownership through pension funds and development of public banks, optimal funding for recovery and development of an alternative system could be effectively provided. Realizing the transition will require concerted promotion, persistent democratic engagement of strategic agencies in multiple social forums, including debate, legislation and voting, as well as continual defence against increasingly desperate capitalist reactions. Some version of "hothouse Earth" may now be unavoidable, but we will have a better chance of a decent tolerable survival with some sort of economic democracy than the torturous times almost certainly coming for most of us with continuation of variants of neoliberal globalized capitalism.

Fourth, we know that technical roadmaps for rapid conversion to the renewable energy systems needed to respond to global warming are readily available and these means are widely desired. The case for rapid widespread implementation of renewable energy technologies becomes ever more compelling. One of the most compelling features is the possibility that the billions in the Global South, with less investment in fossil fuel technologies and infrastructure, may be enabled to develop distributed renewable systems at least as quickly as countries burdened by stronger fossil fuel interests. The basic argument that those with the least vested interest in an established technology may have the best prospects for taking advantage of new technologies has been made by many.[47] That is not only morally essential; it is also the only way a global movement for basic change can be assembled with coordinated demands and forms of international cooperation. In any event, rapid implementation in the Global South will be at least as vital to equitable global futures as changes in current advanced capitalist countries.

Fifth, we know through many means of public expression, from the various opinion surveys reported here to the unprecedented popular protests of recent times and the increasing emergence of modelled alternatives, that large majorities in most class positions, as well as of most racial backgrounds, sexual orientations and all ages would actively support or tacitly accept a transition to a more democratic, environmentally sustainable system. Further surveys to update the class-based measures and trends found in this inquiry are now relatively inexpensive and technically easy to conduct. They should be done in all relevant countries, sponsored by public interest organizations and involving teams of competent researchers, to inform progressive actions. Access to the survey instruments used in this inquiry is readily available to aid all interested in further comparative studies (see Canada Work Learning Surveys 1998–2016).[48] It is far too long since the leading edge surveys in Chapters 6 and 7.

Finally, we should know that however frequently corporate capitalists collude in forums such as Davos and however many rhetorical wishes for global salvation they might utter, the most powerful capitalists remain forever divided by their competitive pursuit of profits through exploiting the rest of us. The globalization that they have fomented has also led to the development of several international organizations, including the United Nations and its associated institutions, and many others, such as the Global Environment Facility, International Renewable Energy Agency, International Institute for Democracy and Electoral Assistance, World Organization for Animal Health and Conference on Disarmament. These organizations are fundamentally designed for cooperation for human survival and betterment.[49] Local to global sociolegal infrastructures enabling cooperative democratic action now exist. There is nothing as essential as capitalists' divisive pursuit of profits preventing us from enhanced cooperation if we value human survival. The need for international cooperation of mass social movements, open exchange of information about environmental and social risks, creation of agreements with mechanisms of accountability to deal with global risks and active ongoing cooperation between progressive agencies of all sorts to effect meaningful global change has never been more obvious. In addition to the intransigence of corporate capitalists and their declining minions, a difficult obstacle is the divisions of political power within and between nation-states in navigating a continually changing global capitalist economy. The evidence presented in this book suggests that class conscious private sector industrial workers and predominantly public sector professional employees in advanced capitalism are well placed and disposed to lead movements outside and inside the state for economic and environmental justice. As we approach this tipping point, the ultimate question is whether they and their many allies focused on racialization, gender, age-based and other important social rights can use their strategic agencies more fully to mobilize for these goals that nearly all of humanity share. It is no exaggeration to say our future depends on it.

My Irish grandmother used to say, "It's a long road that has no turning." As testified by the evidence in this book, many exploited and oppressed people sense that the capitalist road is about done. Desperate people can do extraordinary things. Let's turn off before we go over the cliff.

Notes

1. See United Nations Development Programme (2019).
2. See IPCC (2022) for one of the latest documentations reflecting the consensual view of virtually the entire global scientific community.
3. For a general international perspective, see Piketty (2014). For the most detailed data, for the US case, see Stone et al. (2020).
4. For an insightful historical account of the nuclear threat in current context, see Ord (2020).
5. For suggestive comparative historical perspectives, see Tainter (1990) and Diamond (2011).
6. Many of the most viable alternatives involve variants of economic democracy to be specified below. For fuller development, see Cumbers (2020).
7. See Livingstone (2009; 2019a; 2019b).
8. See American Institute of Physics (2021).
9. For an activist account, see McKibben (2019).
10. See <www.wedonthavetime.org>, the world's largest social network for climate action.
11. See Strohl (2019).
12. See Mishel and Kandra (2020).
13. See Buchanan, Bui and Patel (2020).
14. See, for example, Avalanche Research (2020).
15. See Balko (2013).
16. As Erica Chenoweth (2020), the original formulator of this 3.5 percent participation threshold rule has later noted, this criterion was derived from specific sorts of campaigns, for removal of regime leaders or territorial independence. It is unclear whether a similar criterion might apply to campaigns to undo systemic racism or protect or expand rights for climate action, as well as applicability to campaigns including *reactive* unarmed violence (see Anisin 2020).
17. This "alternatives" survey was designed by me and conducted by Leger Research Intelligence Group in June 2020 with a representative random national sample of Canadians over age 18 (N=3177). Further information on design and data is available at Canada Work Learning Surveys 1998–2016. Leger 2020 Alternatives Survey.
18. Beyond Cumbers (2018), further information on the design of this research project, Transforming Public Policy through Economic Democracy, and on the dataset generated may be found at the UK Research and Innovation website <https://gtr.ukri.org/projects?ref=ES%2FN006674%2F1>.
19. See Cumbers (2020) for a recent accessible overview.
20. But it needs to be said that at the same time support for capitalism as "a good thing" also increased while uncertain responses were greatly reduced and political polarization therefore grew.
21. See, for example, Foster (2020).
22. See Wikipedia, "Socialism."
23. See Alperovitz (2004) and Quarter, Mook and Armstrong (2017).
24. For example, Cruz, Alves and Delbridge (2017).
25. For a recent extensive review, se Pérotin (2016).
26. See Cumbers (2020) for descriptions of the current range of these initiatives.
27. For a brief overview of origins and recent development of deliberative democracy

models, see Wikipedia, "Deliberative Democracy."
28. For a recent analysis of the most extreme US case of elite political dominance, see Lessig (2021).
29. For an outline of elements in this process, see Fishkin (2011).
30. For relevant evidence, see Wilkinson and Pickett (2009); Wheatley (2017).
31. See Jacobson and Delucchi. (2011).
32. As examples spanning the past century, consider the Regina Manifesto of 1933 (Boyko 2021) and the Socialist Manifesto of 2019 (Sunkara 2019). The most detailed models were probably generated by the guild socialism movement (Cole 1920).
33. See Brenner (2020).
34. See, for example, Pontusson and Kuruvilla (1992); Furaker (2016).
35. By "gray capitalism," Blackburn is referring to the rapid aging of the labour force eligible for retirement and the failure of pension fund managers to properly represent the interests of the ultimate beneficiaries of these funds.
36. See, for example, the current orientation of the Ontario Teachers' Federation, one of the largest pension plans in Canada <https://www.otffeo.on.ca/en/pensions/socially-responsible-investment/>.
37. See, for example, Earth Charter Cities (n.d.).
38. See for example, International Database of De-Privatised Public Services Transnational Institute. (2021).
39. See della Porta and Doerr (2018).
40. See Treisman 2020.
41. See Dettmer (2020).
42. See, for example, Oesch and Rennwald (2018).
43. See Abou-Chadri and Wagner (2019).
44. See Gidron and Hall. (2017), Oesch and Rennwald (2018) and Visser et al. (2014) for suggestive evidence.
45. Historical parallels are generally complicated. But, as Arendt (1951) observed, strong early support for antisemitism and the Nazi Party came from the aristocracy in alliance with members of traditionalist, monarchist conservative parties, and antisemitism became a most effective wider mobilizer in Nazi politics. Trump's attempts to retain and regain state power have been sustained through alliances with reactionary corporate and media forces, and the arrested January 6 insurrectionists have been mainly white males in business and managerial classes from areas experiencing increasing ethnic diversity (see Pape 2021).
46. See Climate Change News 2019.
47. With regard to energy transformation, one of the most notable cases was made by Service (1960).
48. For a guide to the full set of research projects, publications and data bases, see https://discover.research.utoronto.ca/27054-dw-livingstone/.
49. For an illustrative list of intergovernmental organizations, see Wikipedia, "List of Intergovernmental Organizations."

Appendices

Appendix 1
The Challenge of Identifying Managers

Most official national surveys of employment and occupations to date have underestimated the numbers of managerial personnel. Many surveys have failed to distinguish some with formally designated managerial roles because these roles have been conflated with non-managerial roles in some of the types of occupations respondents reported. As noted in Chapter 4, the International Labour Office (2015) data set on employment by occupation relies on the highly regarded International Standard Classification of Occupations (ISCO). However, in addition to incorporating employers and self-employed in ISCO occupations, numerous ISCO titles also combine managerial employees with non-managerial employees in the same non-managerial occupations, thereby underestimating numbers of managers.

The international Class Structure and Class Consciousness (CSCC) project led by Erik Olin Wright in the 1980s attempted to address this problem. Wright's (1978; 1985; 1997) own conception of class structure in advanced capitalism went through several versions. But most of the associated 1980s project surveys gathered sufficient information from respondents to distinguish them in terms of status of employment (employer or self-employed), whether they had managerial authority or whether they were non-managerial hired employees, as well as their specific occupational titles. Wright's (1997) own final version of class structure identified employers, self-employed, managers, "experts" (who were deemed to be non-managerial employees with specialized knowledge in occupations generally recognized as professional) and "workers" (non-managerial employees in occupations generally recognized as skilled or unskilled). Wright's final class structure distributions estimated from six national surveys in the early 1980s with sufficient data using these distinctions are summarized in Table A1.1.

Table A1.1 Wright's Final Employment Class Structure circa 1982: Combined Status in Employment and Employment by Occupation, 6 Countries (% of Employed Labour Force)

Country	Employers	Self-Employed	Managers	Experts	Skilled + Unskilled Workers
Canada	4	13	23	3	(22 + 35) =57
Japan	8	23	21	1	(11 + 36) = 47
Norway	4	10	23	4	(21 + 37) =58
Sweden	5	5	20	3	(17 + 49) =66
UK	7	7	24	2	(17 + 43) = 60
US	8	7	29	3	(13 + 41) = 54

Source: Circa 1982 Wright 1997, Figure 2.1, p. 47.

Wright's final survey-based estimates for employment class structure circa 1982 in Table A1.1 can be compared with the closest available ILO KILM5 census-based estimates for the same six countries in 1992 in Table 4.1 in the text. First, while employers and self-employed are distinguished from hired employees in Wright's early 1980s data in Table A1.1, owners and hired employees are mixed together in the 1992 (and 2016) KILM5 occupational data in Table 4.1 in the text. But the major difference between these Wright and KILM5 data sources is that there are from two to four times more managers in the 1980s class structure estimates by Wright than in the later KILM5 employment by occupation data. Some owners with managerial designations are buried in the later 1992–2016 KILM5 occupational data. Significant numbers of managerial-supervisory employees must also remain buried in the professional occupations, service workers and industrial workers occupational positions in the later ILO KILM5 data. Second, there are large and growing numbers in the professional occupations in the ILO surveys from 1992 onward but very few "experts" in the Wright 1980s survey final estimates. It is clear from Wright's subgroupings (i.e., expert managers, expert supervisors) that professional employees who reported any indication of informal workplace authority were designated as managers. More seriously, Wright's chosen authority criteria allowed both lead hands with informal job control and janitors with grandiose subjective views to be identified as managers. Conversely, both the KILM5 categories and my class logic in the current study keep employees in their professional, service work or industrial work positions unless they have a formal managerial-supervisory occupational title. A person just saying they have some sort of workplace advisory role should not be sufficient to attribute managerial status.

In addition, the use of imputed skill levels to distinguish between experts and the working class as well as between skilled and unskilled workers is, as Wright (1997, 53) himself recognized, "notoriously difficult," and he went through several different estimating processes. Unfortunately, the ISCO scheme was not widely available when the 1980s surveys were conducted and retroactive comparisons using it for imputing skill levels are both complicated and may be of limited accuracy for most countries. In any case, comparisons of the total proportion of skilled and unskilled workers in these early 1980s surveys with the total proportion of service and industrial workers in the 1992–2016 ILO KILM5 data suggest that non-managerial skilled and unskilled workers continue to make up around half of the employed labour force in these six advanced capitalist countries. We can also be reasonably sure from the data on employers and self-employed in Figure 4.3 in the text that by 1992 they made up less than 15 percent of the labour force in all six countries.

Given that the ILO KILM and CSCC data are the best available survey sources of relevant empirical evidence, a major challenge for comparative employment class structure analysis is to reconcile Wright's large final estimates for managers in the early 1980s and very low estimates for experts/professional employees with the reverse patterns in the ILO KILM5 data figures for 1992 onward. In addition to distinguishing employers and self-employed, we need to identify those with genuine managerial job titles and to compare the traditional working class of non-managerial service workers and industrial workers with the emerging class of professional employees.

Fortunately, it has been possible to make these class distinctions using the same national survey for Canada that Wright (1997) used for his 1982 class estimates for Canada. This is the Canadian Class Structure Survey (CCS), conducted by Wallace Clement and John Myles (1994) as part of the general CSCC project; the data are available for public use.[1] There is sufficient information in the CCS survey data to distinguish employers and self-employed as well as to use concordance with ISCO occupational titles to distinguish those with formal managerial-supervisory job titles as well as non-managerial professional employees, service workers and industrial workers.

A comparison of my composite class structure model with Wright's initial and final estimates for Canada in 1982 is summarized in

Table A1.2. Wright's initial logic, here designated as Wright I, refers to the logic formulated in Wright (1978) and applied by me to the ccs 1982 Canada survey data. Wright's final logic, here designated as Wright II, is as computed later by Wright and reported for Canada in Wright (1997, 47). Similar variations have been found for other cscc survey countries.

Table A1.2 Employment Class Structure, Canada, circa 1982, Three Logics (% of Employed Labour Force)

Class Logic	Wright I	Wright II	Livingstone
Employers	5	4	4
Self-employed	12	13	13
Managers	27	23	9
Professional employees	13	3	12
Service + industrial workers	(25+18) =43	(22 + 35) =57	(33 +30) =63

Source: Wright I computed by the author from ccs survey data; Wright II Wright 1997, Figure 2.1, p. 47; Livingstone: Livingstone and Watts 2018.

All three estimates for employers and self-employed in the 1982 Canadian survey data are predictably virtually identical — they rely on the same simple survey questions. Both Wright's initial logic and mine identified over 10 percent as professional (or "semi-autonomous") employees. The major difference was for managers. The initial Wright I criteria generate about three times as many managers as mine (27 percent versus 9 percent). Much of the difference is Wright's attribution of managerial status to non-managerial workers who claimed informal authority without managerial titles. This accordingly reduced the proportion of (non-managerial) "workers" to less than half (43 percent) of the 1982 labour force, compared with over 60 percent using my composite class logic. But, with the exception of Wright's overestimation of managers by inclusion of lead hand workers, estimates for 1982 based on his initial model are broadly comparable with mine.

If we further compare the Wright II (1997) revised class logic with my composite model, the main change is his use of attributed "skill assets" to reduce the 1982 numbers of non-managerial semi-autonomous employees cum "experts" and thereby increase the traditional working class of industrial and service workers to the majority (57 percent). Managers remain around a quarter of the labour force while experts/professional employees shrink to near zero (3 percent).

In retrospect, Wright's initial decision to include lead hands as managers clearly generated overestimates for 1982. The later use of skill asset criteria served to reduce to almost nothing the expert/professional employee class that ILO and other sources later suggested to be substantial and increasing.

Wright (2010) went on to do valuable research on economic alternatives. Unfortunately, he effectively left the field of empirical class analysis before his untimely recent death. The CSCC data archive will continue to serve as an important part of his legacy. The data generated by Wright and his international colleagues remain invaluable for further comparative empirical research on class structure and class consciousness in advanced capitalism. For the early 1980s, the CSCC network provides the most adequate cross-national data available for empirical estimates of both class structure and class consciousness. The data in the CSCC archive is used in Chapter 6 for general analyses of class consciousness in the early 1980s for countries with comparable data. The estimates of employment class structure in Figure 4.1 in the text based on the Wright I initial class model are also used in Chapter 7 to analyze connections between class structure and class consciousness.

Note

1. Information on the 1982 CCS survey is available at Canada Work Learning Surveys 1998–2016; 1982 CCS National Dataset.

Appendix 2
Class Consciousness Composite Forms Logic, 1982–2016

Table A2.1 Class Consciousness Composite Forms Logic, 1982–2016

Item	Hegemonic Capitalist Consciousness	Oppositional Capitalist Consciousness	Capitalist Sympathizer	Contradictory Class Consciousness	Labour Sympathizer	Oppositional Labour Consciousness	Revolutionary Labour Consciousness
Class identity	Upper or upper middle class	Upper or upper middle class	Lower, working or lower middle class, or no class identity declared	Any class Identity	Upper or upper middle class, or no class identity declared	Lower, working or lower middle class	Lower, working or lower middle class
Opposed class interests							
Replacement workers	Disagree (4,5)	Disagree (4,5)	Disagree (4,5)	Any agree-disagree combo on both items	Agree (1,2)	Agree (1,2)	Agree (1,2)
Corporate owners gain	Disagree (4,5)	Disagree (4,5)	Disagree (4,5)		Agree (1,2)	Agree (1,2)	Agree (1,2)
Preferred future							
Non-profit economy	Disagree (4,5)	Any other combo besides disagree/disagree on both items	Any response on both items	Any response on both items	Any response on both items	Any other combo besides agree/agree on both items	Agree (1,2)
Worker self-management	Disagree (4,5)						Agree (1,2)

Original Source of Items: CSCC (1980s) US questionnaire, which are reproduced in Table 6.1.

References

Abelard, P. 1976 [1121]. *Sic et non: A Critical Edition*. Chicago: University of Chicago Press.

Abercrombie, N., S. Hill, and B. Turner. 1980. *The Dominant Ideology Thesis*. London: Allen & Unwin.

Abou-Chadri, T., and M. Wagner. 2019. "The Electoral Appeal of Party Strategies in Postindustrial Societies: When Can the Mainstream Left Succeed?" *The Journal of Politics* 81, 4: 1405–1419.

Adams, T.L., and D.W. Livingstone. 2020. "Self-Regulating Professionals and Experts in the 'Knowledge Economy': Autonomy and Authority Compared." Working paper for the Changing Workplaces in a Knowledge Economy Project. https://www.oise.utoronto.ca/clsew/UserFiles/File/Expert_paper_for_CLSEWwebsite_Final-Nov24_2020.pdf.

Adler, P. 2019. *The 99 Percent Economy: How Democratic Socialism Can Overcome the Crises of Capitalism*. Oxford: Oxford University Press.

Albert, M., and R. Hahnel. 1978. *Unorthodox Marxism: An Essay on Capitalism, Socialism and Revolution*. Boston: South End Press.

Albus, J. 1976. *Peoples' Capitalism: The Economics of the Robot Revolution*. New World Books. https://www.robotictechnologyinc.com/images/upload/file/Albus%20Peoples%20Capitalism%20Book.pdf.

Alizada, N., R. Cole, L. Gastaldi, et al. 2021. "Autocratization Turns Viral. Democracy Report 2021." Gothenburg University of Gothenburg, *V-Dem Institute*, March 22. v-dem.net/static/website/files/dr/dr_2021.pdf.

Allen, J.P., S. Pavlin, S., and R.K.W. van der Velden. 2011. "Competencies and Early Labour Market Careers of Higher Education Graduates in Europe." *University of Ljubljana*. ROA External Reports 01, 01. https://www.researchgate.net/publication/265085425_Competencies_and_Early_Labour_Market_Careers_of_Higher_Education_Graduates_in_Europe.

Allen, K. 2018. "Why Exchange Values Are Not Environmental Values: Explaining the Problem with Neoliberal Conservation." *Conservation and Society* 16, 3: 243–256.

Alperovitz, G. 2016. "Socialism in America Is Closer Than You Think." *The Nation*, February 11. thenation.com/article/archive/socialism-in-america-is-closer-than-you-think/.

___. 2004. *America Beyond Capitalism: Reclaiming Our Wealth, Our Liberty, and Our Democracy*. New York: John Wiley & Sons.

American Institute of Physics. 2021. "The Discovery of Global Warming." https://history.aip.org/climate/index.htm.

Amin, S. 1974. *Accumulation on a World Scale*. New York: Monthly Review Press.

Anderson, C.H. 1974. *The Political Economy of Social Class*. Englewood Cliffs, NJ: Prentice-Hall.

Anderson, P. 1976. *Considerations on Western Marxism*. London: N.L.B.

Anisin, A. 2020. "Debunking the Myths Behind Nonviolent Civil Resistance." *Critical*

Sociology 46, 7–8: 1121–1139.

Archer, P., and R. Orr. 2011. "Class Identification in Review: Past Perspectives and Future Directions." *Sociology Compass* 5, 1: 104–115.

Arendt, H. 1951. *The Origins of Totalitarianism*. New York: Houghton Mifflin Harcourt.

Ares, M. 2020. "Changing Classes, Changing Preferences: How Social Class Mobility Affects Economic Preferences." *West European Politics* 43, 6: 1211–1237.

Aries, P. 1962. *Centuries of Childhood*. New York: Vintage Books.

Aronowitz, S. 1973. *False Promises: The Shaping of American Working-Class Consciousness*. New York: McGraw-Hill.

Atkinson, W. 2009. "Rethinking the Work-Class Nexus: Theoretical Foundations for Recent Trends." *Sociology* 43, 5: 896–912.

Avalanche Research. 2020. *Avalanche Insights 2020 Impact Report*. https://static1.squarespace.com/static/5ed6ba258b17cb3ec2d0521d/t/60136bb1765d6108f9b4a219/1611885492027/Avalanche+Insights+2020+Impact+Report.pdf.

Ayers, B. 2013. "Trudge Toward Freedom: A Review of 'After Capitalism.'" Online University of the Left. http://ouleft.sp-mesolite.tilted.net/?page_id=1220.

Baldwin, J.R., and D. Beckstead. 2003. *Knowledge Workers in Canada's Economy, 1971–2001*. Ottawa: Statistics Canada.

Balko, B. 2013. *Rise of the Warrior Cop: The Militarization of America's Police Forces*. New York: Public Affairs.

Banaji, J. 2010. *Theory as History: Essays on Modes of Production and Exploitation*. Leiden: Brill.

___. 1977. "Modes of Production in a Materialist Conception of History." *Capital and Class* 1, 3.

Baradaran, M. 2020. "The Neoliberal Looting of America by Private Equity Funds." *New York Times*, July 2. nytimes.com/2020/07/02/opinion/private-equity-inequality.html?action=click&module=Opinion&pgtype=Homepage.

Barley, S.R., and G. Kunda. 2004. *Gurus, Hired Guns and Warm Bodies: Itinerant Experts in a Knowledge Economy*. Princeton: Princeton University Press.

Barrientos, A., and D. Neff. 2010. "Attitudes to Chronic Poverty in the 'Global Village.'" GIGA *Research Programme: Socio-Economic Challenges in the Context of Globalisation* 134 (May). files.ethz.ch/isn/116236/wp134.pdf.

Bell, D. 1976. *The Coming of Post-Industrial Society: A Venture in Social Forecasting*. New York: Basic Books

___. 1962. *The End of Ideology: On the Exhaustion of Political Ideas in the Fifties*. Cambridge: Harvard University Press.

Bell, J., J. Poushter, M. Fagan, and C. Huang. 2021. "In Response to Climate Change, Citizens in Advanced Economies Are Willing to Alter How They Live and Work." Pew Research Center, September 14. pewresearch.org/global/2021/09/14/in-response-to-climate-change-citizens-in-advanced-economies-are-willing-to-alter-how-they-live-and-work/.

Bellamy-Foster, J., B. Clark, and R. York. 2010. *The Ecological Rift: Capitalism's War on the Earth*. New York: Monthly Review Press.

Benda, J. 1928. *The Treason of the Intellectuals*. New York: William Morrow.

Bengtsson, M., T. Berglund, and M. Oskarson. 2013. "Class and Ideological Orientations Revisited: An Exploration of Class-Based Mechanisms." *The British Journal of Sociology* 64, 4: 691–716.

Bergman, M., and D. Joye. 2005. "Comparing Social Stratification Schemas: CAMSIS, CSP-CH, Goldthorpe, ISCO-88, Treiman, and Wright." Cambridge: Cambridge Studies

in Social Research. https://www.sociology.cam.ac.uk/system/files/documents/cs10.pdf.
Berry, C., and L. Macfarlane. 2019 "A New Public Banking Ecosystem: A Report to the Labour Party Commissioned by the Communication Workers Union and the Democracy Collaborative." labour.org.uk/wp-content/uploads/2019/03/Building-a-new-public-banking-ecosystem.pdf.
Blackburn, R. 2006. "The Global Pension Crisis: From Gray Capitalism to Responsible Accumulation." *Politics & Society* 34, 2 (June): 135–186.
Bloch, E. 1989 [1959]. *The Principle of Hope*. 3 volumes. Cambridge: MIT Press.
Bohm, S., and C. Land. 2012. "The New 'Hidden Abode': Reflections on Value and Labour in the New Economy." *The Sociological Review* 60, 2.
Boswell, T., and W. Dixon. 1993. "Marx's Theory of Rebellion: A Cross-National Analysis of Class Exploitation, Economic Development, and Violent Revolt." *American Sociological Review* 58, 5: 81–702.
Bottomore, T. 1978. "Marxism and Sociology." In T. Bottomore and R. Nisbet (eds.), *A History of Sociological Analysis*. London: Heinemann.
Bourdieu, P. 1989. "The Corporatism of the Universal: The Role of Intellectuals in the Modern World." *Telos* 81 (October).
___. 1991. "The Peculiar History of Scientific Reason." *Sociological Forces* 5, 3–26.
Boyd, M. 2008. "A Socioeconomic Scale for Canada: Measuring Occupational Status from the Census." *Canadian Review of Sociology* 45, 1: 51–91.
Boyko, J. 2021. "Regina Manifesto." *The Canadian Encyclopedia*. thecanadianencyclopedia.ca/en/article/regina-manifesto-1933.
Braun, S. 2020. "Pope Francis and Economic Democracy: Understanding Pope Francis's Radical (yet) Practical Approach to Political Economy." *Theological Studies* 81, 1: 203–224.
Braverman, H. 1974. *Labor and Monopoly Capital: The Degradation of Work in the Twentieth Century*. New York: Monthly Review Press.
Brenner, R. 2020. "Escalating Plunder." *New Left Review* 123 (May-June): 5–22.
___. 1976. "Agrarian Class Structure and Economic Development in Pre-Industrial Europe." *Past and Present* 70: 30–74.
Brick, H. 2019. *Anti-Capitalist Thought and Utopian Alternatives in America*. Oxford Research Encyclopedia of American History.
Bridges, D. 2017. *Philosophy in Educational Research*. Dordrecht, Netherlands: Springer.
Brighton Labour Process Group. 1977. "The Capitalist Labour Process." *Capital and Class* 4, 1 (Spring).
Brödner, P. 2000. "The Future of Work in a Knowledge-Based Economy." ICT/CIREM *International Seminar on 'Economy and Work in the Knowledge Society,'* February 24–25, 2000. iat.eu/aktuell/veroeff/ps/broedner00a.pdf.
Bromley, D. 1991. *Environment and Economy: Property Rights and Public Policy*. New York: Basil Blackwell.
Brunner, J. 1994. "Looking into the Hearts of the Workers, or: How Erich Fromm Turned Critical Theory into Empirical Research." *Political Psychology* 15, 4 (December): 631–665.
Bryer, R.A. 2005. "Marx, Accounting and the Labour Theory of Value: A Critique of Marxist Economics." Paper presented to 5th European Critical Accounting Studies Conference, University of Warwick, Coventry, June, 2005. researchgate.net/publication/229054105_Marx_Accounting_and_the_labour_theory_of_value_a_critique_of_Marxist_Economics.

Brym, R.J. 1980. *Intellectuals and Politics*. London: Allen & Unwin.
Buchanan, L., Q. Bui, and J.K. Patel. 2020. "Black Lives Matter May Be the Largest Movement in U.S. History." *New York Times*. July 3. nytimes.com/interactive/2020/07/03/us/george-floyd-protests-crowd-size.html.
Buchheit, P. 2017. "Inequality Out of Control: The Average 1% Household Made Over $2.5 Million in the Past Year." Common Dreams, November 20. commondreams.org/views/2017/11/20/inequality-out-control-average-1-household-made-over-25-million-past-year.
Bulmer, M. (ed.). 1975. *Working Class Images of Society*. London: Routledge & Kegan Paul.
Burawoy, M. 2016. "The Promise of Sociology: Global Challenges for National Disciplines." *Sociology* 50, 5.
___. 1979. *Manufacturing Consent*. London: Verso.
Burke, M.J., and J.C. Stephens. 2018. "Political Power and Renewable Energy Futures: A Critical Review." *Energy Research & Social Science* 35 (January): 78–93.
Burnham, J. 1941. *The Managerial Revolution: What Is Happening in the World*. New York: Day.
Burris, V. 1990. "Classes in Contemporary Capitalist Society: Recent Marxist and Weberian Perspectives." In S. Clegg (ed.), *Organization Theory and Class Analysis: New Approaches and New Issues*. New York: Walter de Gruyter.
___. 1987. "The Neo-Marxist Synthesis of Marx and Weber on Class." In N. Wiley (ed.), *The Marx–Weber Debate*. Newbury Park, CA: Sage.
Business Roundtable. 2019. "Statement on the Purpose of a Corporation." August 19. purpose.businessroundtable.org.
Camfield, D. 2022. *Future on Fire: Capitalism and the Politics of Climate Change*. Black Point, NS: Fernwood Publishing.
___. 2016. "Theoretical Foundations of an Anti-Racist Queer Feminist Historical Materialism." *Critical Sociology* 42, 2.
Campbell, J., et al. 1974. *Changing Images of Man*. Menlo Park, CA: Stanford Research Institute.
Canada, Employment and Immigration, Occupational and Career Information Branch. n.d. *Conversion Tables: CCDO to NOC*. https://publications.gc.ca/site/eng/9.608781/publication.html.
Canada Work Learning Surveys. 1998–2016. "Corporate Executive Surveys 1980–2000." <https://borealisdata.ca/dataverse/CanadaWorkLearningSurveys1998-2016>.
Canadian Labour Congress. 2020. "Affiliates: Who We Are." canadianlabour.ca/who-we-are/affiliates/.
Canning, J. 1996. *A History of Medieval Political Thought: 300–1450*. London: Routledge.
Carchedi, G, 2022. "The Ontology and Social Division of Knowledge: The Internet and Quantum Time." *International Critical Thought*. doi.org/10.1080/21598282.2022.2113170.
___. 2011. "Behind and Beyond the Crisis." *International Socialism: A Quarterly Review of Socialist Theory* 132 (October 11). isj.org.uk/behind-and-beyond-the-crisis/
___. 1977. *The Economic Identification of Social Classes*. London: Routledge and Kegan Paul.
___. 1975. "On the Economic Identification of the New Middle Class." *Economy and Society* 4, 1: 1–83.
Cardoso Machado, N.M. 2013. "The Money of the Mind and the God of Commodities – The Real Abstraction According to Sohn-Rethel." MPRA paper 48961, University

Library of Munich, Germany. ideas.repec.org/p/pra/mprapa/48961.html

Carroll, W. 2010. *The Making of a Transnational Capitalist Class: Corporate Power in the 21st Century*. London and New York: Zed Books.

Carter, B. 2021. "Defending Marx and Braverman: Taking Back the Labour Process in Theory and Practice." *International Socialism Journal* 2: 171–196.

———. 1995. "A Growing Divide: Marxist Class Analysis and the Labour Process." *Capital & Class* 19, 1: 33–72.

———. 1985. *Capitalism, Class Conflict and the New Middle Class*. London: Routledge and Kegan Paul.

Case, A., and A. Deaton. 2020. *Deaths of Despair and the Future of Capitalism*. Princeton: Princeton University Press.

Castells, M. 2000. *The Information Age: Economy Society and Culture: The Rise of the Network Society*, vol. 1, 2nd ed. Hoboken, NJ: Blackwell.

Castells, M. 1980. *The Economic Crisis and American Society*. Princeton: Princeton University Press.

Centers, R. 1949. *The Psychology of Social Classes; A Study of Class Consciousness*. Princeton: Princeton University Press.

Chaudhry, V. 2018. "Knowing Through Tripping: A Performative Praxis for Co-Constructing Knowledge as a Disabled Halfie." *Qualitative Inquiry* 24, 1: 70–82.

Chenoweth, E. 2020. "Questions, Answers, and Some Cautionary Updates Regarding the 3.5% Rule." *Carr Center*, April 4. carrcenter.hks.harvard.edu/publications/questions-answers-and-some-cautionary-updates-regarding-35-rule.

———. 2013. "My Talk at TEDxBoulder: Civil Resistance and the '3.5% Rule.'" *Rational-Insurgent*, November 4. rationalinsurgent.wordpress.com/2013/11/04/my-talk-at-tedxboulder-civil-resistance-and-the-3-5-rule/.

Chenoweth, E., S. Dahlum, S. Kang, et al. 2019. "This May Be the Largest Wave of Nonviolent Mass Movements in World History. What Comes Next?" *Washington Post*, November 16. washingtonpost.com/politics/2019/11/16/this-may-be-largest-wave-nonviolent-mass-movements-world-history-what-comes-next/.

Chenoweth, E., J. Pinckney, and O. Lewis. 2018. "Days of Rage: Introducing the NAVCO 3.0 Dataset." *Journal of Peace Research* 554: 524–534.

Chenoweth, E., and M. J. Stephan. 2012. *Why Civil Resistance Works: The Strategic Logic of Nonviolent Conflict*. New York: Columbia University Press.

Chhabra, G. 2020. "Turning a Blind Eye to Employers' Discrimination? Attitudinal Barrier Perceptions of Vision Impaired Youth from Oslo and Delhi." *Disability & Society* 36, 10. https://doi.org/10.1080/09687599.2020.1816905.

Chudacoff, H. 1992. *How Old Are You? Age Consciousness in American Culture*. Princeton: Princeton University Press.

Cimbala, S. 2016. "Nuclear Deterrence in Cyber-ia: Challenges and Controversies." *Air & Space Power Journal* (Fall): 54–63.

Clandfield, D., B. Curtis, G-E Galabuzi, et al. 2014. *Restacking the Deck: Streaming by Class, Race and Gender in Ontario Schools*. Ottawa: Canadian Centre for Policy Alternatives.

Clarke, H.D., A. Kornblum, and W. Mishler. 1982. *Representative Democracy in the Canadian Provinces*. Toronto: Prentice-Hall.

Clement, W. 1974. *The Canadian Corporate Elite*. Toronto: McClelland and Stewart.

Clement, W., and J. Myles. 1994. *Relations of Ruling: Class and Gender in Post-Industrial Societies*. Montreal: McGill-Queen's University Press.

Climate Change News. 2019. "Denmark adopts climate law to cut emissions 70% by

2030." https://www.climatechangenews.com/2019/12/06/denmark-adopts-climate-law-cut-emissions-70-2030/.

Cockshott, P., A. Cottrell, and G. Michaelson. 1995. "Testing Marx: Some New Results from UK Data." *Capital and Class* 19, 1: 103–129.

Cohen, R. 1980. "Resistance and Hidden Forms of Consciousness Among African Workers." *Review of African Political Economy* 19: 8–22.

Cole, G.D.H. 1920. *Guild Socialism Re-Stated*. London: Leonard Parsons.

Collins, R. 1998. *The Sociology of Philosophies: A Global Theory of Intellectual Change*. Cambridge, MA: Harvard University Press.

___. 1980. "Weber's Last Theory of Capitalism: A Systematization." *American Sociological Review* 45, 6.

Comparative Political Economy Data Base. https://borealisdata.ca/dataverse/CPEDB.

Connell, R., and N. Dados. 2014. "Where in the World Does Neoliberalism Come From? The Market Agenda in Southern Perspective." *Theory and Society* 43, 1: 117–138.

Corak, M. 2001. *Are the Kids All Right? Intergeneration Mobility and Child Well-Being in Canada*. Statistics Canada, Analytical Studies Branch Research Paper No. 171.

Corman, J., D.W. Livingstone, M. Luxton, and W. Seccombe. 1993. *Recasting Steel Labour: The Stelco Story*. Halifax, NS: Fernwood Publishing.

Corman, J., and M. Luxton. 2001. *Getting by in Hard Times: Gendered Labour at Home and on the Job*. Toronto: University of Toronto Press.

Coulthard, G. 2014. *Red Skin, White Masks: Rejecting the Colonial Politics of Recognition*. Minneapolis: University of Minnesota Press.

Crompton, R., and J. Gubbay. 1977. *Economy and Class Structure*. London: Macmillan.

Cruz, L.B., M.A. Alves, and R. Delbridge. 2017. "Next Steps in Organizing Alternatives to Capitalism: Toward a Relational Research Agenda." *M@n@gement* 204: 322–335.

CSCC (Class Structure and Class Consciousness Series).1980s. Data Archive. https://www.icpsr.umich.edu/web/ICPSR/series/115.

Cumbers, A. 2020. *The Case for Economic Democracy*. London: Wiley.

___. 2018. "A New Definition of Economic Democracy – And What It Means for Inequality." democraticaudit.com/2018/03/01/a-new-definition-of-economic-democracy-and-what-it-means-for-inequality/.

Cuneo, C. 1984. "Class Struggle and Measurement of the Rate of Surplus Value." *Canadian Review of Sociology and Anthropology* 19, 3: 377–425.

Curtis, B., D.W. Livingstone, and H. Smaller. 1992. *Stacking the Deck: The Streaming of Working-Class Kids in Ontario Schools*. Toronto: Our Schools/Our Selves.

Curtis, J. 2013. "Middle Class Identity in the Modern World: How Politics and Economics Matter." *Canadian Review of Sociology* 50, 2: 203–226.

Dahlum, S., C.H. Knutsen, and T. Wig. 2019. "Who Revolts? Empirically Revisiting the Social Origins of Democracy." *The Journal of Politics* 81, 4: 1494–1499.

David, P.A., and D. Foray. 2002. "An Introduction to the Economy of the Knowledge Society." *International Social Science Journal* 54, 171: 9–23.

Davis, H. 1979. *Beyond Class Images: Explorations in the Structure of Social Consciousness*. London: Croom Helm.

Davis, M. 2005. *Planet of Slums*. London: Verso.

Day, G. 2006. *Community and Everyday Life*. London: Routledge

Day, M. 2019. "The Short Happy Life of the Affluent Working Class: Consumption, Debt and Embourgeoisement in the Age of Credit." *Capital and Class* 44, 3: 305–324.

della Porta, D., and N. Doerr. 2018. "Deliberation in Protests and Social Movements." In A. Bächtiger, J.S. Dryzek, J. Mansbridge, and M.E. Warren (eds.), *The Oxford Hand-*

book of Deliberative Democracy. Oxford: Oxford University Press.
Derber, C. 1983. "Managing Professionals: Ideological Proletarianization and Postindustrial Labor." Theory and Society 12, 3: 309–341.
Dettmer, J. 2020. "The Reinvention of Emmanuel Macron." VOA, July 07. voanews.com/a/europe_reinvention-emmanuel-macron/6192317.html.
Devlin, K., S. Schumacher, and J.J. Moncus. 2021. "Many in Western Europe and U.S. Want Economic Changes as Pandemic Continues." Pew Research Center, April 22. pewresearch.org/global/2021/04/22/many-in-western-europe-and-u-s-want-economic-changes-as-pandemic-continues/.
Diamond, J. 2011. Collapse: How Societies Choose to Fail or Succeed, revised edition. New York: Penguin Books.
Dimon, J. 2020. "Unless We Change Capitalism, We Might Lose it Forever." Time, January 16. time.com/collection-post/5764098/jamie-dimon-capitalism/.
DiVito, E., and A. Sojourner. 2021. "Americans Are More Pro-Union—and Anti-Big Business—Than at Any Time in Decades." The Guardian, May 13. theguardian.com/commentisfree/2021/may/13/americans-are-more-pro-union-and-anti-big-business-than-at-any-time-in-decades.
Doane, A. 2017. "Beyond Color-Blindness: Re Theorizing Racial Ideology." Sociological Perspectives 60, 5 (October): 975–991.
Drucker, P. 1998. Peter Drucker on the Profession of Management. Cambridge: Harvard University Press.
Duménil, G., and D. Lévy. 2018. Managerial Capitalism: Ownership, Management, and the Coming New Mode of Production. London: Pluto Press.
Durkheim, E. 1964 [1895]. The Rules of Sociological Method. New York: The Free Press.
Eagleton, T. 1991. Ideology. An Introduction. London: Verso.
Earth Charter Cities. n.d. https://earthcharter.org/library/earth-charter-cities-manifesto/.
Economic Policy Institute. 2020. "CEO Pay Increased 14% in 2019, and Now Make 320 Times Their Typical Workers." Press release, August 18. epi.org/press/ceo-pay-increased-14-in-2019-and-now-make-320-times-their-typical-workers/.
Edwards, R. 1978. "The Social Relations of Production at the Point of Production." Insurgent Sociologist 8, 2–3 (Fall): 109–125.
Ehrenreich, B. 1989. Fear of Falling: The Inner Life of the Middle Class. New York: Pantheon Books.
Ehrenreich, B., and J. Ehrenreich. 2013. "Death of a Yuppie Dream: The Rise and Fall of the Professional–Managerial Class." Rosa Luxemburg Stiftung. rosalux.de/fileadmin/rls_uploads/pdfs/sonst_publikationen/ehrenreich_death_of_a_yuppie_dream90.pdf.
___. 1977. "The Professional–Managerial Class." Radical America 11, 2: 7–32.
Eichler, M. 1980. The Double Standard: A Feminist Critique of the Social Sciences. London: Palgrave Macmillan.
Erikson, R., and J. Goldthorpe. 1992. The Constant Flux: A Study of Class Mobility in Industrial Societies. Oxford: Clarendon Press.
Espinosa, J., and A. Zimbalist. 1978. Economic Democracy. New York: Academic Press.
Evans, M.D.R., and J. Kelley. 2004. "Subjective Social Location: Data from 21 Nations." International Journal of Public Opinion Research 16: 3–38.
EVS/WVS. 2020. "European Values Study and World Values Survey: Joint EVS/WVS 2017–2021 Dataset – Variable Report (Documentation/Tables). Version 1." November 13. europeanvaluesstudy.eu/joint-evs-wvs-2017-2021-dataset/.
Ewart, P. 2020. "BlackRock – The Super Cartel." Tony Seed's Weblog, June 16. tonyseed.wordpress.com/2020/06/16/blackrock-the-super-cartel/.

Fantasia, R. 1995. "From Class Consciousness to Culture, Action, and Social Organization." *Annual Review of Sociology* 21: 269–287.
Federal Reserve System, Board of Governors. 2021. "US, Households and Nonprofit Organizations; Debt Securities and Loans; Liability, Level." FRED, March 25. fred.stlouisfed.org/series/CMDEBT.
Fight Inequality Alliance, Institute for Policy Studies, Oxfam, and Patriotic Millionaires. 2022. "Taxing Extreme Wealth: An Annual Tax on The World's Multi-Millionaires and Billionaires: What It Would Raise and What It Could Pay For." Institute for Policy Studies, January 19. ips-dc.org/wp-content/uploads/2022/01/Report-Taxing-Extreme-Wealth-What-It-Would-Raise-What-It-Could-Pay-For.pdf.
Fikentscher, W. 1995. *Modes of Thought: A Study in the Anthropology of Law and Religion*. Tubingen, Germany: Mohr Siebeck.
Financial Times/Harris Poll. 2019. "New Survey Finds Little Enthusiasm for Free Market Capitalism." American Management Association, Jan 24. amanet.org/articles/new-survey-finds-little-enthusiasm-for-free-market-capitalism/.
Fisher, M. 2009. *Capitalist Realism: Is There No Alternative?* Winchester, UK: Zero Books.
Fishkin, James 2011. *When the People Speak*. New York: Oxford University Press.
Florida, R. 2014. *The Rise of the Creative Class—Revisited*. New York: Basic Books.
Foley, D. 2013. "Rethinking Financial Capitalism and the 'Information' Economy." *Review of Radical Political Economics* 45, 3: 257–268.
Foster, J.B. 2020. "China 2020: An Introduction." *Monthly Review*, October 1. monthlyreview.org/2020/10/01/china-2020-an-introduction/.
Foucault, M. 1970. *The Order of Things: An Archaeology of the Human Sciences*. London: Tavistock Publications.
Frank, R. 2021. "25 Highest-Paid Hedge Fund Managers Made $32 Billion in 2020, a Record." CNBC, February 22. cnbc.com/2021/02/22/-25-highest-paid-hedge-fund-managers-earned-record-setting-32-billion-in-2020.html#:~:text=in%20financial%20markets.-,The%20top%20earner%20was%20Israel%20%E2%80%9CIzzy%E2%80%9D%20En.
Fredrickson, G. 1988. *The Arrogance of Race: Historical Perspectives on Slavery, Racism and Social Inequality*. Middletown, CT: Wesleyan University Press.
Friedman, A. 1977. *Industry and Labour: Class Struggle at Work and Monopoly Capitalism*. London: MacMillan.
Fritz, M., and M. Koch. 2019. "Public Support for Sustainable Welfare Compared: Links Between Attitudes Towards Climate and Welfare Policies." *Sustainability* 11, 15: 4146.
Fuchs, C. and E. Fisher (eds.). 2015. *Reconsidering Value and Labour in the Digital Age*. London: Palgrave Macmillan.
Furåker, B. 2016. "The Swedish Wage-Earner Funds and Economic Democracy: Is There Anything to Be Learned from Them?" *Transfer, The European Review of Labour and Research* 22, 1: 121–132.
Galbraith, J. 1967. *The New Industrial State*. Boston: Houghton Mifflin.
Gallie, D. 1978. *In Search of the New Working Class: Automation and Social Integration Within the Capitalist Enterprise*. London: Cambridge University Press.
Garcia, R., and J. Tomlinson. 2021. "Rethinking the Domestic Division of Labour: Exploring Change and Continuity in the Context of Redundancy." *Sociology* 55, 2: 300–318.
Geoghegan, V. 2008. *Utopianism and Marxism*. Bern: Peter Lang.
Gidron, N., and P.A. Hall. 2017. "The Politics of Social Status: Economic and Cultural

Roots of the Populist Right." *The British Journal of Sociology* 68, 1: 57–84.
Gilbert, D. 2003. *The American Class Structure: In an Age of Growing Inequality*. CA: Thompson Wadsworth.
Gilens, M., and B. Page. 2014. "Testing Theories of American Politics: Elites, Interest Groups, and Average Citizens." *Perspectives on Politics* 14, 3 (September): 564–581.
Gindin, S. 2015. "Bringing Class Back In." *Global Labour Journal* 6, 1 (January). doi.org/10.15173/glj.v6i1.2465.
Girard, J.P., and J. Girard. 2015. "Defining Knowledge Management: Toward an Applied Compendium." *Online Journal of Applied Knowledge Management* 3, 1: 1–20.
Goertzel, T.G. 1979. "Class in America: Qualitative Distinctions and Quantitative Data." *Qualitative Sociology* 1, 3: 53–76.
Goldthorpe, J. 2016. "Social Class Mobility in Modern Britain: Changing Structure, Constant Process." *Journal of the British Academy* 4: 89–111.
Goldthorpe, J., D. Lockwood, F. Bechhofer, and J. Platt. 1969. *The Affluent Worker: Political Attitudes and Behaviour*. Cambridge: Cambridge University Press.
Goldthorpe, J.H., and A. McKnight. 2004. "The Economic Basis of Social Class." London: Centre for Analysis of Social Exclusion. February. core.ac.uk/download/pdf/93872.pdf.
Goody, J. 2006. *The Theft of History*. Cambridge: Cambridge University Press.
Gornick, J., and N. Johnson. 2020. "Income Inequality in Rich Countries: Examining Changes in Economic Disparities." Social Science Research Council. May 5. https://items.ssrc.org/what-is-inequality/income-inequality-in-rich-countries-examining-changes-in-economic-disparities/.
Gorz, A. 1982. *Farewell to the Working Class: An Essay on Post-Industrial Socialism*. London: Pluto Press.
___. 1976. *Division of Labour: Labour Process and Class Struggle in Modern Capitalism*. London: Harvester.
Goyder, J.C. 1975. "A Note on the Declining Relation between Subjective and Objective Class Measures." *British Journal of Sociology* 26, 1.
Graeber, D. 2011. *Debt: The First 5,000 Years*. New York: Melville House.
Gramsci, A. 1971. *Selections from the Prison Notebooks*. New York: International Publishers.
Green, F., A. Felstead, D. Gallie, and G. Henseke. 2016. "Skills and Work Organization in Britain: A Quarter Century of Change." *Journal for Labour Market Research* 49: 121–132.
Green, F., and G. Henseke. 2016. "Should Governments of OECD Countries Worry About Graduate Underemployment?" *Oxford Review of Economic Policy* 32, 4: 514–537.
Grusky, D., and K. Weeden. 2001. "Decomposition Without Death: A Research Agenda for a New Class Analysis." *Acta Sociologica* 44, 3: 203–218.
Guinan. J. 2019. "Socialising Capital: Looking Back on the Meidner Plan." *International Journal of Public Policy* 151, 2: 38–58.
Gurin, P., A. Miller, and G. Gurin. 1980. "Stratum Identification and Consciousness." *Social Psychology Quarterly* 43, 1: 30–47.
Guterres, A. 2022. "Remarks to Press Conference Launch of IPCC Report. Geneva, February 28." ipcc.ch/site/assets/uploads/2022/02/UN_SG_statement_WGII_Pressconference-.pdf
Güveli, A., A. Need, and N.D. de Graaf. 2007. "The Rise of 'New' Social Classes within the Service Class in the Netherlands: Political Orientation of Social and Cultural Specialists and Technocrats Between 1970 and 2003." *Acta Sociologica* 50, 2: 129–46.

Hall, S. 1986. "The Problem of Ideology: Marxism Without Guarantees." *Journal of Communication Inquiry* 10, 2. 28–44.

Hall, S., K. Leary and H. Greevy. 2014. "Public Attitudes to Poverty." York: The Joseph Rowntree Foundation, September. jrf.org.uk/report/public-attitudes-towards-poverty.

Harris Poll. 2007. "Six Nation Survey Finds Little Enthusiasm for Free Market Capitalism in Western Europe or the United States!" https://www.amanet.org/articles/new-survey-finds-little-enthusiasm-for-free-market-capitalism/ /.

Harvey, D. 2005. *A Brief History of Neoliberalism*. Oxford: Oxford University Press.

Harvie, D. 2005. "All Labour Produces Value for Capital and We All Struggle Against Value." *The Commoner* 10 (Spring/Summer): 132–171.

Häusermann, S., T. Kurer, and H. Schwander. 2015. "High-Skilled Outsiders? Labor Market Vulnerability, Education and Welfare State Preferences." *Socio-Economic Review* 13, 2: 235–258.

Häusermann, S., M. Pinggera, M. Ares, and M. Enggist. 2019. "Class and Social Policy in the Knowledge Economy." University of Zurich. June. welfarepriorities.eu/wp-content/uploads/2019/06/CES_Class_Haeusermannetal.pdf.

Hayward, T. 2013. "Human Rights vs Property Rights." Just World Institute, University of Edinburgh. timhayward.wordpress.com/2013/10/14/human-rights-vs-property-rights/.

Hazelrigg, L. 1973. "Aspects of the Measurement of Class Consciousness." In M. Axner and A. Grimshaw (eds.), *Comparative Social Research*. New York: John Wiley.

Hebson, W. 2013. "Renewing Class Analysis in Studies of the Workplace: A Comparison of Working-Class and Middle-Class Women's Aspirations and Identities." *Sociology* 43, 1: 27–44.

Hickel J., D.W. O'Neill, A.L. Fanning, and H. Zoomkawala. 2022. "National Responsibility for Ecological Breakdown: A Fair-Shares Assessment of Resource Use, 1970–2017." *The Lancet Planetary Health*, April. thelancet.com/journals/lanplh/article/PIIS2542-5196(22)00044-4/fulltext.

Hiroyoshi, H. 2005. *Marx's Labour Theory of Value: A Defence*. Lincoln, NE: iUniverse Inc.

Hooker, L. 2022. "Millionaires at Davos Say 'Tax Us More'." BBC *News*, May 23. bbc.com/news/business-61549155.

Hornborg, A. 2016. "Post-Capitalist Ecologies: Energy, 'Value' and Fetishism in the Anthropocene." *Capitalism Nature Socialism* 27, 4: 61–76.

Howard, C., A. Freeman, A. Wilson and E. Brown. 2017. "Poverty." *Public Opinion Quarterly* 81, 3 (Fall): 769–789.

Howard, T., S. Dubb and S. McKinley. 2014. "Economic Democracy." In D. Rowe (ed.), *Achieving Sustainability: Visions, Principles & Practices*, Volume 1, 231–39. New York: Macmillan Reference USA.

Hughes, H.S. 1958. *Consciousness and Society: The Reorientation of European Social Thought*. New York: Vintage Books.

Huws, U. 2019. *Labour in Contemporary Capitalism: What Next?* London: Palgrave Macmillan.

___. 2014. "The Underpinnings of Class in the Digital Age: Living, Labour and Value." In L. Panitch, G. Albo and V. Chibber (eds.), *Registering Class: Socialist Register 2014*. London: Merlin Press.

Ikeler, P., and J. Crocker. 2021. "The Continuity of Work: Class Consciousness in Service and Non-Service Jobs." *Economic and Industrial Democracy* 42, 3: 401–425.

ILO (International Labour Organization). 2015. *Key Indicators of the Labour Market, ILOSTAT database.* ilo.org/wcmsp5/groups/public/---dgreports/---stat/documents/publication/wcms_498929.pdf.

___. 2003. *Key Indicators of the Labour Market. Employment by Sector.* https://labordoc.ilo.org/discovery/fulldisplay/alma993603863402676/41ILO_INST:41ILO_V2

Independent Panel for Pandemic Preparedness and Response. 2021. "COVID-19: Make It the Last Pandemic A Summary." https://theindependentpanel.org/wp-content/uploads/2021/05/Summary_COVID-19-Make-it-the-Last-Pandemic_final.pdf.

Innovative Research Group. 2020. "Half of Canadians Believe that the Economy Needs to Be Radically Transformed in Light of COVID-19." June 3. innovativeresearch.ca/canada-this-month-transforming-the-economy.

International Database of De-Privatised Public Services Transnational Institute. 2021. https://www.tni.org/en/topic/water-justice.

International Institute for Democracy and Electoral Assistance. 2021. "The Global State of Democracy 2021: Building Resilience in a Pandemic Era." idea.int/publications/catalogue/global-state-democracy-2021?lang=en.

International Institute of Management. n.d. "Gross National Happiness and Wellbeing (GNH/GNW) Index — A Policy White Paper." iim.education/gross-national-happiness/index.htm

IPCC. 2022. *Climate Change 2022: Impacts, Adaptation and Vulnerability.* ipcc.ch/report/ar6/wg2/.

Ireland, P., and G. Meng. 2017. "Post-Capitalist Property." *Economy and Society* 46, 3–4 (August–November): 369–397.

Ishay, M. 2008. *The History of Human Rights: From Ancient Times to the Globalization Era.* Berkeley: University of California Press.

Jackman, N., and R. Jackman. 1983. *Class Awareness in the United States.* Berkeley: University of California Press.

Jacobson, M.Z., and M.A. Delucchi. 2011. "Providing All Global Energy with Wind, Water, and Solar Power, Part I: Technologies, Energy Resources, Quantities and Areas of Infrastructure, and Materials." *Energy Policy* 39, 3: 1154–1169.

Jacques, R. 2000. "Theorizing Knowledge as Work: The Need for a Knowledge Theory of Value." In C. Pritchard et al. (eds.), *Managing Knowledge.* London: Macmillan.

Jaros, S. 2005. "Marxian Critiques of Thompson's (1990) 'Core' Labour Process Theory: An Evaluation and Extension." *Ephemera: Theory & Politics in Organization* 5, 2: 5–25.

John, M. 2020. "Capitalism Seen Doing 'More Harm Than Good' in Global Survey." *Reuters*, January 20. reuters.com/article/us-davos-meeting-trust-idUSKBN1ZJ0CW.

Johnson, T. 1977. "The Professions in the Class Structure." In N.R. Scase (ed.), *Industrial Society: Class, Cleavage and Control.* London: Allen & Unwin.

Johnston, W., and M. Ornstein. 1985. "Social Class and Political Ideology in Canada." *Canadian Review of Sociology and Anthropology* 22, 3: 369–393.

Jones, J.M. 2019. "As Labor Day Turns 125, Union Approval Near 50-Year High." *Gallup*, August 28. news.gallup.com/poll/265916/labor-day-turns-125-union-approval-near-year-high.aspx.

Joseph, P.E. 2020. "It Really Is Different This Time." *Politico Magazine*, June 4. politico.com/news/magazine/2020/06/04/protest-different-299050.

Kallevig, M.M. 2005. "Ownership Function of the Norwegian State." oecd.org/daf/ca/35175246.pdf.

Kapur, N. 2018. *Japan at the Crossroads: Conflict and Compromise after Anpo.* Cam-

bridge: Harvard University Press.
Karabel, J. 1996. "Towards a Theory of Intellectuals and Politics." *Theory and Society* 25, 2.
Kasler, Dirk. 1988. *Max Weber: An Introduction to His Life and World*. Chicago: University of Chicago Press.
Katz, L., and A. Krueger. 2016. "The Rise and Nature of Alternative Work Arrangements in the United States, 1995–2015." Princeton University and NBER, March 29. scholar.harvard.edu/files/lkatz/files/katz_krueger_cws_v3.pdf.
Kazan, O. 2020. "How the Corona Virus Could Create a New Working Class." *The Atlantic*, April 15. theatlantic.com/health/archive/2020/04/coronavirus-class-war-just-beginning/609919/.
Keefer, L.A., C. Goode, and L. Van Berkel. 2015. "Toward a Psychological Study of Class Consciousness: Development and Validation of a Social Psychological Model." *Journal of Social and Political Psychology* 3, 2: 253–290.
Kenney, M. 1997. "Value Creation in the Late Twentieth Century: The Rise of the Knowledge Worker." In J. Davis, T.A. Hirschl, and M. Stack (eds.), *Cutting Edge: Technology, Information Capitalism and Social Revolution*. New York: Verso.
Kharas, H., and K. Hamel. 2018. *A Global Tipping Point: Half the World Is Now Middle Class or Wealthier*. Washington, DC: Brookings Institute, September 27. brookings.edu/blog/future-development/2018/09/27/a-global-tipping-point-half-the-world-is-now-middle-class-or-wealthier/.
Kingston, P.W. 2000. *The Classless Society*. Stanford, CA: Stanford University Press.
Kivinen, M. 1989. "The New Middle Classes and the Labour Process." *Acta Sociologica* 32, 1: 53–73.
Klare, M. 2019. "Cyber Battles, Nuclear Outcomes? Dangerous New Pathways to Escalation." *Arms Control Today*, November. https://www.armscontrol.org/act/2019-11/features/cyber-battles-nuclear-outcomes-dangerous-new-pathways-escalation.
Klein, N. 2016. "Let Them Drown: The Violence of Othering in a Warming World." *London Review of Books* 38, 11 (June)2. lrb.co.uk/v38/n11/naomi-klein/let-them-drown.
___. 2007. *The Shock Doctrine: The Rise of Disaster Capitalism*. London: Penguin.
Kluckhohn, F., and F.L. Strodtbeck. 1961. *Variations in Value Orientations*. Bloomington, IN: Row, Peterson and Co.
Kolokowski, L. 1978. *Main Currents of Marxism, Volume 3. The Breakdown*. London: Oxford University Press.
Konrad, G., and I. Szelenyi. 1979. *The Intellectuals on the Road to Class Power*. Brighton, Sussex: Harvester Press.
Kovel, J., and M. Lowy. 2001 "An Ecosocialist Manifesto." Environment and Ecology. environment-ecology.com/political-ecology/436-an-ecosocialist-manifesto.html
Krause, E.A. 1996. *Death of the Guilds: Professions, States, and the Advance of Capitalism, 1930 to the Present*. New Haven: Yale University Press.
Kuhn, T. 1962. *The Structure of Scientific Revolutions*. Chicago: University of Chicago Press.
Kurzman, C., and L. Owens. 2002. "The Sociology of Intellectuals." *Annual Review of Sociology* 28.
Lambert, R., J. Curtis, S. Brown, and B. Kay. 1986. "Canadians' Beliefs about Differences Between Social Classes." *Canadian Journal of Sociology* 11, 4.
Laurence Fink Net Worth. 2021. Wallmine. wallmine.com/people/48979/laurence–fink. (On 12/22, URL shows net worth as of 11/22).

Lavoie, M., R. Roy, and P. Therrien. 2003. "A Growing Trend Toward Knowledge Work in Canada." *Research Policy* 32, 5: 827–844.
Lefebvre, H. 1971. *Everyday Life in the Modern World.* New York: Harper Torchbooks.
Legatum Institute. 2015. "What the World Thinks of Capitalism." The Legatum Institute Foundation. social.shorthand.com/montie/3C6iES9yjf/what-the-world-thinks-of-capitalism.
Leger. 2020. "Alternatives Survey, June 12-24, 2020." Project number 81872_019. CanadaWorkLearningSurveys1998-2016.
Leggett, J. 1979. "The Persistence of Working-Class Consciousness in Vancouver." In J. Fry (ed.), *Economy, Class and Social Reality.* Toronto: Butterworths.
———. 1968. *Class, Race and Labor: Working Class Consciousness in Detroit.* New York: Oxford University Press.
Leiulfsrud, H., I. Bison, and H. Jensberg. 2005. *Social Class in Europe: European Social Survey 2002/3.* Trondheim: Norwegian University of Technology and Science.
Lenin, V. 1973 [1917]. *Imperialism, the Highest Stage of Capitalism.* Peking: Foreign Languages.
———. 1963 [1902]. *What Is to Be Done?* London: Oxford University Press.
Lenton, T.M., J. Rockström, O. Gaffney, et al. 2019. "Climate Tipping Points — Too Risky to Bet Against: The Growing Threat of Abrupt and Irreversible Climate Changes Must Compel Political and Economic Action on Emissions." *Nature*, 27 November. media.nature.com/original/magazine-assets/d41586-019-03595-0/d41586-019-03595-0.pdf.
Lessig, L. 2021. *They Don't Represent Us: And Here's How They Could—A Blueprint for Reclaiming Our Democracy.* New York: Dey Street Books.
Levine, R. 1981. "Class Science and Scientific Truth." *Working Papers on Marxism and Science,* Winter.
Levitin, M. 2015. "The Triumph of Occupy Wall Street." *The Atlantic,* June 10. theatlantic.com/politics/archive/2015/06/the-triumph-of-occupy-wall-street/395408/.
Lindh, A., and L. McCall. 2020. "Class Position and Political Opinion in Rich Democracies." *Annual Review of Sociology* 46: 419–41.
Livingstone, D.W. 2023. "Professional Employees' Transformative Potential: Labour Aristocracy or New Working Class." *Alternate Routes* 33, 1: 17-35.
———. 2021. "The Rise and Polarisation of Managers and Professional Managers." In D.W. Livingstone, T.L. Adams and P.H. Sawchuk, *Professional Power and Skill Use in the 'Knowledge Economy': A Class Analysis.* Leiden/Boston: Brill/Sense.
———. 2019a. "Underemployment of Highly Qualified Labour in Advanced Capitalism: Trends and Prospects." *Journal of Education and Work* 32, 4: 305–319.
———. 2019b. "Proletarianization of Professional Employees and Underemployment of General Intellect in a 'Knowledge Economy': Canada, 1982–2016." *Labour/Le Travail* 84 (Fall): 141–166.
———. 2014. "Interrogating Professional Power and Recognition of Specialized Knowledge: A Class Analysis." *European Journal for Research on the Education and Learning of Adults* 5, 1: 13–29.
——— (ed.). 2010 *Lifelong Learning in Paid and Unpaid Work: Survey and Case Study Findings.* London: Routledge.
———. 2009. *Education and Jobs: Exploring the Gaps.* Toronto: University of Toronto Press.
———. 2004. *The Education–Jobs Gap: Underemployment or Economic Democracy.* Toronto: Garamond Press and Clinton Corners, NY: Percheron Press.
———. 2003. "Ideological Class Struggle." Invited entry for Historisch-kritisches

Wörterbuch des Marxismus (HKWM). https://hdl.handle.net/1807/111171.

___. 1987. "Class Position, Class Consciousness and Political Party Preference in Hard Times." In R. Argue et al. (eds.), *Working People in Hard Times*. Toronto: Garamond Press.

___. 1985. "Class Consciousness." In D.W. Livingstone, *Social Crisis and Schooling*. Toronto: Garamond Press.

___. 1983a. *Class, Ideologies and Educational Futures*. London and New York: Falmer Press and International Publishing Services.

___. 1983b. "Class Structure and Class Consciousness in the Current Crisis." Revised version of a paper presented at the Annual Meetings of the Canadian Sociological and Anthropological Association, Vancouver. University of Toronto, June 1983. hdl.handle.net/1807/111350.

___. 1976. "On Hegemony in Corporate Capitalist States: Material Structures, Ideological Forms, Class Consciousness and Hegemonic Acts." *Sociological Inquiry* 46, 3–4.

Livingstone, D.W., T.L. Adams and P.H. Sawchuk. 2021. *Professional Power and Skill Use in the 'Knowledge Economy': A Class Analysis*. Leiden/Boston: Brill/Sense.

Livingstone, D.W., and E. Asner.1996. "Feet in Both Camps: Household Classes, Divisions of Labour, and Group Consciousness." In D.W. Livingstone and J. Marshall Mangan (eds.), *Recast Dreams: Class and Gender Consciousness in Steeltown*. Toronto: Garamond Press. 72–99.

Livingstone, D.W., and D. Guile 2012. *The Knowledge Economy and Lifelong Learning: A Critical Reader*. Rotterdam: Sense Publishers.

Livingstone, D.W., and D.G. Lake. 1977. "Preferred Images of the Future: Twentieth Century Bourgeois and Socialist Visions." *McGill Journal of Education* 12, 1 (Spring): 95–110.

Livingstone, D.W., and M. Luxton. 1989. "Gender Consciousness at Work: Modification of the Male Breadwinner Norm Among Steelworkers and Their Spouses." *Canadian Review of Sociology and Anthropology* 26, 2 (May): 240–275.

Livingstone, D.W., and J.M. Mangan (eds.). 1996a. *Recast Dreams: Class and Gender Consciousness in Steeltown*. Toronto: Garamond Press.

Livingstone, D.W., and J.M. Mangan. 1996b. "Men's Employment Classes and Class Consciousness: An Empirical Comparison of Marxist and Weberian Class Distinctions." In D.W. Livingstone and J.M. Mangan (eds.), *Recast Dreams: Class and Gender Consciousness in Steeltown*. Toronto: Garamond Press.

Livingstone, D.W., K. Pollock, and M. Raykov. 2016. "Family Binds and Glass Ceilings: Women Managers' Promotion Limits in a 'Knowledge Economy.'" *Critical Sociology* 42, 1: 145–166.

Livingstone, D.W., and P.H Sawchuk. 2000. "Beyond Cultural Capital Theory: Hidden Dimensions of Working-Class Learning." *Review of Education, Pedagogy and Cultural Studies* 22, 2: 203–224.

Livingstone, D.W., and A. Scholtz. 2016. "Reconnecting Class and Production Relations in an Advanced Capitalist 'Knowledge Economy': Changing Class Structure and Class Consciousness." *Capital & Class* 40, 3: 469–493.

Livingstone, D.W., D.E. Smith, and W. Smith. 2011. *Manufacturing Meltdown: Reshaping Steel Work*. Black Point. NS: Fernwood Publishing.

Livingstone, D.W., and B. Watts. 2018. "The Changing Class Structure and Pivotal Role of Professional Employees in an Advanced Capitalist 'Knowledge Economy': Canada, 1982–2016." *Studies in Political Economy* 99, 1: 79–96.

Locke, J. 1689. *Two Treatises on Government*. London: Awnsham Churchill.

Lopreato, J., and L.E. Hazelrigg. 1972. *Class, Conflict, and Mobility: Theories and Studies of Class Structure*. Worcester, MA: Chandler House Press.

Ludovici, A.M. 1932. *The Sanctity of Private Property*. London: Heath Cranton Limited.

Lukács, G. 1971 [1923]. *History and Class Consciousness*. London: Merlin Press.

Luria, A.R. 1976. *Cognitive Development: Its Cultural and Social Foundations*. Cambridge: Harvard University Press.

Maas, I., and M.H.D. van Leeuwen. 2002. "Intergenerational Mobility in Sweden." *Acta Sociologica* 45, 3: 179–194.

Macdonald, D. 2018. *Climbing Up and Kicking Down: Executive Pay in Canada*. Ottawa: Canadian Centre for Policy Alternatives.

Macpherson, C.B. 1962. *The Political Theory of Possessive Individualism: From Hobbes to Locke*. Toronto: University of Toronto Press.

___. 1942. "The Meaning of Economic Democracy." *University of Toronto Quarterly* 11, 4 (July): 403–420.

Malleson, T. 2014. *After Occupy: Economic Democracy for the 21st Century*. Oxford: Oxford University Press.

Mallet, S. 1975. *The New Working Class*. Nottingham, UK: Spokesman Books.

Mann, M. 2013. "The End of Capitalism?" *Análise Social* 209, xlviii (4.º). analisesocial.ics.ul.pt/documentos/AS_209_f02.pdf.

___. 1973. *Consciousness and Action Among the Western Working Class*. London: Macmillan.

___. 1970. "The Social Cohesion of Liberal Democracy." *American Sociological Review* 35, 3 (June): 423–439.

Mannheim, K. 1985 [1929]. "The Sociological Problem of the 'Intelligentsia.'" *Ideology and Utopia*. San Diego, CA: Harcourt Brace Jovanovich.

___. 1936. *Ideology and Utopia: An Introduction to the Sociology of Knowledge*. London: Bradford.

Mansbridge, J.J., and A. Morris (eds.). 2001. *Oppositional Consciousness: The Subjective Roots of Social Protest*. Chicago: University of Chicago Press.

Marois, T. 2021. *Public Banks: Decarbonisation, Definancialisation and Democratisation*. Cambridge: Cambridge University Press.

Marx, I., B. Nolan, and J. Olivera. 2014. "The Welfare State and Anti-Poverty Policy in Rich Countries." Antwerp: Institute for the Study of Labour. Discussion Paper No. 8154, April. ftp.iza.org/dp8154.pdf.

Marx, K. 2010 [1879]. "Marginal Notes to A. Wagner's Lehrbuch der Politischen Oekonomie." in K. Marx and F. Engels, *Marx & Engels: Collected Works, Volume 24*. London: Lawrence & Wishart.

___. 1970 [1859]. *A Contribution to the Critique of Political Economy*. Moscow: Progress Publishers.

___. 1967 [1894]. *Capital, Volume 3. The Process of Capitalist Production as a Whole*. New York: International Publishers.

___. 1967 [1867]. *Capital, Volume 1*. New York: International Publishers.

___. 1964 [1859]. *The Economic and Philosophical Manuscripts of 1844*. New York: International Publishers.

___. 1947 [1865]. *Wages, Prices and Profit*. Moscow: Progress Publishers.

___. 1938. "A Workers' Inquiry." *New International* 4, 12 (December): 379–381. marxists.org/history/etol/newspape/ni/vol04/no12/marx.htm.

Matutinovic, I. 2020. "The End of Neoliberal Ideology." *Green European Journal*, July 6. greeneuropeanjournal.eu/the-end-of-neoliberal-ideology/.

Mayer, R. 1997. "Plekhanov, Lenin and Working-Class Consciousness." *Studies in East European Thought* 49, 1: 159–185.
McCall, L. 2005. "The Complexity of Intersectionality." *Signs: Journal of Women in Culture and Society* 30, 3: 1771–1800.
McCrystal, S. 2010. *The Right to Strike in Australia*. Sydney: Federation Press.
McGaughey, E. 2015. "The Codetermination Bargains: The History of German Corporate and Labour Law." SSRN, March 27. LSE Legal Studies, Working Paper No. 10.
McKenzie, R.T., and A. Silver. 1968. *Angels in Marble: Working Class Conservatives in Urban England*. London: Heinemann Educational.
McKibben, B. 2019. *Falter: Has the Human Game Begun to Play Itself Out?* New York: Henry Holt and Co.
McNall, S., and R. Levine (eds.). 1991. *Bringing Class Back In: Contemporary and Historical Perspectives*. Boulder, CO: Westview Press.
McNally, D., and C. Post. 2021. "Beyond Electoralism: Mass Action and the Remaking of the Working Class." *Spectre*, June 12. https://spectrejournal.com/beyond-electoralism/.
McNeill, W. 1963. *The Rise of the West: A History of the Human Community*. Chicago: University of Chicago Press.
Meidner, R. 1993. "Why Did the Swedish Model Fail?" In R. Miliband and L. Panitch (eds.), *Socialist Register*. London: Merlin.
___. 1981. "Collective Asset Formation Through Wage-Earner Funds." *International Labour Review* 120, 3: 303–317.
Menu, Thibault. 2021. "Denmark: A Case Study for a Climate-Neutral Europe." *Études de l'Ifri*, Ifri, April. https://www.ifri.org/sites/default/files/atoms/files/menu_denmark_climate_neutral_europe_2021.pdf.
Miller, S.M. 1994. "A New/Old Frontier of Inequalities: Respect and Self-Respect as Policy Issues." In H. Lustiger-Thaler and D. Salee (eds.), *Artful Practices: The Political Economy of Everyday Life*. Montreal: Black Rose Books.
Mills, C.W. 1963. "The Social Role of the Intellectual." *Power, Politics and People*. New York: Ballantine.
Mishel, L., and J. Kandra. 2020. "CEO Compensation Surged 14% in 2019 to $21.3 million." Economic Policy Institute, August 18. https://www.epi.org/publication/ceo-compensation-surged-14-in-2019-to-21-3-million-ceos-now-earn-320-times-as-much-as-a-typical-worker/.
Moorhouse, H. 1976. "Attitudes to Class and Class Relationships in Britain." *Sociology* 10, 3: 469–96.
Moraitis, A.B., and J. Copley. 2017. "Productive and Unproductive Labour and Social Form: Putting Class Struggle in Its Place." *Capital and Class* 41, 1: 91–114.
Morin, R 2012. "Rising Share of Americans See Conflict Between Rich and Poor." *Pew Research Center*, January 11. pewresearch.org/social-trends/2012/01/11/rising-share-of-americans-see-conflict-between-rich-and-poor/.
Moskvichov, L. 1974. *The End of Ideology Theory: Illusions and Reality*. Moscow: Progress.
Moyser, M. 2017. *Women in Canada: A Gender-Based Statistical Report*. Ottawa: Statistics Canada. Catalogue Number 89–503–X.
Muntaner, C., C. Borrell, C. Vanroelen, et al. 2010. "Employment Relations, Social Class and Health: A Review and Analysis of Conceptual and Measurement Alternatives." *Soc Sci Med*, December. pubmed.ncbi.nlm.nih.gov/21075495/.
Mustosmaki, A., T, Oinas, and T. Anttila. 2016. "Abating Inequalities? Job Quality at the

Intersection of Class and Gender in Finland 1977–2013." *Acta Sociologica* 60, 3: 228– 245.

Myrdal, G. 1945. *An American Dilemma*. New York: Harper and Row.

Negt, O., and A. Kluge. 1993. *Public Sphere and Experience: Toward an Analysis of the Bourgeois and Proletarian Public Sphere*. Minneapolis: University of Minnesota Press.

Neilson, D. 2007. "Formal and Real Subordination and the Contemporary Proletariat: Re-Coupling Marxist Class Theory and Labour-Process Analysis." *Capital and Class* 31, 1: 89–123.

Neilson D., and T. Stubbs. 2011. "Relative Surplus Population and Uneven Development in the Neoliberal Era: Theory and Empirical Application." *Capital & Class* 35, 3: 435–453.

Nisbet, M.C., and T. Myers. 2007. "Trends: Twenty Years of Public Opinion about Global Warming." *The Public Opinion Quarterly* 71, 3 (Autumn): 444–470.

Noble, D. 1986. *Forces of Production: A Social History of Industrial Automation*. Toronto: Oxford University Press.

Nunlee, M. 2016. *When Did We All Become Middle Class?* London: Routledge.

O'Brien, M. 1981. *The Politics of Reproduction*. London: Routledge & Kegan Paul.

O'Connor, J. 2010. "Marxism and the Three Movements of Neoliberalism." *Critical Sociology* 36, 5: 691–715.

O'Donnell, D., M. Tracey, L.B. Henriksen, et al. 2006. "On the 'Essential Condition' of Intellectual Capital: Labour!" *Journal of Intellectual Capital* 7, 1.

Oddsson, G.A. 2010. "Class Awareness in Iceland." *International Journal of Sociology and Social Policy* 30: 292–312.

OECD. 2020. *Innovative Citizen Participation and New Democratic Institutions: Catching the Deliberative Wave*. Paris: OECD.

___. 2019. "OECD Labour Force Statistics 2019." Paris: OECD Publishing. oecd-ilibrary.org/employment/oecd-labour-force-statistics-2019_g2g9fb3e-en.

___. 2018. *Risks that Matter: Main Findings from the 2018 OECD Risks that Matter Survey*. Paris: OECD.

Oesch, D. 2006. *Redrawing the Class Map: Stratification and Institutions in Britain, Germany, Sweden, and Switzerland*. New York: Palgrave Macmillan.

Oesch, D., and L. Rennwald. 2018. "Electoral Competition in Europe's New Tripolar Political Space: Class Voting for the Left, Centre-Right and Radical Right." *European Journal of Political Research* 57, 4: 783–807.

Ollman, B. 1972. "Toward Class Consciousness Next Time: Marx and the Working Class." *Politics and Society* 3, 1 (Fall): 1–24.

Ord, T. 2020. *The Precipice: Existential Risk and the Future of Humanity*. New York: Hachette Book Group.

Oxfam America. 2020. *Pandemic Profiteers Exposed*. Washington, DC: Oxfam. oxfamamerica.org/explore/research-publications/pandemic-profits-exposed.

Pacthod, D., and D. Pinner. 2021. "Time Is Running Out for Business Leaders Who Don't Have a 'Net Zero' Strategy." Mckinsey Sustainability, May 11. https://www.mckinsey.com/capabilities/sustainability/our-insights/sustainability-blog/time-is-running-out-for-business-leaders-net-zero-strategy.

Page, B.I., L.M. Bartels, and J. Seawright. 2013. "Democracy and the Policy Preferences of Wealthy Americans." *Perspectives on Politics* 11, 1 (March): 51–73.

Pakulski, J., and M. Waters. 1996. *The Death of Class*. Thousand Oaks, CA: Sage Publications.

Pan, L., and X. Zhou. 2018. "CEO Compensation in Japan: Why So Different Than the United States?" *Journal of Financial and Quantitative Analysis* 53, 5: 1–32.

Panitch, L. 2020 "Erik Olin Wright's Optimism of the Intellect." *New Political Science* 42, 1: 42–51.

Panitch, L., and S. Gindin. 2012. *The Making of Global Capitalism: The Political Economy of American Empire*. New York: Verso.

Pape, R., and K. Ruby. 2021. "The Face of American Insurrection. Right-Wing Organizations Evolving into a Violent Mass Movement." Department of Political Science, University of Chicago, January 28. d3qi0qp55mx5f5.cloudfront.net/cpost/i/docs/americas_insurrectionists_online_2021_01_29.pdf?mtime=1611966204.

Parkin, F. 1971. *Class Inequality and Political Order*. London: Paladin.

Pels, D. 1998. "The Proletarian as Stranger." *History of the Social Sciences* 11, 1.

Pérotin, V. 2016. "What Do We Really Know About Worker Co-Operatives?" Co-operatives UK. uk.coop/sites/default/files/2020-10/worker_co-op_report.pdf.

Pew Research Center. 2017. "The Partisan Divide on Political Values Grows Even Wider." October 5. pewresearch.org/politics/2017/10/05/the-partisan-divide-on-political-values-grows-even-wider/.

___. 2015. "The American Middle Class Is Losing Ground: No Longer the Majority and Falling Behind Financially." December 9. pewresearch.org/social-trends/2015/12/09/the-american-middle-class-is-losing-ground/.

Piketty, T. 2014. *Capital in the Twenty-First Century*. Cambridge: Belknap Press.

Pineo, P., J. Porter, and H. McRoberts. 1977. "The 1971 Census and the Socioeconomic Classification of Occupations." *Canadian Review of Sociology and Anthropology* 14, 1: 91–102.

Pink, D. 2009. *Drive: The Surprising Truth About What Motivates Us*. New York: Rivethead Books.

Pontusson, J., and S. Kuruvilla. 1992. "Swedish Wage-Earner Funds: An Experiment in Economic Democracy." *Industrial and Labor Relations Review* 45, 4: 779–791.

Pope Benedict XIV. 1745. "On Usury and Other Dishonest Profit." Vix Pervenit. Encyclical of Pope Benedict XIV promulgated on November 1. catholicculture.org/culture/library/view.cfm?recnum=3853.

Portes, A. 2000. "The Resilient Importance of Classes: A Nominalist Interpretation." *Political Power and Social Theory* 14: 249–284.

Poulantzas, N. 1975. *Classes in Contemporary Capitalism*. London: N.L.B.

Powell, L.F. 1971. "Attack on American Free Enterprise System." Mimeo, U.S. Chamber of Commerce, August 23. law2.wlu.edu/deptimages/Powell%20Archives/PowellMemorandumTypescript.pdf.

Prakesh, M.S., and G. Esteva. 1998. *Escaping Education: Living as Learning Within Grassroots Cultures*. New York: Peter Lang.

Procyk, S., W. Lewchuk, and J. Shields. 2017. *Precarious Employment: Causes, Consequences and Remedies*. Halifax: Fernwood Publishing.

Quarter, J., L. Mook, and A. Armstrong. 2017. *Understanding the Social Economy: A Canadian Perspective*, 2nd Edition. Toronto: University of Toronto Press.

Quinney, R. 1974. *Critique of Legal Order*. Boston: Little and Brown.

Rathgeb, P. 2019. "No Flexicurity Without Trade Unions: The Danish Experience." *Comparative European Politics* 17, 1: S. 1–21.

Raykov, M., and D.W. Livingstone. 2014. "Interest in Unions and Associations in a Knowledge-Based Economy: Canadian Evidence." *Just Labour* 22: 3–23.

Reed, A. 2002. "Rejoinder." In D.E. Davis (ed.), *Political Power and Social Theory* 15:

301–315. doi.org/10.1016/S0198-8719(02)80030-8.
Reid, I. 1981. *Social Class Differences in Britain*. London: Grant McIntyre.
Resnick, S., and R. Wolff. 1987. *Knowledge and Class*. Chicago: University of Chicago Press.
Rikowski, G. 2001. "After the Manuscript Broke Off: Thoughts on Marx, Social Class and Education." academia.edu/6069069/After_the_Manuscript_Broke_Off
Roberts, B. 2014. "Productive/Unproductive: Conceptual Topology." *Rethinking Marxism* 26, 3: 336–359.
Robinson, R., and J. Kelley. 1979. "Class as Conceived by Marx and Dahrendorf: Effects on Income Inequality, Class Consciousness, and Class Conflict in the U.S. and Great Britain." *American Sociological Review* 44, 1: 38–58.
Rodrigues de Moraes-Neto, B. 2013. "On the Labor Process and Productive Efficiency: Discussing the Socialist Project." *Rethinking Marxism* 25, 3: 434–441.
Roediger, D. 2014. *Seizing Freedom: Slave Emancipation and Liberty for All*. London: Verso.
Roemer, J. 1982. *Value, Exploitation and Class*. London: Harwood Academic Publishers.
Rugemer, W. 2019. *The Capitalists of the 21st Century*. Cologne: Tradition.
Saad, L. 2019. "Socialism as Popular as Capitalism Among Young Adults in U.S." November 25. gallup.com/poll/268766/socialism-popular-capitalism-among-young-adults.aspx.
Sakellaropoulos, S., and P. Sotiris. 2015. "From Territorial to Nonterritorial Capitalist Imperialism: Lenin and the Possibility of a Marxist Theory of Imperialism." *Rethinking Marxism* 27, 1: 85–106.
Satgar, V. 2022. "The US, Russia and Ukraine: Thinking Beyond the New Cold War and World War 3." March 28. https://socialistproject.ca/2022/03/us-russia-ukraine-thinking-beyond-new-cold-war-ww3/.
Savage, M. 2000. *Class Analysis and Social Transformation*. Buckingham: Open University Press.
___. 2015. *Social Class in the 21st Century*. London: Pelican.
Savage, M., F. Devine, N. Cunningham, et al. 2013. "A New Model of Social Class: Findings from the BBC's Great British Class Survey Experiment." *Sociology* 47, 2: 219–250.
Sawyer, J.E., and A. Gampa. 2020. "Work Alienation and Its Gravediggers: Social Class, Class Consciousness, and Activism." *Journal of Social and Political Psychology* 8, 1: 198–219.
Sayer, D. 1979. "Science as Critique: Marx vs. Althusser." In J. Mepham and D.H. Ruben (eds.), *Issues in Marxist Philosophy. Volume 3, Epistemology, Science, Ideology*. Brighton, Sussex: Harvester Press.
Scambler, G. 2019. "Sociology, Social Class, Health Inequalities, and the Avoidance of 'Classism.'" *Frontiers in Sociology* 4 (July): 56. ncbi.nlm.nih.gov/pmc/articles/PMC8022477/.
___. 2018. *Sociology, Health and the Fractured Society: A Critical Realist Account*. London: Routledge.
Schreiber, E.M. 1980. "Class Awareness and Class Voting in Canada." *Canadian Review of Sociology and Anthropology* 17, 1.
Schreiber, E.M., and G.T. Nygreen. 1968. "Subjective Social Class in America: 1945–68." *Social Forces* 48 (October).
Scott, J.C. 1990. *Domination and the Arts of Resistance*. New Haven, CT: Yale University Press.

Seccombe, W. 1992. *A Millennium of Family Change: Feudalism to Capitalism in Northwestern Europe*. London: Verso.
Seccombe, W. and D.W. Livingstone. 1999 *'Down to Earth People': Beyond Class Reductionism and Post-Modernism*. Toronto: Garamond Press.
Seider, M. 1974. "American Big Business Ideology." *American Sociological Review* 39, 5: 802–815.
Sennett, R., and J. Cobb. 1972. *The Hidden Injuries of Class*. New York: Knopf.
Serfati, C. 2014. "The New Configuration of The Capitalist Class." In L. Panitch, G. Albo, and V. Chibber (eds.), *Registering Class: Socialist Register 2014*. London: Merlin Press.
Service, E. 1960. "Law of Evolutionary Potential." In M. Sahlins and E. Service, *Evolution and Culture*. Ann Arbor, MI: University of Michigan Press.
Shahinian, S. 2016. "Being an 'Insider-Outsider' and Its Impact on Innovation and Creativity." Oct 16. stephan-shahinian.medium.com/becoming-an-insider-outsider-and-its-impact-on-innovation-a515a083da6.
Shapin, S. 1996. *The Scientific Revolution*. Chicago: University of Chicago Press.
Sitaraman, G. 2019. "The Collapse of Neoliberalism." *The New Republic*, December 23. newrepublic.com/article/155970/collapse–neoliberalism.
Skerrett, K., J. Weststar, S. Archer, and C. Roberts (eds.). 2017. *The Contradictions of Pension Fund Capitalism*. Ithaca, NY: Cornell University Press.
Sklar, H. (ed.). 1980. *Trilateralism: The Trilateral Commission and Elite Planning for World Management*. Boston: South End Press.
Smith, C., and P. Thompson. 1999. "Re-Evaluating the Labour Process Debate." In M. Wardell, T. Steiger, and P. Meiksins (eds.), *Rethinking the Labor Process*. New York: State University of New York Press.
Smith, D.E. 1987. *The Everyday World as Problematic: A Feminist Sociology*. Boston: Northeastern University Press.
___. 1975. "An Analysis of Ideological Structures and How Women Are Excluded: Considerations for Academic Women." *Canadian Review of Sociology* 12, 4 (November): 353–369.
Smith, D.N. 1998. "The Ambivalent Worker: Max Weber, Critical Theory and the Antinomies of Authority." *Social Thought & Research* 21, 1–2: 35–83.
Sohn-Rethel, A. 1978. *Intellectual and Manual Labour: A Critique of Epistemology*. Atlantic Highlands, NJ: Humanities.
Spates, J. 1983. "The Sociology of Values." *Annual Review of Sociology* 9: 29–47.
Spencer, C. 1977. *Blue Collar: An Internal Examination of the Workplace*. Chicago: Vanguard Books.
Speth, G., and K. Courrier (eds.). 2020. *The New Systems Reader: Alternatives to a Failed Economy*. London: Routledge.
Standing, G. 2011. *The Precariat: The New Dangerous Class*. London: Bloomsbury Academic.
Stanford, J. 2020. "The Surprising Resilience of Trade Unionism in Canada." Centre for Future Work, August 26. centreforfuturework.ca/2020/08/26/the-surprising-resilience-of-trade-unionism-in-canada/.
Stansbury, A., and L.H. Summers. 2020. "The Declining Worker Power Hypothesis: An Explanation for the Recent Evolution of the American Economy." Cambridge: National Bureau of Economic Research, Working Paper 27193. nber.org/papers/w27193.
Statistics Canada. 2018. "-10-0238-01 Distribution of Market, Total and After-Tax In-

come of Individuals, Canada, Provinces and Selected Census Metropolitan Areas." www150.statcan.gc.ca/n1/en/catalogue/1110023801.

___. 2011. *Concordance: International Standard Classification of Occupations (ISCO) 2008 to National Occupational Classification (NOC)*. https://www.statcan.gc.ca/en/subjects/standard/noc/2011/isco2008-noc2011.

Steffen, W., J. Rockström, K Richardson, et al. 2018. "Trajectories of the Earth System in the Anthropocene." *PNAS* 115, 33. pnas.org/doi/pdf/10.1073/pnas.1810141115.

Stone, C., D. Trisi, A. Sherman, and J. Beltrán. 2020. "A Guide to Statistics on Historical Trends in Income Inequality." Washington, DC: Center on Budget and Policy Priorities. https://www.cbpp.org/research/poverty-and-inequality/a-guide-to-statistics-on-historical-trends-in-income-inequality.

Streeck, W. 2016. *How Will Capitalism End? Essays on a Failing System*. London: Verso.

Strohl, D. 2019. "Fact Check: Did a GM President Really Tell Congress 'What's Good for GM Is Good for America'?" September 5. hemmings.com/stories/2019/09/05/fact-check-did-a-gm-president-really-tell-congress-whats-good-for-gm-is-good-for-america.

Sunkara, B. 2019. *The Socialist Manifesto: The Case for Radical Politics in an Era of Extreme Inequality*. London: Verso.

Sutton, F., S.E. Harris, C. Kaysen, and J. Tobin. 1956. *The American Business Creed*. Cambridge, MA: Harvard University Press.

Svallfors, S. 2006. *The Moral Economy of Class: Class and Attitudes in Comparative Perspective*. Stanford: Stanford University Press.

Tainter, J. 1990. *The Collapse of Complex Societies*. Cambridge: Cambridge University Press

Tanuro, D. 2014. *Green Capitalism: Why It Can't Work*. Black Point, NS: Fernwood Publishing.

Terkel, S. 1974. *Working: People Talk About What They Do All Day and How They Feel About What They Do*. New York: Pantheon Books.

Terray, E., and J. Serrano. 2020. "Exploitation and Domination in Marx's Thought." *Rethinking Marxism* 31, 4: 412–424.

Therborn G. 2014. "New Masses?" *New Left Review* 85(January–February): 7–16

___. 1980. *The Ideology of Power and the Power of Ideology*. London: Verso.

___. 1976. "Working Class Struggles and Theoretical Breaks: The Social and Theoretical Formation of Historical Materialism." *Science, Class and Society*, London: N.L.B.

Thompson, P. 1990. "Crawling from the Wreckage: The Labour Process and the Politics of Production." In D. Knights and H. Willmott (eds.), *Labour Process Theory*. London: Macmillan.

___. 1983. *The Nature of Work*. London: MacMillan.

Thompson, S., and M. Yar (eds.). 2011. *The Politics of Misrecognition*. London: Routledge.

Thomson, G. 1955. *The First Philosophers: Studies in Ancient Greek Society*. London: Lawrence and Wishart.

Tigar, M. 2002. *Fighting Injustice*. Chicago: American Bar Association.

Tigar, M.E., and M. Levy. 1977. *Law and the Rise of Capitalism*. New York: Monthly Review Press.

Timpanaro, S. 1975. *On Materialism*. London: N.L.B.

Tinel, B. 2014. "Revisiting the Issue of Class Structure in Labor and Monopoly Capital." *Cadernos EBAPE.BR* 12, 4 (October/December). scielo.br/j/cebape/a/ZBXpryHsvwWNrqcwJLJ8w5w/?format=pdf&lang=en.

Tinker, T. 2002. "Spectres of Marx and Braverman in the Twilight of Postmodernist La-

bour Process Research." *Work Employment & Society* 16, 2: 251–281.
Tormey, S. 2004. *Anti-Capitalism: A Beginner's Guide*. Oxford: Oneworld Publications.
Touraine, A. 1966. *La Conscience Ouvriere*. Paris: Editions du Seuil.
Treisman, R. 2020. "Essential Workers Hold Walkouts and Protests in National 'Strike for Black Lives.'" NPR, July 20. npr.org/sections/live-updates-protests-for-racial-justice/2020/07/20/893316011/essential-workers-hold-walkouts-and-protests-in-national-strike-for-black-lives.
Tressell, R. 1955 [1914]. *The Ragged Trousered Philanthropists*. London: Lawrence Wishart.
Tushnet, M. 1992. "Civil Rights and Social Rights: The Future of the Reconstruction Amendments." *Loyola of Los Angeles Law Review*, June 1. digitalcommons.lmu.edu/llr/vol25/iss4/6.
United Nations. 1948. *Universal Declaration of Human Rights*. un.org/en/udhrbook/pdf/udhr_booklet_en_web.pdf.
United Nations Development Programme. 2021. "People's Climate Vote: Results." New York: United Nations, January 26. undp.org/publications/peoples-climate-vote.
___. 2019. "Human Development Report 2019. Beyond Income, Beyond Averages, Beyond Today: Inequalities in Human Development in the 21st Century." December 9. hdr.undp.org/content/human-development-report-2019.
United Nations Population Division. 2018. "World Urbanization Prospects: 2018." population.un.org/wup/.
Vanneman, R.D., and L.W. Cannon. 1987. *The American Perception of Class*. Philadelphia: Temple University Press.
Vanneman, R.D., and F.C. Pampel. 1977. "The American Perception of Class and Status." *American Sociological Review* 42 (June).
Victorsson, M.T., and S. Gowan. 2017. "Revisiting the Meidner Plan." *Jacobin*, August 22. jacobin.com/2017/08/sweden-social-democracy-meidner-plan-capital.
Visser, J. 2006. "Union Membership Statistics in 24 Countries." *Monthly Labor Review* 129, 1: 38–49.
Visser, M., M. Lubbers, G. Kraaykamp, and E. Jaspers. 2014. "Support for Radical Left Ideologies in Europe." *European Journal of Political Research* 53, 3: 541–558.
Vitali, S., J. Glattfelder, and S. Battiston. 2011 "The Network of Global Corporate Control." *PLoS ONE*, October 26. journals.plos.org/plosone/article?id=10.1371/journal.pone.0025995.
Volscho, T. 2017. "The Revenge of the Capitalist Class: Crisis, the Legitimacy of Capitalism and the Restoration of Finance from the 1970s to Present." *Critical Sociology* 43, 2: 249–266.
Vrousalis, N. 2020. "Public Ownership, Worker Control, and the Labour Epistocracy Problem." *Review of Social Economy* 79, 3: 439–453.
___. 2013. "Exploitation, Vulnerability, and Social Domination." *Philosophy & Public Affairs* 41, 2: 131–157.
Wagar, W. 1972. *Good Tidings: The Belief in Progress from Darwin to Marcuse*. Bloomington, IN: Indiana University Press.
Wallace, M., and A. Junisbai. 2003. "Finding Class Consciousness in the New Economy." *Research in Social Stratification and Mobility* 20: 385–421.
Wallace-Wells, D. 2019. *The Uninhabitable Earth: Life after Warming*. New York: Tim Duggan Books.
Weber, M. 1978 [1922]. *Economy and Society: An Outline of Interpretive Sociology*. Berkeley: University of California Press.

———. 1961 [1923]. *General Economic History*. New York: Collier Books.
Western, J. 1999. "Who Thinks What About Capitalism? Class Consciousness and Attitudes to Economic Institutions." *Journal of Sociology* 35, 3: 351–370.
Wheatley, D. 2017. "Autonomy in Paid Work and Employee Subjective Well-Being." *Work and Occupations* 44, 3: 296–328.
Wike, R., J. Fetterolf, S. Schumacher and J. Moncus. 2021. "Citizens in Advanced Economies Want Significant Changes to Their Political Systems." *Pew Research Center*, October 21. pewresearch.org/global/2021/10/21/citizens-in-advanced-economies-want-significant-changes-to-their-political-systems/.
Wikipedia. "Black Death." en.wikipedia.org/wiki/Black_Death.
———. "Deliberative Democracy." en.wikipedia.org/wiki/Deliberative_democracy.
———. "G7." https://en.wikipedia.org/wiki/G7.
———. "Knowledge Management." https://en.wikipedia.org/wiki/Knowledge_management.
———. "List of Intergovernmental Organizations." en.wikipedia.org/wiki/List_of_intergovernmental_organizations.
———. "Organization for Economic Cooperation and Development." en.wikipedia.org/wiki/OECD.
———. "Right to Property." en.wikipedia.org/wiki/Right_to_property.
———. "Socialism." en.wikipedia.org/wiki/Socialism.
Wilkinson, R., and K. Pickett. 2009. *The Spirit Level: Why Greater Equality Makes Stronger Societies*. New York: Bloomsbury Press
Wilkinson, W. 2019. "The Density Divide: Urbanization, Polarization, and Populist Backlash." June 26. niskanencenter.org/the-density-divide-urbanization-polarization-and-populist-backlash/.
Willener, A. 1970. *The Action-Image of Society on Cultural Politicization*. London: Tavistock Press.
Wittke, C.F. 1950. *The Utopian Communist: A Biography of William Weitling*. Baton Rouge: Louisiana State University Press.
Wong, C. 2017. "Canada's Debt-to-Household-Income Ratio Rises to 171 Percent, Stat Can Says." *Toronto Star*, December 14.
Woodburn, J. 1982. "Egalitarian Societies." *Man, New Series* 17, 3 (September): 431–451.
Wright, E.O. 2019. *How to Be an Anti-Capitalist*. New York: Verso.
———. 2010. *Envisioning Real Utopias*. London: Verso.
——— (ed.). 2005. *Approaches to Class Analysis*. Cambridge: Cambridge University Press.
———. 1997. *Class Counts: Comparative Studies in Class Analysis*. Cambridge: Cambridge University Press.
———. 1989. "The Comparative Project on Class Structure and Class Consciousness: An Overview." *Acta Sociologica* 32, 1: 3–22.
———. 1985. *Classes*. London: Verso.
———. 1980. "Class and Occupation." *Theory and Society* 9, 1: 177–214.
———. 1978. "The Class Structure of Advanced Capitalist Societies." In E.O. Wright, *Class, Crisis and the State*. London: Verso.
Xhafa, F. 2016. "The Right to Strike Struck Down? An Analysis of Recent Trends." *Friedrich-Ebert-Stiftung*, October. library.fes.de/pdf-files/iez/12827.pdf.
Xie, J., S. Sreenivasan, G. Korniss, et al. 2011. "Social Consensus Through the Influence of Committed Minorities." *Physics and Society*, February 18. arxiv.org/abs/1102.3931.
Zuboff, S. 2019. *The Age of Surveillance Capitalism: The Fight for the Human Future at the New Frontier of Power*. New York: Public Affairs.

Index

abstraction
    determinate abstraction, 23, 34, 36-39, 41
    formalistic abstraction, 38, 98
    simple abstraction, 36-39, 41, 44, 99
activism, 3, 18-19, 151, 237, 274, 289
advanced capitalist mode of production, 14, 38, 40, 75, 77, 79, 81, 83, 85, 87, 89, 91, 93, 95, 97
alignment, 25-29, 44
alliances, 7, 20, 154, 240, 266, 271-272, 274, 290, 306, 308, 310, 320
alternative visions, 211, 213, 226, 233, 239, 256, 261

bourgeois mode of thought, 15-16, 19, 166, 179, 230

capitalist labour process, 5, 40, 82, 85, 89, 98, 101, 108, 113, 147, 273-274
capitalist mode of production, 12, 16, 19, 37, 39, 40, 75, 78, 80-81, 84-86, 97, 107, 139, 152, 160, 166
capitalist mode of thought, 147, 150-153, 155, 157, 159-161, 163, 165, 167, 169, 171, 173, 175, 177, 179, 180, 182
class and class consciousness, 9, 100, 211, 227, 229, 231, 233, 235, 237-239, 241, 243, 245, 247, 249, 251, 253, 255, 257, 259, 261, 263, 265-267, 269, 271-273, 275
class consciousness
    capitalist class consciousness, 182
    contradictory class consciousness, 7, 182, 183, 206, 215, 216, 226
    labour class consciousness, 182, 266, 306
    levels of class consciousness 5-7, 9, 15, 147, 154, 171, 173, 181, 183, 185-187, 192-193, 198-201, 211, 215, 217-218, 221-223, 225, 230, 233-235, 239, 244, 256, 261, 265, 277
class identity
    class models and class identity, 55, 61
    class position and class identity, 244, 247
    middle-class identity, 51-53, 68, 195, 208, 210, 241, 244, 246-247
    relevance of class identity, 198
    standard class identity, 50, 51, 192, 209, 225
    subjective class identity, 47, 57, 196, 207, 210, 222, 234, 241
    upper-middle-class identity, 56, 190, 194-195, 210, 241, 246, 275
    working-class identity, 52, 60, 187, 192-193, 195, 208, 241, 243-245, 248
class struggle, 72, 98, 114, 139, 154, 171, 179, 315
concentration of capital, 11, 80, 97, 103, 172
conflict approach, 33
consciousness
    hegemonic capitalist consciousness, 7, 182, 210, 215-217, 221, 223, 226, 241, 261-265, 303
    pro-capital class consciousness, 277
    pro-labour class consciousness, 7, 193, 205, 218, 220, 255, 286
    revolutionary class consciousness, 185, 188, 210-211, 217-218, 225, 227-228, 239, 256, 261-269, 272-273, 286, 303, 306, 313
consensual approach, 34
control of the labour process, 75, 78, 80, 84, 95, 211
corporate capitalist, 7, 29, 79-80, 102,

110, 114, 125-126, 136, 142-146, 165, 178, 192, 227-228, 238, 240, 242-243, 245-247, 249, 252, 257, 259-260, 262-267, 269, 271, 275-277, 287-288, 292, 297, 301, 304, 311, 316-318

debt
    credit card debt, 282
    consumer debt, 144-145, 279
    ecological debt, 10, 14
    government debt, 298, 300
    household debt, 144
    personal debt, 299-300
    private debt, 11
demographics, 134
dominant mode of thought, 41, 152, 178

economic democracy, 17-8, 94, 98, 170-171, 289-291, 293, 295-296, 300, 305, 317, 319
employment class model, 108
employment class structure, 5-7, 100, 103, 107, 112-116, 119, 123-125, 128-130, 132-134, 137, 139, 143, 145-146, 148, 243, 322-325
enclaves, 17, 19, 75, 93, 155, 166, 276
environmental rights, 167, 169, 179
exploitation, 8, 45, 94-95, 102-103, 105, 113, 177, 211, 227-228, 230-232, 235, 272, 274, 291

feudal mode of production, 75, 76, 276
feudal mode of thought, 155
forces of production, 20, 37, 89, 147, 316
forms of labour, 1, 38, 40, 76-77, 85-87, 152, 182

G7, 13, 75, 94-95, 115-117, 119, 121-122, 128-130, 290-291, 314
global warming, 4, 11, 180, 218, 220-221, 223-224, 226, 266, 269, 271, 277, 279, 282, 286, 296, 303, 316 317

health, 18, 67, 100, 127, 135, 145-146, 157, 164-165, 236, 278, 280, 289, 297, 298, 311, 318
historical materialism, 39, 42

ideological hegemony, 154, 160, 166, 171-172, 265
ideologies
    class based ideologies, 100, 154, 178
    radical ideologies, 166, 167, 171
    subordinate ideologies, 166
ideology
    bourgeois ideology, 150, 159, 167-169, 171-172, 179, 212
    dominant ideology, 160, 164, 166, 171, 222, 250
    liberal democratic ideology, 161
    neoliberal ideology, 161,165
    technocratic ideology, 160
images of class, 47, 222
income level, 55, 101, 290
industrial workers, 54, 64, 86, 100, 106, 110, 115-116, 121, 123-124, 126-127, 129, 134-135, 137, 139, 141-142, 144, 154, 193, 195-196, 230-232, 238-239, 242-250, 252-255, 258, 260-267, 271, 273, 275, 303, 306, 311, 315, 318, 322-324
inside-outsider, 23, 28, 31
intellectual standpoint, 24, 25, 27, 28, 31

knowledge economy, 2, 12, 16, 75, 88, 92-93, 99, 101, 103-105, 107, 109, 111, 113, 115, 117, 119, 121, 123, 125, 127-129, 131, 133, 135, 137, 139, 141, 143, 145, 147, 149, 161
knowledge workers, 7, 16, 94, 104, 106, 112, 127, 277, 290

labour rights, 132, 152, 160, 163, 177, 200, 207, 216, 229, 235, 238, 250
labour theory of value, 23, 37-38, 101-105, 113, 230, 231
machinofacture, 81-84
material production, 32, 34, 41, 185
mechanization, 81-82, 84, 89, 107
mobility, 13, 37, 100-101, 126, 134, 139-143, 147, 195, 277

new working class, 130-132, 211, 232
Nordic countries, 13, 75, 94-95, 115-117, 119, 121, 128-130, 137, 147, 216, 223, 268, 290-291, 306, 314

oppositional class consciousness, 197, 200, 216-217, 219, 222, 224-226, 229, 245, 248, 250, 253-254, 259-261, 266, 278, 280, 284, 287, 291
  contradictory oppositional class consciousness, 248
  pro-capital oppositional class consciousness, 250, 255
  pro-labour oppositional class consciousness, 207, 208, 210, 256, 286
oppression, 8, 9, 42, 45, 95, 157, 180, 228, 272, 289, 291
organic intellectuals, 26, 29, 150, 153
other bases of social division, 71

personal class model, 50-51, 56
post-capitalist rights, 166
poverty, 2, 11-12, 49, 56, 59, 61-67, 73, 92, 94, 143-144, 147, 164, 168, 180, 219-220, 223-224, 226, 228, 266, 268-269, 271, 277-278, 286, 291, 298, 303
professional employees 7, 16, 21, 100, 104, 106, 109-111, 115-116, 123-124, 127-132, 137-139, 141-142, 144, 148, 192-193, 232-233, 235-236, 238, 242, 244, 246, 248, 250-255, 258, 260-261, 263-265, 270-271, 273-275, 277, 290, 303-304, 306, 311, 313, 315, 318, 322-324
profit maximization, 40, 82, 85-87, 91, 102, 106, 164, 172-175, 177, 180, 201-202, 204, 212-213, 217, 223, 231, 260, 287, 297, 302
profit squeeze, 164
property rights, 76-77, 98, 107, 157, 159, 163, 165, 168-169, 172, 179, 281, 305

reserve army, 82, 106, 111-112, 114, 139, 147, 273, 280
right to profit, 158, 173, 177, 179, 182, 201-202, 204, 314
right to strike, 167, 171-173, 175-177, 182-183, 201-204, 207, 215, 217, 223, 229, 248, 262, 286

separation of powers, 163
service workers, 40, 110, 115-116, 120-121, 123-124, 126-8, 129, 134-135, 138-139, 141, 144, 147, 192, 232, 235-236, 238, 242, 246, 248, 250, 252, 255, 258, 260, 263-265, 274-275, 304, 306, 322-324
social background, 55, 71, 282
social discipline, 81-82, 84
social division of labour, 107, 191
social rights, 159-160, 162-164, 169, 171-172, 181, 271, 281, 299, 314, 318
steelworkers, 16, 19, 57-60, 69-70, 72-73, 224

technical division of labour, 84, 101, 107
technocratic ideology, 160
tipping point, 8-14, 20, 145, 168, 220, 263, 266, 270-271, 273, 276-281, 288, 291, 299, 311, 315, 318
traditional intellectuals, 26, 29
transformation, 11-12, 14, 76, 84, 88, 112, 132, 145, 151, 170, 211, 217-218, 248, 261, 270, 274, 276, 288, 292, 304, 305, 310, 320
trans-historical conceptual framework, 31, 41
tripartite class model, 68, 100

vantage point, 24-30, 42, 45, 100, 150, 231

wealth, 3, 6, 11, 15-16, 23, 46, 49, 54-56, 58, 64, 92, 95, 99, 100, 134, 142-145, 147, 155, 168, 178, 197, 202, 219, 226, 229, 240-241, 254, 261, 302
working class, 5, 30, 50-54, 56-59, 63, 64, 65, 66, 100-101, 112, 116, 124, 128-129, 142, 185, 189, 191-195, 197, 206, 208-209, 211, 225, 229-230, 234-238, 241-248, 262, 274-275, 305-306, 315, 323-324